Knowledge Management in Organizations

Knowledge Management in Organizations

A Critical Introduction

THIRD EDITION

Donald Hislop

OXFORD
UNIVERSITY PRESS

Great Clarendon Street, Oxford OX2 6DP,
United Kingdom

Oxford University Press is a department of the University of Oxford.
It furthers the University's objective of excellence in research, scholarship,
and education by publishing worldwide. Oxford is a registered trade mark of
Oxford University Press in the UK and in certain other countries

First edition published 2005
Second edition published 2009

Impression: 5

British Library Cataloguing in Publication Data
Data available

ISBN 978-0-19-969193-7

Printed in Great Britain by
Ashford Colour Press Ltd, Gosport, Hampshire

For all the women in my life!

Publisher's Acknowledgements

We are grateful to the following for permission to reproduce copyright material.

Wiley-Blackwell for the case studies in Chapter 2: Motivating Workers to Develop Firm-Specific Knowledge via the Use of Different Governance Mechanisms, drawn from Wang, He, and Mahoney, 'Firm-Specific Knowledge Resources and Competitive Advantage: The Role of Economic- and Relationship-Based Employee Governance Mechanisms', *Strategic Management Journal*, 30 (2009), 1265–85; and in Chapter 5: The Linkages between Learning Orientation, Knowledge Assets, and HR Practices in Professional Service Firms, drawn from Swart and Kinnie, 'Organisational Learning, Knowledge Assets and HR Practices in Professional Service Firms', *Human Resource Management Journal*, 20/1 (2010), 64–79; and in Chapter 8: The Impact of Team Reflexivity and Stress on Unlearning and Innovation in New Product Development Teams, drawn from Lee and Sukoco, 'Reflexivity, Stress, and Unlearning in the New Product Development Team: The Moderating Effect of Procedural Justice', *R&D Management*, 41/4 (2011), 410–23; in Chapter 9: Problems with the Management of Patient Safety Knowledge within the UK's National Health Service, drawn from Currie, Waring, and Finn, 'The Limits of Knowledge Management for UK Public Services Modernization: The Case of Patient Safety and Service Quality', *Public Administration*, 86/2 (2008), 363–85; and in Chapter 10: Communities of Practice and Career Trajectories in the British Advertising Industry, drawn from McLeod, O'Donohue, and Townley, 'Pot Noodles, Placements and Peer Regard: Creative Career Trajectories and Communities of Practice in the British Advertising Industry', *British Journal of Management*, 22 (2011), 114–31; and in Chapter 15: Leadership, Trust, Knowledge Sharing, and Team Performance, drawn from Kase, Paauwe, and Zupan, 'HR Practices, Interpersonal Relations, and Intrafirm Knowledge Transfer in Knowledge Intensive Firms: A Social Network Perspective', *Human Resource Management*, 48/4 (2009), 615–39.

Institute for Operations Research and the Management Sciences for the case study in Chapter 3: A Practice-Based Perspective on Telemedicine, drawn from Nicolini, 'Practice as the Site of Knowing: Insights from the Field of Telemedicine', *Organization Science*, 22/3 (2011), 602–20.

Sage for the case studies in Chapter 4: The Relationship between the Structure/Strategy of Multinational Corporations and Patterns of Knowledge Sharing within them, drawn from Kasper, Lehrer, Mühlbacher, and Müller, 'Integration-Responsiveness and Knowledge-Management Perspectives on the MNC: A Typology and Field Study of Cross-Site Knowledge-Sharing Practices', *Journal of Leadership and Organizational Studies*, 15/3 (2009), 283–303; and in Chapter 6: The Role of Time and Discontinuities in shaping the Complex Dynamics of Organizational Learning, drawn from Berends and Lammers, 'Explaining Discontinuity in Organizational Learning: A Process Analysis', *Organization Studies*, 31/8 (2011), 1045–68; and in Chapter 11: The Negotiation of Meaning within Multidisciplinary Medical Teams, drawn from Oborn and Dawson, 'Knowledge and Practice in Multidisciplinary Teams: Struggle, Accommodation and Privilege', *Human Relations*, 63/12 (2010), 1835–57; and in Chapter 12: Power/Knowledge Struggles between HR Practitioners, drawn from Heizmann, 'Knowledge Sharing in a Dispersed Network of HR Practice: Zooming in on Power/Knowledge Struggles', *Management Learning*, 42/4 (2011), 379–93; and in Chapter 14: The Impact of HR Practices on Interpersonal Relations and Knowledge Processes, drawn from Kase, Paauwe, and Zupan, 'HR Practices, Interpersonal Relations, and Intrafirm Knowledge Transfer in Knowledge Intensive Firms: A Social Network Perspective', *Human Resource Management*, 48/4 (2009), 615–39.

Taylor & Francis for the case study in Chapter 7: Enabling Knowledge Creation within Nissan's Oppama Production Plant, drawn from Matsudaira, 'The Continued Practice of "Ethos": How Nissan Enables Organizational Knowledge Creation', *Information Systems Management*, 27 (2010), 226–37.

MIS Quarterly Executive for the case study in Chapter 13: Using Web 2.0 Technology to Help Build a Knowledge Sharing Culture, drawn from Teo, Nishant, Goh, and Agarwal, 'Leveraging Collaborative Technologies to Build a Knowledge Sharing Culture at HP Analytics', *MIS Quarterly Executive*, 10/1 (2011), 1–18.

Brief Contents

Detailed Contents

List of Figures

List of Tables

The Contemporary Importance of Knowledge and Knowledge Management

Introduction

Some think the 'knowledge turn' a matter of macro-historical change; citing Drucker, Bell, Arrow, Reich or Winter, they assert we have moved into an Information Age wherein knowledge has become the organization's principal asset.

(Spender and Scherer 2007: 6)

The physical toil of manufacturing is being replaced by a world where we work more with our heads than our hands.

(Sewell 2005: 685–6)

A firm's competitive advantage depends more than anything on its knowledge: on what it knows—how it uses what it knows—and how fast it can know something new.

(HR Magazine 2009: 1)

In a textbook on knowledge management it is important to put the subject in context, as this helps explain the interest in it. The explosion of interest in knowledge management among academics, public policy-makers, consultants, and business people began as recently as the mid-1990s. The level of interest in knowledge management since then is visible in a number of ways. First, the knowledge society rhetoric is used by and shapes the business and educational policy-making of a number of governments including the UK, Scotland, Australia, and the European Union (Fleming *et al.* 2004; Mandelson 2009; Warhurst and Thompson 2006). While it is impossible to accurately quantify the number of business organizations which have attempted to develop and implement knowledge management systems, various surveys suggest that a significant number of organizations have undertaken such initiatives (Coakes *et al.* 2010; Griffiths and Moon 2011; KPMG 2000, 2003). Finally, a search of any search engine such as Google or Google Scholar using the key term 'knowledge management' reveals the vast number of articles, books, and reports that have been written on the topic since 1995.

The late 1990s also witnessed an exponential increase in the number of academic articles and books published on the topic of knowledge management. Thus, surveys by both

Scarbrough and Swan (2001) and Wilson (2002) revealed that prior to the mid-1990s interest in the topic was virtually non-existent, but from about 1996 onwards, the number of publications on knowledge management grew exponentially. Both these articles, however, suggested that there was a risk that knowledge management was a passing fad (Wilson is particularly scathing and talks of knowledge management as a bandwagon 'without wheels'), and that there was likely to be an 'impending decline' of interest in the topic (Scarbrough and Swan 2001: 56). However, contemporary analysis suggests such a decline has not occurred, and that the early years of the twenty-first century saw a sustained interest in the topic. For example, Hislop (2010) found that between 2000 and 2008 the number of academic publications on the topic of knowledge management increased quite significantly. A fuller discussion of this topic is undertaken in Chapter 16, at the end of this book.

The ongoing academic interest in knowledge management is also visible in a number of other ways, such as in the emergence of a number of conferences on the topic which have become regular annual events (see web links), as well as the topic of learning and knowledge now becoming a regular theme at many long-standing management and organization conferences. Finally, in relation to academic journals, papers on learning and knowledge in organizations have consistently been published in top-tier journals (such as *Journal of Management Studies*, *Organization Studies*, *Organization Science*) and there has also been the birth of a number of journals specifically concerned with issues of learning and knowledge management. Serenko *et al.* (2010) conducted an analysis of eleven peer-reviewed journals on the topic of knowledge management and intellectual capital, and suggest that there are at least twenty peer-reviewed academic journals in this field.

Key Assumptions in the Knowledge Management Literature

The central idea uniting and underpinning the vast majority of the knowledge management literature, that it is important for organizations to manage their workforce's knowledge, flows from a number of key assumptions embodied in the three quotations which open the chapter. First, Spender and Scherer's quotation illustrates the assumption that the end of the twentieth century witnessed an enormous social and economic transformation which resulted in knowledge becoming the key asset for organizations to manage. A second key assumption, flowing from the first one, and illustrated by Sewell's quotation, is that the nature of work has also changed significantly, with the importance of intellectual work increasing significantly. The third, related, key assumption, illustrated by the third quotation, is that the effective management by an organization of its knowledge base is likely to provide a source of competitive advantage (see also Swart 2011, and the illustration by Bognor and Bansal).

While the growth of interest in knowledge management only took off during the mid-1990s the theoretical foundation for the assumptions it makes resonate with, and to some extent flow from, Daniel Bell's post-industrial society concept (Bell 1973). Thus it is useful to examine his work in a little detail.

> ### ⊙ Illustration   Knowledge creation and the link to business performance
>
> Bogner and Bansal (2007) conducted research which tested certain aspects of the knowledge-based view of the firm (see Chapter 2 for a detailed exploration of the knowledge-based view of the firm). Specifically they examined whether an organization's ability to create and utilize new knowledge was linked to business performance. In their study they used patents as a measure of knowledge creation, and studied patent data in five patent-intensive industries (pharmaceuticals, semiconductors, forest products, oil and gas, and automotive). Two of the hypotheses that their research data supported, which they argued provided support for the knowledge-based view of the firm, were that first, business performance was strongly linked to an organization's level of knowledge creation and, secondly, that business performance was also linked to an organization's ability to 'recycle' new knowledge and use it to improve future organizational knowledge creation activities.

The Knowledge Society Concept and its Links to Bell's Post-Industrial Society Concept

The knowledge management literature is typically based on an analysis which suggests that, since approximately the mid-1970s, economies and society in general have become more information and knowledge intensive, with information/knowledge-intensive industries replacing manufacturing industry as the key wealth generators (see e.g. DeFillippi *et al.* 2006; Neef 1999). Arguably, the main source of inspiration for this vision was, and is, Daniel Bell's seminal book *The Coming of Post-Industrial Society*, which was first published in 1973. While earlier writers, notably von Hayek (1945) and one of his pupils, Machlup (1962), developed a similar analysis, Bell's work has provided the main inspiration for contemporary writers in the area of knowledge management. As a consequence, Bell's post-industrial society and contemporary conceptualizations of knowledge society bear more than a passing resemblance to each other. Burton-Jones (1999: 4), for example, explicitly links his knowledge capitalism model to Bell's thesis. Further, Bell himself has, over time, used the terms knowledge and information societies interchangeably with the post-industrial society concept (Webster 1996).

Bell's analysis is based on a typology of societies characterized by their predominant mode of employment (Webster 1996). Thus, an industrial society is characterized by an emphasis on manufacturing and fabrication: the building of things. In a post-industrial society, however, which is argued to evolve out of an industrial society, the service sector has replaced the manufacturing sector as the biggest source of employment (see Figure 1.1). Another crucial characteristic of Bell's post-industrial society is that knowledge and information play a much more significant role in economic and social life than during industrial society, as work in the service sector is argued to be significantly more information and knowledge intensive than industrial work.

Finally, Bell suggests that not only has there been a quantitative increase in the role and importance of knowledge and information, but there has also been a qualitative change in the type of knowledge that is most important. In a post-industrial society, theoretical knowledge has become the most important type of knowledge. Theoretical knowledge represents abstract knowledge and principles, which can be codified or at least embedded

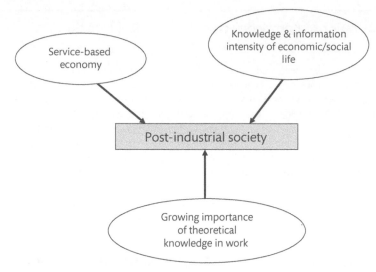

Figure 1.1 Characteristics of Post-Industrial Society

in systems of rules and frameworks for action. This is to a large extent because, for Bell, in post-industrial societies professional service work is of central importance, and this type of work typically involves the development, use, and application of abstract, theoretical knowledge more than manual work ever did. This relates not just to technical knowledge, such as may be used in R&D processes, but also encompasses a large and growing diversity of jobs which increasingly require the application and use of such knowledge—for example, formulation of government policy, architecture, medicine, software design, etc. This topic is returned to and elaborated in Chapter 4, when the debates regarding how to define knowledge work and knowledge-intensive firms are examined.

> **DEFINITION Post-industrial society**
>
> A society where the service sector is dominant and knowledge-based goods/services have replaced industrial, manufactured goods as the main wealth generators.

An important element of Bell's analysis is that post-industrial societies represent an advancement on industrial societies, as in general more wealth will be generated and workers individually will have better, more fulfilling jobs. In fact, there is a tendency towards utopianism in aspects of Bell's vision, as he argues that unpleasant, repetitive jobs will decline in number significantly; social inequality will reduce; (all) individuals will have increased amounts of disposable income to spend on personal services; society will be better able to plan for itself; and social relations will become less individualistic and provide greater scope for community development and collective support.

In order to empirically test and substantiate such claims, statistical evidence is typically mobilized to show the increasing importance of service work, and the simultaneous decline of

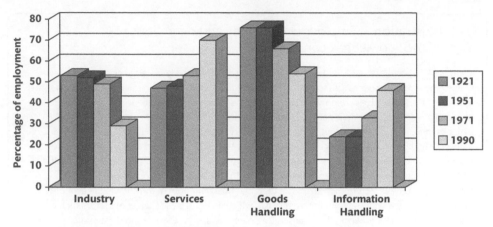

Figure 1.2 The Changing Character of the Economy of the USA in the 20th Century
Source: Castells 1995: table 4.8, p. 296.

manufacturing employment. Thus, statistics on the US economy in the mid-1970s were argued to show that 46 per cent of its economic output was from the information sector, and 47 per cent of the total workforce was employed in this sector (Kumar 1995). Castells (1998), in articulating his vision of a network/information society, mobilized an impressive amount of evidence from a wide range of economies which showed the long-term, historical shift from industry to services, and from goods-handling to information-handling work (Figure 1.2).

Some empirical evidence on the growing skill intensity of much work also supports Bell's thesis. For example, Zuboff (1988) suggested that advances in computer technology had the potential to make work more knowledge and skill intensive, through the potential for problem-solving and abstraction these technologies provide workers. This perspective is supported by research conducted by Gallie *et al.* (1998) in the UK in the mid-1990s, where almost 65 per cent of workers surveyed reported experiencing an increase in the skill levels of their jobs. Further evidence also reinforces these conclusions (Felstead *et al.* 2000; NSTF 2000).

Overall, therefore, aggregate statistical evidence appears to support the knowledge society/post-industrial society thesis. However, Bell's thesis has been the subject of a sustained and not insignificant critique, much of which has relevance to the knowledge society vision developed by contemporary writers on knowledge management. The following section changes focus to consider these criticisms.

A Critical Evaluation of the Knowledge Society Concept

One of the main criticisms of the arguments made by knowledge society or post-industrial society theorists is that they typically conflate knowledge work with service sector jobs. Thus, as outlined, aggregate statistics on the size of service sector employment is usually used to indicate the transition to a knowledge society (see Figure 1.2). However, not all service sector work can be classified as knowledge work, as the service sector is a residual employment category for all types of work which are neither manufacturing nor agricultural. Thus the service sector encompasses an enormously heterogeneous range of

Illustration   Employment, gender, and definitions of the knowledge economy

Walby's (2011) central focus is on how issues of gender relate to the knowledge economy/society. One element in her paper relates to how the gender composition of employment varies dependent upon how the knowledge economy is defined. Walby utilizes three separate definitions of the knowledge economy. One definition focuses on high-technology manufacturing work, which includes industries such as computers, office machinery, and consumable electronic goods. The second definition of the knowledge economy used by Walby focuses on information and ICT-related industries, which includes sectors such as publishing, mass media, telecommunications, computer and related activities such as software development. Both of these definitions focus heavily on technology-intensive sectors/industries. The third and final definition of the knowledge economy utilized by Walby is knowledge-intensive services, which includes a wide range of sectors such as air transport, telecommunications, financial services, computers, and research and development. Walby presents data which show that in the UK in 2005, 1 per cent of employment was in high-technology manufacturing, 4 per cent was in the information and IT sector, and 42 per cent was in knowledge-intensive services. The proportions of employment in each area reflect the specificities of the UK economy, and are likely to vary significantly between countries.

Arguably, the knowledge economy could be defined as the aggregate total of these separate definitions/sectors. However, by disaggregating the knowledge economy Walby is able to highlight gender-related differences in each of the three sub-sectors. In examining the gender composition of employment in the knowledge economy, Walby again focuses solely on the UK, and utilizes data from the UK government's Labour Force Survey. These data show that the gender composition of employment varies significantly in each sub-sector, with high-technology manufacturing industries being particularly male-dominated, with only 32 per cent of jobs in these industries being done by women. While the information sector is also male-dominated in employment terms (36 per cent female employment), knowledge-intensive services are female-dominated (61 per cent female employment). Walby's conclusion is that the more centred definitions of the knowledge economy are on technology and manufacturing, the more male-dominated the knowledge economy is, and the more definitions focus on services, the more female-dominated the knowledge economy becomes.

Walby also argues that, as female employment levels in knowledge-intensive services (61 per cent) are higher than for all manufacturing industries (26 per cent female employment) and the service sector as a whole (56 per cent female employment), as these sectors expand and grow employment opportunities for women are likely to be good.

job types, including consultants and cleaners, as well as scientists and security guards. Thus, the service sector does not represent a coherent and uniform category of employment. While some service sector work such as consultancy, research, etc. can be classified as being knowledge intensive, other types of service work, such as security, office cleaning, and fast food restaurant work is low-skilled, repetitive, and routine (Thompson *et al.* 2001). Therefore to suggest that all service sector employment is knowledge-intensive work does not acknowledge the reality of much service sector work.

The transition from an industrial to a post-industrial knowledge economy should produce an increase in the proportion of jobs that are knowledge intensive, and a more general increase in the knowledge intensity of work. There is some evidence for this, as statistical analyses typically show that managerial and professional work, work which is typically regarded as knowledge intensive, has been one of the fastest growing occupational groups since the 1980s (Elias

> **⊡ Time to reflect**   Call centres and knowledge-intensive work
>
> While customer service work in call centres is typically highly controlled, routine, and repetitive, it also involves the use of computers and a significant amount of interaction with customers. To what extent can such work be regarded as more skilled and knowledge intensive than skilled or semi-skilled factory work?

and Gregory 1994; Fleming *et al.* 2004). However, focusing on this trajectory alone provides a partial and over-simplistic overview of the way work has been changing.

Simultaneous to the growth in professional and managerial work there has been an equally significant growth in low-skilled, service work (Thompson *et al.* 2001). This is leading to what Mansell and Steinmueller (2000: 403) suggest is 'a growing polarization of the labour market between highly skilled, highly paid jobs, and low skilled, lower paid jobs', a conclusion reached by a growing number of writers (Fleming *et al.* 2004; Littler and Innes 2003; Warhurst and Thompson 2006). Thus, rather than there being a single trajectory in the direction of upskilling and increasing knowledge intensity, there are two simultaneous trends moving in opposite directions. A detailed statistical analysis of employment statistics in Australia conducted by Fleming *et al.* (2004) provides empirical support for this 'polarization thesis'. Thus while such analyses provide some support for the knowledge society thesis, they also suggest that the idea that there is a universal increase in the knowledge intensity of work in general is simplistic and a little misleading.

Questions have also been raised regarding the way knowledge was conceptualized by Bell. His conception of theoretical knowledge as codifiable and objective draws on classical images of scientific knowledge. However, much contemporary analysis views knowledge as having substantially different characteristics, being partial, tacit, subjective, and context dependent (see Chapters 2 and 3 for these debates).

While aspects of the analytical frameworks developed by post-industrial society and knowledge society theorists can be criticized and challenged, this does not mean that society and economies have remained unchanged, or that every aspect of these analyses is unfounded. Thus, it is undeniable that the last quarter of the twentieth century was a period of profound change. For the advanced, industrial economies there was not only a significant change in the type of products and services produced, and the nature of work itself, but the role of information and knowledge in many aspects of social and economic life also increased substantially. However, it is arguably going too far to suggest that these changes represent a fundamental rupture, witnessing the birth of a new type of society. This is because, while much change has occurred, there have also been significant elements of continuity: organizations remain driven by the same imperatives of accumulation, and the general social relations of capitalism remain unchanged. Thus, Kumar (1995: 31) suggests, 'capitalist industrialism has not been transcended, but simply extended, deepened and perfected'.

Such a conclusion is reinforced by McKinlay (2005: 242), who suggests that one of the key drivers for knowledge-intensive firms, such as those in the pharmaceutical industry, to develop knowledge management systems is 'new competitive pressures within capitalism for perpetual innovation in products, services and organization by leveraging the tacit knowledge of their employees'.

Thus to challenge Bell's conceptualization of a post-industrial society as representing a fundamental rupture with existing social and economic structures is not to suggest that there has been no change. Equally, such critiques cannot be used to conclude that knowledge is not important to contemporary business organizations.

Aims, Philosophy, and Structure

The final objective of this chapter is to articulate the general aims and philosophy of this book, as well as outlining the themes and issues examined in each chapter. A useful way to articulate the aims and philosophy of this textbook is to sketch out an overview of the various perspectives on knowledge and knowledge management that exist in the academic literature and locate the perspective adopted here within this framework. As will be seen, one of the features of this academic literature is the diversity of perspectives that exist. However, despite the heterogeneity of the literature on knowledge management, a number of broad perspectives can be identified.

One of the key distinctions in the knowledge management literature relates to epistemology. As outlined in the introduction to Part 1 on epistemology (see Table I in the introduction to Part 1), there is a general consensus that two identifiable perspectives on epistemology dominate. These perspectives are here labelled the objectivist and practice-based perspectives on knowledge. The objectivist perspective assumes that knowledge is an entity that can be codified and separated from the people who possess and use it. In contrast, the practice-based perspective challenges this conceptualization of knowledge and instead assumes that knowledge is embedded in, developed through, and is inseparable from people's workplaces, practices, and the contexts in which they occur. In Part 1, which follows, Chapters 2 and 3 are devoted to fully articulating each of these two epistemologies.

Another useful framework that helps to characterize the knowledge management literature, and simultaneously highlight issues which are typically neglected in it, was developed by Schultze and Stabell (2004), and is itself based on Burrell and Morgan's (1979) sociological paradigms framework. As with Burrell and Morgan's (1979) work, they articulate a two-dimensional framework which produces four distinctive knowledge management discourses. Due to the different perspectives on epistemology, outlined above, this is one of the dimensions in their framework. What is here labelled the objectivist perspective, Schultze and Stabell label the epistemology of dualism, and what is here referred to as the practice-based perspective, Schultze and Stabell label as the epistemology of duality.

What is distinctive about Schultze and Stabell's framework is that they add a second dimension to the epistemology one. The second dimension in their framework relates to social order, with differences existing on the extent to which existing social relations are regarded as consensual and unproblematic. In relation to the social order dimensions Schulze and Stabell suggest two distinct perspectives dominate. The consensus perspective is where existing social relations are regarded as unproblematic and where challenging them is not considered. The dissensus perspective, by contrast, assumes that existing social relations are problematic, that conflict is rife, that they typically reinforce power differentials that result in exploitation. The four discourses on knowledge management that emerge when these dimensions are put together are illustrated in Figure 1.3.

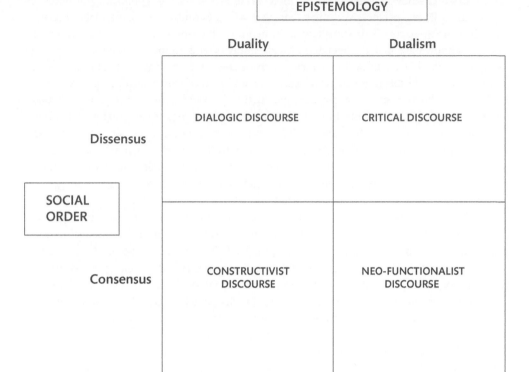

Figure 1.3 Schultze and Stabell's (2004) Four Discourses on Knowledge Management
Source: Schultze and Stabell (2004).

What this analysis reveals, and one of the key insights flowing from Schultze and Stabell's framework, is the extent to which the consensus-based perspective on social order predominates in the knowledge management literature. Thus most literature on the topic regards the management of organizational knowledge as being positive and progressive, and unquestioningly benefiting all organizational members, which consequently results in issues of conflict, power, and disagreement being marginalized, if not ignored.

Further, of the four discourses outlined by Schultze and Stabell, the neo-functionalist one is by far the most dominant in the knowledge management literature (a conclusion also drawn by Goles and Hirscheim 2000). This literature not only assumes that the management of knowledge is positive and has potential benefits for all organizational members, but also that the object-like status of knowledge in organizations makes it a resource amenable to managerial control.

This book, while describing the neo-functionalist discourse on knowledge management (see Chapter 2), is concerned with giving voice to and drawing on work from the other three knowledge management discourses. Thus, its primary purpose is to provide readers with a rich understanding of the debates and diversity of perspectives that exist through drilling down below the surface assumptions that typically go unquestioned in the mainstream knowledge management literature (regarding both the manageability of knowledge and the extent to which knowledge management involves conflict, power, and politics). This necessarily means utilizing perspectives other than that which Schultze and Stabell label the neo-functionalist discourse. This will allow an in-depth exploration of the issues underlying the theme of knowledge management and provide students with an insight into the debates and disagreements that continue to characterize the knowledge management literature, which would remain invisible if the focus was narrowly on the neo-functionalist perspective.

Thus, the book provides a critical introduction to knowledge management through examining ideas and assumptions that typically are not questioned in the mainstream knowledge management literature. Undertaking such an analysis reveals fundamental and important questions, which are likely to be of perennial interest, such as what is knowledge? Can it be controlled? Can it be codified? What are the difficulties involved in sharing or codifying it? Why might people be unwilling to participate in knowledge management initiatives? How these issues are structured in the book is described below.

The book is organized into four distinctive parts, each of which is focused around a particular theme. Part 1 addresses one of the fundamental questions in the knowledge management literature, how knowledge is conceptualized. This issue is explored in detail in Chapters 2 and 3. These chapters separately examine the two dominant perspectives on epistemology that predominate in the knowledge management literature. Chapter 2 focuses on elaborating the objectivist perspective on knowledge, which Schultze and Stabell label the epistemology of dualism. While Schultze and Stabell's (2004) analysis links two discourses with this perspective on knowledge (the neo-functionalist and the critical), the central focus here is largely on the neo-functionalist discourse alone. This is primarily because, as outlined, it represents the mainstream perspective of the knowledge management literature, and few analysts utilize the critical discourse. Issues raised by writers who adopt what Schultze and Stabell (2004) label the critical discourse are examined later, in Chapter 12, on power, politics, and conflict.

Chapter 3 then elaborates the practice-based perspective on knowledge, which Schultze and Stabell label the epistemology of duality. As with Chapter 2, while Schultze and Stabell (2004) identify two knowledge management discourses as being associated with this epistemology (the dialogic and constructivist discourses), the focus in Chapter 3 is narrowly on what they label the constructivist discourse. This is largely because substantially more writing on knowledge management has utilized the constructivist discourse. Of Schultze and Stabell's (2004) four discourses the dialogic discourse is the least utilized.

Part 2 is concerned with examining and elaborating key concepts and is organized into three chapters. Chapter 4 engages with the questions of what knowledge management is and shows that providing a simple definition is problematic. This is due to the wide range of strategies that have been advocated and adopted for managing knowledge in organizations. A number of different typologies and frameworks are then utilized to categorize and structure them. Chapter 5 focuses on the key and related concepts of knowledge work, knowledge workers, and knowledge-intensive firms. The chapter examines and explores the debates that have developed around all these concepts, which, as with the idea of knowledge management itself, make providing a straightforward definition for them difficult. Chapter 6, the final chapter in Part 2 engages with the topic of organizational learning and the learning organization, exploring how the concepts and practices of learning and knowledge management in organizations are closely related. The chapter also examines the contrasting viewpoints on the learning organization that have emerged, specifically engaging with the debate on whether the learning organization increases opportunities for self-development or simply represents a new method of control and exploitation of workers.

The two chapters in Part 3 focus on processes of organizational innovation, but each examines quite different aspects of it. Chapter 7 looks at innovation through the creation and use of new knowledge. The central focus of this chapter is on Nonaka and his various collaborators, whose work on knowledge creation is arguably the most well known and used of all writing on knowledge management. The chapter provides a critical evaluation of his work, highlighting a number of ways in which it has been criticized.

Chapter 8 examines an equally important aspect of organizational innovation processes, though one which is often neglected in the knowledge management literature: the process of unlearning or giving up knowledge which may be perceived as not having contemporary relevance.

Part 4, the last, but largest section of the book examines a diverse range of human and social issues related to managing knowledge in organizations, all of which have emerged as being important to organizational attempts at knowledge management. Chapter 9 considers the question of how knowledge processes in organizations are intimately linked to the topic of motivation. The chapter challenges the assumption that people are likely to be willing to share their knowledge, and explores why this is the case. This chapter utilizes the now copious literature that argues for a greater sensitivity to human and social factors.

Chapters 10 and 11 look at the dynamics of knowledge sharing and knowledge generation in two distinctive types of group situation. These chapters illustrate different aspects of the collective and shared nature of much organizational knowledge. Chapter 10 uses the community of practice concept to consider the dynamics of knowledge sharing and knowledge production in a homogeneous group context, where the people working together have well-established social relations, a significant degree of common knowledge, and a sense of collective identity. It closes by examining the potential dark side of communities of practice, which has been relatively unexplored in the communities of practice literature. Chapter 11 considers knowledge processes in more heterogeneous group contexts, where there are limited social relations, a limited degree of common knowledge, and a limited sense of collective identity (for example, in international project teams). This chapter shows how the dynamics of knowledge sharing and production in such a context are significantly different from those that are typical within communities of practice.

Chapter 12 builds on some of the issues touched on in Chapter 9: how knowledge processes are shaped by the conflict and politics that are an inherent part of organizational life. In general, the chapter considers how and why knowledge and power are inextricably linked, and specifically examines how conflicts in the development and use of knowledge can also be linked to the fundamental character of the employment relationship. The chapter examines the contrasting perspectives on knowledge and power developed within what Schultze and Stabell label the critical and discursive discourses on knowledge management.

Chapter 13 covers one of the most heated debates in the knowledge management literature, the role that information technology can play in knowledge management processes. The chapter considers two broad ways in which IT systems can facilitate knowledge management, first via the codification, organization, and sharing of knowledge, and secondly via facilitating processes of interpersonal communication (such as via interactive Web 2.0 technologies).

Chapter 14 examines the way that organizations have shaped and can attempt to shape the knowledge behaviours of their staff through utilizing specific HRM policies and practices such as recruitment, rewards, and training. Chapter 15, the final chapter in Part 4, looks at the topics of leadership and organizational culture. These topics are considered together due to the significant role that organizational leaders can play in shaping the culture within an organization. The chapter considers the role of senior management in organizations in facilitating or inhibiting knowledge management processes, and also how organizational culture can shape workers' attitudes towards the management of their knowledge.

The book then concludes in Chapter 16 by considering the extent to which knowledge management is likely to continue being a topic of great importance, reflecting on how the level of interest in it by business organizations, academics, and consultants has evolved over time.

 ## Review and Discussion Questions

1. What is your position on the knowledge society debate? Do you believe that the economy and society in the country in which you live has the characteristics of a knowledge society? What evidence supports and undermines your argument?

2. Why do you think academic interest in the topic of knowledge management has been sustained since it first became a topic of interest in the mid-1990s?

3. The critical and dialogical discourses raise the idea that knowledge management initiatives may not always be in the best interests of everyone working in an organization. To what extent do knowledge management initiatives create conflicts of interest between senior managers and workers in business organizations?

4. To what extent is the dissensus-based perspective on knowledge management (the critical and dialogical discourses) neglected in the knowledge management literature. Can you think of any examples of work which utilizes either of these perspectives?

 ## Suggestions for Further Reading

1. **R. DeFillippi, M. Arthur, and V. Lindsay (2006)** *Knowledge at Work: Creative Collaboration in the Global Economy* **(London: Blackwell).**
This represents a good example of a text clearly embracing the knowledge society thesis and examining the implications of it for organizations and managers.

2. **S. Walby (2011) 'Is the Knowledge Society Gendered?',** *Gender, Work and Organization*, **18: 1–29.**
Not only examines how issues of gender links to knowledge work and the knowledge society, but also presents different definitions of what constitutes the knowledge economy.

3. U. Schultze and C. Stabell (2004) 'Knowing What you Don't Know? Discourses and Contradictions in Knowledge Management Research', *Journal of Management Studies*, 41: 549–73.

A useful analysis which provides a way to categorize the diverse range of work published on knowledge management.

Take your learning further: Online Resource Centre

Visit the Online Resource Centre for resources which will extend your understanding of knowledge management in organizations. As well as web links to sites of interest, the author has provided case studies looking at knowledge management in virtual and knowledge-intensive firms, and in global multinationals. These will help you with your research, essays, and assignments; or you may find these additional resources helpful when revising for exams.

 www.oxfordtextbooks.co.uk/orc/hislop3e/

Part 1

··

Epistemologies of Knowledge in the Knowledge Management Literature

· ·

Chapter 1 has introduced the idea that increasingly knowledge is seen as representing the most important asset organizations possess, and that society has witnessed a significant increase in both the number of knowledge workers and knowledge-intensive organizations. This begs a number of questions, not least of which is: what is knowledge? This represents one of the most fundamental questions that humanity has grappled with, and has occupied the minds of philosophers for centuries. Furthermore, even in contemporary times, interest in the topic of knowledge stems from more than the growth of interest in knowledge management. For example, postmodern philosophy has raised questions about the assumed objectivity of knowledge, and in the process has sparked an enormous debate. Therefore, in engaging with the question of the fundamental character of knowledge, it is tempting to look beyond the knowledge management literature and engage with the wider historical and philosophical literature on the topic. However, this temptation is resisted here, for two primary reasons.

First, it is way beyond the scope of this book to attempt to provide any kind of adequate review, however brief, of the debates regarding the nature of knowledge (such as what distinguishes knowledge from belief, opinion, etc.), or to describe, compare, and contrast the different perspectives on knowledge that have been developed by different writers (from Plato and Aristotle to later philosophers such as Hume, Kant, and Nietzsche to twentieth-century writers such as Ryle or Polanyi[1]). The second reason for not engaging with such issues and writers here is that few writers on knowledge management do so. Styhre (2003) suggests two reasons for this. First, writers on knowledge management appear less interested in knowledge *per se*, instead having a narrow focus on knowledge in workplaces that has practical utility and can contribute to an organization's competitive advantage. Further, writers on knowledge management appear unwilling to embrace the idea that knowledge is not ultimately amenable to

[1] Anyone interested in developing an understanding of such issues should find and read one/some of the many books which provide an introduction to, and overview of, the philosophy and theory of knowledge.

management control. However, where knowledge management writers do engage directly with such issues and philosophers, such as the use of Polanyi's work in discussions of tacit knowledge, or Foucault's concept of power/knowledge, reference will be made to relevant philosophers.

Thus, this section of the book deliberately chooses to focus narrowly on how knowledge is conceptualized in the knowledge management literature. Even with this restricted focus, addressing the question of the nature of knowledge is by no means simple. This is to a large extent because in the contemporary literature on knowledge management there are an enormous range of definitions, and from the way knowledge is described by different writers it is obvious that it is conceptualized in hugely divergent ways. Thus, rather than suggest that there is one single 'true' definition of what knowledge is, the book reflects the fragmented nature of the contemporary debate on this topic and presents various definitions and descriptions. As will be seen, the competing conceptualizations examined are based on fundamentally different epistemologies.

DEFINITION Epistemology

Philosophy addressing the nature of knowledge. Concerned with questions such as: is knowledge objective and measurable? Can knowledge be acquired or is it experienced? What is regarded as valid knowledge, and why?

As outlined in Chapter 1, Schultze and Stabell (2004), drawing on Burrell and Morgan's (1979) analysis of sociological paradigms, suggested that two distinctive epistemologies exist in the knowledge management literature. This is a similar conclusion to that reached by a number of other writers (see Table I), who label their epistemologies differently from Schultze and Stabell. This part of the book is structured to reflect these findings and a separate chapter is devoted to each epistemology, with Chapter 2 examining what is here labelled the objectivist perspective, and Chapter 3 what is here labelled the practice-based perspective (see Table I).

These chapters examine not only how knowledge is conceptualized within each perspective, but also how the management and sharing of knowledge is characterized, based on their different assumptions about knowledge. Therefore, to best understand these competing perspectives, and to allow an effective comparison of their differences, it is useful to read these chapters in parallel, and consider them as being two halves of a debate.

While the objectivist epistemology represents the dominant perspective in the knowledge management literature (Schultze and Stabell 2004), as will be seen in Chapters 3 and 16 the popularity of the practice-based perspective has grown over time. In fact, it has become such a widely utilized perspective that Corradi *et al*. (2010) refer to the 'bandwagon' of practice-based studies. Thus having an understanding of both perspectives is useful. These represent probably the most difficult chapters to read, as they deal with relatively abstract ideas. However, they provide a useful foundation to the issues addressed in the remainder of the book. A thorough grasp of these issues should facilitate a deeper understanding of what follows.

Table I Competing Epistemologies

Author	Objectivist Perspective	Practice-based Perspective
Schultze and Stabell (2004)	Epistemology of dualism	Epistemology of duality
Werr and Stjernberg (2003)	Knowledge as theory	Knowledge as practice
Empson (2001a)	Knowledge as an asset	Knowing as a process
Cook and Brown (1999)	Epistemology of possession	Epistemology of practice
McAdam and McCreedy (2000)	Knowledge as truth	Knowledge as socially constructed
Scarbrough (1998)	'Content' theory of knowledge	'Relational' view of knowledge

The Objectivist Perspective on Knowledge

Introduction

The purpose of this chapter is to fully articulate the objectivist perspective on knowledge. In this book the term 'objectivist' perspective is used instead of the various terms adopted by other writers (see Table I in the introduction to Part 1 of the book). This is because this label embodies and highlights what are here regarded as two of this perspective's foundational assumptions: not only that much organizational knowledge is typically considered as being objective in character, but also that such knowledge can be separated from people via codification into the form of an object, or entity (explicit knowledge).

This chapter is structured as follows. First, it begins by outlining the key assumptions and characteristics of the objectivist perspective on knowledge. The characteristics of this perspective are further elaborated in the second section which examines and gives examples of work utilizing the knowledge-based theory of the firm, which, as outlined, is one of the most important and well-known theories associated with the neo-functionalist variant of the objectivist perspective. The third section of the chapter examines the development of knowledge typologies that highlight and differentiate between distinctive categories of knowledge (the most well-known being tacit and explicit knowledge). The final section of the chapter concludes by considering how those adopting an objectivist perspective on knowledge typically conceptualize the sharing and management of organizational knowledge.

Objectivist Perspectives on Knowledge

The primary aim of this section is to describe the principles and characteristics of the objectivist epistemology of knowledge, outlining the way it characterizes knowledge, which can be summarized as having four distinctive features (see Table 2.1). Cook and Brown (1999) refer to this perspective as the 'epistemology of possession', as knowledge is regarded as an entity that people or groups possess.

Within the objectivist perspective the entitative character of knowledge is the primary characteristic. Knowledge is regarded as an entity/commodity that people possess, but which can exist independently of people in a codifiable form. From this perspective,

Table 2.1 The Objectivist Character of Knowledge

Character of Knowledge from an Objectivist Epistemology
Knowledge is an entity/object
Based on a positivistic philosophy: knowledge regarded as objective 'facts'
Explicit knowledge (objective) privileged over tacit knowledge (subjective)
Knowledge is derived from an intellectual process

knowledge can be codified, made explicit, and separated from the person who creates, develops, and/or utilizes it. Such knowledge can exist in a number of forms, including documents, diagrams, computer systems, or be embedded in physical artefacts such as machinery or tools. Thus, for example, a text-based manual of computer operating procedures, whether in the form of a document, CD, or web page, represents a form of explicit knowledge. King and Marks illustrate this assumption through talking about how IT-based knowledge management systems 'capture' (2008: 131) people's individual knowledge.

A further assumption about the nature of knowledge is that it is regarded as objective. The assumption is that it is possible to develop a type of knowledge and understanding that is free from individual subjectivity. This represents what McAdam and McCreedy (2000) described as the 'knowledge is truth' perspective, where explicit knowledge is seen as equivalent to a canonical body of scientific facts and laws which are consistent across cultures and time. The idea that explicit knowledge can exist in a textual form stems from a number of assumptions about the nature of language, including that language has fixed and objective meanings. These ideas are deeply rooted in the philosophy of positivism, the idea that the social world can be studied scientifically, i.e. that social phenomena can be quantified and measured, that general laws and principles can be established, and that objective knowledge is produced as a result.

DEFINITION Positivism

While Comte, a nineteenth-century French philosopher, founded what is now called Positivism, Durkheim was arguably the first to translate these ideas into the realm of sociology. Durkheim was concerned to make sociology into a science, and advocated the use of positivistic philosophy. This philosophy assumes that cause and effect can be established between social phenomena through the use of observation and testing, and that general laws and principles can be identified. These general laws and principles constitute objective knowledge.

The third key element of the objectivist epistemology is that it privileges explicit knowledge over tacit knowledge. Primarily, explicit knowledge is regarded as equivalent to objective knowledge. Tacit knowledge on the other hand, knowledge which is difficult to articulate in an explicit form, is regarded as more informal, more personal and individualized, less rigorous and highly subjective, being embedded within the cultural values and assumptions of those who possess and use it. Nonaka *et al.* (2000), for example, make this explicit by suggesting that 'explicit knowledge can be expressed in formal and systematic language and shared in the form of data, scientific formulae . . . In contrast, tacit knowledge is highly personal . . . Subjective insights, intuitions and hunches fall into this category of knowledge.'

However, a key element of Nonaka's perspective on epistemology, as will be seen in Chapter 7, is that he challenges the privileging and prioritization of explicit knowledge, which he regards as being characteristic of the way knowledge is conceptualized in 'western' societies, and suggests that greater attention should be paid to the role of tacit knowledge.

The final major assumption is that knowledge is regarded as primarily a cognitive, intellectual entity (but which is ultimately codifiable). As Cook and Brown (1999: 384) suggest, knowledge 'is something that is held in the head'. From this perspective, the development and production of knowledge comes from a process of intellectual reflection (individual or collective), and is primarily a cognitive process.

The Knowledge-Based Theory of the Firm

The knowledge-based theory of the firm represents the dominant theory which adopts the objectivist perspective on knowledge. For example, Nonaka and Peltokorpi's (2006) analysis of the twenty most cited knowledge management articles found that articles using or developing the knowledge- (and/or resource-) based theory of the firm were prominent in this list. Hence it is worth spending time examining it in a little detail.

The knowledge-based theory of the firm, which represents a specific development from the resource-based view of the firm, was initially articulated and developed by a number of writers including Spender (1996), Kogut and Zander (1996), and Grant (1996). Over time the theory has been developed and refined partly through theoretical development, and partly through empirical testing (Berman *et al.* 2002; Bogner and Bansal 2007; Cuervo-Cazurra and Un 2010; Haas and Hansen 2007; Nahapiet and Ghoshal 1998; Sullivan and Marvel 2011; Wang *et al.* 2009). Finally, it is a perspective that underpins much knowledge management literature (Donate and Guadamillas 2010; King and Marks 2008; Stock *et al* 2010; Voelpel *et al.* 2005; Williams 2011). There are two central tenets to the knowledge-based theory of the firm. First, it assumes that knowledge which is difficult to replicate and copy can be a significant source of competitive advantage for firms. Knowledge that is assumed to be difficult to replicate is firm-specific knowledge, which builds from and links to existing knowledge within an organization, and which is related to firm-specific products, services, or processes (Wang *et al.* 2009). Secondly, it assumes that organizations provide a more effective mechanism than markets do for the sharing and integration of knowledge between people. Thus, two of the key focuses of research which utilizes the knowledge-based theory of the firm are on the development of firm-specific knowledge (see e.g. Nag and Gioia 2012), and the relationship between the development and use of such knowledge and firm performance (see e.g. Bogner and Bansal 2007).

The compatibility of the knowledge-based view of the firm with Schultze and Stabell's (2004) neo-functionalist discourse is visible in the fundamental, unquestioned assumptions made by those adopting this perspective (such as those listed in the previous paragraph) that organizational knowledge is an increasingly important source of competitive advantage for firms and, further, that the interests of workers and organizational managers and owners in attempting to protect this are compatible and not contradictory.

The compatibility of the knowledge-based view of the firm with the characteristics of the objectivist perspective on knowledge just outlined is also typically quite apparent. For example, such work typically adopts an entitative view of knowledge (see e.g. Szulanski 1996), with Glazer (1998: 176) explicitly talking about 'knowledge as a commodity'. Second, this perspective is also founded on the idea that there are separate and distinctive types of knowledge, such as tacit and explicit, and group and individual knowledge (see e.g. Berman *et al.* 2002; Haas and Hansen 2007; Williams 2011). Finally, assumptions in this perspective regarding the objective character of knowledge are apparent in the view that the quality and character of organizational knowledge can be quantified and measured. For example, one of the key objectives of Glazer's article is to facilitate efforts to 'develop reliable and valid measures of knowledge' (1998: 176). Further, Haas and Hansen, in examining how the acquisition of tacit and explicit knowledge can improve task performance, assume unproblematically that it is possible to measure the quality of both types of knowledge (defined as 'rigour, soundness and insight', 2007: 1137) through asking relevant questions in a survey.

Finally, the compatibility of those utilizing and developing the knowledge-based theory of the firm with the objectivist perspective on knowledge is evident in the use of positivistic methods to investigate and analyse organizational knowledge and knowledge management processes. This is apparent in the assumptions that the variables under investigation can be objectively measured (typically via quantitative methods involving the collection of large bodies of statistical data), and that objective causal relationships between these variables can be revealed via the development and testing (via statistical analysis) of specific hypotheses. Such characteristics are visible in the various illustrated examples provided in this chapter.

At this point it is useful to briefly link to the concept of 'intellectual capital accounting', as it builds on the principles of the knowledge-based view of the firm, being concerned with finding a way to objectively measure, in accounting terms, the contribution that the intellectual assets of an organization's workforce can make to organizational value and organizational performance. When interest in knowledge management was in its infancy a number of writers suggested that the increasing contribution of knowledge to organizational performance meant that accounting systems required to be adapted to take account of this (see e.g. Seetharaman *et al.* 2002). However, attempts to find a way of formally defining what intellectual capital is and how exactly it contributed to the value and share price of companies failed. Ultimately, no consensus was reached on how this could be done, and very few companies have attempted to quantitatively and formally account for the contribution of intellectual capital to their financial performance (Andrikopoulos 2010). Thus, while intellectual capital accounting was regarded by some as an important topic in the early 2000s, it has now become an almost forgotten footnote in the evolving knowledge management literature. However, the failure of intellectual capital accounting did not mean that the assumptions of the knowledge-based view of the firm became questioned or the way it conceptualized knowledge in organizations became any less popular, as the knowledge-based view of the firm has continued to be one of the dominant models underpinning knowledge management initiatives and studies.

Typologies of Knowledge

As has been outlined, one of the primary features of the objectivist perspective on knowledge is the privileging of explicit/objective knowledge over tacit/subjective knowledge. This distinction between tacit and explicit knowledge, which are regarded as quite separate and distinct types of knowledge, flows from the either/or logic of binary oppositions which is a fundamental characteristic of this perspective (see Figure 1.3, and also Nonaka and Peltokorpi 2006). Thus, one feature of the writing of those adopting an objectivist perspective on knowledge is to make and develop typologies that identify and distinguish between fundamentally different types of knowledge. Two of the most common distinctions made which are examined here are between tacit and explicit knowledge, and individual and collective or group knowledge.

Tacit and explicit knowledge

The tacit–explicit dichotomy is ubiquitous in analyses of organizational knowledge. Explicit knowledge, from an objectivist perspective, is synonymous with objective knowledge, therefore, it is unnecessary to restate in detail its characteristics (see Table 2.2). Suffice to say that explicit knowledge is regarded as objective, standing above and separate from both individual and social value systems and, secondly, that it can be codified into a tangible form.

Tacit knowledge on the other hand represents knowledge that people possess, and which may importantly shape how they think and act, but which cannot be fully made explicit. It incorporates both physical/cognitive skills (such as the ability to juggle, to do mental arithmetic, to weld, or to create a successful advertising slogan), and cognitive frameworks (such as the value systems that people possess). The main characteristic of tacit knowledge is therefore that it is personal and is difficult, if not impossible, to disembody and codify. This is because tacit knowledge may not only be difficult to articulate, but may even be subconscious (see Table 2.2). Two of the most commonly referred to examples of tacit knowledge are the ability to ride a bike or to swim, with the knowledge possessed by people of how to carry out these activities being difficult to communicate, articulate, and share. Examples of work-related tacit knowledge include the ability to write good computer software, the ability of a skilled craftsman to produce high-quality goods, the ability to be an effective leader, and the ability to solve complex problems.

This distinction between tacit and explicit knowledge is by no means unique to the objectivist epistemology of knowledge, but the specific way that the distinction is theorized within this perspective is quite particular. Importantly, as will be seen later in the chapter, some major implications flow from this depiction of the dichotomy in terms of the way

Table 2.2 The Characteristics of Tacit and Explicit Knowledge

Tacit Knowledge	Explicit Knowledge
Inexpressible in a codifiable form	Codifiable
Subjective	Objective
Personal	Impersonal
Context-specific	Context independent
Difficult to share	Easy to share

knowledge-sharing processes are conceptualized. Within the objectivist epistemological framework an either/or logic predominates, resulting in tacit and explicit knowledge being regarded as separate and distinctive types of knowledge. This characterization of the dichotomy is explicit in the following quotation, '[t]here are two types of knowledge: explicit knowledge and tacit knowledge' (Nonaka *et al.* 2000). From this perspective, tacit and explicit knowledge do not represent the extremes of a spectrum, but instead represent two pure and separate forms of knowledge.

Typically, this polarized dichotomy is argued to be based on the work of Michael Polanyi (1958, 1983). Nonaka makes this derivation explicit. However, as will be shown in Chapter 3, there is another, distinctly different interpretation of Polanyi's work, which questions this conceptualization of the tacit–explicit dichotomy. More details on Nonaka's conceptualization of knowledge are presented in Chapter 7.

 Illustration   The role played by the acquisition of tacit and explicit knowledge in improving task productivity

Haas and Hansen (2007) examined the impact that the acquisition by work groups of tacit and explicit knowledge from beyond their group/team had on what they called task productivity. This was done within the empirical context of sales teams in a large management consultancy firm in the USA. The management consultancy firm examined provided tax and audit advice to clients in a wide range of industries including energy, communications, healthcare, automotive, and financial services. The study focused narrowly on the acquisition and use of knowledge in the work done by sales teams in pitching for business with prospective clients. One of the key elements involved in preparing such bids, the knowledge-sharing/acquisition process examined by Hass and Hansen, was to draw on and utilize knowledge or experience from previous bids that was felt to be relevant. The data on the knowledge and work processes they examined were acquired from surveys that were distributed to the team leaders of a random selection of sales bids carried out during the time of the research. Three dimensions of task productivity were examined, including time saved, task quality, and the extent to which the bid team were considered to be competent by external stakeholders such as clients. In terms of knowledge sharing, two mechanisms were examined, with one being related to each type of knowledge that was examined. Fundamentally it was assumed that explicit knowledge was shared through the acquisition and use of documentation, whereas tacit knowledge was acquired through person-to-person interaction.

The most fundamental and general finding of their study was that the acquisition of both tacit and explicit knowledge from outside the bid teams did positively impact on task productivity, but in quite different ways. For example, the acquisition of explicit knowledge did have positive time-saving benefits, but the acquisition of tacit knowledge did not. Further, the higher the quality of the explicit/codified knowledge that was used, the greater the time saving. By contrast, the sharing of tacit knowledge improved both task quality and client's perception of competence, with both being positively related to the quality of the tacit knowledge that was shared. This study does not privilege tacit over explicit knowledge and shows that both tacit and explicit knowledge have their own distinctive benefits for task productivity.

1. Does this empirical evidence undermine assumptions regarding the superiority of explicit over tacit knowledge?

Individual–group knowledge

While some argue that knowledge can only ever exist at the level of the individual, this idea is disputed by a range of writers. These writers argue that, while much knowledge does reside within individuals, there is a sense in which knowledge can reside in social groups in the form of shared work practices and routines, and shared assumptions or perspectives (Collins 2007; Ebbers and Wijnberg 2009; Hecker 2012). This insight is used as the basis for a further dichotomy of knowledge types: into individual- and group/social-level knowledge. One of the most well-known advocates of such a perspective is Spender (1996), who combined the tacit–explicit dichotomy with the individual–group dichotomy to produce a two-by-two matrix with four generic types of knowledge (Table 2.3).

Objectified knowledge represents explicit group knowledge, for example a documented system of rules, operating procedures or formalized organizational routines. *Collective* knowledge on the other hand represents tacit group knowledge, knowledge possessed by a group that is not codified. Examples of this include informal organizational routines and ways of working, stories and shared systems of understanding. For example, the value systems that people possess have a collective element, as they are related to values and ideas that circulate within the particular social milieu that people work within. The massive expansion of the culture management industry that has occurred since the mid-1980s, which attempts to inculcate specific value systems within organizations, suggests that there is an optimism amongst organizational management that such shared systems of values can be developed.

However, collective knowledge can exist within different types of community, of different sizes and characteristics. For example, at a relatively small-scale level, collective knowledge can exist within teams or communities. One specific example of this small-scale community knowledge that is increasingly being referred to is that possessed and held within communities of practice (see Chapter 10). However, other types of group or community within which collective knowledge can be developed include departments, sites, organizations, or business units within multinational corporations. At a more macro level, Lam (1997) also found that the national cultural context could play an important role in shaping the nature of organizational knowledge.

One of the most detailed analyses of collective knowledge was produced by Hecker (2012). Constraints of space make it impossible to fully articulate the model of collective knowledge developed by Hecker. However, it is worth highlighting the distinction Hecker makes between three types of collective knowledge (see Table 2.4). The first type of collective knowledge identified by Hecker is shared knowledge. This represents knowledge that is possessed by a range of different members within a community.

Table 2.3 Generic Knowledge Types

	Individual	Social
Explicit	Conscious	Objectified
Tacit	Automatic	Collective

Source: Adapted from Spender 1996.

Table 2.4 Hecker's (2012) Three Types of Collective Knowledge

Type of Collective Knowledge	Definition	Locus	Relationship to Individual Knowledge	Origin
Shared Knowledge	Knowledge held by individuals in a group	Individuals	Overlapping, common knowledge	Shared experiences
Complementary Knowledge	Knowledge regarding the division of expertise within a group	Interdependencies between individual knowledge		Specialized division of knowledge within group
Artefact-Embedded Knowledge	Knowledge embedded in collective, group artefacts	Artefact	Combinations of individual knowledge in an articulated form	Codification and articulation of knowledge

---

Illustration   Collective tacit knowledge within temporary project teams in the film industry

Ebbers and Wijnberg (2009) examine the development of collective knowledge and its impact on performance within temporary project teams in the film industry. While their analysis is focused around the concept of organizational memory, in terms of the Hecker (2012) framework just outlined, what they examine can be referred to as complementary knowledge. The data presented by Ebbers and Wijnberg are taken from a qualitative study where twenty-four interviews were conducted with different film producers and directors. What is presented here is not the central argument developed by Ebbers and Wijnberg, which relates to the relationship between two different types of organizational memory, with the focus instead being narrowly on how collective knowledge was developed, and the benefits this provided to teams where such collective knowledge existed.

In the film industry, collective knowledge develops when the same people work together on successive film projects. Fundamentally, collective knowledge is developed through shared experiences. In the context of film production, when people collaborate together on a particular project they develop insights into each other's tastes and habits, and their ways of working. Collaborating with the same people on successive projects thus has a number of potential benefits. First, it gives people insights into each other's abilities, thus one director said he preferred to work with the same people, 'because of what they are capable of and because they are pleasant to work with' (p. 486). Another benefit of having such complementary knowledge is that it can speed up decision-making processes, and film production in general. Thus, as one director said, 'if you know what to expect from someone, and you collaborate often, you will work more efficiently' (p. 486). Another director talking about serial collaboration expressed similar sentiments saying, 'I only need to signal to make clear what I mean. That way you can communicate very fast' (p. 486).

For example, within a sales team, this may be shared knowledge regarding how to manage customer interactions. The second type of collective knowledge identified by Hecker is complementary knowledge. This is where there is a knowledge-based division of labour within a community, where people possess different bodies of (overlapping) but specialized knowledge. The shared, complementary knowledge in this context is the knowledge and understanding people have about the distribution of expertise within the community, where community members' knowledge of each other's expertise helps them to effectively coordinate their work activities such that their collective efforts are greater than the sum of their individual knowledge and efforts. The third and final type of collective knowledge identified by Hecker is knowledge embedded in artefacts which are developed and used collectively by community members. Examples of such artefacts are documentation (such as a shared presentation or database), or technological artefacts, such as collectively developed products.

An Objectivist Perspective on the Sharing and Management of Knowledge

Having examined both the fundamental character of knowledge, and the way knowledge can be categorized into different types, the final section of the chapter looks at the implications of these ideas for the sharing and management of knowledge. This section begins by making explicit the general model of knowledge sharing which flows from objectivist assumptions regarding knowledge, before concluding by outlining the way knowledge management processes are characterized.

Conduit model of knowledge sharing

The assumptions in the objectivist perspective outlined earlier that knowledge can be externalized from people into a separate and discrete object or entity, and that knowledge can also be objective, have profound implications for how knowledge-sharing processes are conceptualized.

Building from such assumptions the sharing of knowledge from an objectivist perspective represents what has been referred to as the conduit or transmitter/receiver model (see Figure 2.1). This model suggests that knowledge is shared by the transferral of explicit, codified knowledge (in the form of text, a diagram, or an electronic document, etc.) from an isolated sender to a separate receiver. The metaphor of knowledge sharing as being similar to the posting of a letter is thus appropriate. The idea behind this model is that the sender, in isolation from the receiver, can produce some wholly explicit knowledge, and then

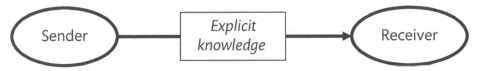

Figure 2.1 The Conduit Model of Knowledge Sharing

transfer it remotely to the receiver. The receiver then takes this knowledge and is able to understand it and use it without any other form of interaction with the sender. Further, it is assumed that no important aspects of this explicit knowledge are lost in the transfer process, and that both sender and receiver derive the same meaning from the knowledge.

Such assumptions are often made explicit. For example, Szulanski, while acknowledging that most organizational knowledge has tacit components, and can be embedded in organizational routines, suggests that knowledge sharing involves 'the exchange of organizational knowledge between a source and a recipient' (1996: 28). Voelpel *et al*.'s (2005) case study of Siemens' ShareNet knowledge management initiative (which is examined at the end of Chapter 4) also reveals similar assumptions, as utilizing the resource-based theory of the firm, they use terms such as 'source unit's knowledge', 'transmission channels' and 'receiving unit' (p. 10) to conceptualize knowledge transfer processes. Finally, Williams, who utilizes the knowledge-based view of the firm to analyse the sharing of knowledge between some clients and offshore engineers they work with, says that 'knowledge transfer involves both [the] transmission of knowledge from sender to recipient, as well as its integration and application by the recipient' (2011: 338).

Knowledge management processes

Building from these assumptions regarding the sharing of knowledge, we can now examine the nature of knowledge management processes from an objectivist perspective (Table 2.5).

Based on the strict dichotomy on which the objectivist perspective is founded, where tacit and explicit knowledge are regarded as distinctive and separate types of knowledge with quite specific characteristics, the sharing of tacit and explicit knowledge are also regarded as being fundamentally different processes (the case study by Haas and Hansen is a good illustration of this, as is the study by Williams 2011). From this perspective, while the sharing of tacit knowledge is acknowledged to be difficult, complex, and time-consuming, the sharing of explicit knowledge is regarded as much more straightforward. In fact, from the objectivist perspective, the easy transferability of explicit knowledge represents one of its defining characteristics. For example, Grant (1996: 111) suggests that 'explicit knowledge is revealed by its communication. This ease of communication is its fundamental property.'

The typical starting point in objectivist conceptualizations of knowledge management is the processes of codifying relevant knowledge, converting tacit to explicit knowledge (a process which Nonaka and his collaborators refer to as 'externalization'—see Chapter 7). From this perspective there is an acknowledgement that much organizational knowledge may be tacit. But this is accompanied by an optimism that it is possible to convert much of this knowledge to an explicit form. For example, while all the assembly instructions for

Table 2.5 An Objectivist Perspective on Knowledge Management

Knowledge Management: Objectivist Perspective
Convert tacit to explicit knowledge (codification)
Collect knowledge in central repository
Structure/systematize knowledge (into discrete categories)
Information and Communication Technologies play a key role

putting together a car, or all the stages in a telesales customer interaction, may not be totally explicit, with effort and work it is assumed to be possible to make all this knowledge explicit, and codify it into a complete set of instructions/body of knowledge. This can be achieved by getting relevant workers to articulate all their knowledge about such processes, making explicit all the assumptions, behaviours, and actions they utilize in accomplishing the task being examined.

Thus, the first stage in any knowledge management initiative, from this perspective, is to identify what knowledge is important and then make it explicit. The typical optimism that exists with regard to the extent to which tacit knowledge can be made at least partially explicit means that the difficulties involved in sharing tacit knowledge, and the nature of such processes are not typically central to objectivist models of knowledge management.

 Time to reflect 'Externalizing' tacit knowledge

Think about an example of tacit knowledge that you possess. To what extent could this knowledge be converted into an explicit form? Could it be codified such that someone else could utilize it? Further, how easy and how time-consuming is this process likely to be?

The next stage in the knowledge management process involves collecting all the codified knowledge together into a central repository, and then structuring it in a systematic way to make it easily accessible to others (Durcikova and Gray 2009). Thus for example, the knowledge may be collected in a central database, where it is not only stored, but also categorized, indexed, and cross-referenced. The importance of doing this effectively is related to the next part of the knowledge management process: making this knowledge accessible to all people who may want to use it. One of the primary rationales for organizations managing their knowledge is to allow knowledge to be more widely and effectively shared within organizations (so that 'best practices' can be shared, etc.). This makes organizing knowledge, and making it accessible, equally as important as the codification process. The knowledge management system examined by King and Marks (2008) fits with these objectives, being described as a 'repository' whose purpose is to facilitate the dissemination of best-practice knowledge among the case study organization's globally dispersed workforce.

Finally, information and communication technologies (ICTs) typically play a key role in knowledge management processes utilizing the objectivist perspective. For example ICTs can play an important role in almost every element of the knowledge management process (Gilbert *et al.* 2010). First, they can provide a repository (for example, databases) in which codified knowledge can be stored (Cha *et al.* 2008). Secondly, they can play a role in the organizing of knowledge (for example, with electronic cross-referencing systems). Finally they can provide conduits and mechanisms through which knowledge can be transferred into or extracted from a central repository (for example, through an intranet system or search engine). It is thus no surprise that many studies into the role of ICTs in knowledge management initiatives utilize an objectivist perspective on knowledge (see e.g. King and Marks 2008; Voelpel *et al.* 2005). The role of ICTs in knowledge management processes is examined more fully in Chapter 13.

Conclusion

This chapter has outlined the defining characteristics of the objectivist perspective on knowledge, which represents the mainstream perspective in the knowledge management literature on how to conceptualize knowledge. The most fundamental features of this perspective on knowledge are that it assumes that knowledge can take the form of a discrete entity, separate from people who may understand or use it. While within this perspective there is an acknowledgement that knowledge can take different forms, most importantly between tacit and explicit knowledge, there is an assumption and optimism that much of the organizational knowledge possessed by workers can be codified into an explicit form. Some subsidiary features of this perspective on knowledge are that tacit and explicit knowledge are regarded as quite separate and distinctive types of knowledge, with explicit knowledge typically being privileged and prioritized over tacit knowledge. This is largely because explicit or codified knowledge is typically characterized as being objective, while tacit knowledge is, in contrast, assumed to be more personal, subjective, and context-specific.

These assumptions about the nature of knowledge have significant implications for how the management and sharing of knowledge are conceptualized. The privileging of explicit knowledge within this perspective means that there is a bias towards and focus upon the management and sharing of explicit, codified knowledge. The emphasis on codified knowledge is also due to assumptions that it is much easier to manage and share codified knowledge than it is to manage and share tacit knowledge. The optimism regarding the codifiability of knowledge means that those adopting an objectivist perspective on knowledge typically emphasize processes of codification. Thus, from this perspective, an initial step in the management and sharing of knowledge is to codify as much knowledge as possible. The sharing of such knowledge between people has the characteristics of a 'transmitter–receiver' model, where it is assumed codified, explicit knowledge can be passed from one person to another unmodified. This perspective on knowledge typically also suggests that computer and communication technologies can play a key role in knowledge management processes, through providing one important medium, or conduit, via which codified knowledge can be shared.

 Case study   Motivating workers to develop firm-specific knowledge via the use of different governance mechanisms

Wang *et al.* (2009) make both an empirical and conceptual contribution to the knowledge-based view of the firm. They do this by developing hypotheses that address some significant gaps in knowledge and then testing them empirically. The gap in knowledge they address is the extent to which different governance mechanisms motivate workers to contribute to the development of organization-specific knowledge resources. This is a neglected topic as the literature on the resource/knowledge-based view of the firm typically doesn't question or address the issue of employee motivation, generally assuming that such motivation is unproblematic.

Wang *et al.* (2009) argue that, in line with the knowledge-based view of the firm, the development of firm-specific knowledge is likely to benefit the firm. Further, they argue that the development of such knowledge does not happen automatically, and is dependent on the activity of key organizational employees. However, they argue that workers may not necessarily be willing to invest the effort necessary to develop this knowledge. This is because contributing to the development of firm-specific resources does little to improve the marketability of workers in external labour markets, as the firm-specific knowledge they are contributing to the development of has limited relevance and transferability beyond the firm. The main way in which employees can benefit from the development of such knowledge is via being rewarded by their employer. If workers have concerns regarding whether they will be adequately rewarded by their employer for such efforts they may be unwilling to contribute to the development of firm-specific knowledge resources. Thus, for firms to ensure that their workers are willing to contribute to the development of such resources, they need to motivate them to do so. Wang *et al.* investigate the extent to which two different governance mechanisms were able to provide this motivation.

The governance mechanisms they examined were economic (rewarding employees by giving them some company stocks and shares) and relationship-based (developing long-term employee loyalty to the firm). In relation to rewarding employees via giving them company stock, this is argued to help align the interests of the employee with that of the company. Thus it is hypothesized that there will be a positive relationship between levels of organization-specific knowledge and the provision of this type of economic governance mechanism. Another way in which to align the interests of the employee and the company is via the development of employee trust and loyalty in the firm. Wang *et al.* argue that such trust and loyalty can be developed via providing long-term employee benefits, such as giving access to training, having team-based appraisal, and using long-term employment policies. They hypothesize that there will be a positive relationship between the provision of such resources, and the levels of firm-specific knowledge a firm possesses.

The hypotheses were tested via the analysis of data that were collected from a range of different databases, but were restricted to manufacturing companies in the USA. The composite dataset that was developed contained information on 211 companies. The existence of firm-specific knowledge was measured via looking at patent data and counting the number of self-citations in patent applications. It was assumed that, if a patent application included citations of other company patents, this represented evidence of the development of firm-specific knowledge, which is developed cumulatively and iteratively. The provision of long-term employee benefits was measured via data on factors as diverse as whether companies had good union relations, had 'no layoff' policies, encouraged employee involvement, and had good health and safety records.

The analysis of the empirical data that was undertaken provided support for both of the hypotheses that were tested. Thus it was found that there was a positive relationship between levels of firm specific knowledge, and the provision of both economic and relationship-based governance mechanisms. Overall therefore it was concluded that employees are motivated to contribute to the development of firm-specific knowledge by the provision of either type of governance mechanism.

1. Of the two types of governance mechanism examined here, do you think one of them is likely to provide a greater level of motivation for employees to develop firm-specific knowledge than the other?

2. Can you think of other factors, such as the provision of promotion opportunities, which may provide a similar motivation to employees to develop firm-specific knowledge?

Source: Wang, H., He, J., and Mahoney, J. (2009) 'Firm-Specific Knowledge Resources and Competitive Advantage', *Strategic Management Journal*, 30: 1265–85.

 ## Review and Discussion Questions

1. Do you agree with the idea that the objectivist perspective on knowledge represents the most dominant perspective in the knowledge management literature? Think about what you regard as being the most well-known and important works on the topic of knowledge management. Do they represent examples of the objectivist perspective on knowledge or the knowledge-based view of the firm? What features of their assumptions and analysis reveal their perspective on knowledge?

2. Think about your experience of social/group knowledge in the workplace. Is it largely tacit or explicit? Did it exist in the form of systems of rules, routines, stories, etc.?

3. National culture and communities of practice have been discussed as two types of social context/setting where collective knowledge can be seen to exist. In what other social contexts, in your own experience, have you witnessed collective knowledge to exist—organization, family, geographic region, peer group, friendship network, profession?

4. In your experience, is it common that explicit/codified knowledge tends to be privileged and regarded as more objective than tacit knowledge?

 ## Suggestions for Further Reading

1. R. Grant (1996) 'Towards a Knowledge Based Theory of the Firm', *Strategic Management Journal*, 17 (Winter Special Issue): 109–22.

One of the earliest papers explicitly concerning itself with articulating and theoretically developing the knowledge-based view of the firm.

2. H. Wang, J. He, and J. Mahoney (2009) 'Firm-Specific Knowledge Resources and Competitive Advantage: The Role of Economic- and Relationship-Based Employee Governance Mechanisms', *Strategic Management Journal*, 30: 1265–85.

Makes an empirical and conceptual contribution to the development of the knowledge-based view of the firm by examining what influences workers to use and share their knowledge.

3. J. Ebbers, and M. Wijnberg (2009) 'Organizational Memory: From Expectations Memory to Procedural Memory', *British Journal of Management*, 20: 478–90.

An interesting empirical example of how collective tacit knowledge is developed, and the value it can provide to people and groups.

4. A. Hecker (2012) 'Knowledge Beyond the Individual? Making Sense of a Notion of Collective Knowledge in Organization Theory', *Organization Studies*, 33/3: 423–45.

A conceptual paper which considers the different ways in which collective knowledge is conceptualized.

Take your learning further: Online Resource Centre

Visit the Online Resource Centre for resources which will extend your understanding of knowledge management in organizations. As well as web links to sites of interest, the author has provided case studies looking at knowledge management in virtual and knowledge-intensive firms, and in global multinationals. These will help you with your research, essays, and assignments; or you may find these additional resources helpful when revising for exams.

 www.oxfordtextbooks.co.uk/orc/hislop3e/

The Practice-Based Perspective on Knowledge

Introduction

Chapter 2 provided one specific answer to the question 'what is knowledge?' However, the objectivist perspective has been widely challenged, and for a number of different reasons. Arguably the most fundamental challenge and critique of it is that it is based on flawed epistemological assumptions. Chapter 3 therefore presents an alternative answer to the question 'what is knowledge?' This chapter is based on fundamentally different epistemological assumptions and, as will be seen, characterizes knowledge and knowledge management practices quite differently from the objectivist perspective.

The practice-based perspective conceptualizes knowledge not as a codifiable object/entity, but instead emphasizes the extent to which it is embedded within and inseparable from work activities or practices. Cook and Brown (1999) labelled this perspective an 'epistemology of practice' due to the centrality of human activity to its conception of knowledge. Ripamonti and Scaratti adopted a similar perspective talk about knowledge being 'action-oriented and implicit . . . [and] acquired by experience in a specific context' (2011: 185). Thus, the embedded-ness of knowledge in human activity (practice) represents one of the central characteristics of this epistemological perspective. This is therefore why the label practice-based epistemology is here preferred to Schultze and Stabell's (2004) terminology, the epistemology of duality.

DEFINITION Practice

Practice refers to purposeful human activity. It is based on the assumption that activity includes both physical and cognitive elements, and that these elements are inseparable. Knowledge use and develop-ment is therefore regarded as a fundamental aspect of activity.

While the objectivist perspective was closely aligned with a positivistic philosophy, the practice-based one is compatible with a number of different philosophical approaches (Table 3.1). For example, Nicolini (2011) distinguishes between three different perspec-tives within the literature adopting a practice-based epistemology, but constraints of space prevent a comparison of these perspectives here.

Table 3.1 Theoretical Perspective Related to the Practice-Based Perspective

Writer	Theoretical Perspective
Empsom (2001*a*)	Interpretive
Blackler (1995)	Activity Theory
Tsoukas (1996)	Ethnomethodology/interpretive philosophy
Cook and Brown (1999)	American Pragmatists
Lave and Wenger (1991)	Situated Learning Theory
Suchman (2003)	Actor Network Theory

Table 3.2 Practice-Based Characteristics of Knowledge

Characteristics of Knowledge from Practice-Based Epistemology
1. Knowledge is embedded in practice
2. Knowledge as multidimensional and non-dichotomous
3. Knowledge is embodied in people
4. Knowledge is socially constructed
5. Knowledge is culturally embedded
6. Knowledge is contestable

The chapter follows a similar structure to Chapter 2, and begins by outlining the way knowledge is characterized within the practice-based perspective. The chapter then examines how knowledge management processes are conceptualized. As the chapter proceeds, the vast differences that exist between practice-based and the objectivist perspective on knowledge will become more apparent.

Features of a Practice-Based Perspective on Knowledge

The practice-based epistemology can be understood in terms of six specific, but interrelated factors, each of which are now examined in turn (Table 3.2).

The embeddedness of knowledge in practice

Perhaps the most important difference between the objectivist and practice-based epistemologies of knowledge is that the practice-based perspective challenges the entitative conception of knowledge. From this perspective, knowledge is not regarded as a discrete entity/object that can be codified and separated from people. Instead, knowledge, or as some of the writers from this perspective prefer, knowing, is inseparable from human activity (Corradi *et al.* 2010; Gherardi 2006; Orlikowski 2002). Thus all activity is, to some extent, knowledgeable, involving the use and/or development of knowledge. Conversely, all knowledge work, whether using it, sharing it, developing it, or creating it, will involve an element of activity. Nicolini (2011: 604) summed this up as follows, 'knowledge is inherently tied to the pursuit of an activity and is constituted and renovated as actors engage with the organizational world in practice'.

As well as challenging the knowing–doing dichotomy, this perspective also challenges the mind–body dichotomy that is inherent in the objectivist perspective (see more detail in the later 'Knowledge is Embodied' section). As outlined, the objectivist perspective, drawing on the classical images of science, conceptualizes knowledge as being primarily derived from cognitive processes, something involving the brain but not the body. The practice-based perspective instead views knowing and the development of knowledge as occurring on an ongoing basis through the routine activities that people undertake. Knowing thus can be seen as less of a purely cognitive process, and more of a holistic one involving the whole body (Hindmarsh and Pilnick 2007; Strati 2007). From this perspective, thinking and doing are fused in knowledgeable activity, the development and use of embodied knowledge in undertaking specific activities/tasks. The involvement of the body in processes of knowing is illustrated in the example here. However it is important to say that the involvement of the body in processes of knowing is as much a part of managerial, professional, white-collar work as it is in manual work.

 Illustration   Sensible knowledge and work practices

Strati (2007) contributes to the development of the practice-based perspective on knowledge through the development of the term 'sensible knowledge'. Central to Strati's conceptualization of knowledge is the idea that knowing is not an activity conducted purely within the brain, with knowing involving the whole body. For Strati (p. 67), work practices and processes of knowing in organizations are 'not only mental and logical-analytical but also corporeal and multi-sensorial'. The concept of sensible knowledge relates to knowing that involves workers using the human senses of touch, sight, taste, hearing, and smell, with a number of empirical examples being given to illustrate the arguments being made. One of these examples concerned sawmill workers from the north-east of Italy (Strati 2007: 67–9). In this example, the workers in the mill (who did not wear gloves) were able to identify the thickness of the planks they were moving without formally measuring them, simply through the process of lifting and feeling them. Their sense of touch was such that they were able to differentiate between planks whose thicknesses varied by half a centimetre. For Strati this represented an example of sensible knowing, where the sawmill workers' hands, through their sense of touch, were intimately involved in knowing how thick the planks they handled were.

Knowledge as multidimensional and non-dichotomous

One key difference between the objectivist and practice-based perspectives on knowledge, as highlighted by Schultze and Stabell (2004) is their attitudes towards binary oppositions. Within the objectivist perspective an either/or logic dominates, which results, as outlined in Chapter 2, in the development of taxonomies of distinctive categories of knowledge. From this perspective, knowledge can be either tacit OR explicit, and knowledge can be individual

OR collective in character. However, such a logic is rejected by those advocating and utilizing a practice-based perspective on knowledge, who suggest that, while such an approach may have analytical benefits, it underestimates the complexity of organizational knowledge. Tsoukas (1996), for example, suggests that dichotomies such as tacit–explicit and individual–group are unhelpful as they disguise the extent to which these elements are inseparable and mutually defined. Blackler (1995: 1032) makes a similar point by suggesting that:

> knowledge is multi-faceted and complex, being both situated and abstract, implicit and explicit, distributed and individual, physical and mental, developing and static, verbal and encoded.

Thus the practice-based perspective rejects the taxonomy-based approach to categorizing knowledge into distinctive types which are independent of each other. Instead of the objectivist perspective's either/or logic, a both/and logic predominates. This perspective is most obvious in how those utilizing a practice-based perspective conceptualize the relationship between tacit and explicit knowledge. The practice-based perspective suggests that rather than tacit and explicit knowledge representing separate and distinctive types of knowledge, they represent two aspects of knowledge and in fact are inseparable, and are mutually constituted (Werr and Stjernberg 2003). One consequence of this is that there is no such thing as fully explicit knowledge, as all knowledge will have tacit dimensions. For example, text, which is often referred to as a form of codified knowledge, has tacit components without which no reader could make sense of it. Examples of these tacit elements include an understanding of the language in which they are written, or the grammar and syntax used to structure them. Polanyi (1969: 195) suggests that 'The idea of a strictly explicit knowledge is indeed self-contradictory; deprived of their tacit co-efficients, all spoken words, all formulae, all maps and graphs, are strictly meaningless.'

 Illustration   This book as partially explicit knowledge

This book represents a piece of partially explicit knowledge for two reasons. First, as an author, I have not been able to make fully explicit all the ideas, assumptions, theoretical frameworks, and values which underpin what I have written. From the point of view of the reader it can also be considered partially explicit, as to read it you have to have a good grasp of the English language, and some knowledge of other relevant academic topics.

While, as outlined in Chapter 2, Polanyi's work is often used to justify the idea that tacit and explicit knowledge are two separate and distinctive types of knowledge, a number of writers suggest that this misunderstands his analysis (Brown and Duguid 2001; Tsoukas 2003). These writers suggest that his analysis is grounded more in the practice-based perspective which builds from the assumption that there are tacit and explicit dimensions to all knowledge, and that they are inseparable. Thus, from this perspective, there is no such thing as pure tacit or pure explicit knowledge, as all knowledge contains elements of both.

The both/and logic of the practice-based perspective shapes not only how tacit and explicit knowledge are interrelated, it also extends to understanding how other aspects of knowledge are conceptualized. Three dichotomies, which are challenged by those adopting the practice-based epistemology, are outlined in Table 3.3. For example, those adopting a practice-based perspective (such as Strati and his example of sawmill workers) reject the Cartesian distinction between mind and body, which assumes that knowing is primarily an intellectual and cognitive process related to the brain and instead takes knowing and doing to be inseparable, with all knowing involving some element of doing or action and vice versa (see below section on the embodied nature of knowledge for further elaboration). Finally, those adopting a practice-based epistemology challenge the dichotomy between individual and collective knowledge, suggesting that all knowledge has both individual and collective aspects. For example in relation to communities of practice (see Chapter 10), which are typically examined from a practice-based perspective, the knowledge developed and utilized by people who are part of such communities simultaneously has individual and collective elements. Bouty and Gomez (2010) adopt a similar perspective in their analysis of knowledge developed and utilized by chefs and kitchen staff within a haute cuisine restaurant kitchen (see the example below).

Table 3.3 Challenging Objectivist Dichotomies

Practice-Based Perspective	Objectivist Perspective
Knowledge as tacit and explicit	Knowledge as either tacit or explicit
Knowledgeable activity (knowing and doing)	Knowledge as purely cognitive
Knowledge as both individual and collective	Knowledge as either individual or collective

 Time to reflect   The multidimensionality of knowledge

Think of some specific organizational knowledge that you possess. Can it be classified into a neat category, such as tacit–collective, or does it have multiple dimensions simultaneously?

 Illustration   The individual and collective dimensions of knowledge within the kitchen of a haute cuisine restaurant

The central focus of Bouty and Gomez's (2010) analysis is on the bidirectional and interdependent nature of knowledge, which was empirically examined within the context of the kitchen of a French haute cuisine restaurant. They conducted a longitudinal study of the restaurant that spanned eight years. During this time the restaurant had three different head chefs and they were thus able to examine how each chef influenced the nature of knowledge and practice within the kitchens. They also took account of the social and gastronomic context in which the restaurant was located, through the analysis of reviews of the restaurant in newspapers and magazines. To understand the nature of knowledge/practice within this social field they utilized Bourdieu's concept of 'habitus', which can be

(continued)

defined as a set of socially constructed dispositions and beliefs which shape how people think and act, which people develop through being socialized into and acting within a particular social field.

In their analysis of the knowledge/practice of the three head chefs and how they influenced the knowledge/practice within the restaurant kitchen, they concluded that there was a reciprocal and bidirectional relationship between individual and collective knowledge, with it not being possible to identify knowledge which was purely of one type or the other. For example, in terms of the knowledge that was developed and used by the chefs, this was found to be significantly shaped by the particular way that they were socialized into the field of French gastronomy. Thus their knowledge was partly collective as it was deeply embedded in this context, but also partly individualistic, as each of the chefs had their own preferred style of cooking and culinary preferences. This individualistic aspect of their knowledge was visible, for example, in the distinctive way that the restaurant operated under the management of each head chef.

Knowledge is embodied

The objectivist perspective on knowledge assumes that knowledge can exist in a fully explicit and codified form and can exist independently of human beings. This position is fundamentally challenged by the practice-based perspective on knowledge, which sees all knowledge or knowing as personal. The practice-based perspective therefore assumes that it is impossible to totally disembody knowledge from people into a fully explicit form. This assumption is therefore closely related to and flows from the previous two issues examined, that all knowledge has tacit dimensions and that knowledge is embedded in and inseparable from practice. Thus, knowledge that is embedded in work practices is simultaneously embodied by the workers who carry out these practices (Strati 2007; Yakhlef 2010).

The practice-based nature of knowing/knowledge assumes that knowledge develops through practice: people's knowledge develops as they conduct activities and gain experience. Further, the inseparable and mutually constituted nature of tacit and explicit knowledge means that it is not possible to make such knowledge fully explicit. There will always be an element whereby knowledge resides in the head/body of those who developed and possess it. Thus while it may be possible to partially convert tacit knowledge into an explicit form, in contradiction of the objectivist perspective, the practice-based perspective assumes that such processes can never be complete.

For example, in terms of a situation most readers are likely to be familiar with from one context or another, consider the nature of knowledge sharing in 'master–apprentice' type relations, where someone experienced attempts to share their knowledge with a more inexperienced colleague. The practice-based perspective assumes that the practice-based nature of the knowledge and expertise the 'master' possesses means that this knowledge will be to some extent embodied, and cannot be fully articulated and made explicit. Further, the practice-based perspective assumes that for the apprentice to learn the knowledge of the master requires that they communicate, interact, and work together, typically over an extended period of time. Hindmarsh and Pilnick's (2007) study of pre-operative anaesthetics illustrates the embodied nature of knowledge. In their study they found that anaesthetics staff demonstrated the effectiveness of their knowledge through the way they utilized it to physically manipulate the body of patients in certain ways, as well as coordinate these movements with those of other anaesthetics staff, with these activities having to be done quickly, and with little verbal communication between people.

A further sense in which knowledge is embodied (and simultaneously embedded in practice) relates to what Tsoukas (1996) referred to as the 'indeterminacy of practice', where the essential distinctiveness of all situations that people act in requires them to continually make personal judgements. No matter how explicit and well defined the rules are that may guide action, there will always be some element of ambiguity or uncertainty that creates a need for actors to make inferences and judgements. For example, in applying this insight to the perspective of the 'apprentice' just discussed, no matter how formalized, structured, and explicit the knowledge they have acquired, there will always be circumstances that emerge where an element of judgement will be required. Thus, knowledge/knowing involves the active agency of people making decisions in light of the specific circumstances in which they find themselves. A good example of such decision-making was found by Ripamonti and Scarrati (2011) in a study of dock workers in an Italian port (see example).

 Illustration   The indeterminacy of practice and ad-hoc decision-making in an Italian dock

One of the catalysts for Ripamonti and Scarratti's (2011) study of Italian dock workers was that management were unable to effectively explain the highly variable productivity levels of their dock workers. Management found that the number of containers that could be processed per day varied enormously but were unable to effectively explain this variability. Ripamonti and Scaratti conducted an observation- and interview-based study in order to explain this variability. They felt that to fully understand the nature of the work in question, they had to gain a detailed qualitative understanding of exactly what the dock workers did. They concluded that the key reason for the variability in productivity levels was that the nature of the work they had to do was highly variable, with some jobs being straightforward and others being complex. This variability meant that they couldn't use standardized working practices as what they did was shaped by the specific nature of each ship and cargo. Further, in deciding how to load or unload each cargo, they had to continuously have discussions with each other and make decisions about how to proceed. Thus they argued that the dock workers experienced 'continuous learning to cope with ever-changing circumstances' (p. 193). The reason why management were unable to explain the variable productivity levels was because they assumed that the work of the dockers was routine and low-skilled, and didn't appreciate the extent to which it involved ongoing decision-making.

   To what extent can standardized routines and rules be used in any job? Can you think of other apparently routine jobs which involve a degree of analysis and decision-making to cope with different, unpredictable circumstances?

The socially constructed and culturally embedded nature of knowledge

Two factors that are closely interwoven are that knowledge is socially constructed and culturally embedded. It is therefore necessary to examine them simultaneously. In stark contrast to the 'knowledge is truth' assumption of the objectivist perspective on knowledge, where it is suggested that codified knowledge can exist in an objective form independent of social and cultural values, the epistemology of practice perspective argues that all knowledge is socially constructed in nature, which makes it somewhat subjective and open to interpretation. Thus, knowledge is never totally neutral and unbiased and is, to some extent, inseparable from the values of those who produce it.

As with the objectivist perspective, this viewpoint is based on a particular understanding about the nature of language. The objectivist perspective assumes that language has fixed and objective meanings, and that there is a direct equivalence between words or phrases and their meaning. Instead, the practice-based perspective suggests that language has no such fixed meanings, and that in fact the meaning of language is inherently ambiguous. This subjectivity or interpretive flexibility in language thus undermines any claims about the objective status of any knowledge, whether it is highly tacit and personal, or whether it is partially explicit and codified.

The socially constructed nature of knowledge applies to both its production and its interpretation. Polanyi (1969) referred to these two processes as sense giving and sense reading, while Boland and Tenkasi (1995) used the terms 'perspective making' and 'perspective taking'. Thus both the production of knowledge and the reading/interpretation required to develop an understanding of it involve an active process of meaning construction/inference. For example, a written report is a piece of partially explicit knowledge, whose meaning is constructed by its author/s. However, different readers may infer a different meaning and analysis. This aspect of the practice-based perspective therefore has profound implications for the way knowledge is shared and managed, as the attractive simplicity of the transmitter–receiver model is questioned.

Further, this process of meaning construction/inference is typically culturally embedded. As Weir and Hutchins argue (2005: 89), 'knowledge cannot be understood outside of the cultural parameters that condition its emergence and modes of reproduction'. For example, the meanings people attach to language/events are shaped by the values and assumptions of the social and cultural context in which they live and work. The French restaurant examined by Bouty and Gomez (2010—see above illustration) provides an example of such culturally embedded knowledge. In this case, the knowledge of the chefs that was examined was shaped by the traditions, knowledge, and values of French society, and more specifically, French culinary culture, which has its own distinctive characteristics and values when compared to the national history, values, and culinary culture in other countries.

 Time to reflect   Perspective making and taking

Can you think of an example from any organizational experience you may have where a range of people inferred different meanings from a report? Could these differences partly be explained by the fluidity of meaning in language?

The socially constructed and culturally embedded nature of knowledge becomes visible when examining collaborations which span communities or groups with different and distinctive values and knowledge (see e.g. Hong *et al.* 2010), with the characteristics of such collaborations being the focus of Chapter 11.

The socially constructed and culturally embedded nature of organizational knowledge can also be illustrated through considering how national cultural factors impact on both the nature of organizational knowledge and the character of knowledge management processes. For example, Lam (1997), in examining the knowledge involved in a joint technology development project involving extended collaboration between a Japanese and a UK company, found the knowledge of all relevant staff to be deeply embedded in the social context the engineers were socialized into and worked within and that, further, the knowledge base and organizational context of both organizations were significantly different. While in the UK company there was an emphasis on formalized knowledge, developed through education, in the Japanese company tacit knowledge accumulated through experience was more important. Secondly, in the UK company there was a clear demarcation of job boundaries, limited use of job rotation, and a tendency for people to develop narrowly specialized knowledge bases. In the Japanese company, by contrast, due to the emphasis on team working, the demarcation between jobs was blurred, and due to the use of job rotation, people's knowledge bases were typically broad. Finally, there were also significant differences in the way knowledge was shared and developed throughout the product cycle. In the UK division, product design and the development of detailed specifications were principally the domain of design staff. In the Japanese company, by contrast, production and design staff both had an important role in the development of product specifications. These differences made the process of knowledge sharing and joint technology development extremely complicated. Overall Lam concluded that the socially embedded character of all knowledge means that sharing knowledge between any different social and cultural contexts is likely to be both complex and time-consuming.

The impact of national cultural values on knowledge management activities is also considered in Chapter 9 when examining how national culture affected people's attitudes towards knowledge-sharing activities. Finally, the impact of national cultural values on knowledge management activities is also visible in the analysis of the Nonaka and Takeuchi's (1995) SECI model of knowledge creation, which some writers suggest is not universally applicable as it is based upon social and organizational characteristics that are specific to Japan (Glisby and Holden 2003; Weir and Hutchins 2005). This is an issue that is returned to in Chapter 7, when the work of Nonaka and Takeuchi is considered in detail.

 Time to reflect   The complexity of cross-cultural knowledge sharing

These ideas suggest that the sharing of knowledge between people from different cultures is likely to be difficult. Such situations are likely to be common in multinational corporations. From a management point of view, what, if anything can management in multinationals do to address such problems?

The contestable nature of knowledge

The final key aspect of the practice-based perspective is the acknowledgement that the subjective, socially constructed and culturally embedded nature of knowledge means that what constitutes knowledge is open to dispute (see e.g. Marshall and Rollinson 2004; Yanow 2004). This therefore challenges and undermines the idea central to the objectivist perspective that it is possible to produce truly objective knowledge. Thus, competing conceptions of what constitute 'legitimate' knowledge can occur where different groups/individuals develop incompatible and contradictory analyses of the same events, which may lead to conflict due to attempts by these groups to have their knowledge legitimated (see e.g. Heizmann 2010, the end of chapter case in Chapter 12, the case of Mørk *et al.* 2010 examined in Chapter 10, and the relevant sections in Chapter 12 on conflict regarding the legitimacy of knowledge claims).

One of the main consequences flowing from this, therefore, is that issues of power, politics, and conflict become more important than are acknowledged by the objectivist perspective. Most fundamentally, Foucault's conception of power/knowledge suggests that these concepts are inseparable (Heizmann 2010; Marshall and Rollinson 2004; McKinlay 2000). Finally, Nicolini (2007, 2011) who utilizes a practice-based epistemology argues that the analysis of knowledge and work practices requires issues of power and conflict to be accounted for, as the collaborative nature of work practices and the application of knowledge tends to 'produce and reproduce a landscape of inequalities' (2011: 616). In the case of the medical knowledge/practices examined by Nicolini (see the case study at the end of this chapter), such inequalities exist between doctors, nurses, hospital administrative staff, and patients. The importance of acknowledging and taking account of the contested and political nature of knowledge is magnified by the fact that this aspect of knowledge and knowledge management initiatives is typically either neglected or ignored by the majority of the

---

Illustration   Conflict regarding the application of collaboratively developed knowledge

Marcos and Denyer (2012) present their analysis of a long-term collaboration between academic researchers at a UK management school, and some management consultants. The collaboration lasted for over six years, and evolved through four different stages, with Marcos and Denver collecting data throughout the lifetime of the collaboration. The central focus of this illustration is on the dissemination phase of the collaboration, which occurred during its fifth year. The collaboration was initiated by the management consultancy company which wanted help in developing its reputation for 'thought leadership'. The core project team in the collaboration involved two academic staff and two consultants. The collaboration was focused around a research centre that was to be created within the management school and which was to be funded by the consultancy company.

As some of the consultancy company's clients were involved in high-hazard industries the research centre was tasked with examining the topic of high-reliability organizations, and was given the task of reviewing and analysing relevant literature on this topic, with the aim being to 'synthesize key principles to design "failure-free" organizations'. As the project evolved and the analysis was undertaken, it became apparent that the findings of much of the research they examined were contradictory, making it hard both to summarize it succinctly and to provide definitive answers to their questions.

Over time there was pressure on the project team to use their analysis to produce value for the consultancy company. Efforts to do this were initially focused around presenting some of the key findings at various meetings involving consultants as well as some of their key clients, with these presentations being received favourably. After this there was an expectation from the consultants that these findings could be utilized to derive material, financial value from the research, generating revenue and profit. It was at this point that conflict emerged within the project, when one of the consultants gave a presentation to clients which deviated from and abandoned the carefully developed research findings, and gave an analysis that was more based on 'personal opinion'. Due partly to the negative fallout that occurred after this presentation, and also because two of the core project team from the consultancy company left their jobs, the project was abandoned, and funding for the research centre discontinued.

---

1. Have you had experience of similar situations where there has been disagreement among a project team or working group regarding what the findings of a collaborative project mean, or how they are to be presented? Is such conflict and disagreement inevitable?

knowledge management literature. These issues are examined more fully in Chapter 12. However, the example illustrates these issues through considering a case where conflict emerged over how some collaboratively developed knowledge was described and used.

A Practice-Based Perspective on the Management and Sharing of Knowledge

Having considered in detail how the practice-based epistemology conceptualizes knowledge, it is now time to examine the implications of these ideas for understanding the character of organizational knowledge-sharing and knowledge management processes (see Table 3.4). Fundamentally, the assumptions in this epistemology that knowledge cannot be codified into a discrete entity as it is deeply embodied in people and simultaneously embedded in and inseparable from people's work practices, means that knowledge isn't regarded as something which can be directly managed. Instead, those adopting this perspective conceptualize the active role of management as attempting to shape knowledge processes to involve facilitating interpersonal communication and collaboration between people.

One of the central components of the practice-based perspective on knowledge management is that it eschews the idea that it is possible for organizations to create a disembodied library or repository of codified knowledge, or for middle and senior managers to fully understand the knowledge of those who work for them (Goodall and Roberts 2003). Tsoukas (1996: 15), quoting Hayek, suggests that a belief in the ability to achieve such a state represents the 'synoptic delusion . . . that knowledge can be surveyed by a single mind'. Thus managerial understanding of organizational knowledge will always be fragmented and incomplete, and attempts to collect knowledge in a central location likely to be limited. The following quotation from Tsoukas (1996: 22) sums this up, and points towards the practice-based perspective's conceptualization of knowledge-sharing processes: 'the key to achieving coordinated action does not so much depend on those "higher up" collecting more and more knowledge, as on those "lower down" finding more and more ways to get connected and interrelating the knowledge each one has'.

The practice-based perspective further suggests that the transmitter–receiver model of knowledge sharing is questionable because the sharing of knowledge does not involve the

Table 3.4 A Practice-Based Perspective on Knowledge Management

Knowledge Management from a Practice-Based Epistemology
1. Knowledge sharing/acquisition requires 'perspective making' and 'perspective taking'—developing an understanding of tacit assumptions
2. Knowledge sharing/acquisition through   • 'rich' social interaction   • immersion in practice—watching and/or doing
3. Management role to facilitate social interaction

simple transferral of a fixed entity between two people. Instead, the sharing of knowledge involves two people actively inferring and constructing meaning. The adoption of a practice-based epistemology implies that to be effective the sharing of knowledge requires individuals to develop an appreciation of (some of) the tacit assumptions and values on which the knowledge of others is based—the processes of 'perspective making' and 'perspective taking' outlined earlier (Boland and Tenkasi 1995). This challenges the assumption embedded in the transmitter–receiver model that the knowledge exchanged in such processes is unchanged. Bolisani and Scarso (2000) suggest the practice-based perspective on knowledge sharing represents a 'language game', due to the importance of dialogue and language to such processes. Boland and Tenkasi (1995: 358) argue that effective knowledge sharing involves 'a process of mutual perspective taking where distinctive individual knowledge is exchanged, evaluated and integrated with that of others in the organization'.

> **DEFINITION Perspective making and taking**
>
> Perspective making is the process through which an individual develops, strengthens and sustains their knowledge, beliefs and values. Perspective taking is the process through which people develop an understanding of the knowledge, values and 'worldview' of others.

The logic of the 'language game' model complicates the nature of knowledge-sharing processes, as the inherent ambiguity of language, combined with the fact that those involved in the knowledge-sharing process have different cognitive frameworks, means that there is always scope for differing interpretations. Thus, as you read this book, a piece of partially explicit knowledge, the meaning you take from it may vary from the meaning I intend to convey.

These perspective-making and perspective-taking processes typically require an extensive amount of social interaction and face-to-face communication. The acquisition and sharing of knowledge typically occur through two distinct, but closely interrelated processes (see Table 3.4): immersion in practice and 'rich' social interactions between people. These processes are interrelated because learning by doing is likely to simultaneously involve an element of social interaction, and vice versa.

Immersion in practice is the process whereby people develop, share, and communicate knowledge through either undertaking a particular task or closely observing (and communicating with) someone else who is carrying out a particular task. An example of such a process is presented by Bouty and Gomez (2010) which describes the way in which knowledge in restaurant kitchens is communicated and shared between the chefs and other kitchen staff, which occurs via actually preparing food for customers. Another example of knowledge sharing/development via a process of 'immersion in practice' is the collective problem-solving of the dock workers highlighted by Ripamonti and Scaratti (2011). Here knowledge was developed through the dock workers having to find ways to deal with the highly variable types of cargo they had to process. Rich social interactions can take an almost infinite range of forms, but to be 'rich' they need to allow people to be able to effectively communicate their knowledge, values, and assumptions with each other. Listed below

is a range of ways in which this could be done. A specific example from the academic literature of a successful rich interaction was the process of 'imagineering' or brainstorming
identified by Marcos and Denyer (2012) in the collaborative research project they examined. This 'imagineering' process involved open dialogue and communication between
people who had read the same (complex and ambiguous) research findings, and provided a
mechanism for people to integrate their individual perspectives and develop a sense of
shared understanding.

From a practice-based perspective, the managerial role in facilitating the management
and sharing of knowledge is therefore to encourage and facilitate the type of communication and social interaction processes that will allow effective perspective making and taking
to occur. This can be done through an enormously diverse range of ways including (to highlight just a few examples):

- developing a knowledge sharing culture (through rewarding people for sharing);
- facilitating the development of organizational communities of practice;
- providing forums (electronic or face-to-face) which create opportunities for social
  interaction between people;
- implementing a formalized 'mentoring' system to pair experienced and inexperienced
  workers;
- designing job roles to facilitate and encourage interpersonal communication and
  collective problem-solving.

These issues are examined in more detail in subsequent chapters, with Chapter 9
looking at general issues of motivation to share knowledge, Chapters 10 and 11
at the specific dynamics of knowledge sharing within and between communities of
practice, Chapter 12 at the political nature of knowledge sharing, while Chapter 13 considers the role that information systems may be able to play in facilitating perspective-
making and taking processes. Finally, Chapter 14 considers the role that organizations
can play through their human resource management policies and culture management
practices.

 ## Conclusion

Chapters 2 and 3 have outlined two distinctive epistemological perspectives, which
characterize knowledge in extremely different ways. These perspectives also conceptualized
knowledge-sharing and knowledge management processes differently. They therefore have
very different managerial implications with regard to how knowledge management efforts
should be organized and structured:

- *Objectivist perspective:* focus on the codification and collection of knowledge, create
  mechanisms to allow this knowledge base to be searched and accessed, such as setting
  up a searchable database and encouraging staff to codify their knowledge and store it there.
- *Practice-based perspective:* facilitate interpersonal knowledge sharing and processes of
  perspective making and taking through diverse forms of interaction and communication.

Case study   A practice-based perspective on telemedicine

Nicolini (2011) utilizes a practice-based epistemology to analyse the work of nurses. The nurses examined were involved in what was defined as telemedicine, which involved making extensive use of ICTs to manage the ongoing care of patients. More specifically, the focus was on patients with heart problems who required continuous monitoring between regular hospital visits, with the monitoring process being carried out by nurses regularly calling the patients to check up on them at home. The central focus of Nicolini's analysis is on the practices and knowing of the nurses as they called patients and managed their care. Nicolini's paper makes both a conceptual and empirical contribution to knowledge, and limitations of space make it impossible to fully articulate the conceptual contribution being made, or to describe all aspects of the empirical data presented and analysed.

Nicolini explicitly adopts a practice-based epistemology, for example arguing that 'knowing is always a practical accomplishment and practice is where knowledgeability manifests itself' (p. 602), However, the conceptual contribution made by Nicolini is to shift the unit of analysis from the individual workers to the various interrelated practices they undertake, and the knowing that is embedded within them. In doing so Nicolini suggests that attention should be paid to the site within which these practices are carried out. For Nicolini, a 'site' is a network of interconnected practices rather than a physical location. For example, in looking at the telephone interactions between nurses and patients in their home, there is no single physical site where the practices being examined are undertaken, as the nurse is located in the hospital, the patient at home. Thus, in this context, the 'site' of knowing is the conversation the nurses have with their patients, where various practices are constructed via the interaction between the nurse and the patient, and within which the knowing of the nurses (and the patients) is embedded.

The analysis undertaken by Nicolini was derived from a three-year study undertaken in Northern Italy which was ethnographic in nature. Thus data were collected via observing the work of the nurses, attendance at meetings of nurses and other clinical staff, and informal interviews with a range of clinical staff, as well as via the analysis of relevant documentation. Research was undertaken at more than one hospital, but the focus here is narrowly on the telemedicine practices in one particular hospital.

Before articulating the knowing that is embedded in the work of the nurses, Nicolini gives a detailed account of their day-to-day work routines. Here, only a very superficial overview is provided, which focuses centrally on the telephone calls the nurses made to their patients. These phone calls represented the primary way that patient care was managed in between formal visits. These phone calls involved checking on the general health of the patients, identifying any problems they were experiencing, and checking whether they were taking their medication as prescribed and whether this medication was causing any problems. For the heart patients who were being monitored these phone calls were very important, as they provided hospital staff with information that could help identify the early signs of possible heart problems. After describing the work practices of the nurses, Nicolini shifts focus to highlight the knowing that is embedded within them. In doing so he identifies seven different ways in which knowing emerges and becomes visible. Here only two of these instances are examined.

First, knowing is embedded within and emerges through what the nurses and patients say to each other, and how the nurse makes sense of and responds to what the patients tell them. Thus, nurses (attempt to) manage the conversation in order to gain particular types of information from the patient, which typically involves trying to organize the conversation according to a particular sequence. However, they need to be active in managing this, as due to patients developing an understanding of what is being sought, they may not give information in the order that it is sought, or they may not be willing to reveal some information easily to the nurses. Secondly, knowing emerges from what Nicolini calls the 'process of material mediation', whereby a range of non-human artefacts are utilized, such as the range of paper and computer-based medical records that nurses possess. In talking with patients these records play an important role, as they give the nurses crucial information on the patient's health, such as blood pressure and heart rate data, etc. However, Nicolini argues that these records do not 'carry' codified knowledge, with the knowledge they contain emerging from how the nurses read and make sense of them.

Nicolini concludes his analysis by emphasizing the interconnected nature of practice(s), arguing that all practices are part of a web of different interconnected practices involving different people, who may not be collocated. One example of the interconnectedness of practice highlighted, which is referred to as 'translation at a distance', involves the sharing and dissemination of information across different locations, which occurs via different 'mediators' (objects or artefacts such as documents, diagrams, or equipment). For example, data on the patient's heart rate patterns are transferred from their home to the hospital via a number of 'mediators', including the heart rate monitoring equipment in the patients home, the equipment in the hospital to which this information is sent, and the graphs of paper onto which this information is translated. However, this process of 'translation at a distance' does not involve the passive transferral of codified knowledge. This information only becomes knowing to the nurse when they read, interpret, and make sense of this information, and use it to develop an understanding of the patient's health, and the type of questions that should be asked in subsequent phone calls.

1. Do you agree with Nicolini's analysis of codified information embedded in medical records etc., that it only becomes knowledge when it is read, and made sense of by medical staff?

Source: Reprinted by permission, Nicolini (2011) 'Practice as the Site of Knowing', *Organization Science*, 22/3: 602–20, The Institute for Operations Research and the Management Sciences (INFORMS), 7240 Parkway Drive, Suite 300, Hanover, MD 21076 USA.

 ## Review and Discussion Questions

1. Think about an example of partially explicit knowledge you are familiar with, for example a set of instructions for how to conduct a certain task. What tacit knowledge is necessary for you to make sense of them? What does this say about the inseparability of tacit and explicit knowledge?

2. Think about interactions you have had with people of different nationalities. Have there been examples from these interactions where people's contrasting understandings of the same phenomenon have revealed the socially constructed and culturally embedded nature of knowledge?

3. Compare the two perspectives on knowledge outlined in Chapters 2 and 3. Which one more closely models the nature of knowledge in the organizations that you have worked in?

 ## Suggestions for Further Reading

1. **G. Corradi, S. Gherardi, and L. Verzzonneli (2010) 'Through the Practice Lens: Where is the Bandwagon of Practice-Based Studies Heading?', *Management Learning*, 41/3: 265–83.**
Presents a good overview of the literature which utilizes a practice-based epistemology.

2. **I. Bouty and M.-L. Gomez (2010) 'Dishing Up Individual and Collective Dimensions of Organizational Knowing', *Management Learning*, 41/4: 545–59.**
A useful case study which highlights the inseparability of the individual and collective aspects of knowledge.

3. A. Strati (2007) 'Sensible Knowledge and Practice-Based Learning', *Management Learning*, 38/1: 61–77.

Illustrates how the practice-based perspective challenges the mind–body dualism through considering the role of human senses in processes of knowing and learning.

4. A. Yakhlef (2010) 'The Corporeality of Practice-Based Learning', *Organization Studies*, 31/4: 409–30.

An interesting conceptual overview of the role played by the human body in processes of knowing and learning.

Take your learning further: Online Resource Centre

Visit the Online Resource Centre for resources which will extend your understanding of knowledge management in organizations. As well as web links to sites of interest, the author has provided case studies looking at knowledge management in virtual and knowledge-intensive firms, and in global multinationals. These will help you with your research, essays, and assignments; or you may find these additional resources helpful when revising for exams.

 www.oxfordtextbooks.co.uk/orc/hislop3e/

Part 2

·······································

An Introduction to Key Concepts

·······································

Part 2 contains three chapters, each of which examines concepts that are fundamental to the topic of knowledge management. As has already been outlined, the knowledge management literature contains a wide range of perspectives on the question of the nature of knowledge, and this diversity extends to all of the concepts examined here. Thus a separate chapter is required to fully explore and elaborate the diversity of perspectives and debates that surround each topic.

Chapter 4 examines the topic of knowledge management itself. Fundamentally the chapter shows that there is no single, simple, agreed definition of what knowledge management is, and that there is an enormous diversity of ways in which organizations can attempt to manage their knowledge. The chapter explores the range of perspectives on this topic by suggesting that in exploring the topic of knowledge management what 'management' constitutes requires as much attention as the nature of organizational knowledge. The chapter then examines the diversity of factors, including the type of strategy adopted by organizations, that shape the type of approach to knowledge management that organizations should adopt, as well as examining some of the most well-known typologies developed to characterize the diversity of knowledge management strategies that exist.

As Chapter 1 outlined, the knowledge society rhetoric suggests that much work has become increasingly knowledge-intensive. However, there is still a debate within the knowledge management literature over what constitutes knowledge work and which organizations can be defined as knowledge-intensive. Chapter 5 engages with and examines the different perspectives that exist on these debates.

Chapter 6 closes this section by examining the linkages between the related topics of knowledge management and learning in organizations, which will involve engaging with the debate on the question of the character of the 'learning organization' concept, as well as examining Crossan's influential model on the learning organization which links processes of individual- and organizational-level learning.

What is Knowledge Management?

Introduction

Now it is time to consider what is meant by the term 'knowledge management'. A whole chapter is needed to explore this topic to take account of the heterogeneous ways in which knowledge management is defined and in which organizational knowledge can be managed. Almost every book or article published on the topic of managing knowledge in organizations has a different definition of knowledge management. Thus, two relatively recent analyses of the literature on knowledge management (Lloria 2008; Mehrizi and Bontis 2009) emphasize the lack of consensus regarding how knowledge management is defined and conceptualized. One general distinction that can be made in terms of how to manage knowledge is between technology-centred and people-centred approaches. Thus, while some suggest that knowledge management can be equated with the implementation and use of particular types of information and communication technologies (see Chapter 13 for more detail on the role of ICTs in knowledge management), others focus on more indirect methods of managing knowledge, via managing the people who possess and utilize knowledge (see Chapters 14 and 15 for further details on this approach to knowledge management).

However, before exploring these issues, the question of what is management is considered. In understanding what knowledge management is this question is as important as the nature of knowledge. Despite this, the knowledge management literature has devoted more space to knowledge than to management, and typically the nature of management is not examined. Here we look at the work of Alvesson and Kärreman (2001), one of the few papers on knowledge management to systematically consider the nature of management. After this the chapter explores the diverse range of factors that influence the approach to knowledge management that firms adopt. Finally, the chapter examines three frameworks and taxonomies that have been developed to categorize how the management of organizational knowledge can be achieved.

What is Management?

Alvesson and Kärreman (2001) suggest that the mainstream knowledge management literature is weak at defining the term 'management', with its meaning typically being regarded as both self-evident and unproblematic, making any discussion or definition of it seem unnecessary. They argue that such an assumption is misguided and that in defining the term 'knowledge management' it is as important to talk about management as it is knowledge. While their analysis is of the early knowledge management literature, arguably their conclusions are still relevant now, as there has been little further conceptualization of management in subsequent knowledge management literature.

DEFINITION Management

Management as a term can be used as both a noun and an adjective. The term 'management', used as a noun, refers to a group of people who have responsibility for managing people and other organizational resources. Used as an adjective, management refers to the process by which people and organizational resources are controlled and coordinated with the intention of achieving particular objectives.

There is a vast academic literature concerned with explaining and understanding the role of senior and middle managers in organizations, with whole books being devoted to the topic (e.g. Hales 1993; Watson 1994). Alvesson and Kärreman (2001) characterize the range of management philosophies that exist as varying along two dimensions. First, they differentiate between management philosophies focused on directly controlling and monitoring workers' behaviours versus those concerned with controlling and shaping workers' attitudes. Taylorism, or Fordism, arguably the most widely used managerial system of the twentieth century, is an archetypal example of a behavioural control system. Under Taylorized control systems, workers' behaviour is typically highly proscribed, with workers having little discretion or autonomy to decide how work tasks should be carried out. Under such systems, for example, as in call centres, workers typically have day-to-day performance targets which management rigorously monitor. Further, in such contexts there are strict controls over how workers behave and talk to clients. Attitudinal-based management, which can also be referred to as culture-based management or normative control is a quite different philosophy of management that began to emerge in the 1980s and which has now become widely used (Ogbonna and Harris 2002). Attitudinal-based management represents a more indirect form of management which, rather than being focused on worker behaviours, concentrates on shaping workers' attitudes and values, with the assumption being that if the right attitudes and values can be developed in workers they are likely to be committed workers, who control their own behaviour and act in ways that management deem appropriate.

 Time to reflect   A neglect of the term 'management'?

To what extent do you agree with Alvesson and Kärreman (2001) that the knowledge management literature typically fails to define and discuss what is meant by the term 'management'? To investigate this topic pick a well-known book on knowledge management and, looking at its index and contents pages, reflect on the extent to which it discusses the concept of management and defines the way it utilizes the term.

The other distinction made by Alvesson and Kärreman (2001) to characterize the variety of management philosophies which exist is between strong and weak forms of intervention.

Strong management philosophies are characterized by the use of specific, detailed targets for worker performance, whereas weak forms of management play more of a coordinating role, with the use of performance targets being minimal. Alvesson and Kärreman conclude by suggesting that the particular management philosophy used in an organization is likely to influence the way management attempt to manage knowledge and they use their framework of management philosophies to develop a typology of four different approaches to knowledge management, which is examined later in this chapter.

Factors Influencing Organizational Approaches to Knowledge Management

In the previous section it was suggested that the way in which management personnel in an organization attempt to manage knowledge is likely to be shaped by the particular approach to management that is adopted. This section builds on this insight to look at the diverse range of factors that influence both the wide range of distinctive knowledge-based issues/challenges different types of organization face, as well as the approaches to managing knowledge that they adopt. The first issue explored here is the link between an organization's general business strategy and its approach to knowledge management. After this, a range of factors related to both the nature of the business environment and the characteristics of organizations are considered. What this section attempts to illustrate is that the enormous diversity in the strategies that firms utilize, in the character of their business environment, and in basic organizational features, means that there is likely to be a vast range of ways in which organizations attempt to manage knowledge. This diversity is reflected here in the heterogeneous range of illustrations, examining knowledge management in small firms, multinational corporations, and a public sector organization.

A number of writers and analysts suggest that it is essential to link knowledge management initiatives to concrete business strategies (Hansen *et al.* 1999; Hunter *et al.* 2002; McDermott and O'Dell 2001; Pan and Scarbrough 1999). The logic of such perspectives is that an organization's knowledge management strategy should link to and flow from its business strategy. This is done via developing an understanding of the role of knowledge resources and processes in an organization's business strategy, and developing a knowledge management strategy to sustain and enhance these knowledge resources/processes. For example, contrast the situations of two different companies in the same industry pursuing different strategies, such as the car manufacturers Nissan and Jaguar. While both companies design, manufacture, and sell cars, the nature of their products and the strategies pursued by the companies are vastly different, with Nissan primarily focusing on high-volume family cars, while Jaguar is more focused on the luxury car market. Fundamentally, the type of knowledge-based challenges they face, the type of knowledge processes they have to manage (creation, codification, sharing . . .), and thus the approaches to managing knowledge that they adopt are consequently likely to be different.

Writers examining the link between business strategy and knowledge management activities typically propose neat sequential stage models for linking knowledge-related issues into strategy-making processes. For example, Massingham's (2004) model of knowledge-based strategy making is outlined in Table 4.1. Zack (1999) and Earl (2001) develop similar

Table 4.1 Massingham's (2004) Model of Knowledge-Based Strategy-Making Processes

Stage Number	Stage Title	Actions
1	Clarify strategy	Decide on the generic strategy to be used and get buy in to it from senior management
2	Identify strategic themes	Determine the activities that are key to achieving this strategy
3	Identify knowledge resources	Identify the role of knowledge resource in the activities which are key to the agreed strategy
4	Evaluate knowledge resources	Evaluate whether the firm's existing knowledge resources are adequate to allow the effective execution of the firm's strategic activities
5	Knowledge decision	Decide what actions are necessary to develop and/or sustain the firm's knowledge resources

models to conceptualize the relationship between business and knowledge management strategies. However, such a conceptualization of the knowledge management–strategy relationship has idealistic and rationalistic overtones. Thus, there are assumptions that business strategies are developed on the basis of thorough and objective analyses of the business/market environment, and that the implications of these business strategies are then used in a logical and structured fashion to determine organizational practices (such as HRM policies, IT strategy).

In Mintzberg *et al*.'s terms (1998), such a conceptualization of strategy making follows the Design School or Planning School models, which neglects the extent to which strategy is *ad hoc*, emergent, based on limited searches and hunches, or that business strategies are as much the result of political battles as careful market analyses. Arguably, this is because the issue of strategy has been given inadequate attention in the knowledge management literature, and that as a consequence strategy models are relatively basic and unsophisticated. Empirical support for the *ad hoc* and emergent model of strategy making is provided by Meroño-Cerdan *et al*. (2007). They report on a study looking into the knowledge management strategies adopted by a selection of Spanish and Austrian small and medium-sized enterprises (SMEs). One of the main conclusions from their study was few of the SMEs examined had clear, deliberate, and consistent approaches to the management of knowledge.

 Time to reflect The nature of organizational strategy-making processes

To what extent do stage model conceptualizations of organizational strategy making reflect the reality of what happens inside organizations? Do sequential stage models of strategy-making processes provide an unrealistic and over-simplified picture of how such processes occur?

> ### ⊙ Illustration (Informal) knowledge management in small and medium enterprises (SMEs)
>
> Hutchinson and Quintas (2008) report on the findings of a study into knowledge management initiatives within some UK SMEs. They conducted an interview-based study of a diverse range of SMEs, with these including farms, IT consultancies, and a roofing contractor. Of the thirteen SMEs they examined, ten didn't recognize the term 'knowledge management', and didn't engage in any formal knowledge management activities. However, in all thirteen firms examined, they did find extensive evidence of what they refer to as informal knowledge management. Informal knowledge management is defined as knowledge processes/activities that are specifically concerned with the management of knowledge but which are not 'systematized within policies, roles, programmes or budgets that are governed by the terminology or concepts of KM' (p. 141). Thus knowledge management activities were identified but they were relatively ad hoc and personalized. Further, informal examples of knowledge creation, knowledge sharing, knowledge searching, and knowledge synthesis were identified as being undertaken by a range of people in the companies examined. For example, one of the farmers, engaging in what was labelled informal knowledge creation, said, 'I discuss how things could be improved with the butcher that I supply. We make discoveries accidentally. You could say we have a partnership' (p. 141). An example of informal knowledge sharing in one SME simply involved different people chatting and sharing ideas within an open-plan office. Finally, informal knowledge searching within one manufacturing company involved a range of activities including attending industry conferences, developing contacts with two professors at a local university, and chatting with suppliers.
>
> 1. Think about the potential advantages and disadvantages to SMEs such as those of trying to formalize these informal knowledge activities. Do you think the benefits of formalization outweigh the disadvantages?

As outlined above, the type of knowledge-related challenges and approaches to managing knowledge that are appropriate for different firms will be affected not only by the type of strategies that organizations pursue, but also by the characteristics of an organization, and also by the nature of the environment that businesses operate in. Both these issues are briefly examined now, starting with how an organization's characteristics will affect its approach to knowledge management. As the illustration suggests, organizational size, in terms of the number of employees it has, may be an important variable, with the type of knowledge-based challenges faced by small companies likely to be quite different to those faced by a global multinational employing thousands of workers. However, in considering organizational size, it is also necessary to simultaneously take account of other organizational characteristics that are likely to be linked to the number of employees, including the extent to which an organization's workforce is geographically dispersed, and the extent to which an organization's workforce is culturally diverse. Thus, while global multinationals may employ a culturally diverse workforce which is dispersed across sites and locations which are thousands of miles apart, a small firm may be located on only one site and employ a culturally homogeneous workforce. Further, the knowledge-related challenges faced by these two types of company are likely to be significantly different, and they are thus likely to manage knowledge in quite different ways. Such a contrast is visible if the above illustration of informal knowledge management in SMEs is contrasted with the next example of IT-based knowledge management adopted by some multinationals. For example, multinationals

Illustration   The challenges of knowledge sharing across sites within multinationals

Kasper *et al.*'s (2010) paper is concerned with how six multinational firms address a problem that all multinationals face, that of sharing knowledge across sites. Sharing knowledge between sites can be particularly challenging if the knowledge to be shared is highly tacit, and contextually rich. The generic solution to this challenge adopted by all the multinationals they examined was to give up attempts to share contextually rich knowledge between sites, and to instead focus on the sharing of what they referred to as 'thinned' knowledge. One writer who talked about thick and thin knowledge was Geertz (1973), who contrasted the 'thick', rich, detailed descriptions that ethnographic anthropologists could produce with the thin, briefer, more summarized knowledge of other anthropologists. Another illustration of thin knowledge is two-dimensional technical drawings, which provide a thin (two-dimensional) description of three-dimensional objects. Thin knowledge is thus brief, summarized knowledge that is stripped of its contextual richness. The benefit of thin knowledge in addressing the problem of cross-site knowledge sharing is that such knowledge is relatively easy to transmit.

While Kasper *et al.* (2010) argue that all six multinationals shared thin knowledge between sites, they identified three different thinning strategies, with the strategies they adopted being related to the nature of the work done within them, and the type of knowledge that needed to be shared. Two of the multinationals examined were consultancies. In both these companies what was labelled a *topographical approach* to thinning was adopted. This involved developing electronic expertise maps, which codified details of who possessed what expertise and knowledge and where in the organization they were located, but not the details of the knowledge. These electronic maps could be accessed and searched by anyone within the company who was interested in locating people with specific expertise. This was typically people-centred knowledge. This type of knowledge was important in these organizations as it allowed both consultants to advertise their knowledge and experience to others in the organization, and project leaders to identify relevant people for their projects.

An alternative *statistical approach* to thinning knowledge was adopted by the two industrial materials companies that were examined. In these companies, the type of knowledge that needed to be shared between sites was site-specific knowledge, related to a site's performance, which allowed people to benchmark and compare performance across sites. With the statistical approach to thinning, the thinned knowledge was statistical information (on topics such as product quality levels, productivity levels, error levels, etc.), with collections of such statistical information presenting thin knowledge on site performance. The third and final approach to knowledge thinning adopted by the two high-technology companies was referred to as a *diagrammatic approach* to thinning. In both these organizations product design responsibilities were highly centralized with dispersed sites being responsible for the standardized production of products that were designed at the corporate centre. In this context, the knowledge to be shared between the corporate centre and production sites was product design specifications, which were shared in the form of diagrams and technical drawings.

Overall therefore, all six multinationals examined dealt with the challenge of sharing knowledge across sites by thinning knowledge of its contextual richness, allowing it to be more easily transmitted and shared. However, the specific approach to knowledge thinning that was utilized in each company varied dependent on the company strategy, the type of products and services being produced, and the type of knowledge that required to be shared across sites.

are likely to face the challenge of sharing knowledge between workers of different cultures (see Chapter 9 and Chapter 11), and may need to make extensive use of information technology to facilitate communication and knowledge sharing between workers who are geographically dispersed (see Chapter 13). Overall therefore, factors such as the structure, size, and cultural diversity of an organization are likely to have a significant impact on the ways in which it attempts to manage knowledge.

The final range of factors examined here that affect an organization's approach to knowledge management relates to the character of the environment that organizations operate in. First, due to the embodied and tacit nature of much knowledge, the nature of the labour markets that organizations recruit from can have significant implications for their knowledge management strategies. For example, research on knowledge-intensive work suggests that labour market shortages in particular sectors can make it easy for knowledge workers to move between firms, making the retention of such workers difficult (see Chapter 14). In such circumstances, methods developed to retain such workers can be conceived of as an important element of an organization's knowledge management strategy.

Secondly, the nature of an organization's markets and the character of competition in them are also likely to be important factors. Thus, whether markets are highly competitive or not and whether competition is on the basis of cost, product quality, or product/service innovation are likely to affect the strategic role of knowledge processes within firms. For example, in business sectors such as pharmaceuticals, IT/software, mobile technologies and consumer goods such as televisions, levels of technological change are high, thus for companies involved in the development of products in these sectors processes of knowledge creation are likely to be important. By contrast in business sectors such as furniture manufacture and sales or food production, where levels of technological innovation are lower, organizations are likely to place less emphasis on knowledge creation processes.

Relatedly, the degree of standardization of an organization's products or services will influence the type of knowledge processes that are important. For example, if an organization is focused on producing and selling standardized products, processes of knowledge codification or knowledge sharing, between workers and between sites, may be particularly important. In contrast, if an organization develops and provides products or services which require to be customized to the specific needs of different customers, as is the case generally with architects, processes of knowledge creation, to find unique solutions to individual customer challenges, may be particularly important.

Finally, whether an organization is a private business, which has to make profit etc., or whether it is a public sector organization or a charity, is fundamental to the type of knowledge processes that are likely to be important. While the vast majority of research on knowledge management is focused on private business, some studies have been done on knowledge management activities in other types of organizations, such as public sector organizations (Dawes *et al.* 2009; Kothari *et al.* 2011; Seba *et al.* 2012; Waring and Currie 2009: see illustration) and not-for-profit organizations (Cruz *et al.* 2009; Hume and Hume 2008; Matzkin 2008).

Conceptualizing the Diversity of Knowledge Management Strategies

It should now be obvious that there is not one single way for an organization to manage knowledge. Arguably there are virtually an infinite number of ways organizations can attempt to manage the knowledge of their workforce. To take account of this diversity, the following, generic and broad-brush definition of knowledge management is developed.

Illustration   The knowledge management challenges within a UK hospital

Waring and Currie (2009) examine the dynamics involved with the implementation of a knowledge management system in an English hospital that focused on managing patient safety knowledge. The purpose of this illustration is not to give details on the implementation of this knowledge management system, but to instead focus on highlighting how the dynamics of the implementation were significantly shaped by the institutional context/environment of the National Health Service in the UK. The knowledge management system being implemented was focused on issues of patient safety. Issues of patient safety were regarded as an important topic due to the number of errors and 'adverse incidents' that can occur during the delivery of care. The knowledge management system to be implemented had three stages. First, clinicians were responsible for reporting the details of adverse incidents to hospital risk managers. Secondly, risk managers then analysed this knowledge to identify the underlying cause/s of the incidents. Thirdly, risk managers then made recommendations regarding changes that were required to be implemented to reduce the risk of similar adverse incidents recurring.

However, to understand the varied, but generally hostile and suspicious response of medical practitioners to this initiative, it is necessary to understand the historical and institutional context surrounding the knowledge management initiative. Fundamentally, the initiative was regarded as representing a (further) way in which the autonomy of medical professionals was being challenged and undermined by non-clinical managers. The knowledge management initiative was thus seen as providing a potential means by which the doctor's knowledge could be detached from them, and the clinical context in which it was utilized, and be made amenable to control by non-clinical managers (the risk managers). These aims were seen as being compatible with historical trajectory which had seen market principles and managerial practices being increasingly utilized to govern patient care and which were regarded as blurring the boundaries between managerial and professional roles as well as undermining the autonomy of clinical professionals to provide care.

Thus this historical/institutional context played a significant role in shaping the actions of the doctors in relation to the patient safety knowledge management system, which involved utilizing a range of different strategies to attempt to manage and control the knowledge management system themselves, rather than allow it to be managed by hospital risk managers.

DEFINITION   Knowledge management

Knowledge management is an umbrella term which refers to any deliberate efforts to manage the knowledge of an organization's workforce, which can be achieved via a wide range of methods including directly, through the use of particular types of ICT, or more indirectly through the management of social processes, the structuring of organizations in particular ways or via the use of particular culture and people management practices.

While the focus thus far in the chapter has been on the general and strategic factors which can shape the type of KM strategies organizations adopt, the focus shifts here to provide some specific details of three of the most influential frameworks and typologies that have been developed to characterize some of the key features of different approaches to the management of organizational knowledge. While the three frameworks examined were published between 1999 and 2001, they still have continued relevance and influence. Further, a recent review of the literature on knowledge management suggests that there have been no significant, more recent attempts to develop a typology of knowledge management strategies (Lloria 2008).

Hansen *et al.*'s (1999) codification versus personalization framework

One of the earliest, but arguably most influential typologies of knowledge management approaches was developed by Hansen *et al.* (1999). The extent of its influence is visible in the fact that according to Google Scholar it had been cited more than 3, 400 times by May 2012. Examples of recent studies which have linked to their framework include Kumar and Ganesh (2011—see illustration), Lin (2011) and Jasimuddin *et al.* (2012). Of the three knowledge management typologies examined here, Hansen *et al.*'s is the simplest, as it only differentiates between two broad knowledge strategies: codification and personalization (see Table 4.2). The codification strategy is argued to be most relevant for companies whose competitive advantage is derived from the reuse of codified knowledge and is centrally concerned with creating searchable repositories for the storage and retrieval of codified knowledge. The personalization strategy, by contrast, is most relevant for companies whose competitive advantage is derived from processes of knowledge creation and the provision of innovative, customized products/services. The personalization knowledge strategy assumes that much of the key knowledge of its workers is tacit and cannot be codified, and thus focuses on ways to improve the face-to-face sharing of this tacit knowledge between workers.

In terms of the link between knowledge management and HRM, Hansen *et al.* (1999) make clear that the HRM implications of the codification and personalization knowledge strategies are different, and argue that it is thus important for organizations to ensure that their knowledge and HRM strategies are aligned (see Table 4.2). For example, with the codification strategy, the main motivation issue is persuading workers to codify their knowledge, whereas with the personalization strategy it is related to persuading people to share

Table 4.2 Codification and Personalization Knowledge Strategies

Knowledge Strategy	Codification	Personalization
Business–Knowledge Link	Competitive advantage through knowledge reuse	Competitive advantage through knowledge creation
Relevant Knowledge Process	Transferring knowledge from people to documents	Improving social processes to facilitate sharing of tacit knowledge between people
HRM Implications	Motivate people to codify their knowledge Training should emphasize the development of IT skills Reward people for codifying their knowledge	Motivate people to share their knowledge with others Training should emphasize the development of interpersonal skills Reward people for sharing knowledge with others

Source: Hansen *et al.* 1999.

Illustration   The use of codification and personalization strategies within Indian manufacturing companies

Kumar and Ganesh (2011) undertook a survey-based study of the knowledge management strategies utilized within the product development facilities of some Indian manufacturing companies. They examined both the extent to which codification and personalization strategies to manage knowledge were adopted, and also the extent to which product development performance was linked to the use of either approach to knowledge management. They found that, in virtually every product development unit they examined, both approaches to knowledge management were utilized simultaneously. However, in general terms significantly greater use was made of the personalization-based approach to knowledge management. Secondly, in terms of the link between the use of these knowledge management strategies, and product development performance, which was measured in terms of the extent to which product development activities were carried out according to planned cost and time schedules, they found a positive link between both approaches and product development performance. Thus, both approaches to knowledge management appeared to facilitate product development performance.

Kumar and Ganesh also analysed the differences between firms in terms of the extent to which they utilized each knowledge management approach. In terms of the use of a codification-based approach they found little variation between firms, with this being argued to be due to the increasing standardization of IT facilities that were being used by Indian manufacturing firms. However, they did find some variation between firms in terms of the extent to which the personalization-based approach to knowledge management was used. It was suggested that this variation may be related to differences between firms, both in terms of the types of knowledge they utilized, and the types of business strategies they adopted. Fundamentally, the more orientated a firm is to the creation of new knowledge, the more important a personalization-based approach to knowledge management is likely to be.

their knowledge with others. HRM policies and practices thus need to be directed towards the achievement of these quite different objectives. Thus for example, in terms of recruitment and selection, it will be important to identify and recruit people with suitable personalities to implement these different knowledge activities (knowledge reuse versus knowledge creation). Equally, training and development implications also have to be different, with companies pursuing codification strategies needing to emphasize the development of IT skills, whereas those organizations pursuing a personalization strategy require a substantially greater emphasis on developing the social networking and interpersonal skills of their workers. Finally, payment and appraisal systems should reward behaviours appropriate to the organization's knowledge strategy. The IT implications of these two strategies are also obviously different, with codification strategy being much more IT based, and the personalization strategy being much more HRM based.

Earl's (2001) seven schools of knowledge management

The second taxonomy of knowledge management approaches was developed by Michael Earl, a professor of information management (Earl 2001). The extent of its influence is visible in the fact that, according to Google Scholar, it had been cited more than 700 times by May 2012. This is a more complicated taxonomy than Hansen *et al*.'s as it identifies seven specific schools which are organized into three broad approaches (see Table 4.3). This taxonomy takes account of the choices organizations face with regard to the role they allocate in knowledge management initiatives to IT systems and HRM practices through the varying extent and character of the role they play in each of the seven schools.

Earl to some extent acknowledges the complexity of the choices organizations have to make about the role of IT systems in their knowledge management initiatives by identifying three different and distinctive schools of knowledge management, all of which give a prominent (but different) role to IT systems, which are classified together as making up the technocratic approach to knowledge management.

The first of the technocratic approaches to knowledge management is the *Systems School*. With the systems school the main concern is with the codification of knowledge into databases, with this knowledge then being available for use as an organizational resource. Knowledge sharing thus occurs not in a direct face-to-face exchange between people, but indirectly via people codifying knowledge which others then subsequently utilize.

Earl's second IT-based approach to knowledge management is the *Cartographic School*. With this approach IT systems are used to facilitate the creation of interpersonal connections between people who possess relevant expertise through the creation of searchable directories of expertise which effectively provides a map of an organization's knowledge base. With such systems, anyone seeking a source of particular expert knowledge can use such directories to find and develop links with relevant people. Thus, while IT systems play a key role in this school, ultimately knowledge sharing typically occurs directly between people, once relevant sources of knowledge and expertise have been identified.

The third and final IT-based approach to knowledge management identified by Earl is the *Engineering School*. With this school IT systems are used to provide people with task and process oriented knowledge on operational processes and procedures through the codification of knowledge in databases that are available to relevant people. The difference between this approach and the systems school of knowledge management is the focusing of knowledge around operational tasks and processes.

The second broad approach to knowledge management identified by Earl is the economic approach, which has only one specific school of knowledge management, the *Commercial School*. With this approach to knowledge management the main aim of knowledge management activities is to effectively commercialize an organization's knowledge such that an organization can achieve measurable economic benefits from these efforts. With this approach knowledge activities are focused on producing products and services that add value, and attempting to protect such knowledge assets via patents, trademarks, etc.

The final broad approach to knowledge management identified by Earl, within which he identified three distinctive schools, is the behavioural approach to knowledge management. This approach contrasts with the technocratic approach as its emphasis is much more on people management practices and processes than on managing knowledge via the use of IT systems. Fundamentally, this approach is focused on creating processes, spaces, and mechanisms which facilitate the interpersonal sharing of knowledge between people.

The first of the behavioural approaches is the *Organisational School*. This school of knowledge management is concerned with facilitating the creation of interpersonal networks, or communities of people who have common interests and who can benefit from sharing their knowledge and experience with each other. The success of such efforts

Table 4.3 Earl's Seven Schools of Knowledge Management

| | Technocratic | | | Economic | Behavioural | | |
	Systems	Cartographic	Engineering	Commercial	Organizational	Spatial	Strategic
Focus	Technology	Maps	Processes	Income	Networks	Space	Mindset
Aim	Kn. bases	Kn. directories	Kn. flows	Kn. assets	Kn. pooling	Kn. exchange	Kn. capabilities
Unit	Domain	Enterprise	Activity	Know-how	Communities	Place	Business
IT Role	Kn. based systems	Internet directories	Shared databases	Intellectual asset register	Groupware and intranets	Access tools	Eclectic
Philo-sophy	Codification	Connectivity	Capability	Commercializ'n	Collaboration	Contactivity	Consciousness

Source: Adapted from Earl 2001: table 1.

depends upon the people participating in such communities developing a strong sense of identity with them, and also on there being adequate levels of trust between people within them to facilitate knowledge sharing. While such communities can interact on a face-to-face basis, there is also scope for IT systems to play a role in such communities through the role they can have in supporting the remote, IT-mediated interaction of community members.

The second of the behavioural approaches to knowledge management is the *Spatial School*. This method of knowledge management is focused on the creation of spaces, both physical and virtual, which can provide opportunities to bring people together, and allow them to share knowledge and experiences when they do so. Examples of physical spaces that can be developed for such purposes are formal meeting and training rooms, or more informal meeting spaces such as water-coolers and kitchens. McKinlay (2002) provided an example of a virtual space that was created for such purposes in his research on a global pharmaceutical company which developed an online, virtual café which workers could enter and share knowledge relatively informally via discussion boards and chatrooms.

The final of the behavioural approaches to knowledge management identified by Earl is the *Strategic School*. This approach to knowledge management is concerned with shaping

 Illustration   The spatial approach to knowledge management at the BBC

Chaundy (2005) describes a knowledge management activity utilized by the BBC's Nations and Regions division to facilitate interpersonal knowledge sharing. The Nations and Regions division is both large (employing nearly 7,000 staff) and highly dispersed, being spread over more than fifty separate sites in the UK. Most sites were focused on the provision of local and regional television and radio news. However, the physical separation of staff across such a large number of sites made it difficult to share knowledge and experience between offices. One solution developed and supported by the BBC's knowledge management team was the creation of a training site which would allow staff from different regional offices to come together and share their experiences. This site, named SON&R (Sharing Opportunities across Nations and Regions), was developed in Bristol in an existing BBC building.

The idea of SON&R was to facilitate knowledge sharing through bringing together people from different sites who performed similar functions for two- to five-day workshops during which they would have the opportunity to develop social relations and share experiences. Overall, the idea was to create an 'exciting and safe atmosphere where participants would feel happy to share their experiences and be inspired to enhance working practices' (p. 25). The centre opened in September 2002 and by the time Chaundy wrote her article over 3,500 Nations and Regions staff had attended an event at the SON&R facility. Role-based sessions have brought together people performing a range of different jobs, including sports journalists, weekend producers, assistant editors, football commentators, religious producers, weather presenters, and 'front of house staff'. For example, in 2003, thirty 'front of house staff' such as receptionists and security guards had a workshop. Prior to its start, ten of the staff participated in a job swap, while ten others visited front of house functions in other organizations. Participants in these events gave feedback on their experiences during the workshops. All participants in the workshop felt they had had a positive experience, had learnt something new, and had developed a sense of being part of a wider community.

attitudes and values which facilitate effective knowledge management behaviours rather than directly shaping knowledge processes. It can be labelled the 'culture management based approach to knowledge management' as it uses a wide range of mechanisms, such as vision statements, business plans, communication programmes, and training activities, to develop a consciousness within employees that knowledge management processes matter. The expectation with this approach is that, if such interventions are successful, people will voluntarily choose to undertake and participate in relevant knowledge management processes.

Alvesson and Kärreman's (2001) four knowledge management approaches

Finally, it is useful to examine Alvesson and Kärreman's (2001) typology of knowledge management strategies. First, it is a well-referenced and influential framework, with over 350 citations in May 2012. Secondly, it builds on and links to their typology of management strategies and explicitly links the varying nature of management practices to the different approaches to knowledge management that organizations adopt. Alvesson and Kärreman (2001) used the framework of four management philosophies outlined earlier as the basis for developing four specific approaches to knowledge management (see Figure 4.1). Alvesson and Kärreman, as with Earl, make clear that the distinctions they make between the four different approaches to knowledge management are analytical rather than empirical. Thus they suggest that organizations are unlikely to exclusively use one approach to knowledge management and that management in any particular organization are likely to simultaneously use a combination of their four approaches. The four approaches to knowledge management they identify are structured around two dimensions: the mode of managerial intervention and the medium of interaction (see Figure 4.1). The mode of managerial intervention dimension relates to the strength of managerial control dimension outlined earlier, with the 'coordination' mode relating to a relative weak philosophy of management, and the 'control' mode referring to a stronger form of management control. The medium of interaction dimension relates to the distinction, outlined earlier, between management systems focused on controlling behaviour and those focused on workers' attitudes, with the 'social' dimension relating to attitudinal control, and the 'technostructural' dimension relating to behavioural controls. The four approaches that result from the combination of these dimensions are described below.

Starting at the bottom left of Figure 4.1 is the *Extended Library* approach to knowledge management, which combines technostructural focused controls with a relatively weak form of coordinated management. This approach to knowledge management is relatively bureaucratic, centrally controlled, and top–down in character. IT systems play an important role in this approach, with senior management creating central databases and archives where employees are encouraged to codify their knowledge and experiences. Such databases are searchable and can be accessed by staff looking for sources of particular types of knowledge.

The *Community* approach to knowledge management combines the coordinated form of weak and limited managerial interventions with socially focused managerial controls.

MODE OF MANAGERIAL INTERVENTION

	Coordination: 'weak' Management	Control: 'strong' Management
Social: Attitude Centred	COMMUNITY: Sharing of Ideas	NORMATIVE CONTROL: Prescribed Interpretations
Technostructural: Behaviour Focused	EXTENDED LIBRARY: Information Exchange	ENACTED BLUEPRINTS: Templates for Action

MODE OF INTERACTION

Figure 4.1 Alvesson and Kärreman's Knowledge Management Approaches

Source: Adapted from Alvesson and Karreman (2001).

This approach to knowledge management gives a very limited role to IT systems, due to the acknowledgement that much organizational knowledge is highly tacit, with it being focused around encouraging the direct sharing of knowledge between people. Management efforts in this approach are focused on creating a positive environment, context, or culture which is likely to encourage staff to share knowledge with each other, for example through facilitating the development of communities of practice.

The *Normative Control* approach to knowledge management combines the same focus on socially focused control as the community approach, but allies it with a stronger form of managerial intervention. This is knowledge management via culture management, whereby management invest significant efforts in creating a culture which encourages, values, and rewards employee participation in organizational knowledge processes, and encourages employees to 'buy into' the culture.

Alvesson and Kärreman's final approach to knowledge management is the *Enacted Blueprints* method which combines a strong form of managerial intervention with technostructural type managerial controls. As with the normative control approach to knowledge management, the enacted blueprints model involves significant managerial efforts. These efforts are focused on creating codified databases of knowledge on particular roles and tasks, that provide employees with templates to guide their action. This means of knowledge management is intended to facilitate the codification and dissemination of 'best practice' ways of work. However, the way in which this method limits the scope of workers to use their autonomy leads Alvesson and Kärreman to label it a form of Taylorism.

Conclusion

Following on from Chapters 2 and 3, where two different perspectives on the character of knowledge in the knowledge management literature were examined, this chapter moved on to grapple with the question of what knowledge management is. The general conclusion of the chapter, which was illustrated through examining three separate knowledge management typologies (those of Earl, Hansen *et al.*, and Alvesson and Kärreman) was that there is a large diversity of ways in which to manage knowledge in organizations. The chapter also considered the factors that influence the approach to knowledge management that organizations adopt. In this respect it was found that a large diversity of heterogeneous factors came into play, including the types of business strategies that organizations pursue, the characteristics of organizations such as number of employees, level of geographic dispersal, etc., and the nature of the environment that organizations operate in. Another important factor examined, which also influences the approach to knowledge management organizations adopt, but which is typically neglected in the knowledge management literature, is the approach to management adopted by an organization. Using Alvesson and Kärreman's (2001) analysis, the concept of management was examined and unpacked, with it being concluded that 'management' itself doesn't represent a unified and coherent set of objectives or practices and that there are a diversity of ways for organizations to manage.

⊙ Case study   The relationship between the structure/strategy of multinational corporations and patterns of knowledge sharing within them

The key question investigated by Kasper *et al.* (2009), in a study of eight multinationals (MNCs), was whether differences in the strategies and structures of multinational corporations affected the nature of knowledge sharing within them. In defining the different type of strategies and structures utilized by MNCs Kasper *et al.* utilized the most common typology in the literature on MNCs. This typology is based on the extent to which multinationals emphasize the global integration of their business activities, and the extent to which they emphasize local responsiveness of business units to the individual and distinctive needs of their particular markets. This framework produces three distinctive type of strategy for MNCs:

- Global MNCs—which are focused on achieving high levels of global integration, and where levels of local responsiveness are relatively low;
- Multidomestic MNCs—which are focused on achieving high levels of local responsiveness, and where levels of global integration are relatively low;
- Transnational MNCs—which attempt to achieve high levels of global integration, while simultaneously sustaining high levels of local responsiveness.

The assumptions made by Kasper *et al.* regarding the structure and hypothesized knowledge-sharing patterns within these different types of MNC are summarized in Table 4.4. Further, Kasper *et al.* (2009) hypothesized that the greatest quantity of knowledge sharing between business units and between HQ and subsidiaries would be in transnational MNCs, with the lowest levels being in multidomestic MNCs.

Kasper *et al.* (2009) adopted a qualitative multiple case study approach to investigating their research questions. Research was conducted in eight different MNCs, all of whose HQs were either in Europe or North America. Interviews were conducted with staff from both the headquarters and at least two different subsidiaries in all eight MNCs researched. The MNCs involved in the research were from a range of different business sectors, including management consulting, the capital goods industry, high-technology sectors, IT services, and logistics.

Table 4.4 Relationship between MNC Strategy, Structure, and Hypothesized Knowledge-Sharing Patterns

	Global MNC	Multidomestic MNC	Transnational MNC
Degree of Global Integration (I) and Local Responsiveness (R)	High I and Low R	High R and Low I	High I and High R
Structure	Global hierarchy	Federation of heterogeneous, autonomous businesses	Heterarchical network
Hypothesized Pattern of Knowledge Sharing	HQ: global innovator Subsidiaries: local implementers	HQ and Subsidiaries: both local innovators	HQ and subsidiaries: integrated players

The most distinctive and arguably important finding from their research related to the patterns of knowledge sharing that were found. The research findings partly supported the hypotheses developed, and partly challenged them. As hypothesized, the greatest level of knowledge sharing was found in the transnational MNCs. However, in opposition to another hypothesis there were virtually non-existent levels of knowledge sharing in the global MNCs. The focus now is on explaining the contrast in knowledge-sharing patterns between these two types of MNC.

In the transnational MNCs examined attempts were made to sustain both high levels of global integration and high levels of local adaptability. In these organizations subsidiaries typically had high levels of autonomy to pursue strategies and develop innovations that were deemed by their management to be appropriate to their specific markets. However, simultaneously and in tension with this, there were demands on subsidiaries to develop and use standardized solutions and project structures. In terms of knowledge sharing, there was evidence of reasonable levels of knowledge sharing both between subsidiaries and between subsidiaries and HQ.

In the global MNCs that were researched quite different strategies were pursued, and very contrasting patterns of knowledge sharing were found. In these MNCs the strategic focus was on the global integration of products and services. Subsidiaries had no autonomy to develop customized products/services and were tasked with providing globally standardized products/services in their particular local markets. In these MNCs innovations on products and services were only ever developed by the HQ, which monopolized strategically important knowledge. Subsidiaries were thus constrained to implement the strategies and innovations of the HQ and were not involved in knowledge sharing with the HQ as they were never involved in strategic decision-making processes regarding products and services.

Overall therefore, the type of strategy pursued by the MNCs was found to play a crucial role in shaping the patterns of knowledge sharing that occurred between the HQ and subsidiaries.

1. Do these findings suggest that there isn't a single best model of knowledge sharing within MNCs and that what is more important is that the knowledge-sharing patterns that exist reflect the particular strategy adopted?

Source: Kasper, H., Lehrer, M., Mühlbacher, J., and Müller, B. (2009) 'Integration-Responsiveness and the Knowledge Management Perspectives of the MNC: A Typology and Field Study of Cross-Site Knowledge Sharing Practices', *Journal of Leadership and Organizational Studies*, 15/3: 287–303.

Review and Discussion Questions

1. McKinlay (2002) suggested that one of the limits that exist to managerial efforts to control and manage knowledge relate to the difficulty of managing informal, unregulated encounters, such as when groups of colleagues socialize together. What, if anything, can organizations do to manage knowledge in such contexts?

2. Think about the link between the three taxonomies of knowledge management examined. What similarities and overlaps exist between the different approaches to knowledge management identified? For example, to what extent is Earl's systems approach similar to Hansen *et al.*'s codification-based strategy?

3. Earl suggests that organizations can adopt more than one school of knowledge management simultaneously. For example, an organization could simultaneously utilize a strategic and commercial approach to knowledge management. Can you identify any of Earl's schools of knowledge management which are unlikely to be compatible with each other?

 Suggestions for Further Reading

1. **M. Mehrizi, and N. Bontis (2009) 'A Cluster Analysis of the KM Field',** *Management Decision*, **47/5: 792–805.**
A relatively up to date article which gives an overview of the literature on knowledge management.

2. **A. Haesli and P. Boxall (2005) 'When Knowledge Management Meets HR Strategy: An Exploration of Personalization-Retention and Codification-Recruitment Configurations',** *International Journal of Human Resource Management*, 16/11: 1955–75.
Makes use of Hansen *et al.*'s knowledge management typology to analyse how two organizations link their knowledge management (and human resource management) strategies to their different business strategies.

3. **H. Kasper, M. Lehrer, J. Mühlbacher, and B. Müller (2010) 'Thinning Knowledge: An Interpretive Field Study of Knowledge Sharing Practices of Firms in Three Multinational Contexts',** *Journal of Management Inquiry*, 19/4: 367–81.
Examined cross-site knowledge sharing, one of the key challenges faced by knowledge-related multinationals, as well as highlighting a diversity of responses to it which are shaped by different organizational factors.

4. **V. Hutchinson and P. Quintas (2008) 'Do SMEs do Knowledge Management? Or Simply Manage What they Know?',** *International Small Business Journal*, 26/2: 131–54.
Highlights the significance of informal knowledge management practices within small companies.

Take your learning further: Online Resource Centre

Visit the Online Resource Centre for resources which will extend your understanding of knowledge management in organizations. As well as web links to sites of interest, the author has provided case studies looking at knowledge management in virtual and knowledge-intensive firms, and in global multinationals. These will help you with your research, essays, and assignments; or you may find these additional resources helpful when revising for exams.

    www.oxfordtextbooks.co.uk/orc/hislop3e/

5 Knowledge-Intensive Firms and Knowledge Workers

Introduction

As was discussed in Chapter 1, many commentators and writers characterize contemporary society as being a knowledge society, with the importance of knowledge to work and economic activity having grown enormously in the last quarter of the twentieth century. The growing importance of knowledge to the world of work is also argued to have transformed the character of the work activities people undertake, as well as the nature of organizations. Key to these transformations has been the growing importance of knowledge workers and knowledge-intensive firms. In fact, if contemporary society is a knowledge society, then almost by definition knowledge-intensive firms and knowledge workers represent constituent elements of it.

This chapter has two primary purposes. First, it provides a detailed definition of the terms 'knowledge-intensive firms' and 'knowledge workers' and, secondly, it examines the character of work and the dynamics of the knowledge processes within knowledge-intensive firms. However, as the chapter progresses, it will be shown that a number of debates exist on these topics, most fundamentally about the definition of knowledge workers and the extent to which they are distinctive from other types of worker (Bosch-Sijtsema *et al.* 2010; Hislop 2008).

The chapter begins by looking at how writing on knowledge workers and knowledge-intensive firms is typically embedded in the knowledge society rhetoric. Next we consider how knowledge-intensive firms are defined and the overlap that exists between knowledge-intensive firms and professional service firms. Following this, the next two sections present different perspectives on the definition of knowledge work, starting with the mainstream 'professional knowledge work' perspective, and then moving on to the alternative 'all work is knowledge work' perspective. Next we consider the nature of the work carried out within knowledge-intensive firms, examining the extent to which ambiguity represents a distinguishing feature of, and inherent element in, knowledge work. A following sixth section considers the character of knowledge processes within knowledge-intensive firms, which links to the topic of social capital. The chapter concludes by examining the debate regarding the extent to which knowledge workers represent the ideal employee, being always willing to participate in relevant knowledge processes, and work long hours for their employers. A topic not examined here, as it is dealt with in Chapters 14 and 15, is what organizations can do to manage knowledge workers.

The Knowledge Economy and the Growing Importance of Knowledge-Intensive Firms and Knowledge Workers

Since approximately the mid-1970s, as discussed in Chapter 1, the character of work has changed enormously. These changes are argued to have produced an enormous expansion in the number of knowledge workers, and knowledge-intensive firms (Huang 2011; Joo 2010; Matson and Prusak 2010). More specifically, such analyses typically utilize the knowledge society rhetoric and argue that, not only have the number of knowledge workers and the knowledge intensity of work increased, but the effective use of knowledge is now a significant source of competitive advantage for many companies (Bosch-Sijtsema *et al.* 2010; Carleton 2011; Dul *et al.* 2011), and that abstract and theoretical knowledge has taken on a heightened level of importance (Giauque *et al.* 2010; Huang 2011; Joo 2010).

One writer who was among the first to popularize such analyses was Robert Reich (Blackler 1995; Rifkin 2000). Reich's analysis was focused largely on the USA, but his argument was relevant to all of the most industrialized economies (Reich 1991). He argued that the shift towards high-value-added, knowledge-intensive products and services in these economies gave rise to a category of workers he labelled 'symbolic analysts'. These are workers who, first, 'solve, identify and broker problems by manipulating symbols' (p. 178) and, secondly, need to make frequent use of established bodies of codified knowledge (p. 182). Thus, typical of symbolic analytical occupations are research and product design (problem-solving), marketing and consultancy (problem identification), and finance/banking (problem brokering). According to Reich's analysis, by the late 1980s this category of work had grown to account for 20 per cent of employment in the USA, and was one of the USA's three key occupational categories. Statistical analysis from the UK suggests that the proportion of professional/knowledge-intensive workers in Britain was also 20 per cent in the early 1990s (Elias and Gregory 1994). As outlined immediately above, contemporary writing on knowledge workers and knowledge-intensive firms restates these claims, but as these assertions are typically assumed to be so obviously true that they do not require substantiation, few people provide contemporary statistical data in support of them.

 Time to reflect   How important are knowledge workers?

If knowledge workers constitute approximately 20 per cent of the workers in the most industrialized nations, does this suggest that their importance to these economies has been exaggerated, or is their contribution to knowledge creation and wealth generation disproportional to their numbers?

Chapter 1 presented a critique of the knowledge society rhetoric on which much of the literature on knowledge work and knowledge-intensive firms is founded and there is no need to revisit it here. The main purpose of linking back to the concept of the knowledge economy here was to highlight the way in which the concepts of knowledge work and knowledge-intensive firms are so closely tied to it. The chapter now shifts focus to consider the challenges involved in providing a precise definition of what a knowledge-intensive firm is.

Defining and Characterizing Knowledge-Intensive Firms

In considering the characteristics of knowledge-intensive firms and how to define them, it is necessary to begin by acknowledging that not only are a wide range of diverse organizations labelled as knowledge-intensive, but also there is no consensus on how to define a knowledge-intensive firm. Thus some of the types of organization labelled as knowledge-intensive include IT service companies (Grimshaw and Miozzo 2009), law firms (Malhotra *et al.* 2010), biotechnology companies (Bunker Whittington *et al.* 2009; Luo and Deng 2009), and business consultancies and engineering services (He and Wong 2009). In the case of law firms it also needs to be acknowledged that there is an overlap and inter-relationship between knowledge-intensive firms and professional service firms.

In terms of the diversity of definitions, they vary from those which are relatively broad, such as Alvesson (2000: 1101) who defines them as 'companies where most work can be said to be of an intellectual nature and where well qualified employees form the major part of the workforce', to Swart *et al.* (2003) who define them in terms of a wide range of features which distinguish them from more traditional, hierarchical organizations, including the way they are structured, the character of their workforce, the nature of work processes within them, and the character of their products and services.

 Illustration IT service firms as knowledge-intensive

Grimshaw and Miozzo (2009) examine the HRM practices within two global IT service firms which they define as knowledge-intensive. These organizations are labelled knowledge-intensive firms as the work/service they provide (IT services) involves supplying and maintaining complex high-level technological systems for their clients, which requires a significant proportion of their workforce to possess both specialized skills and professional knowledge. The need for this type of service has grown significantly in recent years as many large organizations have shifted to 'outsource' and contract such work to external firms rather than provide such services themselves. This work often involves the transferral of employees to client firms, and the work requires detailed knowledge not only of IT systems and services, but also the specific and distinctive requirements and needs of individual clients, which typically vary greatly.

In discussing the character of knowledge-intensive firms the taxonomy of knowledge-intensive firms developed by von Nordenflycht (2010) is utilized. Not only is this sensitive to the diversity of firms that can be labelled knowledge-intensive, but it also links to the concept of professional service firms. While some writers link professional service firms and knowledge-intensive firms together by arguing that professional service firms are simply a specialized subset of a wider population of knowledge-intensive firms (see e.g. Malhotra *et al.* 2010), von Nordenflycht develops a taxonomy with three dimensions.

The three dimensions in von Nordenflycht's taxonomy of knowledge-intensive firms are the knowledge intensity of work carried out within them, their level of capital intensity, and the extent to which their workforce is professionalized (see Table 5.1). The knowledge intensity of a firm is defined in terms of the extent to which the development and use of complex knowledge is involved in the creation of its outputs (products/services). In terms of capital intensity, von Nordenflycht argues that knowledge-intensive

Table 5.1 Von Nordenflycht's (2010) Taxonomy of Knowledge-Intensive Firms

Category	Knowledge Intensity	Low Capital Intensity	Professionalized Workforce	Exemplars
Technology developers	X			Biotechnology firms and R&D laboratories
Neo- professional service firms	X	X		Consultants and advertising agencies
Professional campuses	X		X	Hospitals
Classic professional service firms	X	X	X	Accountants and architects

firms have a low capital intensity, which means that their output is not dependent upon significant amounts of non-human assets such as factories, equipment, patents, copyrights, etc. The third dimension in von Nordenflycht's taxonomy is the extent to which a firm employs a professionalized workforce, being defined not only by the possession of specialized knowledge, but also where this knowledge is institutionally regulated (such as by a professional body/association), and where a code of ethics governs behaviour. In applying this taxonomy (see Table 5.1) von Nordenflycht argues that knowledge-intensive firms vary in their degree of professional service intensity, with law firms having a high level and biotechnology firms having a low level of professional service intensity.

Defining Knowledge Workers: The Professional Knowledge Work Perspective

As with the concept of knowledge-intensive firms, providing a precise definition of knowledge workers is not straightforward as there is a lack of general consensus on the topic (Bosch-Sijtsema *et al.* 2010). To reflect this debate two different definitions are presented in the chapter, with this section beginning by presenting the mainstream definition of knowledge work/ers, before introducing the critique of this perspective in the following section, which leads to another definition of knowledge work/ers.

Precise definitions vary from paper to paper, with some being relatively broad and others being more specific. For example, one of the broadest (and vaguest) definitions of knowledge work is provided by Dul *et al.* (2011) who define knowledge workers as people, 'who perform "brain work"' (p. 722). In contrast, a more detailed definition is provided by Bosch-Sijtsema *et al.* (2010), who define knowledge workers as 'anyone who creates, develops, manipulates, disseminates or uses knowledge to provide a competitive advantage or some other benefit contributing towards the goal of the organization' (p. 183). Such definitions also typically suggest that knowledge workers possess high-level, formal academic qualifications (see e.g. Giauque *et al.* 2010; Huang 2011; Joo 2010). Despite the enormous variation in definitions of knowledge workers, a number of features are typically common to all of what is here labelled the mainstream perspective on knowledge work. These common elements are that knowledge workers constitute an elite and quite distinctive element of the contemporary workforce, that they possess high-level formal qualifications, that their output typically contributes significantly to their employers' performance, that their work is highly creative and involves a significant amount of problem-solving as well as the creation and use of knowledge. Finally, this definition of knowledge work fits with Reich's definition of symbolic analysts.

DEFINITION Knowledge worker ('professional knowledge work' perspective)

Someone whose work is primarily intellectual, creative, and non-routine in nature, and which involves both the utilization and creation of abstract/theoretical knowledge.

Based on such definitions, an enormous range of occupations can be classified as knowledge work. Typical of the sort of occupations so characterized are: IT and software designers (Bosch-Sijtsema *et al.* 2010; Swart and Kinnie 2003), lawyers (Hunter *et al.* 2002; Malhotra *et al.* 2010), consultants (Dul *et al.* 2011; Robertson and Swan 2003; Swart and Kinnie 2010), advertising executives (Alvesson 1995; Beaumont and Hunter 2002; Swart and Kinnie 2010), accountants (Morris and Empson 1998), scientists and engineers (Beaumont and Hunter 2002; Huang 2011), and architects (Frenkel *et al.* 1995). Definitions of knowledge workers therefore overlap with and include the classical professions (such as lawyers, architects, etc.), but also extend beyond them to include a wide variety of other occupations (such as consultants, advertising executives, IT developers, etc.).

One problem with the definitions of knowledge workers outlined is that they are a little vague. However, Frenkel *et al.*'s (1995) somewhat neglected framework develops a more detailed definition, and conceptualizes knowledge work in relation to three dimensions (see Table 5.2). The first dimension, creativity, is defined as a process of 'original problem solving', from which an original output is produced (p. 779), with the level of creativity in work varying on a sliding scale from low to high. Thus work with a high level of creativity would include software design, where programmers design and produce new software to meet the specific requirements of their clients. The second dimension is the predominant form of knowledge used in work, with knowledge being characterized as being either theoretical or contextual. Theoretical knowledge represents codified concepts and principles, which have general relevance, whereas contextual knowledge is largely tacit, and non-generalizable, being related to specific contexts of application. The third and final dimension is skill, with the skills involved in work being divided into three categories: intellective skills, social skills, and action-based skills. Action-based skills relate to physical dexterity, social skills to the ability to motivate and manage others, while intellective skills are defined as the ability to undertake abstract reasoning and synthesize different ideas.

Table 5.2 Frenkel *et al.*'s Three Dimensional Conceptualization of Work

Dimensions	Characteristics
Creativity	Measured on a sliding scale from low to high
Predominant form of knowledge used	Characterizes work as involving the use of two predominant forms of knowledge 1. Contextual knowledge 2. Theoretical knowledge
Type of skills involved	Characterizes work as involving three main categories of skill: 1. Intellective skills 2. Social skills 3. Action-based skill

Source: Frenkel *et al.* 1995.

Using these dimensions, Frenkel *et al.* (1995) define a knowledge worker as anyone who, first, has a high level of creativity in their work, secondly, has to make extensive use of intellective skills, and finally also makes use of theoretical rather than contextual knowledge. This framework fits within the professional knowledge work perspective as the label 'knowledge worker' is restricted to those whose work has the above listed three characteristics.

Also common within the mainstream perspective on knowledge workers and knowledge-intensive firms is the use of the term 'knowledge-intensive work', which provides the same function as Frenkel *et al.*'s framework in maintaining the idea that knowledge workers represent an elite and exclusive element in the contemporary workforce. Thus what distinguishes knowledge workers from other types of worker is the intensity of their knowledge use. However, as Alvesson (2000) makes clear, knowledge intensiveness is a somewhat vague concept and Alvesson suggests in a later paper that 'any evaluation of "intensiveness" is likely to be contestable' (2001: 864). Thus, arguably, there will always be room for debate on which occupations can be defined as knowledge-intensive work. The chapter now examines an alternative definition of knowledge work that can be found in some of the knowledge management literature.

Defining Knowledge Workers: The 'All Work is Knowledge Work' Perspective

Explicitly embedded in Frenkel *et al.*'s conceptualization of knowledge work is the privileging of theoretical knowledge over contextual knowledge (Hislop 2008). Thus occupations that involve the use of high levels of contextual knowledge, and low levels of theoretical knowledge, such as the care workers examined by Nishikawa (2011) or the highly skilled flute makers examined by Cook and Yanow (1993), are not classified as knowledge work by Frenkel *et al.* This privileging of abstract/theoretical knowledge is typical, either explicitly or implicitly in the mainstream conceptualization of knowledge work, and provides the basis of one of the main critiques of such definitions.

Such a privileging of theoretical knowledge, and the use of the term 'knowledge worker' to refer to an exclusive group of workers is a subjective and somewhat arbitrary definition. The main problem with such definitions is that the privileging of abstract and theoretical knowledge in them typically leads to the significance, role, and even legitimacy of (often tacit) contextual knowledge in work being downplayed. The 'all work is knowledge work' perspective suggests that, when such knowledge is taken account of, virtually all types of work can be considered to be knowledge work (Alvesson 2000; Grant 2000; Thompson *et al.* 2001). Knights *et al.* (1993) make such an argument, drawing on Giddens's (1979) argument that all behaviour involves a process of self-reflexive monitoring and is thus knowledgeable. Such arguments lead to an awareness that most types of work involve the development and use of tacit knowledge. Further, Beaumont and Hunter (2002) report the findings of a study which concluded that knowledge generation/creation was not simply the domain of a small, elite group of workers and that knowledge was created at all levels within organizations (Cutcher-Gershenfeld *et al.* 1998).

Nishikawa's (2011) argument that care workers can be labelled as knowledge workers is compatible with the 'all work is knowledge work' perspective. The lack of formalized, codified knowledge in care work means that it is not classified as knowledge work using the professional knowledge work perspective outlined above. However, Nishikawa argues that tacit and collectively developed knowledge of the specific context in which care is provided is fundamentally important to the quality of care and that, if account is taken of this contextual knowledge, care workers could be defined as knowledge workers.

Key to this perspective on knowledge work is that account is taken of tacit and contextual knowledge, as well as abstract and codified forms of scientific knowledge. Those adopting a practice-based perspective on knowledge typically adopt this perspective, and have examined the role of knowledge in a wide range of workers from flute makers (Cook and Yanow 1993), construction workers (Styhre *et al.* 2006), copier engineers (Orr 1996), open-source software developers (Hemetsberger and Reinhardt 2006) to manual workers in a sawmill (Strati 2007).

Further, Hislop (2008) developed an analysis which suggested that Frenkel *et al.*'s (1995) framework outlined earlier, due to the fact that it takes account of both contextual and theoretical knowledge as well as the range of skills involved in work, could be adapted to be compatible with the 'all work is knowledge work' perspective, by stripping it of its exclusivist 'professional knowledge work' assumptions. From this perspective, any job involving the use of a reasonable amount of theoretical and/or contextual knowledge can be classified as a form of knowledge work.

DEFINITION Knowledge worker ('all work is knowledge work' perspective)

Anyone whose work involves the use of a reasonable amount of tacit and contextual and/or abstract/conceptual knowledge.

Illustration   Office equipment service engineers as knowledge workers

Hislop (2008) illustrated the way Frenkel *et al.*'s framework could be made compatible with the 'all work is knowledge work' perspective by using the modified framework to describe and understand the work of some management consultants and office equipment service engineers as knowledge workers. Data on the engineers were collected in three small office equipment servicing companies based in the same city in the English Midlands. Using the modified Frenkel framework, these workers were classified as knowledge workers, with the skills, knowledge, and level of creativity involved in their work being summarized in Table 5.3.

Table 5.3 The Knowledge, Skills, and Creativity involved in Office Equipment Service Engineering

Skills	Action-Based	Medium
	Social	Medium—social interaction with customers and colleagues is important
	Intellectual	Medium—regular need to draw on experience to solve non-standard problems
Knowledge	Contextual	Medium-Important
	Theoretical	Low
Degree of Creativity		Low–Medium

Source: Adapted from Hislop 2008: table 2.

First, the level of creativity required by the engineers was relatively low. This was because the majority of the jobs done by the engineers were common, simple, and required little diagnostic analysis by the engineers. In terms of the skills involved in their work, there was an identifiable need to make a reasonable use of all three skill types. First, action-based skills were needed as most jobs involved some amount of physically disassembling and reassembling equipment. Social skills were also necessary to allow effective communication not only with clients, but also with colleagues (typically via mobile phones).

The repetitiveness and apparent simplicity of most jobs undertaken by the engineers disguised the extent to which intellectual skills were used. This was because these skills were relatively tacit, and were developed on the job, over time, through experience. What such 'experience' provided was summed up by one engineer as follows:

> when you have first done a machine because you have not got experience on it you spend a lot of time fault finding, figuring out what the faults are. But once you get to know the machine you walk in and straight away a customer says it is doing this and you know what it is and you will go in there and you will fit the part.

Finally, in terms of knowledge, while the engineers made little if any use of theoretical knowledge, they did develop and utilize contextual knowledge. This knowledge consisted of an understanding, developed over time, of not only what the business needs and uses of their client's office equipment was, but how this impacted on the type of problems that could develop. One engineer described this as follows: 'you get to know what they expect from the machine, which might be quite different from what someone else's identical machine expects'.

Thus, the way clients used office equipment affected the type of faults that their equipment developed, and having an understanding of this constituted contextual knowledge that the engineers drew on in their efforts to diagnose and repair these faults. As with the engineer's conceptual skills, such knowledge was relatively tacit in nature.

1. If the contextual knowledge and conceptual skills of the engineers were developed through experience, 'on the job', rather than through a process of formal education and training, what can the employers of such workers do to facilitate the development of their skills and knowledge?

Knowledge Work and Ambiguity

Thus far this chapter has shown the ambiguity that exists in defining knowledge workers and knowledge-intensive firms. Alvesson (2001, 2011), in an interesting critique of the mainstream perspective on knowledge workers/knowledge-intensive firms, argues that such ambiguity actually represents one of the defining characteristics of the work done in knowledge-intensive firms. The arguments regarding the ambiguity in knowledge-intensive firms were initially developed in 2001, but are revisited in the 2011 article, which reflects on the ideas developed in the original article. The argument developed by Alvesson suggests that these mainstream conceptions are too closely wedded to objectivist perspectives on knowledge, and that greater account should be taken of the way knowledge is conceptualized from a practice-based perspective. Fundamentally, Alvesson suggests that doing so reveals three key areas of ambiguity that are irresolvable, and represent an intrinsic element of the work carried out by knowledge workers (see Table 5.4). Thus for

Table 5.4 The Ambiguities Inherent in Knowledge Work

Topic	Mainstream Perspective	Area of Ambiguity
Knowledge: what it is and what it is like.	Knowledge is codified, objective, scientific.	Knowledge is subjective, socially constructed, context-specific, equivocal.
The significance of knowledge as an element of knowledge work.	Using institutionalized knowledge systematically and creating knowledge are the core activities of knowledge workers.	The systematic utilization of formal bodies of knowledge, the need for high-level cognitive capabilities are not necessarily the most significant elements in knowledge work.
The results of knowledge work.	The contribution of the knowledge and intellectual effort of knowledge workers in the provision of client solutions, and in underpinning the economic performance of knowledge intensive firms is regarded as transparent.	The complexity of the work undertaken by knowledge workers makes the quality of their advice/solutions/products difficult to establish, and makes the unambiguous establishment of the contribution of the efforts of knowledge workers to such products/services problematic.

Source: Alvesson 2001.

Alvesson, there are ambiguities not only in the nature of the knowledge possessed by workers in knowledge-intensive firms, but there are also ambiguities regarding both the extent to which their work involves the use of knowledge, and also regarding the measurability of the impact of their work.

One example of the ambiguity inherent in the work of knowledge workers is provided by Swart *et al.* (2003). They suggest that a key source of ambiguity in knowledge-intensive firms that knowledge workers have to deal with relates to the nature of their client's needs and requirements. Fundamentally they suggest that, particularly in the early stages of a project's development, clients may have quite broad, vague, and unclear requirements, with one of the tasks of knowledge workers being to try and reduce such ambiguity through communicating with clients in order to develop a more detail understanding of their needs and requirements. This point is reinforced by both Matson and Prusak (2010) and Carleton (2011), who argue that there are significant ambiguities in the nature of their work and the type of problem-solving activities they commonly have to undertake.

 Illustration   The ambiguous impact and output of some management consultants

Alvesson's 2011 article is largely conceptual, presenting a sceptical perspective on the mainstream claims about knowledge-intensive firms. However, within the article there is a short anecdote that usefully illustrates his arguments regarding the ambiguity involved in knowledge-intensive work. The anecdote relates to the impact of some consulting work that was done by a firm of global management consultants for a large life science firm.

Alvesson suggests that, on the basis of the research that was done, three types of ambiguity existed regarding the consultants' work. First, and most fundamentally, there were ambiguities regarding what work they actually did, with different interviewees giving significantly different stories regarding the consultants' intervention. Another ambiguity in the case related to the benefits the client firm derived from the consultants' work. The senior consultant, perhaps unsurprisingly, argued that their work had provided significant and positive benefits to the company, and any limitations in the impact of their work related to problems in the client firm. This perspective was challenged to some extent by some junior consultants who argued that the benefits derived by the client were somewhat limited, with this being the fault of the client firm, which failed to effectively implement the majority of the consultants' proposals. A third perspective was presented by the client managers who dealt with the consultants who argued that the benefits derived from the consultants' work were limited, as the proposals made typically took too little account of the cost to implement them.

A third area of ambiguity related to the impact of the consultants' presentations. Client managers typically emphasized the extent to which the consultants utilized presentations to outline their proposals and recommendations. While some client managers regarded these presentations as simply self-publicity exercises that contained little in the way of effective advice, other client managers felt that these presentations were effective and helped sustain the idea that the consultants' work had been successful.

1. The ambiguities outlined in this case flow from the variation in perspectives possessed by different people in both the consultancy and client firms. Would it be possible to reduce these ambiguities through a detailed investigation of the various claims made, or are these ambiguities and differences unavoidable?

Knowledge and Knowledge Processes in Knowledge-Intensive Firms

As the definitions section has made clear, the utilization of knowledge represents one of the defining aspects of the work undertaken in knowledge-intensive firms. Thus to understand the character of knowledge-intensive firms, and the knowledge management challenges which exist within them, it is necessary to develop a fuller understanding of the type of knowledge processes undertaken by knowledge workers. The key knowledge processes within knowledge-intensive firms, which are overlapping and closely interrelated, are knowledge creation and knowledge integration/application.

Knowledge creation

One of the key aspects of the work in knowledge-intensive firms is that it is typically not routine, repetitive work. Instead knowledge-intensive firms provide customized, specifically designed products/services, rather than off the shelf ones. For example, Robertson and Swan (2003: 833) suggest one of the key characteristics of knowledge-intensive firms is 'their capacity to solve complex problems through the development of creative and innovative solutions'. The production/creation of such client-specific, customized solutions requires and involves both the application of existing bodies of knowledge and the creation of new knowledge (Dul *et al.* 2011; Morris 2001). Thus, the ongoing creation and development of knowledge represents an important and intrinsic feature of a knowledge worker's work. This helps explain why there is a significant body of research into the topics of knowledge creation and innovation within knowledge-intensive firms (see e.g. Amara *et al.* 2009; Bunker-Whittington *et al.* 2009; Dul *et al.* 2011; Liu and Deng 2009).

Knowledge integration/application

The development of client-specific, customized solutions involves more than the creation of knowledge, it also involves the integration and application of different bodies of knowledge, both between workers in knowledge-intensive firms and between the workers in knowledge-intensive firms and staff from client organizations (Amara *et al.* 2009; Fosstenløkken *et al.* 2003). Due to this need to acquire and share knowledge, and the limits to codification that exist, most typically this is done through interpersonal interaction. For example, two specific mechanisms that can be utilized to achieve this process of knowledge integration/application are through extensive interactions between workers from knowledge-intensive firms and their clients (see He and Wong 2009) or through a process of outsourcing which involves having staff from knowledge-intensive firms work on extended secondments with client firms (see Grimshaw and Miozzo 2009). To understand the character and dynamics of such social interactions/networking and knowledge processes the concept of social capital is useful, a concept utilized by a number of analysts examining knowledge-intensive firms (Kärreman 2010; Swart and Kinnie 2003; Yli-Renko *et al.* 2001).

Social capital relates to the networks of personal relationships that people possess and are embedded within, and the resources people can draw on and utilize through such networks.

Social capital theory is typically predicated on the assumption that the resources available to people through such networks can aid action. However, the close and inseparable relationship that exists between the networks of relations that people possess and the resources they have access to through them means that there is a lack of consensus within the social capital literature about the precise definition of social capital. For some, social capital refers purely to the networks of relations people possess, while to others it encompasses not only these networks, but also includes the resources people have access to through them (Nahapiet and Ghoshal 1998). Here it is used in the narrow sense, to refer purely to the networks of social relationships that people have. Further, Nahapiet and Ghoshal (1998) suggest that social capital has three key dimensions or facets: the structural, the relational, and the cognitive (see Table 5.5).

In the context of knowledge-intensive firms, the importance of social capital to knowledge workers is that it is only through having it that they are able to access the client-specific knowledge that they require in order to be able to do their work effectively (Swart and Kinnie 2003). This is because for people to be willing to share knowledge with others some degree of interpersonal trust is required (a topic discussed more extensively in Chapters 9 and 11), and the existence of social capital implies that an element of trust exists between people (the relational dimension of social capital).

The types of knowledge that knowledge workers use in their work requires their networks of social capital to include both staff from their own organization (but who may be working on different projects), and staff in client firms (Grimshaw and Miozzo 2009; He and Wong 2009; Swart *et al.* 2003; Yli-Renko *et al.* 2001). As outlined, the typically project-based nature of work in knowledge-intensive firms means that the knowledge base within knowledge-intensive firms is typically fragmented, with different workers possessing different bodies of expertise linked to different client firms and projects. Having a network of social relations (social capital) that spans such project boundaries thus provides knowledge workers with a way of accessing potentially relevant knowledge possessed by colleagues working on other projects (Swart and Kinnie 2003). The importance for knowledge workers of possessing social capital with representatives of client firms is that such networks can provide access to relevant client knowledge which is necessary for their work. However, as outlined, the need for knowledge workers to continually interact with representatives of their client firms over the course of a project typically means that social

Table 5.5 The Three Dimensions of Social Capital

Dimension	Character
Structural	The overall pattern of social relations a person possesses. For example, the number of contacts, and the type of people in the network.
Relational	The strength of the relationship between people. Can vary from weak relations to strong relationships involving high levels of trust. This dimension of social capital typically built up over time, through repeated interactions.
Cognitive	The extent to which people have shared cognitive resources such as shared knowledge, common assumptions, interpretations, and beliefs.

capital and good relations with specific client staff are often not difficult to develop (Alvesson 2000; Fosstenløkken *et al.* 2003).

The Willingness of Knowledge Workers to Participate in Knowledge Processes: Contrasting Perspectives

One of the key themes developed and examined in Part 4 of this book is that the willingness of any worker to participate in organizational knowledge management processes should *not* be taken for granted. In fact, dealing with such motivational issues, and creating a socio-cultural environment where workers are prepared to participate in knowledge management initiatives represents one of the key challenges and difficulties of knowledge management. However, another area of divergence in the literature on knowledge workers and knowledge-intensive firms relates to the extent to which knowledge workers are always willing to participate in knowledge management processes and initiatives, with two contrasting perspectives existing, both of which are outlined below.

Knowledge workers: The ideal employee?

A reasonable amount of (largely case study) evidence exists to suggest that in many ways knowledge workers represent the ideal employees. Primarily, this evidence suggests that such workers are prepared to invest significant amounts of time and effort into their work, and that motivating them to do so is typically not difficult (Alvesson 1995; Deetz 1998; Robertson and Swan 2003). As these workers are prepared to make such efforts with minimal levels of supervision, and without regarding such effort as problematic, Alvesson suggests such workers represent the ideal subordinates (2000: 1104). Alvesson (2000) suggests four reasons why knowledge workers are prepared to make such efforts:

1. They find their work intrinsically interesting and fulfilling.
2. Such working patterns represent the norms within the communities they are a part of.
3. A sense of reciprocity, whereby they provide the organization with their efforts in return for good pay and working conditions.
4. Such behaviour reinforces and confirms their sense of identity as a knowledge worker, where hard work is regarded as a fundamental component.

Robertson and Swan (2003) provide a further explanation: the structure of the employment relationship is less clear than for other workers, and the potential for conflict on the basis of it thus becomes dissipated. Primarily they suggest that the employer/employee, manager/managed relationship is not as clear cut in knowledge-intensive firms as in other, more hierarchically based organizations. In knowledge-intensive firms such boundaries are fuzzy, and evolve over time, and therefore the interests of employers and employees are more likely to be shared.

Factors inhibiting knowledge workers' work efforts and knowledge management activities

As will be discussed in more detail in Chapters 9 and 12, two general factors which may inhibit workers from participating in organizational knowledge management efforts are the unavoidable potential for conflict between workers and their employers embedded in the employment relationship and the potential for intra-organizational conflict (between people and groups/teams) that arguably exists in all organizations. In contrast to the perspective of writers adopted in the previous section, some analysts suggest that these two potential sources of conflict are as likely in knowledge-intensive firms as in any other type of organization, and that the willingness of knowledge workers to participate in knowledge management initiatives should not be taken for granted. Thus Starbuck (1993) described the knowledge-intensive company he examined as being 'internally inconsistent, in conflict with itself . . . An intricate house of cards.' Further, Empson (2001b) presented an example of a knowledge-intensive firm in a post-merger situation, where workers from the two pre-merger companies were unwilling to share their knowledge with each other. Kärreman (2010) in reviewing the contribution of Starbuck's (1993) article also emphasized the importance of the attention it paid to issues of power and conflict.

A number of writers highlight the issue of the conflicting sense of identities that knowledge workers may experience, and how this may shape and inhibit their willingness to participate in organizational knowledge management processes (Alvesson 2000). Due to the amount of time that many knowledge workers can spend working with individual client organizations and particular staff within them (see previous section), one source of identity-based conflict knowledge workers can experience is feeling a sense of belonging to both their employer and to their client's firm (Swart *et al.* 2003). Ravishankar and Pan (2008) present a case of where such client-based identity on the part of the knowledge workers they studied (an Indian IT outsourcing vendor) resulted in some staff being unwilling to participate in their employer's knowledge management initiatives. Grimshaw and Miozzo's (2009) study of outsourcing with IT-based business services reached similar conclusions, talking about 'the tensions of the competing claims on the identity of knowledge workers in a context of inter-organizational networks' (p. 1544).

Other evidence which suggests that knowledge workers may have divergent interests from their employers relates to the problem many knowledge-intensive firms experience in trying to retain their employees for extended periods. Fundamentally many knowledge-intensive firms have quite high turnover rates, which suggests that knowledge workers have only a limited amount of loyalty to their employing organization. This is partly due to labour market conditions, where the skills and knowledge of knowledge workers are typically relatively scarce, creating conditions for knowledge workers which are favourable to labour market mobility (Flood *et al.* 2001; Huang 2011; Malhotra *et al.* 2010; Von Nordenflycht 2010).

Having a high turnover rate is a potentially significant problem for knowledge-intensive firms (Alvesson 2000; Beaumont and Hunter 2002; Flood *et al.* 2000). For example, client knowledge or social capital, the knowledge of and relationships with key individuals within their client organizations, can be a key source of knowledge for knowledge-intensive firms.

Individual knowledge workers develop such knowledge and social capital through working closely with clients. Such knowledge is typically tacit and highly personal. Therefore, when a knowledge worker leaves their job, they take such knowledge with them. Not only that, but through the social capital they possess with individuals in client firms there is also a risk for their employer that when a knowledge worker leaves they may take some clients with them. The question of how to develop the loyalty and commitment of such workers is one of the key issues addressed in Chapter 14.

 ## Conclusion

The importance of knowledge workers and knowledge-intensive firms is closely tied to the rhetoric regarding the contemporary rise and emergence of the knowledge society. In the debate over defining knowledge workers two perspectives were identified. While the mainstream perspective suggests that knowledge workers are a distinctive and elite element in the contemporary workforce, others argue that this fails to account for the extent to which all work is knowledge work, and thus how all workers can be defined as knowledge workers. With regard to knowledge-intensive firms, a multiplicity of definitions were found to exist.

In relation to the work in knowledge-intensive firms it was shown that the possession and use of client-related knowledge was as important as the possession of formalized technical knowledge. Further the acquisition of such knowledge requires knowledge workers to possess and utilize any networks of social capital they have and that such knowledge is acquired from both their colleagues (who may work on different projects) and staff from the clients they work with.

Finally, while some case study evidence suggests that knowledge workers arguably represent the ideal employee, due to their willingness to work autonomously, others suggest that for a number of reasons, such as tensions that may exist between a knowledge worker and their employer over how their knowledge is utilized, knowledge workers cannot always be assumed to be willing to participate in the knowledge management processes their employers may desire.

 Case study   The linkages between learning orientation, knowledge assets, and HR practices in professional service firms

Swart and Kinnie (2010) report the findings of a study conducted on a diverse range of sixteen professional service firms from the UK and US that included law firms, management consultants, software development companies, and advertising agencies. The conceptual focus of their paper is on the links between a firm's learning orientation, and the types of knowledge assets needed to sustain it, as well as the type of HR practices which help facilitate it. In the paper they define organizational learning as involving both the refinement and renewal of organizational knowledge.

In doing this they develop a conceptual framework which distinguishes between four separate learning orientations. The learning orientation framework they develop is based on two key dimensions: the mode of learning undertaken by an organization and the temporal frame in which learning and knowledge creation have to occur. With respect to the mode of learning they differentiate between exploration-based learning and exploitation-based learning (see Chapter 6). While exploitation-based learning is concerned with the incremental innovation related to the development of an organization's existing knowledge, services, and products, exploration-based learning is concerned with the development of new knowledge, products, and services. With respect to the

(continued)

temporal frame, they differentiate between accelerated timescales, where learning has to be undertaken quickly, and planned timescales, which are more long term. When these two dimensions are linked, four different learning orientations are created.

For each of these four learning orientations Swart and Kinnie examine the type of knowledge assets necessary to sustain them and the type of HR practices that facilitate them. Constraints of space mean that it is not possible to examine all the links between these variables for all four learning orientations. Thus, only two are examined here.

First is what is labelled the Creative Combination learning orientation, which combines an accelerated timescale with exploration-based learning. This type of learning thus involves and underpins the creation of new products or services in short timescales. A specific example of the need for this learning orientation was created within one advertising agency where a client gave the company a week to develop a brief to highlight the music-playing potential of a mobile phone. In terms of knowledge assets, Swart and Kinnie found that this learning orientation required a combination of creativity, experimentation, and quick adaptability of ideas. Further, they found that these knowledge assets were facilitated by a range of different HR practices. First, to facilitate creativity and experimentation, recruitment and selection processes need to emphasize these skills. Secondly, to facilitate quick adaptability, they argued that people need to work with a range of different clients who have their own unique specific demands, which can be facilitated by regularly rotating people between different projects, or getting people to work on different projects simultaneously. Finally, to facilitate and support people's efforts to be creative and experimental, organizations need to have cultures which encourage risk-taking and which don't automatically punish failure.

Another of the learning orientations examined by Swart and Kinnie is labelled Expert Solutions. In contrast to Creative Combination, this learning orientation links exploitation-based learning with planned timescales. This type of learning is thus quite different from Creative Combination, and is concerned with the incremental development of existing products and services for established clients over long-term timescales. An example of this mode of learning was found in law firms where well-established procedures were utilized for personal injury or employment law cases. For this learning orientation Swart and Kinnie found that people needed good client capital (knowledge of and relationships with clients and their needs), procedure-based organizational capital, where people had a good knowledge of established procedures, and project-based knowledge, where people have experience working on long-term projects. Swart and Kinnie found a range of HR practices that facilitated these knowledge assets. For example, one way of developing good client capital was through the recruitment of staff from clients, which not only gave the firms good knowledge of their clients' needs and expectations, but also gave them people with good social capital within client firms. Secondly, procedure-based knowledge was found to be facilitated by a combination of on-the-job training and one-to-one coaching.

While Swart and Kinnie identified four specific learning orientations, they do not argue that companies typically only utilize one. Instead, they argue that all of the companies examined had to utilize a range of learning orientations, and had to be flexible and adaptable in utilizing the appropriate learning orientation at the appropriate time.

1. Given that each learning orientation is linked to a particular timescale and mode of learning, requires the use of different knowledge assets, and is facilitated by different HR practices, how challenging is it likely to be for any organization to utilize more than one learning orientation, and flexibly switch between them when appropriate?

Source: Swart, J., and Kinnie, N. (2010) 'Organizational Learning, Knowledge Assets and HR Practices in Professional Service Firms', *Human Resource Management Journal*, 20/1: 64–79.

Review and Discussion Questions

1. What do you think of the 'all work is knowledge work' perspective? Can all forms of work be defined as knowledge work even if they don't require the use of abstract/conceptual knowledge? Think about a range of jobs and the types of knowledge, skills, and level of creativity involved in them. Can you identify any that you don't feel should be labelled 'knowledge work'?

2. Do you agree with Alvesson's perspective regarding the ambiguity of knowledge work? Is it possible to reduce or eliminate the types of ambiguity identified by Alvesson or are they unavoidable?

3. One of the factors that was found to be a potential source of conflict and tension for knowledge workers, and that could affect their attitude to participating in organizational knowledge management initiatives, was their identification with both their employer and the client firms they work for. Given the nature of the work undertaken by knowledge workers and the typical need that exists to work extensively with their clients, is it likely to be inevitable that knowledge workers will typically always have some level of identification with and loyalty to client firms?

 ## Suggestions for Further Reading

1. **M. Alvesson (2011) 'De-essentializing the Knowledge intensive Firm: Reflections on Sceptical Research Going Against the Mainstream',** *Journal of Management Studies*, 48/7: 1640–61.
A useful review article that highlights Alvesson's sceptical perspective on the claims of the mainstream work on knowledge-intensive firms.

2. **A. von Nordenflycht (2010) 'What is a Professional Service Firm? Towards a Theory and a Taxonomy of Knowledge-Intensive Firms',** *Academy of Management Reviews*, 35/1: 155–74.
Reviews the debate on how to define professional service firms and knowledge-intensive firms and develops a taxonomy that differentiates between distinctive types of knowledge-intensive firm.

3. **D. Hislop (2008) 'Conceptualizing Knowledge Work Utilizing Skill and Knowledge-Based Concepts: The Case of Some Consultants and Service Engineers',** *Management Learning*, 39/5: 579–97.
Elaborates the debate on how knowledge work is defined and illustrates argument via use of two contrasting examples.

4. **J. Swart and N. Kinnie (2010) 'Organizational Learning, Knowledge Assets and HR Practices in Professional Service Firms',** *Human Resource Management Journal*, 20/1: 64–79.
Interesting empirical analysis of learning and HR practices in a range of professional service firms.

Take your learning further: Online Resource Centre

Visit the Online Resource Centre for resources which will extend your understanding of knowledge management in organizations. As well as web links to sites of interest, the author has provided case studies looking at knowledge management in virtual and knowledge-intensive firms, and in global multinationals. These will help you with your research, essays, and assignments; or you may find these additional resources helpful when revising for exams.

 www.oxfordtextbooks.co.uk/orc/hislop3e/

6 Learning and Knowledge Management

Introduction

For a number of reasons the topic of learning in organizations encompasses a vast literature. First, its origins date back more than forty years, and can be traced to the work of March, Simon, and Cyert (Cyert and March 1963; March and Simon 1993). Secondly, it is a subject that is truly multidisciplinary, being written about and conceptualized (quite differently) in a range of academic disciplines from economics, management science, psychology and sociology to anthropology (Easterby-Smith and Lyles 2011a; Styhre *et al.* 2006). Thirdly, since the early 1990s there has been a mushrooming of interest in the topic, with this interest pre-dating the growth of interest in knowledge management by a few years (Scarbrough and Swan 2001). Contu *et al.* (2003) suggest this blossoming of interest in organizational learning connects with a wider interest in and discourse on the value and importance of learning in contemporary globalized, knowledge-based economies/societies. This enormous and diverse literature is characterized by heterogeneity, debate, and a lack of theoretical consensus on a wide range of topics, from whether learning should be conceived primarily in behavioural or cognitive terms, the relationship between individual and organizational learning, to whether organizations learn at all (Antonacopoulou 2006; Berthoin Antal *et al.* 2001; Crossan *et al.* 1999).

To attempt to outline and review all the features, characteristics, and debates in this literature it would be necessary to write a book on the topic (examples of overviews include Easterby-Smith and Lyles 2011a; Starkey *et al.* 2003). Further, the interrelated and overlapping nature of the relationship between learning and knowledge management (Chiva and Allegre 2005; Thomas *et al.* 2003) means that another book could be written on how the topic of learning relates to and connects with knowledge management. In this chapter, there is a deliberately narrow, partial, and specific focus on examining learning in organizations.

This chapter has three primary objectives. First, it aims to give a sense of the diversity of the ways that learning is conceptualized. Secondly, it examines the issue of organizational learning and the complex and dynamic relationship between individual-, group-, and organizational-level learning. In doing this the primary focus is on the influential learning framework developed by Crossan *et al.* (1999, 2011). Finally, it presents two perspectives on the debate surrounding the concept of the learning organization. In presenting the critique of the learning organization the chapter connects both to some themes that will be shown in later chapters to resonate with the knowledge management literature and the objective of the book to adopt a critical perspective to mainstream literature and concepts.

The chapter begins by very briefly examining the difficulties involved in defining what learning is, and considering the diversity of ways in which learning occurs. After this, the next major section examines the dynamics of organizational learning, and the relationship between individual-, group-, and organizational-level learning processes. The largest section in the chapter then examines the debate on the learning organization concept, which provides a useful way of discussing some of the key issues which link the learning and knowledge management literatures. As will be seen, issues raised by the critics of the learning organization rhetoric, such as the need to account for power, as well as the broad context of the employment relationship, link closely with some of the key issues developed in Part 4 of the book, and in Chapters 9 and 12 in particular.

The Heterogeneity of Learning

It would seem sensible to begin the chapter by defining learning and considering the various processes and mechanisms via which learning in organizations can occur. However, such a task is by no means easy due to the diversity of ways in which learning is defined, and the heterogeneity of methods via which it can occur. This section therefore provides a very brief overview of both topics.

Characterizing learning types

The heterogeneity and lack of theoretical consensus in the learning literature means that providing a single, simple definition of learning is impossible. Instead of providing a single definition of learning, Table 6.1 gives an overview of some of the most important ways that learning in organizations has been characterized (for a more detailed examination of the different taxonomies of learning which exist see Pawlovsky 2001). These typologies are not examined in detail because not only do constraints of space make it impossible to do justice to the depth of debate, but the debate on these typologies became somewhat dormant during the mid-1990s (Easterby-Smith *et al.* 2000). Thus, most of the contemporary learning literature makes only passing reference to these frameworks. This overview illustrates the complexity of the topic and the diversity of ways in which learning has been conceptualized.

Learning mechanisms and processes

Due to the diversity of ways that learning is conceptualized and characterized, it is no surprise that the literature suggests that learning can occur via a wide range of different mechanisms and processes. These can be characterized into three distinctive types: learning via formal training and education, learning via the use of interventions in work processes, and learning that is embedded in and emerges from day-to-day work activities (and people's reflections on them).

Table 6.1 Typologies of Learning

Frameworks	Concepts/Levels	Description
Learning Modes	Cognitive	Learning as a change in intellectual concepts and frameworks (at individual or group level).
	Cultural	Change in inter-subjective, group-based values, concepts, or frameworks.
	Behavioural/action-based	Learning occurs primarily through action followed by a process of critical reflection.
Learning Types	Single-loop	Incremental changes within a coherent framework of theory.
	Double-loop	Learning where existing theories/assumptions are questioned and reflected on.
	Deutero	The highest level of learning which involves the process of learning and reflection itself being questioned.
Learning Levels	Individual	Changes in the behaviour or theories and concepts of an individual.
	Group	Changes in group-level, shared understandings or practices.
	Organizational	Institutionalization at organizational level of changes in behaviour/theory.
	Inter-organizational	Learning at supra-organizational level, e.g. within a network or sector.

Before learning became a fashionable idea, it was a relatively neglected backwater and was regarded as being most closely linked to the topics of training and education. From this perspective, learning occurred and was facilitated via workers attending and participating in formal processes of training and education. The growing interest in the topic of learning led to an acknowledgement that learning could also occur in and be facilitated by a range of practices, values, and activities embedded in work processes. From this perspective learning can be facilitated via the creation of 'learning cultures', where learning, reflection, debate, and discussion are encouraged (López *et al.* 2004; Raz and Fadlon 2006), the embedding of learning opportunities in organizational decision-making processes (Carroll *et al.* 2006), and, where project-based work is common, via processes such as post-project reviews (Ron *et al.* 2006; von Zedtwitz 2002). Finally, writers who adopt a practice-based perspective on knowledge see learning as occurring via and embedded in day-to-day work practices (see e.g. Hong and Snell 2008; Styhre *et al.* 2006).

In conclusion, there is significant diversity and disagreement in the literature about learning on what learning is and how it occurs in organizations. The chapter now changes focus to consider the dynamic inter-relationship between individual, group, and organizational levels of learning.

The Dynamics of Organizational Learning

While the central concern of the chapter is on learning within organizations, this does not mean that there is an exclusive focus on organizational-level learning. As will be seen, learning in organizations can be characterized as involving a dynamic reciprocity between learning processes at the individual, group, and organizational level (Berends and Lammers 2011; Crossan *et al.* 2011; Antonacopoulou 2006). Before presenting a conceptual model that outlines the interrelationship between these processes it is useful to define and discuss the term 'organizational learning'. Organizations can be understood to learn, not because they 'think' and 'behave' independently of the people who work within them (they cannot), but through the embedding of individual and group learning in organizational processes, routines, structures, databases, systems of rules, etc. (Shipton 2006). For example, organizational learning would be where insights developed by an individual or group result in a systematic transformation of the organization's work practices/values.

However, it is wrong to see organizational learning as simply the sum of individual and group learning processes (Vince 2001). Organizational learning only occurs when learning at the individual or group level impacts on organizational-level processes and structures. But such a transition is by no means automatic (for a good illustration of this see the case study at the end of this chapter, which examines how discontinuities disrupt the flow of learning between levels). The literature on project-based working also shows how project-based learning is often not transferred to an organizational level (Scarbrough *et al.* 2004*a* and *b*).

> **DEFINITION Organizational learning**
>
> The embedding of individual- and group-level learning in organizational structures and processes, achieved through reflecting on and modifying the norms and values embodied in established organizational processes and structures.

This complex interrelationship between learning at different levels is taken account of in the Crossan/Zietsma framework of organizational learning. This framework was initially devised by Crossan *et al.* (1999), but was usefully modified by Zietsma *et al.* (2002) with the addition of two action-based learning processes to supplement the more cognitively focused processes of Crossan *et al.* The relationship between the six learning processes and three levels of learning in the Crossan/Zietsma framework are illustrated in Figure 6.1. The significance and influence of Crossan *et al.*'s organizational learning framework is that the article in which it was initially articulated (Crossan *et al.* 1999) was the most cited article in the *Academy of Management Review* in the 2000s (Crossan *et al.* 2011).

Descriptions of the learning processes, and the levels at which they exist are outlined in Table 6.2. In the framework, the six learning processes link the three levels of learning through two opposing dynamics: feed forward and feedback loops. The feed forward loop, alternatively referred to as an *exploration*-based learning process, involves the development and assimilation of new knowledge. Exploration thus starts with individual-level learning, through intuition or attending, and then builds to both group- and organization-level

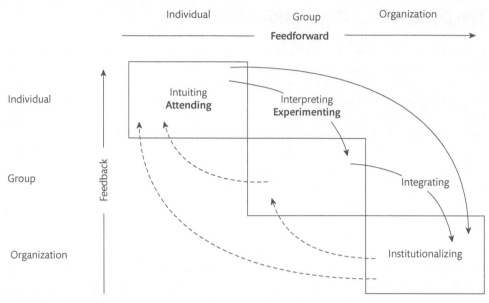

Figure 6.1 The Modified Crossan *et al.* Model (1999)

Source: Zietsma *et al.* (2002).

learning through interpretation, experimentation, integration, and institutionalization processes. The feedback loop, by contrast, referred to as an *exploitation*-based learning process, involves the utilization of existing knowledge, whereby institutionalized learning guides and affects how groups and individuals act and think. However, while feed forward and feedback learning loops involve moving between learning processes at different levels, such movement cannot be assumed to happen automatically, or unproblematically. Thus, for example, it can be difficult for someone to take an individual-level insight, articulate it to a group, and for this to develop into a shared, agreed upon, collective insight.

One of the core themes in the Crossan/Zietsma framework is the tension that exists between exploration (the development and acquisition of new knowledge) and exploitation (the utilization of existing knowledge). This tension exists because processes of exploration may bring into question, challenge, undermine, and even replace institutionalized norms (knowledge and practice) embedded in exploitation processes. This is a potentially serious tension because, as Crossan *et al.* argue (1999: 534), 'learning that has become institutionalized at the organizational level is often difficult to change'. Thus the institutionalization of learning has the potential risk that such a process can introduce rigidities and an inability to adapt and change through a blinkering process that leaves institutionalized norms unquestioned. Thus when institutionalized norms become powerful and dominant, for example through being successful, they can turn into what have been defined as 'competency traps' where organizations become locked in to previously successful routines through not noticing or effectively accounting for changed circumstances (Bettis and Prahalad 1995; Levinthal and March 1993). See Chapter 8 for a further discussion of competency traps in relation to the topic of unlearning.

Table 6.2 Characteristics of Learning Process in Crossan/Zietsma Model

Process Name	Level	Process Description
Intuition	Individual	Cognitive process involving the preconscious recognition of patterns. Intuition is highly subjective and rooted in individual experience.
Attending	Individual	Action-based individual process of actively searching for and absorbing new ideas.
Interpretation	Individual–Group	Explaining personal insights through words or actions. It can be an individual process, where an individual actively interprets their own insights, or a group process where individual insights are shared and discussed collectively.
Experimenting	Individual–Group	Attempting to implement and utilize new learning through actual practices of change.
Integration	Group–Organization	Developing shared understandings and practices, which can occur through both dialogue and coordinated action.
Institutionalization	Organization	The process of ensuring that routinized action occurs through embedding insights in organizational systems and processes.

Despite the tensions between processes of exploitation and exploration, and the difficulties that organizations face when attempting to do both simultaneously, an increasing number of writers suggest that it can be highly beneficial to an organization's dynamic innovative capability to be able to do both simultaneously (Gibson and Birkinshaw 2004; He and Wong 2004). The ability to do so is referred to as ambidextrous learning (Kang and Snell 2009; Turner and Lee-Kelley 2012, see special issue of *Organization Science*, 20/4 (2009), e.g. Raisch *et al.* 2009).

The Learning Organization: Emancipation or Exploitation?

As outlined in the introduction, the literature on organizational learning is characterized by a diversity of theoretical perspectives. One specific topic that has produced an enormous amount of heated argument is the learning organization. It is worth examining the contours of this debate, as this sheds light on some key issues.

Crudely, those engaged in this debate can be classified into two broad camps: the visionaries, or utopian propagandists, and the sceptics, or gloomy pessimists (Friedman *et al.* 2001). The visionary/propagandist camp, whose most well-known and prolific writers include Peter Senge (1990) and Mike Pedler (Pedler *et al.* 1997), is largely dominated by consultants and industrial practitioners (Driver 2002) and is very prescriptive in nature (Shipton 2006). This camp portrays the learning organization as an achievable ideal with significant benefits for both organizations and their workers. The sceptic/pessimistic camp which is largely populated by academics challenges this perspective and pours scorn on the claims of the learning organization propagandists (Levitt and March 1988; Weick and West-ley 1996). Primarily these writers, with Coopey (1995, 1998) being one of the most incisive, argue that, despite the emancipatory rhetoric of the learning organization discourse, in reality it is likely to provide a way to buttress the power of management and is thus likely to lead to increased exploitation of and control over workers, rather than in their emancipa-tion and self-development (Hong and Snell 2008).

This section examines the two dominant perspectives in this debate, uncovering and examining issues such as power, the nature of the employment relationship, and trust, which as will be shown in Chapters 9 and 12 connect the topics of learning and knowledge management as they are factors which can also play a crucial role in shaping organizational knowledge management processes.

The learning organization: the advocates' vision

Constraints of space make it impossible to elaborate all the different learning organization frameworks developed by its different advocates (Pedler, Senge, Garvin, among others—see Shipton 2006). This section focuses centrally on the way Pedler *et al.* and Senge conceptualize it, and the illustrated example links to Senge's learning organization model. However, there is much commonality to these frameworks and a general resonance between the broad characteristics of these different models. Pedler *et al.* (1997: 3) define the learning org-anization as an 'organization which facilitates the learning of all its members and consciously transforms itself and its context'. Their learning organization framework is also elaborated into eleven specific characteristics (see Table 6.3). A key element of this definition is that there is a mutual, positive synergy between the organizational context and the learning of its members. Thus in a learning organization, the organizational context should facilitate the learning of organizational staff, with this learning in turn sustaining and contributing to the ongoing transformation of the organizational context.

One of the articulated organizational advantages of the learning organization framework is that it is appropriate to the contemporary business environment, which is typically character-ized as being highly competitive and turbulent (Harrison and Leitch 2000; Salaman 2001). In such circumstances organizations have to continually adapt and change, with the adoption of the learning organization framework being argued to make this possible. One of the defining characteristics of a learning organization is therefore that it is flexible, and that this provides organizations with the ability to achieve and retain a position of competitive advantage. A number of papers (including Bui and Baruch 2011—see the illustration) examine the extent to which organizations have the characteristics of learning organizations (such as Elkin *et al.* 2011), or the relationship between learning organizations and organizational performance (see e.g. Shieh 2011). Implicitly (and sometimes explicitly) the learning organization is regarded as the antithesis of traditional bureaucracies, which are regarded as having highly centralized and hierarchical systems of management and control (Contu *et al.* 2003). Instead, the learning organization is typically conceptualized as having a relatively flat structure, open communica-tion systems, limited top–down control, and autonomous working conditions (Driver 2002).

However, the advocates such as Pedler are clear that the benefits of utilizing the learning organization framework are by no means confined to improving organizational perform-ance. Instead, an inherent element of these frameworks is that management and workers

Table 6.3 The Learning Company Framework of Pedler *et al.* (1997)

Focus	Core Characteristics	Description
Strategy	1. Learning approach to strategy	Strategy making–implementation–evaluation structured as learning processes, e.g. with experiments and feedback loops.
	2. Participative policy-making	Allow all organizational members opportunity to contribute to making of major policy decisions.
Looking In	3. Informating	Use of IT to empower staff through widespread information dissemination and having tolerance as to how it is interpreted and used.
	4. Formative accounting and control	Use of accounting practices which contribute to learning combined with a sense of self-responsibility, where individuals/groups are encouraged to regard themselves as responsible for cost management.
	5. Internal exchange	Constant, open dialogue between individuals and group within an organization, and encouraging collaboration not competition.
	6. Reward flexibility	New ways of rewarding people for learning contribution which may not be solely financial, and where principles of reward system are explicit.
Structures	7. Enabling structures	Use of loose and adaptable structures which provide opportunities for organizational and individual development.
Looking Out	8. Boundary workers as environmental scanners	The bringing in to an organization of ideas and working practices developed and used externally—an openness and receptivity to learning from others.
	9. Inter-company learning	Use of mutually advantageous learning activities with customers, suppliers, etc.
Learning Opportunities	10. Learning climate	Facilitate the willingness of staff to take risks and experiment, which can be encouraged by senior management taking the lead. People not punished for criticizing orthodox views.
	11. Self-development opportunities for all	Have opportunities for all staff to be able to develop themselves as they see appropriate.

alike will benefit from their adoption. In fact, one of the articulated consequences of utilizing these frameworks is that the divisions between management and workers are likely to become blurred. As is clear from all eleven characteristics of the learning organization framework (see Table 6.3), workers benefit through the creation of a working environment where levels of participation in major decisions are high, where the opinions of all are valued, and where there are opportunities for workers to be creative and develop themselves. These features of learning organizations are presented in a very positive light, as a 'visionary ideal' (Shipton 2006: 240), and as a 'utopia of democracy' (Contu *et al.* 2003: 939).

DEFINITION Learning organization (propagandists)

An organization which supports the learning of its workers and allows them to express and utilize this learning to the advantage of the organization, through having an organizational environment which encourages experimentation, risk-taking, and open dialogue.

 Illustration   Universities as learning organizations

Bui and Baruch (2011) test for Senge's model of the learning organization in two universities, one in the UK and one in Vietnam. They define a learning organization as an organization which 'works to create values, practices and procedures, in which learning and working are synonymous', and which 'align people's learning and development continuously to corporate vision, mission and strategy' (p. 2). They conducted a survey-based study in both universities, and examined not only whether they had the characteristics of a learning organization, but also the extent to which the components of a learning organization they examined were linked to particular antecedents and outcomes. There are five disciplines or elements in Senge's model of a learning organization; systems thinking; personal mastery; mental models; team learning; and shared vision. Systems thinking is the capacity to identify underlying causes in events, personal mastery refers to a person's commitment to learn and develop, mental models are the assumptions people have which shape how they see the world, team learning is the commitment of people to work collaboratively, while shared vision is the extent to which people have shared values and ideas. Senge argues that the existence of these disciplines in an organization will result in positive benefits in terms of both organizational performance and employee satisfaction and commitment.

Bui and Baruch identify particular antecedents linked to each of these disciplines, with, for example, the antecedents of team learning being suggested as being team commitment, leadership, goal setting, development and training, organizational culture, and individual learning. They also examined a range of individual and organizational outcomes including work performance (in terms of teaching, research, and administration), self-efficacy, work–life balance, and knowledge sharing. In terms of outcomes, they looked at the extent to which the existence of the five disciplines of a learning organization were positively linked to these outcomes, and also mediated the relationship between the antecedents and outcomes they examined.

Limitations of space mean that it is only possible to give a broad overview of their research findings. First, they did identify the characteristics of learning organizations in both organizations, and provided support for Senge's learning organization model. All the hypotheses tested were either partially or fully supported, and the existence of the five disciplines of a learning organization was positively linked to the outcomes investigated. One interesting conclusion was that the Vietnamese university scored higher that the UK one on all disciplines of the learning organization model. It was suggested that this might be due to the fact that Vietnam has a more collectivist culture than the UK.

1. Do you think that this final conclusion can be generalized such that, the stronger the sense of collectivism in a country, the easier it will be to create learning organizations?

One element, which is argued to be necessary and central to the creation of such a working environment, is a particular type of leadership style (Biu and Baruch 2011; Crossan *et al.* 2011; Sadler 2001; Snell 2001). For example, leaders in learning organizations are required to be learners as much as teachers, and they should also have roles as coaches or mentors. Such a leadership style is necessary not only to actively stimulate the curiosity and learning of workers, but to also make leaders sensitive and responsive to the opinions of workers. The contradictions of the learning organization advocates regarding the role and style that organizational management should have will be discussed later. Before doing this it is useful to illustrate its application in practice, in one of the few empirical evaluations of this perspective.

The learning organization: the sceptics' perspective

The arguments of the learning organization advocates produced an enormous amount of debate (Easterby-Smith 1997; Tsang 1997). This section examines the critique put forward by those who have been labelled the pessimists, or sceptics. The critique is structured into three broad, but interrelated areas: the nature of the employment relationship, the need to account for power, and how individual factors, such as emotion, shape people's willingness to learn.

Learning and the employment relationship

Central to Coopey's (1995, 1998) critique of the learning organization rhetoric is that there is a fundamental contradiction that is not addressed, regarding the power and authority of management. On the one hand, as outlined previously, Pedler's vision of the learning organization—characterized by the support and encouragement given to open discussion and risk-free critical debate, as well as the importance of democratic decision-making processes—requires organizational managers to share power much more than in traditional organizations. However, on the other hand, Pedler takes for granted the legitimacy of both shareholder rights, enshrined in company law, as well as management's authority and right to manage in their shareholders' interests (Coopey 1995: 195). Thus, while the learning organization rhetoric suggests that more democratic decision-making is necessary, it does not explain how this can be effectively achieved. Given that empirical evidence suggests that organizational management are often unwilling to share power, it is arguably unlikely that such a process will occur voluntarily (Dovey 1997).

 Time to reflect   Authority, law, and democracy

If management's authority to manage is enshrined in company law, does this limit the extent to which organizational decision-making can be made democratic?

Coopey's argument, a perspective also expressed by Contu and Willmott (2003), is that, within the socio-economic context of capitalism, power is structurally embedded in the employment relationship, and that this typically places workers in a subordinate position to management. This issue is returned to in Chapters 9 and 12. Such institutional arrangements are argued to produce a 'democratic deficit' where the values, ideas, and interest of workers are largely downplayed and where the authority and knowledge of management is privileged and taken for granted (Coopey 1998). In such situations it is arguable that the vision of the learning organization articulated by its propagandists is unlikely to be achieved. The relevance of these arguments for the topic of learning is that these features of the employment relationship are likely to significantly shape the nature of organizational learning processes.

Power, politics, and learning

Neglecting to adequately take account of power, politics, and conflict is another critique made against the learning organization propagandists. Such a neglect is typical of the majority of the learning literature (Bunderson and Reagans 2011; Hong and Snell 2008). Further, the propagandists not only downplay such issues but are typically unwilling even to acknowledge that they are relevant to the analysis of learning processes (Driver 2002). However, since the mid-1990s, issues of power and politics have been given a greater level of attention (LaPolombara 2001; Vince *et al.* 2002). The need to account for power and politics in learning processes flows from three closely interrelated factors (see Figure 6.2).

First, as will be discussed more fully in Chapter 12, power and knowledge are either intimately interrelated or totally inseparable (the precise way that the power–knowledge relationship is understood depends on how power is conceptualized). Thus, if learning is about the development and use of knowledge, then account needs to be taken of issues of power (Vince 2001). Coopey (1998) for example, drawing on Foucault, suggests that managerial authority relates to the inseparability of power and knowledge, where management's power is reflected in the privileging of their knowledge, and vice versa. Secondly, as discussed in the previous section, the need to account for power in learning processes relates to the embeddedness of power in the employment relationship. Thirdly, and finally, some argue that power and politics need to be accounted for due to the typical lack of value consensus

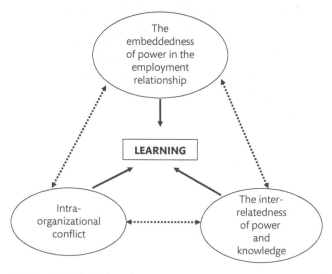

Figure 6.2 Linking Power and Politics to Learning

which exists in most organizations, and the potential for conflict and disagreement this creates (Huzzard and Ostergren 2002; Salaman 2001). This is another issue that is discussed more fully in Chapters 9 and 12.

 Illustration   Power inequalities and cultural differences in learning within Japanese subsidiaries in China

Hong and Snell (2008) conducted a detailed qualitative study into the dynamics of learning within five Japanese subsidiary companies in China. The subsidiary companies they examined were all based in the same region, and were of a reasonable size, employing between 500 and 2,500 staff. The study found that all five of the Japanese parent companies made significant efforts to impose their corporate culture within the subsidiaries, despite the existence of some identified culture differences. One of the culture differences identified between the working style of the Chinese workers and Japanese managers was in relation to teamworking. For the Japanese managers, effective teamworking involved all team members making significant efforts to contribute to group tasks and problem-solving activities. The Japanese managers did not feel that the Chinese workers were prepared to participate in such activities effectively. One manager said, 'within the traditional culture of Canon, we encourage close cross-departmental cooperation and total employee participation . . . the workers here perceive their work differently. They tend to have a clear demarcation of duties, titles and power' (p. 262). Another manager said, 'In general, the Chinese are not aggressive enough to engage in the problem solving process' (p. 263). Hong and Snell argued that these differences were not due to any laziness of the Chinese workers, but to cultural differences.

   Despite these culture differences, no attempts were made to take account of them and make some cultural adjustments. The Japanese managers were totally convinced of the superiority and value of the corporate culture their company had developed, and made great efforts to impose it within the Chinese subsidiary plants. This was achieved through the inflexible imposition of particular types of work practice, combined with an intensive programme of culture management. Hong and Snell found evidence of cultural adjustment over time: 'some of the local Chinese had gradually developed the kinds of work-related attitudes and behaviours that were valued by the Japanese headquarters' (p. 267). Hong and Snell conclude that the power inequalities that existed between the Japanese managers and Chinese workers in the subsidiary factories were such that the former were able to impose their preferred style of culture and work practices on the Chinese staff.

1. In all types of subsidiary organizations, do corporate management have the same level of power to be able to impose their preferred work styles on people, or do workers in such situations have any power to challenge and resist such efforts?

The critics of the learning organization rhetoric argue that the need to take adequate account of these factors means the vision of the advocates is unrealistic, and that there are likely to be some stark contradictions between their rhetoric, and the way the adoption of learning organization practices impact on organizational relations. Thus, rather than workers having a greater potential for creativity and self-development, the use of learning organization practices may mean they are subject to greater levels of control. Further, rather than empowering workers, learning organization practices have the potential to bolster and reinforce the power of management (Driver 2002; Hong and Snell 2008—see the illustration).

The adoption of the rhetoric and practice of the learning organization can be perceived as increasing the potential to control workers, because, as with the use of culture-based management practices generally (Kunda 1992), it involves a form of socially based control, where goal alignment between worker and organization is achieved through persuading workers to internalize the organizational value system (Driver 2002). Such control systems are more subtle, less visible, and have the potential to be more effective than traditional bureaucratic methods (Alvesson and Willmott 2001).

> **DEFINITION Learning organization (sceptics)**
>
> An organization where socially based control systems are used to create value alignment around the benefits to all of learning, which has the potential to reinforce management power, and contradict the logic of emancipation embodied in the learning organization rhetoric.

Some writers however, conclude that conflict is not necessarily detrimental to learning processes, and that if conflict and differences of opinion are managed and negotiated through a certain type of dialogue, they can actually facilitate learning (Coopey and Burgoyne 2000; Huzzard and Ostergren 2002). For example conflict can facilitate learning if it is dealt with in a communication process which does not privilege any particular point of view, where people are able to communicate without fear, where the communication is two-way, and where ultimately the objective of the process is not to achieve a consensus, but for people to develop a greater understanding of the viewpoint of others. Such processes therefore have much in common with the processes of perspective making and taking outlined in Chapter 3, which are an important element of the practice-based perspective on knowledge. Further, while Bunderson and Reagans (2011) highlight how power inequalities within organizations can negatively affects the dynamics of learning processes, they argue that a 'socialized' style of leadership, which is sensitive to such issues, can stimulate and facilitate learning in groups where such power inequalities exist.

Emotion and attitudes to learning

The final factor that the learning organization advocates inadequately account for is the role that people's emotions play in shaping attitudes and behaviours towards learning processes. However, a growing number of writers now acknowledge how emotion importantly affects the dynamics of learning processes (Crossan *et al.* 2011; Shepherd *et al.* 2011; Vince 2001; Zhao 2011). At the individual level, learning can be regarded as potentially positive and exciting: discovering new knowledge, improving levels of understanding, developing more effective ways of working, etc. But, there is also a potential negative side—giving up the familiar, embracing some level of uncertainty—which may be anxiety-inducing for people (Kofman and Senge 1993; Shipton and Sillince 2012). Learning is therefore likely to induce conflicting emotions for people. Learning and changing can also be understood to affect an individual's sense of self-identity (Child 2001), which may be regarded positively or negatively. Arguably, the attractiveness of defensive routines (Argyris 1990) is that they provide people with a sense of security and self-identity (Giddens 1991). Thus, a potentially frightening side of learning is that it can be felt to involve giving up that which makes people feel competent and secure.

Illustration   The impact of emotion, context, and personality on people's ability to learn from errors

Zhao (2011) presents the findings of a laboratory experiment that involved undergraduate students which was centrally concerned with examining the relationship between experiences of negative emotions and people's ability to learn from errors, with it being hypothesized that negatively emotional experiences would be negatively related to people's ability to learn from errors by reducing their motivation to learn. The paper starts from the assumption that, while errors can provide potentially valuable learning opportunities, they often create negative emotions in people that can inhibit them from learning from these experiences. Errors are defined as 'individuals' decisions and behaviours that (a) result in an undesirable gap between an expected and real state; and (b) may lead to actual or potential negative consequences for organizational functioning that could have been avoided' (p. 436). In terms of the relationship between experiences of negative emotionality and learning from errors, three specific hypotheses are tested. First, they hypothesize that experiences of negative emotionality will be negatively related to people's motivation to learn. Secondly, they hyothesize that people's motivation to learn will be positively related to the ability to learn from errors. Finally, they hypothesize that motivation to learn will mediate the relationship between the experience of negative emotionality and the ability to learn from errors.

In the study that was conducted Zhao also examined two antecedents of negative emotionality: people's emotional stability and their perception regarding managerial intolerance of errors. They hypothesize that emotional stability is negatively related to experiences of negative emotion, i.e. the more emotionally stable people are the less likely they are to experience negative emotions. Secondly, they hypothesize that people's perceptions of managerial intolerance of errors will be positively related to experiences of negative emotion. In the tests that were conducted, both of these hypotheses were supported.

In terms of the relationships between negative emotion and learning from errors, while it was found that motivation to learn was positively linked to the ability to learn from errors, their hypothesis that motivation to learn would be negatively related to people's motivation to learn was not supported. In fact, in contradiction to what was expected, experiences of negative emotions were found to be positively linked to people's motivation to learn. Two suggestions were put forward to explain this. First, the level of negative emotions people experienced were relatively low, which may have been due to the fact that the research data were collected in a student simulation test, where participants did not have to experience and deal with the consequences of real errors. Secondly, it was suggested that the level of negative emotion experienced may actually be an important variable. Thus experiencing low levels of negative emotions may motivate people to learn as this does not create a lot of fear, anxiety, etc., whereas if high levels of negative emotions are experienced, this may act to inhibit people's motivation to learn.

Finally, in terms of managerial implications, the study suggests that management behaviour can influence the extent to which people experience negative emotions related to errors. To avoid or minimize this, it is suggested that managers should behave in a manner which indicates a tolerance for making errors and that people should feel safe in admitting to, and discussing the reasons for, any errors they make.

1. To what extent do you agree with the suggestion that the relationship between experiencing negative emotions and people's motivation to learn is affected by the level of negative emotion that people experience?

Finally, as the illustration highlights, learning from errors and mistakes is a situation where emotion can strongly influence the dynamics of learning processes (see also Shepherd *et al.* 2011). This is returned to in Chapter 8 when the topic of unlearning is examined.

 ## Conclusion

The chapter has shown that the enormous literature on organizational learning which has been produced since the mid-1990s is of great relevance to those wishing to understand the dynamics of organizational knowledge processes. This should be relatively unsurprising given the relatedness of learning to knowledge management. Through utilizing the Crossan/Zietsma framework the complexity and multi-level nature of organizational learning was explored, showing how organizational learning cannot simply be regarded as the sum of the learning of an organization's workers.

The chapter also showed how the concept of the learning organization has been the subject of significant debate, with its advocates arguing that it provides both organizations and workers with many benefits, while the critics argue that the emancipatory rhetoric of the learning organization disguises and denies the way in which the practices of the learning organization may impact negatively on workers, for example, leading to increased levels of exploitation and control. This debate was not resolved, but it did provide a useful way of revealing the diversity of factors which make learning within the context of work organizations difficult and complex (see Table 6.4).

Table 6.4 Factors Affecting Learning in Organizations

Factor	Level
The emotional character of learning	Individual
Competency traps and the difficulty of giving up established values and practices	Individual–group–organization
The politics and power involved in implementing learning and challenging established norms	Individual–group–organization
The inter-relatedness of learning, knowledge, and power	Supra-organizational
The embeddedness of power in the employment relationship	Supra-organizational

 Case study   The role of time and discontinuities in shaping the complex dynamics of organizational learning

Berends and Lammers (2010) use Crossan *et al.*'s multi-level model of organizational learning to analyse the dynamics of a knowledge management initiative that was undertaken within a large Dutch bank. They not only apply Crossan *et al.*'s model, but also contribute to its development, through their use of the concept of discontinuities and how they affected the dynamics of learning within the project and wider organization. Discontinuities are defined as occurring when 'one of the four learning processes is interrupted or where learning does not flow from level to level' (p. 1048). Their analysis also highlighted how factors of time, the social context of the organization, and politics played crucial roles in shaping the dynamics of learning. Their analysis was based on a detailed, qualitative study of the knowledge management project that involved both interviewing people at various times, and observing key project meetings. While the knowledge management project was ultimately unsuccessful, their analysis of it provides detailed insights into the dynamics of organizational learning. To give some insights into their analysis, this brief overview presents some examples of the four learning processes within the project, as well as some of the discontinuities that interrupted learning. The way in which factors such as time and the social context impacted on learning in the project is also highlighted.

As outlined earlier, central to Crossan *et al.*'s model of organizational learning are the four processes of intuiting, interpreting, integrating, and institutionalizing, which move learning between individual, group, and organizational levels through feed forward and feedback processes. An example of individual-level intuition in the project occurred at an early phase, when interest in knowledge management was in its infancy and was relatively limited. At this stage interest in the topic, and understanding of the relevance of knowledge management to the bank, occurred through the intuition of various individuals. The growth of interest in knowledge management, which grew out of these intuitions, resulted in knowledge management becoming a topic that the bank considered investing in via a research project. One outcome was the organization of various workshops and meetings that brought relevant people together, and where a group-level process of interpretation began. However, various interruptions to the evolution of the project meant that these initial interpretations of knowledge management were not sustained throughout the project. An example of one such discontinuity occurred immediately after the project was awarded funding, when it was decided to replace the initial project team with a new and highly successful project manager. This decision both delayed the project, as the new project manager wasn't available to start immediately, and resulted in the focus of the project changing, as the new project manager developed his own ideas about how to implement knowledge management. This meant that the initial focus and priorities of the project changed.

An example of knowledge integration occurred later in the project, during the conduct of some small pilot projects within particular departments. Here a process of knowledge integration occurred as the insights developed within the knowledge management project were integrated with local, department-specific knowledge to help address particular local challenges and problems. A partial process of integration also flowed out of this as some of the findings from the pilot projects (though not all) were institutionalized into formalized, departmental procedures. A final example of discontinuity occurred towards the end of the project, at a time when there was growing concern among senior management regarding the organizational benefits that were being derived from the project. After analysis of the knowledge derived from the pilot projects, and the ways in which this understanding could be institutionalized into organizational procedures, senior managers decided not to continue funding the project and to merge the knowledge management project, subsuming it within a new intranet project.

Time crucially shaped the project in various ways. For example, funding for and evaluation of the project's progress was shaped by the timing of various management committees. Further, factors such as when key people were available to participate, as well as the timing of holidays, also impacted on the project's progress. The social structure of the organization also shaped the progress of the knowledge management project and the learning that occurred. The project spanned various departments (such as IT and HRM), and involved people from a wide range of hierarchical levels. This shaped the project in various ways. First, it contributed to the conflict that existed regarding the general character of the knowledge management project, such as the extent to which it should be IT focused. Fundamentally, there was a wide range of different views regarding what the knowledge management project should focus on. Secondly, the social structure of the project and the wider organization also influenced the politics that developed within the project, whereby various actors used different strategies in order to have their vision of knowledge management privileged over others. An example of this occurred early in the project, where an IT-focused view predominated, which led to the downplaying of HRM issues and the exclusion from the project team of HRM staff.

Berends and Lammers's conclusion regarding the general character of organizational learning was that, due to the various discontinuities that occurred, learning was 'fragmented', and that overall learning within and from the project was 'non linear' and 'more complex than process models suggest' (p. 1060), where learning 'resembled a changing delta of meandering flows, some of which get blocked, while new flows emerge and others get reinforced' (p. 1059).

1. While this case is based on a single project, do you think that it is atypical or typical of how learning occurs during the life of large, cross-departmental projects?

Source: Berends, H., and Lammers, I. (2011). 'Explaining Discontinuity in Organizational Learning: A Process Analysis', *Organization Studies*, 31: 1045–68.

 ## Review and Discussion Questions

1. The advocates of the learning organization suggest that critical self-reflection and open debate on norms and values are fundamental to learning organizations. However, Coopey and Burgoyne (2000) suggest few organizations provide the 'psychic space' where such reflection can occur. Do you agree with this analysis? If so, what factors are key in stifling such processes?

2. Compare the two definitions of the learning organization outlined in the chapter. Which do you most agree with, and why?

3. The research of Hong and Snell (2008) suggested that national culture shaped the learning styles of Japanese and Chinese workers. How important is national culture in shaping the way people learn?

4. If experiencing strong negative emotions can negatively influence people's ability to learn, to what extent does experiencing strong positive emotions affect people's willingness to learn?

 ## Suggestions for Further Reading

1. **M. Crossan, C. Maurer, and R. White (2011) 'Reflections on the 2009 AMR Decade Award: Do we Have a Theory of Organizational Learning?', *Academy of Management Review*, 36/3: 446–60.**
A review article which looks at developments in theory on organizational learning which link to and build from the Crossan *et al.* framework.

2. **J. Bunderson and R. Reagans (2011). 'Power, Status, and Learning in Organizations', *Organization Science*, 22/5: 1182–94.**
A conceptual paper, which draws on a range of literature to examine the way in which power and status differences within teams and organizations affect learning processes.

3. **H. Bui and Y. Baruch (2011) 'Learning Organizations in Higher Education: An Empirical Evaluation within an International Context', *Management Learning* (publ. via Onlinefirst, doi: 10.1177/1350507611431212).**
An empirical paper which examines the existence of Senge's learning organization framework within two universities.

4. D. Shepherd, H. Patzelt, and M. Wolfe (2011) 'Moving Forward from Project Failure: Negative Emotions, Affective Commitment and Learning from the Experience'. *Academy of Management Journal*, 54/6: 1229–59.

An empirical study which considers the role that negative emotions (and a number of other variables) have on the extent to which people can learn from experiencing project failure.

Take your learning further: Online Resource Centre

Visit the Online Resource Centre for resources which will extend your understanding of knowledge management in organizations. As well as web links to sites of interest, the author has provided case studies looking at knowledge management in virtual and knowledge-intensive firms, and in global multinationals. These will help you with your research, essays, and assignments; or you may find these additional resources helpful when revising for exams.

 www.oxfordtextbooks.co.uk/orc/hislop3e/

Part 3

Knowledge Creation and Organizational Unlearning

While most chapters in this book take a general approach to knowledge management and do not focus on particular types of knowledge process, the two chapters in this brief section are different. Thus Chapter 7 is concerned narrowly with processes of knowledge creation, while Chapter 8 has an exclusive focus on processes of unlearning (the conscious process of giving up or abandoning existing knowledge and capabilities).

These processes deserve particular attention for a number of reasons. First, as is highlighted in both chapters, the turbulent and dynamic business environments that many companies compete in mean that the ability to innovate and change is a crucial organizational competence. For different reasons, the ability of organizations to innovate is affected by the ability of organizations and people to create new knowledge and to give up or abandon old knowledge. Knowledge creation is important in dynamic contexts as organizations require to regularly adapt and develop new products and/or services. Unlearning, while being examined to a much lesser extent than knowledge creation, is equally crucial to an organization's ability to adapt and change. This is because the ability to innovate and create new knowledge is to some extent predicated on the ability of an organization to reflect on and be willing to give up existing competences, ways of working, products, and services.

In Chapter 7, on knowledge creation, the chapter takes a deliberately narrow focus, examining Nonaka's theory of knowledge creation. There are two fundamental reasons for this focus. First, within a single book chapter it is not possible to effectively examine the various perspectives on innovation and knowledge creation that exist. Secondly, the reason for choosing Nonaka's work as the focus is fundamentally due to its widespread popularity.

Chapter 8 focuses on unlearning. The importance of examining this topic is that it is generally neglected in the learning and knowledge management literatures. Thus, part of the reason for examining organizational unlearning is to suggest that it is a topic which requires greater levels of attention by those interested in the topics of innovation and knowledge management.

Nonaka and Knowledge Creation Theory

Introduction

This chapter has a narrow and specific focus, the description and evaluation of Nonaka's theory of knowledge creation.[1] In examining the topic of knowledge creation it is virtually impossible to ignore Nonaka's theory as it represents the single most influential and widely referenced theory in the knowledge management domain (Güldenberg and Helting 2007; Nonaka *et al.* 2006). The influence of this work is visible in citation data. The two most cited publications which articulate knowledge creation theory are Nonaka's 1994 article in *Organization Science* (Nonaka 1994), and Nonaka and Takeuchi's book *The Knowledge-Creating Company* (Nonaka and Takeuchi 1995), which by May 2012 had been cited over 10,000 and 26,000 times respectively, according to Google Scholar.

Nonaka's work and theory is centrally concerned with processes of organizational innovation, and new product development. While there is an extensive body of research and writing on knowledge management issues related to innovation and new product development processes which does not utilize Nonaka's knowledge creation theory (Almeida *et al.* 2011; Foss and Mahnke 2011), this other work is not examined here. It was not feasible to give an adequate overview of both Nonaka's theory on knowledge creation and the wider literature on innovation-related knowledge processes within the space of a single chapter. Thus, rather than attempt this impossible task it was decided to focus solely on Nonaka's work.

Nonaka's work is very influential; however, there are two other reasons why this chapter focuses on Nonaka. First, the theory is extremely wide-ranging, and Nonaka and his various collaborators have published extensively on various aspects of it. In terms of its scope, not only is it a theory of knowledge, and knowledge creation, it also engages with topics such as space (or Ba), leadership and management, organizational structure/form, and business strategy. In terms of publications, the body of work in which this theory has been developed is substantial, spanning a timescale of more than twenty years, and includes (in terms of English-language publications only) a number of books (Ichijo and Nonaka 2006;

---

[1] This knowledge creation theory has been developed by Nonaka in collaboration with a number of others. However, for simplicity it is referred to here as Nonaka's theory.

Nonaka and Takeuchi 1995; Nonaka *et al.* 2008; von Krogh *et al.* 2000) and more than twenty refereed journal articles (including Nonaka 1991, 1994; Nonaka and Konno 1998; Nonaka and von Krogh 2009; Nonaka *et al.* 2006; von Krogh *et al.* 2012). Thus, even with the chapter's focus being limited to Nonaka's theory of knowledge creation, all that can be done is give an overview of some of its key features.

The final reason for examining Nonaka's knowledge creation theory is that it has been subject to various critiques which are worthy of examination. Two of the most significant relate to Nonaka's epistemology, and the nature of the relationship between tacit and explicit knowledge, which affects the way knowledge creation occurs. The second critique or comment relates to the suggestion that Nonaka's theory may have limited generalizability, being fundamentally related to and developed from the analysis of Japanese companies.

The structure of the chapter is relatively simple. Some of the key components of knowledge creation theory are presented, including the distinctive epistemology it is founded on, how knowledge creation is achieved through the conversion of knowledge from one form to another, the role of space/ba in knowledge creation, and finally the role for management and organizational leaders in facilitating knowledge creation. The chapter concludes by examining some of the main critiques that have been made of knowledge creation theory which relate to its epistemology and its level of cultural generalizability.

The Scope and Evolution of Nonaka's Knowledge Creation Theory

As outlined, the scope of Nonaka's knowledge creation theory is wide-ranging and includes issues of epistemology as well as business strategy and organizational structure. However, another key feature of this theory is that it has evolved and developed over time, partly due to the refinement and elaboration of the theory (such as Nonaka *et al.* 2008, on a process-based view of the knowledge-based theory of the firm, and von Krogh *et al.* 2012, on the topic of leadership), as well as responses to some of the critiques that have been made of it (such as Nonaka and von Krogh 2009, on the topics of tacit knowledge and knowledge conversion). Thus, knowledge creation theory should be understood as dynamic rather than being a static body of ideas which have remained unchanged over time.

This dynamism can be illustrated via a couple of examples, relating to the reduced emphasis on or abandonment of concepts that were prominent in some of the earliest work. First is the concept of the 'hypertext organization', which had a prominent place in both Nonaka's 1994 *Organization Science* paper, as well as in *The Knowledge-Creating Company*. This was argued to be a particular organizational form that facilitated knowledge creation by synthesizing the efficiency achievable in hierarchical organizations with the adaptability of more flexible organizational structures. However, this particular conceptualization of organizational structure was abandoned in later work (see e.g. Nonaka *et al.* 2008). Further, the concept of 'middle-up-down management' also featured prominently in early conceptualizations of the theory. While there is much synergy between the way middle-up-down management is conceptualized and the role of middle and senior management is characterized in later work, the label 'middle-up-down management' appears to have fallen out of favour. In the review presented here the central focus is on the most contemporary conceptualization of the theory.

The Epistemology of Knowledge Creation Theory

There are three fundamental elements to the way knowledge is conceptualized in knowledge creation theory. First, there is the basic definition of knowledge as 'justified true belief'. Secondly, knowledge gives people the ability to define and understand situations and act accordingly. Finally, there is the distinction between tacit and explicit knowledge, which implies that they represent distinctive and different forms of knowledge. Further, one of the themes in knowledge creation theory is the distinction between Japanese and Western epistemology and that the high level of importance attributed to tacit knowledge in knowledge creation theory distinguishes it from the dominant Western epistemology in academia which is argued to be more centrally focused on explicit knowledge. For example, the embedding of knowledge creation theory in Japanese values and philosophies is visible in the subtitle of *The Knowledge-Creating Company*, which is *How Japanese Companies Create the Dynamics of Innovation.*

For Nonaka, defining knowledge as 'justified true belief', refers to the knowledge individuals develop based on their particular experiences and work practices. While distinctions are made in knowledge creation theory between individual, group, and organizational knowledge, and it is argued that through the process of knowledge conversion knowledge can 'move' between these levels (see following section), within knowledge creation theory knowledge is fundamentally individual, being possessed by and embodied within people. In this respect it has resonances with the practice-based perspective on knowledge articulated in Chapter 3 (see e.g. Nonaka *et al.* 2008: ch. 1). Further, it is a highly subjective and relative definition of knowledge, as knowledge constitutes what an individual believes to be true. Thus, Nonaka *et al.* (2006: 1182) say that 'knowledge is never free from human values and ideas'. Ultimately, knowledge conceptualized in this way refers to what an individual can justify as being true, based on their experience of and interaction with the world. However, an important element of people's experiences are their interactions with others, whose understanding of the same events may be different. People's knowledge or justified true beliefs emerge from a process of dialogue with others, where people become exposed to others with different perspectives, with people's knowledge being 'born of the multiple perspectives of human interaction' (Nonaka *et al.* 2008: 12). In this process of dialogue conflict may exist between competing perspectives, with knowledge resulting from the process via which people (attempt to) justify their personal beliefs.

The second feature of knowledge is that it provides people with the ability to define and understand situations and then act in accordance with these insights. Thus knowledge is closely linked to and inseparable from how people act and behave. This implies, as above, that knowledge is highly practice-based and also that the relationship between knowledge and action is two-way. Thus, not only does people's knowledge (justified true beliefs) shape how they act and behave, but the relationship also operates in the opposite direction, with consequences of people's actions shaping their knowledge.

The third key dimension of Nonaka's epistemology is the distinction between tacit and explicit knowledge as being fundamentally different. Thus, 'knowledge that can be uttered, formulated in sentences, captured in drawings and writing, is explicit', while, 'knowledge tied to the senses, movement skills, physical experiences, intuition, or implicit rules of thumb, is tacit' (p. 1182). In this respect, Nonaka's epistemology is closer to the objectivist perspective articulated in Chapter 2. Thus, Nonaka's theory of knowledge creation cannot easily be characterized as embedded in either the objectivist or practice-based perspectives on knowledge, as it embodies elements of both.

This distinction between tacit and explicit knowledge as two distinct and separate types of knowledge is something that has been generally consistent and unchanged in knowledge creation theory (see e.g. Nonaka 1994; Nonaka and Takeuchi 1995; Nonaka *et al.* 2006). However, the conceptualization of the distinction between tacit and explicit knowledge has been refined in later work (Nonaka and von Krogh 2009) in response to various comments and critiques. This refinement of epistemology will be examined later, following the critique that is presented towards the end of the chapter.

SECI and Knowledge Creation/Conversion

The distinction Nonaka makes between tacit and explicit knowledge is fundamental to his model of knowledge creation, as it is via the conversion of knowledge between forms (tacit and explicit) that knowledge is created. In Nonaka's knowledge creation spiral (Figure 7.1) there are four modes of knowledge conversion and the SECI mnemonic with which it is labelled utilizes the first letter of the four knowledge conversion processes (socialization, externalization,

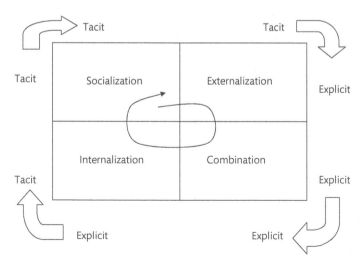

Figure 7.1 The SECI Model of Knowledge Creation

conversion, and internalization). First, socialization involves the conversion of tacit knowledge into new forms of tacit knowledge. Second is externalization, which involves the conversion of tacit knowledge into explicit knowledge. The third conversion process, labelled combination, involves the integration of different forms of explicit knowledge to create new forms of explicit knowledge. Finally, internalization involves the conversion of explicit knowledge into tacit knowledge. For Nonaka, socialization is typically the starting point of knowledge creation processes, as it is the impulse of individuals to collaborate and communicate or share explicit knowledge which provides the initial catalyst for knowledge creation.

It is important to note that knowledge creation evolves through a spiral rather than circular motion. This is because the SECI knowledge conversion/creation processes involve a double, simultaneous conversion. Thus, with each mode of knowledge creation, not only is knowledge created via changing forms, but simultaneously knowledge moves between individual, group, and organizational levels (see Table 7.1). The movement of knowledge 'up' from the individual level, through to group level, and finally to organizational-level knowledge is referred to as a process of amplification (Nonaka *et al.* 2008: 25). Thus at an organizational level knowledge creation contributes to the expansion of an organization's knowledge system. Such systems include not only a store of explicit knowledge codified into IT systems, formalized rules, or operating procedures, but also a body of tacit knowledge existing within an organization's culture and value system. Each mode of knowledge creation/conversion is examined in a little more detail below.

The first process of knowledge conversion is socialization. This process involves the interpersonal sharing of tacit knowledge, where new tacit knowledge for one person is created through gaining access to the tacit knowledge of others as they work together on a day-to-day basis. This type of knowledge creation occurs when people work together collaboratively, and usually occurs over extended periods of time, which allows people to develop not only shared working practices, but also common systems of values and understanding. Thus socialization involves the movement of knowledge from one individual to another.

Table 7.1 Nonaka's four modes of knowledge conversion

	Socialization	Externalization	Combination	Internalization
Knowledge conversion type	Tacit to tacit	Tacit to explicit	Explicit to explicit	Explicit to tacit
Change in level of knowledge	Individual to individual (between people)	Individual to group	Group to organization	Organization to individual
Illustrative example	Where a new member of a work group acquires the tacit knowledge possessed by other group members through dialogue, observation, or cooperative working.	Where an individual is able to make their tacit knowledge explicit, e.g. through a process of communication and dialogue with others.	The linking together of discrete bodies of knowledge, to create a more complex body of knowledge.	Where an individual converts explicit knowledge into tacit knowledge, through applying it to their work tasks.

The second process of knowledge creation, where knowledge is transformed from a tacit to an explicit form, is externalization. This knowledge creation process involves the movement of knowledge from the level of the individual to a group. This is a process via which individuals articulate, communicate, and justify their individual knowledge to a group of peers. It involves transforming knowledge from a tacit to an explicit form via people using language, images, models, and concepts, etc., to begin the process of codifying tacit knowledge. Dialogue is important to this process, as the articulation of knowledge by one person will involve them being questioned (or possibly challenged) by peers to clarify and develop their knowledge and ideas.

The third process of knowledge creation is combination. This involves creating new forms of explicit knowledge from existing forms of explicit knowledge, and involves the

Illustration   The application of Nonaka's SECI model to understanding knowledge creation in new product development projects

Hoegl and Schulze (2005) carried out a survey of participants in new product development projects in Germany, Switzerland, and Austria to investigate the extent to which a range of knowledge management tools supported knowledge creation processes. The survey investigated both which knowledge management tools were utilized, and the respondents' level of satisfaction with them. The paper then used Nonaka's SECI framework to explain how the different knowledge management tools examined facilitated processes of knowledge creation.

The survey found that the most commonly used knowledge management tools were informal social events (used in the organizations of over 80 per cent of respondents), experience workshops (80 per cent of organizations), experience reports, databases, project briefings, and communities of practice (all used by just under 75 per cent of organizations). Further, the knowledge management methods that were most commonly used were also the ones that were regarded as being most effective.

In explaining why these knowledge management methods facilitate knowledge creation processes, Hoegl and Schulze make use of Nonaka's SECI framework by linking each of the knowledge management methods examined to one particular form of knowledge conversion. For example, informal events which encourage conversation and open communication between work colleagues are argued to facilitate processes of socialization (the conversion of tacit knowledge into new forms of tacit knowledge) through the way they allow the development of strong interpersonal relations between people. By contrast, experience workshops, which allow people to share their experiences with colleagues, are argued to facilitate the process of externalization. This is because the process of talking about and reflecting on experiences facilitates the explicit articulation and codification of knowledge and understanding.

1. In Hoegl and Schulze's analysis there is a one-to-one relationship between the knowledge management practices and the forms of knowledge conversion in Nonaka's model, with each form of knowledge management being linked to a particular form of knowledge creation. However, to what extent is it possible that particular knowledge management methods may facilitate more than one form of knowledge conversion? For example, as well as experience workshops facilitating processes of externalization, to what extent can they also facilitate processes of socialization, combination, and/or internalization?

movement of knowledge from the level of the group to the level of the organization. This process involves combining different bodies of somewhat disparate explicit knowledge to create more complex and interrelated systems of knowledge. Further it involves the institutionalization of group-level knowledge into formalized, organizational-level knowledge, such as an organization-wide system of rules or working practices.

The fourth and final process of knowledge creation is internalization. This is where knowledge is converted from an explicit form to a tacit form, and where knowledge moves from the level of the organization to the level of the individual. This is therefore a process of absorption or embodiment, where people's use of explicit knowledge (such as systems of rules, operating manuals, etc.) becomes absorbed into their work practices so that they eventually do not have to utilize the explicit knowledge which has shaped their (tacit) practices. Finally, the process of knowledge creation/conversion is potentially infinite, as the internalization of explicit knowledge by people does not mean that knowledge at this point becomes static and unchanging, as internalization has the potential to lead to and initiate a new process of socialization, whereby new tacit knowledge is created out of the existing tacit knowledge people possess and utilize.

Ba/Space

Ba is a Japanese concept which translates into English as shared space or context. While it was a concept that was not referred to in the earliest formulations of knowledge creation theory (Nonaka 1994; Nonaka and Takeuchi 1995), it was fully articulated by Nonaka in 1998 (Nonaka and Konno 1998) and has evolved to constitute an important element of knowledge creation theory. Ba or space represents an important element of the organizational context which facilitates knowledge creation processes or, in Nonaka's terms, provides the 'enabling conditions' for knowledge creation. Ba enables knowledge creation by facilitating interpersonal interactions between people, whether such interactions are physical or virtual. Such interactions facilitate knowledge creation as they provide an 'existential place where participants share contexts and create new meanings' (Nonaka *et al.* 1994: 34) and which provide a person an opportunity to 'get involved and transcend one's own limited perspective' (p. 36).

While Nonaka's conceptualization of ba includes shared physical space, ba refers to more than simply a shared physical context where people create knowledge through face-to-face collaboration. Ba also includes shared virtual space, where people can communicate, interact, and collaborate via IT systems such as e-mail. Further, ba also refers to shared mental space in terms of common assumptions, values, practices, and knowledge that people can develop and share. For example, Nonaka *et al.* (2006: 1185) suggest that an example of this type of ba in the context of product development activities refers to common interpretations regarding technical data, test results, product features in terms of quality, etc.

Nonaka also suggests that the type of ba that facilitates and supports each type of knowledge conversion is likely to be different (see Table 7.2). For example, with socialization, the type of ba that facilitates knowledge creation is one which allows people to work collaboratively together in a face-to-face environment, and includes elements such as the use of

Table 7.2 Ba and Knowledge Conversion

Knowledge Conversion Mode	Socialization	Externalization	Combination	Internalization
Type of ba	Originating ba	Interacting ba	Cyber ba	Exercising ba
Characteristics of ba	A shared physical space where people develop shared knowledge, ideas, practices via communicating and working collaboratively.	A shared space (not necessarily physical) where groups of people can articulate experiences to each other via metaphors, concepts, etc.	A virtual space within which explicit knowledge can be combined, such as within IT systems, or documents.	A context which allows people to develop, refine, and familiarize themselves with and utilize explicit knowledge, which includes training opportunities, and the ability to repeatedly apply and utilize explicit knowledge.

flexible, team-based work practices which allow people to interact with a range of different people in carrying out their work. Thus, the type of ba which facilitates socialization is a particular type of physical workspace in which people can effectively collaborate. This is referred to as an *originating ba*. In contrast, the type of ba that supports externalization is somewhat different and is defined as *interacting ba*. This is a ba which supports not only people's efforts to articulate their tacit knowledge, but which also facilitates group-based communication. This type of ba may involve a physical space, but is not restricted to this and may also involve a virtual element (shared computer systems) or common values. The type of ba which supports combination is labelled *cyber ba* by Nonaka, as this represents a context in which disparate bodies of explicit knowledge can be integrated and formalized into more complex bodies of explicit knowledge. Finally, the type of ba which supports internalization is labelled *exercising ba* by Nonaka. This is a shared context which facilitates people's efforts to absorb and internalize explicit knowledge, which will be an environment that allows people to familiarize themselves with and experiment with explicit knowledge.

Nonaka argues that the key reason why an appropriate ba is necessary to support knowledge creation is that knowledge creation is a typically fragile social process in which people articulate and justify their knowledge to others in a group-based context. If the organizational context within which this type of activity occurs is inappropriate it is likely to inhibit people's efforts to communicate and interact. However, the concept of ba, and the relationship between different type of ba and particular modes of knowledge conversion, has been largely empirically untested, and remains somewhat abstract. For example, in their 2006 review article Nonaka *et al.* (2006) refer to only a couple of studies on the topic. Further, a recent search of academic papers (in June 2012) did not identify any peer-reviewed academic journal articles which empirically examine the relationship between ba and knowledge conversion, but two papers were identified which develop the concept (Lindblom and Tikkanen 2010; Nakamori 2006).

> ### ⊙ Illustration   Organizational culture facilitating knowledge creation
>
> Song (2008), while not explicitly utilizing the concept of ba, highlights how a certain type of shared organizational context can facilitate knowledge creation. Thus Song links together the concept of learning organization culture and Nonaka's knowledge creation theory to investigate the extent to which they are positively correlated. The model developed by Song was tested by distributing a survey among managers from Korean firms in a range of industries (including electronics, service industries, finance, and IT industries). Song conceptualized a learning organization culture as having seven separate elements, including among other things continuous learning, team-based learning, empowerment, and supportive leadership. Song conceptualized knowledge creation using Nonaka's SECI framework, considering it to involve elements such as knowledge sharing, the creation of concepts, the justification of concepts, and the development of models. Song conducted a statistical analysis on the relationship between these variables through analysing the 471 completed surveys they received. Song's analysis found that there was a strong positive correlation between learning organization culture and knowledge creation, which suggests that developing and possessing such a culture is likely to facilitate people's knowledge creation activities.

Leadership/Management and Knowledge Creation

Another way in which organizations can facilitate knowledge creation processes is via the behaviour of leaders and managers. As knowledge creation theory has developed and evolved over time not only has the importance assigned to leadership and management roles increased, but there has been a significant evolution in the way these roles have been conceptualized. Thus, over time more space has been devoted to the topic of leadership, while the topic of middle-up-down management articulated in Nonaka and Takeuchi (1995) and Nonaka (1994) has been virtually abandoned. For example, in *Managing Flow* (Nonaka *et al.* 2008) while two chapters are devoted to leadership and leading, the only mention of middle-up-down management is made by David Teece in the foreword (see also von Krogh *et al.* 2012).

Before considering separately the role that senior and middle managers can play in facilitating knowledge creation it is useful to highlight two generic features of leadership in knowledge creation processes that are relevant to all types of leadership/management role. First, as outlined in the Nonaka quote in Chapter 15 on leadership, the role of leaders/managers is more to facilitate and enable knowledge creation than to control and direct it. Fundamentally, knowledge is created by workers collaborating and carrying out their work, and the role of leader/managers is to facilitate these efforts (for example, by encouraging them to act autonomously). Secondly, leadership is something that should be distributed within the organization, with a wide range of different people at different hierarchical levels playing leadership roles in different ways. Thus Nonaka *et al.* (2008) say that 'leadership is not exclusive to an elite few' (p. 206).

However, in talking about leadership and management in knowledge creation theory Nonaka distinguishes between senior managers and middle managers. In this chapter, in the following section, when the term 'leadership' is used, it refers to senior/top management, while the term 'management' refers to middle and lower levels of management. The articulated role for each in knowledge creation processes is outlined below.

Fundamentally, the role of leaders is generally concerned with issues of high-level strategy and structure. First, this involves the development of a particular vision and communicating this to others in the organization. The vision of leaders should focus knowledge creation processes into the development of products that provide genuine value to customers. Thus part of the role of leaders is to be external facing, taking account of customer desires and preferences and then translating that into a particular organizational vision. In terms of structure, the role of senior management is to structure the organization to provide an appropriate environment to facilitate knowledge creation, i.e. to create the conditions for appropriate ba to exist. Finally, the role of senior management is to recruit, train, and communicate with middle managers, who themselves then cascade the knowledge vision downwards.

The role of middle managers is to take the high-level vision of organizational leaders and translate it into concepts and frameworks that are relevant to the workers they are responsible for. Thus they are not passive conduits for passing on the ideas of leaders, but actively translate them into different terms. Middle managers have responsibility for communicating this translated vision to workers and motivating them to create knowledge in pursuit of it. Nonaka *et al.* label this role as that of 'knowledge activists' (Nonaka *et al.* 2006; von Krogh *et al.* 1997). A key feature of the knowledge activist role for (middle) managers is to facilitate knowledge creation within teams by acting as boundary spanners, for example through helping to introduce new ideas from the external environment within a team, or by linking a particular team to relevant others. Thus the catalyst for knowledge creation is the bringing together of people with different bodies of specialized local knowledge.

It is worth finishing this section with the same message as the previous one. While Nonaka has done much to articulate and develop the role that leaders and managers can play in knowledge creation processes, and has presented many illustrative examples to support these ideas, few others have empirically tested and evaluated Nonaka's conceptualization of leadership. Thus, for example, while von Krogh *et al.* (2012) review forty-eight academic articles which link leadership with knowledge management activities, very few of these articles explicitly conceptualized leadership using Nonaka's framework on leadership. Thus, much work needs to be done to empirically evaluate and validate Nonaka's ideas.

The Critique of Nonaka's Knowledge Creation Theory

While Nonaka's theory is widely cited, and highly influential, it has also been the subject of a number of criticisms. Three considered here are that the empirical evidence supporting the theory is unconvincing, that the model has conceptual problems, and that its universal applicability is limited as it is only relevant to companies utilizing Japanese business practices. One of the most extensive critiques of Nonaka's knowledge creation theory has been developed by Gourlay (2006), and his work is here utilized in the development of the first two critiques of Nonaka's theory.

Gourlay (2006) argues that one of the main criticisms of Nonaka's theory is that, despite the fact that his work is typically replete with illustrative examples, the evidence supporting it is brief, anecdotal, and unconvincing. In substantiating his argument, Gourlay reviews the evidence and examples presented by Nonaka which are argued to provide illustrative and supporting evidence for each of the four modes of knowledge creation. Here, for illustrative purposes, only the evidence supporting socialization is considered.

In *The Knowledge-Creating Company* (Nonaka and Takeuchi 1995) the key exemplar provided to illustrate the process of socialization (converting tacit knowledge into new forms of tacit knowledge) is how the process of bread making was learnt in the development of a domestic bread-making machine. To overcome some initial problems in the bread-making process (the inability to produce 'tasty bread') it was decided that a member of the product development team would watch a master chef making bread. Through doing this it was realized by the developer that the chef was both twisting and stretching the dough. These insights were then integrated into the design of the bread machine and it was argued that the tasty bread problem had been solved. This process of learning by watching undertaken by the developer is argued to be an example of socialization. While Gourlay acknowledges that this may represent an example of socialization he argues that the anecdotal nature of the example and the lack of detailed evidence makes it far from convincing that what has been revealed is an example of socialization.

Even if Nonaka's many illustrative examples are regarded as convincing, there are other limitations regarding the extent to which the theory has been tested and evaluated by others (as was highlighted in the previous sections on ba and leadership). Teece goes further, questioning whether at present knowledge creation theory is a 'testable theory' (2008: p. xiv), as it is not articulated in the form of testable propositions. However, Teece was generally positive that hypothesis formulation and testing of the theory was possible.

A second critique developed by Gourlay is that there are a number of conceptual problems not only in the SECI model, but in what he argues is a radically subjective definition of knowledge, and the epistemological assumption that it is possible to completely convert tacit knowledge into explicit knowledge. Again, for illustrative purposes, the focus here is narrowly on the extent to which tacit knowledge can be made explicit. While Nonaka draws on Polanyi in making the distinction between tacit and explicit knowledge, and arguing that tacit knowledge can be converted wholly into an explicit form, Gourlay argues that Polanyi's position on these questions is more ambiguous. Further, Gourlay takes the perspective, shared by a number of theorists (Ribeiro and Collins 2007; Collins 2007), that there is an irreducibly tacit element to any and all explicit knowledge, and that it is never possible to make fully explicit any tacit knowledge.

This critique of Nonaka's epistemology was explicitly acknowledged and responded to by Nonaka and von Krogh (2009). The focus here is the response to the critique regarding the nature of tacit and explicit knowledge and the relationship between them. Nonaka and von Krogh's (2009) paper develops a subtle but significantly different way of articulating their relationship. While Nonaka's earlier work, as outlined in the previous section, suggested that tacit and explicit knowledge were separate types of knowledge, in the response to the critique that tacit knowledge cannot be made fully explicit, they argue in their 2009 article that tacit and explicit knowledge exist 'on a continuum' and that 'tacit and explicit knowledge are not two separate types but inherently inseparable' (p. 637). The idea of tacit and explicit knowledge being part of a continuum is reinforced later when they talk about how knowledge 'loses some of its "tacitness"', and 'increasingly explicit knowledge' (both p. 642). Thus while continuing to highlight the important distinction between tacit and explicit knowledge, and with knowledge conversion between forms remaining the centre of knowledge creation theory, Nonaka and von Krogh's (2009) paper represents a retreat from the idea that tacit and explicit represent two separate and distinct forms of knowledge.

The third and final critique of Nonaka's knowledge creation theory questions its tacit universalistic assumptions, arguing that it is based on values very much embedded in Japanese work practices and culture. This is an argument that Nonaka has thus far not responded to. Glisby and Holden (2003), as well as Weir and Hutchins (2005), argue that all knowledge is culturally embedded, and that the universality of Nonaka's knowledge creation model is limited by the fact that it is embedded within and reflects the values and culture of Japanese business. Thus its relevance to business cultures which do not share these values is argued to be limited. Glisby and Holden illustrate their argument by considering the way that Nonaka's conceptualization of each of the four modes of knowledge conversion reflects business practices that are common in Japan, but much less frequently utilized elsewhere.

In examining processes of socialization, Glisby and Holden distinguish between the internal sharing of tacit knowledge by employees within an organization, and the external sharing of knowledge by people across organizational boundaries. Glisby and Holden argue that the external sharing of knowledge referred to by Nonaka reflects the close and inter-locking inter-organizational relations that are typical in Japan. In countries where the management of inter-firm relations is typically more arms length, the sharing of tacit knowledge across organizational boundaries is argued to occur much less frequently. Equally, Glisby and Holden argue that the frequent sharing of tacit knowledge between employees discussed by Nonaka is likely to be shaped by the typically high commitment levels Japanese workers have for the organizations they work for, and that in countries where levels of organizational commitment and loyalty are lower, the sharing of tacit knowledge between employees is also likely to be lower. Glisby and Holden make a similar argument with respect to processes of internalization, the conversion of explicit knowledge into tacit knowledge. For Nonaka, this is closely linked to processes of learning by doing which emerge when job rotation occurs. However the type of job rotation referred to by Nonaka, while being common within Japanese companies, is much less common in other countries. The embeddedness of knowledge creation theory in Japanese values and practices is reinforced by the fact that, almost without exception, the illustrative examples utilized by Nonaka are taken from Japanese companies.

Hong (2012) adds a further contribution to this critique by arguing that the behaviours and assumptions underpinning each of Nonaka's knowledge conversion modes are embedded in particular Japanese cultural values. This argument is developed utilizing Hofstede's perspective on national culture (see Table 7.3). For example, in relation to socialization, the assumption underpinning it is that people have a willingness to identify

Illustration The (partial) applicability of knowledge creation theory in Russia

Andreeva and Ikhilchik (2011) reflect on the extent to which each of the four modes of knowledge creation in Nonaka's SECI model are applicable in Russia. The arguments they present are based on their own direct knowledge of business practices and cultural values in Russia rather than on the collection of any specific research data. To analyse the applicability of the SECI processes to Russia they argue that there are certain societal/organizational conditions, as well as managerial tools/practices, which facilitate each mode of knowledge creation. They then reflect on the extent to which these conditions exist in Russia. Only part of their analysis is presented here, with the focus being on socialization alone.

In relation to socialization they argue that it is facilitated by factors including employees with high levels of loyalty, a willingness among employees to cooperate with each other, organizations which are embedded in collaborative partnerships with other organizations, jobs which allow people to collaborate and share ideas, and good mentoring systems.

In terms of employee commitment and loyalty, Andreeva and Ikhilchik argue that levels of loyalty and commitment are either low or medium rather than high, due to the levels of job insecurity and economic instability most Russian employees have experienced in the recent past. Secondly, in relation to Russian employees' general willingness to cooperate with colleagues, they also argue that such values are typically limited, with it being more usual for employees to have a competitive attitude towards each other that limits their willingness to collaborate extensively with colleagues. In terms of the extent to which Russian companies are linked into collaborative networks, Andreeva and Ikhilchik argue that this varies significantly between industries, but is typically something that Russian companies are not good at. Finally, in terms of having jobs that encourage collaboration and communication, and the existence of extensive mentoring schemes, Adreeva and Ikhilchik argue that these are both types of work practices that are used to a limited extent. For example mentoring is typically limited to new or probationary employees and experienced managers may be unwilling to share their knowledge and experience with others due to a fear of being replaced by younger employees.

In conclusion, they argue that knowledge creation theory has partial applicability in Russia as not all the cultural conditions or business practices necessary to support and facilitate SECI processes exist there.

1. To what extent are the business practices, history, and cultural values that exist within a country likely to affect the extent to which employees are willing to participate in Nonaka's SECI knowledge creation processes?

and work closely with others. Hong argues that this willingness will be facilitated by national cultural values that have a high level of collectivism (as Japan does). Secondly, Hong argues that externalization can be understood as an attempt by people to reduce ambiguities, with people's desire to engage in this type of activity being facilitated by national cultural values concerned with uncertainty avoidance (as is the case with Japan). This line of argument thus implies that in countries where cultural values are different to those in Japan, people may be less likely and willing to engage in SECI knowledge conversion processes, as the behaviours and assumptions they involve are not embedded in their cultural values.

Table 7.3 Assumptions and Cultural Values Underpinning Knowledge Conversion Modes

Mode of Knowledge Conversion	Underlying Assumptions	Embedded Japanese Cultural Values (from Hofstede)
Socialization	A desire to identify with and interact with others	• High collectivism • Large power distance
Externalization	A strong motivation to reduce ambiguity	• High uncertainty avoidance • Masculinity
Combination	Importance of producing things via collaboration with others	• High collectivism • Large power distance
Internalization	Willingness to be open to new ideas, reflect on own ideas/practices and continuously improve	• High uncertainty avoidance • Masculinity

Source: from Hong 2012.

 ## Conclusion

While examining innovation and knowledge creation processes, the focus in this chapter has been deliberately narrow, examining Nonaka's theoretical framework on knowledge creation. The reason for this focus is that it is such a complex model, and highly influential and extensively referenced, that it warranted detailed examination. The majority of the chapter has thus been devoted to briefly articulating some of the key elements of Nonaka's knowledge creation theory. At the centre of this theory is the distinction between tacit and explicit knowledge, with knowledge being created through the conversion of knowledge from one form to another. However, Nonaka's theory also incorporated ideas regarding the type of organizational context and environment likely to facilitate knowledge creation processes. In doing this Nonaka developed the concept of ba, or shared space, to highlight how each type of knowledge creation is facilitated by a different type of interaction between people, with these interactions being shaped by the character of the space they occur in. Finally, Nonaka's theory also articulated particular roles and responsibilities that management and organizational leaders should engage in to encourage knowledge creation. While Nonaka's theory is very influential and extensively referenced, there are still a number of limitations to it, not least that many aspects of it remain to be fully empirically evaluated. Further critiques relate to the way tacit knowledge and knowledge conversion processes are conceptualized and the extent to which it is a theory which is relevant beyond the Japanese business and cultural context that it was developed in. Despite these criticisms, Nonaka's theory has been developed over more than twenty years and represents the single most influential theory in the domain of knowledge management.

 ### Case study   Enabling knowledge creation within Nissan's Oppama production plant

Matsudaira (2010) utilized Nonaka's knowledge creation theory to examine knowledge creation processes within one specific part of Nissan, its Oppama manufacturing plant in Japan. The aim of the research that is reported in the paper was to highlight the micro-level practices of workers and managers that facilitated knowledge creation.

The catalyst for innovation and knowledge creation within the Oppama plant was a desire to reduce the cost of manufacturing at the plant so that production costs were more comparable to those in countries such as Mexico, which had traditionally been able to produce cars at a significantly lower cost. The project to transform the Oppama manufacturing plant was made up of six separate teams, and Matsudaira focused on one, the Integrated Factory Automation (IFA) team. This team consisted of eighteen people from different divisions within Nissan. Matsudaira's research on the IFA involved conducting detailed interviews with a number of IFA team members. The factors which enabled each mode of knowledge creation at the Oppama plant are considered separately below.

In terms of socialization, one important mechanism to facilitate it was getting workers to go to other parts of the organization where similar activities to the ones they are responsible for are carried out. This exposed workers to a range of different ways for carrying out the same work activities, and provided a catalyst for people to implement change. Thus one interviewee said of this initiative, 'after going around and seeing other shops [work sites] anew, there is much astonishment and many discoveries of usable points' (p. 232). Another mechanism which facilitated socialization was bringing groups of workers together for a period of two to three weeks to collaborate and problem solve intensively. Bringing people together for this amount of time created a sense of shared identity and facilitated interpersonal knowledge sharing.

In terms of externalization, one practice that facilitated it was a process of translating concepts that was utilized by team leaders. The team leaders took the relatively general and abstract concepts and goals of the change initiative, and translated them into terms that were relevant to people in their particular team. This activity facilitated the externalization of knowledge as it not only made the change initiative tangible and understandable to people, but also allowed them to develop a commitment to it.

Two key factors which were found to have enabled the process of combination are relatively interrelated. First was to develop in people a holistic view of the production process to help understand the role that their particular area contributed to it. Secondly, and relatedly, people were encouraged to 'break down the walls' (p. 233) between different divisions within the factors and collaborate more extensively with people from all areas of the site.

Finally, a number of practices were identified that facilitated internalization, but only two are outlined here. First, efforts were made to reinforce and embed in people the idea that continuous improvement means that people should be continually looking for ways to innovate and improve the activities they carry out. This was summed up in the slogan, 'there is no such thing as 100% perfection' (p. 233). Secondly, people were encouraged to not only develop their own particular vision of how the plant could be developed and improved, but also discuss their visions with each other. This facilitated a dialogue between people in which they compared and contrasted their specific visions, and which encouraged people to develop and innovate their ideas and working practices.

1. Think about the extent to which these ideas could be utilized to facilitate innovation and knowledge creation within a car factory in Europe or the USA. Think about the factors specific to these locations which you think might facilitate or inhibit the implementation of these practices for supporting knowledge creation.

Source: Matsudaira, Y. (2010) 'The Continued Practice of "Ethos": How Nissan Enables Organizational Knowledge Creation', *Information Systems Journal*, 27: 226–37.

Review and Discussion Questions

1. To what extent, if at all, can tacit knowledge be articulated and made explicit?

2. Think of a country whose culture and business practices you are relatively familiar with and reflect on the extent to which business organizations there would be able to effectively utilize Nonaka's knowledge creation theory.

3. One potential catalyst for knowledge creation is the differences that exist in people's knowledge and understanding, which can act to encourage people to reflect on their knowledge and ideas and potentially modify them. However, to what extent is it also possible that such differences in knowledge and values may be a source of conflict and disagreement between people, requiring issues of politics and conflict to be given a greater level of attention in knowledge creation theory?

4. To what extent do you agree with the critique of Nonaka's knowledge creation framework that the evidence presented by Nonaka in support of it is anecdotal and unconvincing?

 ## Suggestions for Further Reading

1. I. Nonaka, G. von Krogh, and S. Voelpel (2006) 'Organizational Knowledge Creation Theory: Evolutionary Paths and Future Advances', *Organization Studies*, 27/8: 1179–1208.

   A relatively contemporary overview of knowledge creation theory and how it has evolved.

2. S. Gourlay (2006) 'Conceptualizing Knowledge Creation: A Critique of Nonaka's Theory', *Journal of Management Studies*, 43/7: 1415–36.

   One of the most extensive critiques of Nonaka's knowledge creation theory.

3. I. Nonaka and G. von Krogh (2009) 'Tacit Knowledge and Knowledge Conversion: Controversy and Advancement in Organizational Knowledge Creation Theory', *Organization Science*, 20/3: 635–52.

   A response to the epistemological critique of knowledge creation theory made by Gourlay and others.

4. T. Andreeva and I. Ikhilchik (2011) 'Applicability of the SECI Model of Knowledge Creation in Russian Cultural Context: Theoretical Analysis', *Knowledge and Process Management*, 18/1: 56–66.

   Considers the relevance of SECI knowledge creation process to the context of Russia.

Take your learning further: Online Resource Centre

Visit the Online Resource Centre for resources which will extend your understanding of knowledge management in organizations. As well as web links to sites of interest, the author has provided case studies looking at knowledge management in virtual and knowledge-intensive firms, and in global multinationals. These will help you with your research, essays, and assignments; or you may find these additional resources helpful when revising for exams.

    www.oxfordtextbooks.co.uk/orc/hislop3e/

Unlearning and the Deliberate Loss of Knowledge

8

Introduction

While processes of unlearning and forgetting knowledge (accidentally or deliberately abandoning or giving up knowledge) are neglected in the knowledge management literature, and are rarely addressed in knowledge management textbooks, they are arguably a crucial element in organizational knowledge management processes as well as change processes more generally. Primarily, this is because forgetting and unlearning are closely related to learning, and the creation and acquisition of new knowledge (Lee 2011; Zahra *et al.* 2011). Fundamentally, the *in*ability to unlearn or forget can produce a rigidity in thinking and acting and create a blinkering of outlook which prevents change being implemented when it is necessary (Akgün *et al.* 2006*a*; Tsang 2008). This can occur when existing views are never questioned or challenged. Further, the inability to reflect upon and question what may have been successful organizational norms, values, practices, and knowledge can create what have been referred to as 'competency traps' (see Ch. 6, and Shipton 2006), where useful competencies become outdated through never being challenged, revised, or abandoned.

Thus, the ability to unlearn and give up existing knowledge (routines, assumptions, values, behaviours, etc.) can be a catalyst to change, and can allow organizations to be adaptable (Becker 2010). Most fundamentally, the ability to acquire, develop, or create new knowledge is directly related to an organization or person's ability to begin unlearning, through recognizing and acknowledging the limitations of existing knowledge (Tsang and Zahra 2008). In business environments where high levels of turbulence and change occur, the capacity to do so effectively is arguably crucial to organizational performance. This therefore helps explain why unlearning has been examined within the context of change, innovation, or learning processes. For example, studies have examined the role of unlearning in the context of knowledge transfer processes (Tsang 2008; Yildiz and Fey 2010), the implementation of technological change (Becker 2008), processes of exploration- and exploitation-based learning in organizations (Cegarra-Navarro *et al.* 2011), in new product development teams (Akgün *et al.* 2007*b*; Lee and Sukoco 2011), and in processes of internationalization (Casillas *et al.* 2010).

Another reason for examining processes of unlearning is that research suggests that organizations and people find the process of giving up old ways of thinking and doing challenging and difficult. For example, research suggests that even the experience of failure in organizations *rarely* results in the adequacy of existing knowledge/values/ideas/practices being reflected upon and that consequently few organizations are systematically able to un/learn from failure (Baumard and Starbuck 2005; Cannon and Edmondson 2005). This therefore raises questions regarding why people and organizations find such processes so difficult, which is one of the key topics addressed in this chapter.

While the topic of unlearning or forgetting is neglected in the knowledge management literature, and is a generally under-researched topic (Tsang and Zahra 2008), there is a growing body of conceptual and empirical work on topics such as the nature of forgetting, unlearning, and their relationship to change and learning (Akgün *et al.* 2007a; Easterby-Smith and Lyles 2011*b*; Tsang and Zahra 2008), what the antecedents of unlearning are (Cegarra-Navarro *et al.* 2012; Lee 2011), and what the consequences of unlearning are (Casillas *et al.* 2010; Tsang 2008; Wong *et al.* 2012). This chapter will utilize all of this contemporary research. This chapter is

---

 Illustration   The role of unlearning in joint ventures

Tsang (2008) uses the concept of unlearning to understand what inhibited the transfer of knowledge during some international joint ventures involving Chinese companies. Further, in relation to unlearning, Tsang's focus was on the unlearning of organizational routines, with routines, following Feldman and Pentland, being defined as 'repetitive patterns of interdependent actions carried out by multiple organizational members involved in performing organizational tasks' (Tsang 2008: 7). For Tsang unlearning represents a deliberate process, whereby old routines are discarded in favour of newer ones.

In the context of the type of acquisition-based joint ventures Tsang examined, the process of unlearning organizational routines was a stage crucial to their success. This is because, with such joint ventures, the adaptation of an existing site and the retraining of an existing workforce, which are intrinsic elements in such initiatives, require the workers involved to give up and unlearn organizational routines, as well as learn new ones. For Tsang, this process of unlearning is thus both unavoidable and crucially important, as without it workers are unlikely to learn new routines, and in such circumstances joint ventures have a high chance of failing.

Tsang conceptualized the transfer of knowledge during joint ventures as involving four separate, but overlapping and interrelated processes. First, there is the initiation stage, which consists of processes leading up to the decision to undertake the joint venture. Second is the implementation stage, during which knowledge is transferred from one party in the joint venture to the other. Third is the ramp-up stage where the recipients of the acquired knowledge begin to make use of it in carrying out their work. Fourth and finally is the integration stage, whereby the newly acquired knowledge and routines become established and institutionalized. While Tsang's analysis examined what inhibited unlearning during each of these stages, the focus here is purely on the ramp-up and integration stages.

At the ramp-up stage a key indicator of unlearning was that, despite this being a phase when workers were meant to be utilizing the new routines, they often continued to utilize the old work routines they were more familiar with. This was most likely to occur when the joint venture partner only sent a few managers to the site of the joint venture to help with the utilization of the new routines. It was also likely to occur where the old, established routines concerned were highly socially embedded. Finally at the integration, as with the ramp-up phase, a key indicator of unlearning was that a number of workers still continued to use existing routines rather than utilize the new ones. However, over time, as people's memories faded, and the new routines became more familiar, such processes became less pronounced. Time thus facilitated the abandonment of old routines, partly through the fact that staff who had been familiar with the old routines left the organization.

located in a separate section with knowledge creation as the ability to deliberately forget and give up existing knowledge is a necessary and important precursor to the creation and development of new knowledge, which means that deliberately forgetting/giving up knowledge and knowledge creation are closely related topics. The relatedness of learning, unlearning, and forgetting also means numerous links are also made with issues discussed in Chapter 6, as well as there being a brief section in this chapter examining their interlinkages.

Thus far, in talking about giving up, losing, or abandoning knowledge, both the concepts of unlearning and forgetting have been referred to, but the central focus of this chapter will be on unlearning. The chapter differentiates between forgetting and unlearning through examining De Holan and Phillips's (2004) typology of forgetting, which distinguishes between the accidental and deliberate forgetting of knowledge, defining unlearning as a specific type of forgetting concerned with the deliberate giving up of established knowledge. It is also acknowledged that unlearning and forgetting processes are not always positive and can have potentially dysfunctional consequences. Next we examine the close and inseparable inter-relationship that exists between unlearning, learning, and change. The chapter concludes by looking at the different individual- and organizational-level factors which can act as barriers to forgetting and concludes by considering what can be done by organizational management to address them and thus facilitate these processes.

Unlearning as a Type of Deliberate Forgetting

While it has been suggested thus far in the chapter that, in general terms, the ability to unlearn, forget, and give up knowledge can be a useful organizational capability, it is important to make clear that not all forms of abandoning or giving up knowledge are functional for organizations (Easterby-Smith and Lyles 2011b). For example, the loss of a key source of knowledge when specialist staff leave an organization may have quite negative organizational implications (Massingham 2008—see also Chapters 5 and 14).

Distinguishing between what constitutes useful and dysfunctional knowledge loss requires defining and differentiating between the specific and distinctive forms that it can take. One of the most fundamental distinctions that can be made is between the accidental and deliberate loss of knowledge. Accidental knowledge loss is where knowledge and capabilities are lost inadvertently, while deliberate knowledge loss involves a conscious process of giving up and abandoning knowledge, values, and/or practices which are deemed to have become outdated. In general terms, unintentional or accidental processes of forgetting are typically understood as having generally negative and dysfunctional consequences, while deliberate processes of forgetting are regarded as having positive consequences for the organizations which undertake them (De Holan and Phillips 2004; Akgün *et al.* 2006a; Zahra *et al.* 2011). Thus, organizations need to get the balance right between retaining, protecting, and developing knowledge that is useful and important, while simultaneously being able to discard, forget, unlearn, or give up knowledge which has become outdated and of limited contemporary use. Achieving such a balance is by no means easy.

A useful typology which helps differentiate between different types of knowledge loss is De Holan and Phillips's (2004) typology of forgetting (see Figure 8.1). This typology combines the distinction between accidental and deliberate forgetting with one between newly

MODE OF FORGETTING

	Accidental	Intentional
From Existing Stock	MEMORY LOSS	UNLEARNING
Newly Innovated	FAILURE TO CAPTURE	AVOID BAD HABITS

SOURCE OF KNOWLEDGE

Figure 8.1 Typology of Organizational Forgetting

Source: De Holan and Philips (2004).

acquired/developed knowledge and established knowledge, which constitutes an accepted and existing part of an organization's knowledge base.

The first form of forgetting is the accidental forgetting of existing or established knowledge, which De Holan and Philips (2004) define as memory loss. This form of forgetting is typical when knowledge is used infrequently. In such situations organizations may forget knowledge through the loss to the organization of the people who possess it, or where an organization loses the ability to carry out long unused, informal, and uncodified work routines because they have been forgotten through lack of use. The second form of forgetting is the accidental forgetting of new knowledge, which is defined as a failure to capture new knowledge. This occurs when new knowledge is acquired and developed by one individual, or a small group of workers, and which, through not becoming institutionalized, becomes forgotten or lost by the wider organization. A common example of this form of forgetting occurs with project-based working, where project teams often break up with most of the learning they have acquired/developed being lost to the wider organization through not being effectively shared or codified (Scarbrough *et al.* 2004*a*).

 Time to reflect   Technology and unintentional forgetting

To what extent does the development of technology, such as computer and communications technologies, and industrial robotics, lead to particular technical skills and capabilities being forgotten by organizations? Can you think of examples of specific skills (spelling, letter writing) that have been forgotten in this way due to the development of computers and mobile phones? Is the loss of such capabilities likely to ever be a problem for business organizations? Can you think of specific situations where the loss of such technical skills/competencies might cause problems for organizations?

The other two forms of forgetting are quite different, involving the deliberate and conscious process of forgetting organizational knowledge. First is the intentional forgetting of newly acquired knowledge, referred to as avoiding bad habits. This form of forgetting starts from the assumption that not all learning is necessarily positive, and that as a consequence, whenever new knowledge, values, ideas, routines, practices, etc. are learnt, a conscious process of reflection should occur to decide whether they are useful to retain or not. An example of when such a process may be useful is during and after joint ventures, where efforts could be made to ensure any potentially dysfunctional habits learnt do not become institutionalized. Finally, the fourth form of forgetting is the intentional forgetting, loss, or abandonment of established organizational knowledge, referred to by De Holan and Phillips (2004) as unlearning. This definition of unlearning as deliberately abandoning or giving up knowledge is the most common way in which unlearning is defined in relevant literature (Tsang and Zahra 2008). Organizations and their staff generally find this to be a challenging and difficult process. Part of the reason why unlearning is difficult is that it involves reflecting upon and being prepared to give up knowledge and practices which may be taken for granted and which are deeply embedded in organizational routines and cultures.

> **DEFINITION Unlearning**
>
> A conscious and deliberate process of reflecting upon and being prepared to give up existing knowledge, values, and/or practices.

As outlined earlier, this form of forgetting will be the main one focused on in what remains of this chapter. The reason for focusing on unlearning alone is that it is a deliberate rather than an accidental process, and also that the challenges involved in unlearning established knowledge and behaviours link to the themes raised in Chapter 9 and beyond regarding the problems and challenges of motivating workers to participate in knowledge management processes such as unlearning.

Unlearning, Learning, and Change

As outlined earlier, the ability to unlearn is particularly useful during processes of change, as change arguably involves the ability to both unlearn and learn. Thus Hayes (2002: 7) characterizes change as requiring people to both 'unlearn old ways and develop new competencies'. This raises questions regarding the relationship between unlearning, learning, and change, which is the topic that is briefly examined here.

In terms of the relationship between learning and unlearning, Tsang and Zahra (2008) consider that various relationships are possible, and that unlearning may precede learning, occur simultaneously with it, or be independent of it. However, the dominant perspective in the unlearning literature is that unlearning is a distinctive process and is a prerequisite to, and a precursor of, learning (Akgün *et al.* 2007a; Becker *et al.* 2006; Cegarra-Navarro *et al.* 2010). However, there is also another way to conceptualize the relationship between learning and unlearning and that is to consider unlearning as a specific and particular type of learning (Antonacopoulou 2009). This is the perspective that is also utilized by Argyris and Schön (1996: 3–4), who argued that 'we may also speak of the particular kind of learning that consists of "unlearning": acquiring information that leads to subtracting something (an obsolete strategy, for example) from an organization's existing store of knowledge'. Overall therefore, while it is acknowledged that learning and unlearning are closely interrelated, there is no consensus in the unlearning literature regarding the nature of their relationship.

◉ Illustration   Facilitating unlearning during change

Becker (2010) reports the findings of a survey-based study into the factors which facilitated and inhibited unlearning during a process of change in a single Australian company. The company concerned was a large government-owned corporation in the energy sector that had approximately 5,000 employees. The change process examined was the implementation of an organization-wide enterprise information system, and the survey was given to over 200 people who had had a direct role in the change programme. The analysis identified seven factors which had significantly influenced people's attitude to unlearning, with five of these being individual-level factors related to employees, and two of which were organization-level factors. The five individual factors were: having a positive outlook, the extent to which people had negative feelings regarding the change, the extent to which people experience good levels of informal peer support, the extent to which people understood the need for change, and finally, the extent to which people perceived the new ways of working to be an improvement on the old ones.

Here, only two of these factors are considered in detail. First, in terms of feelings and emotions, the survey found that the more negative and apprehensive people felt about the change that was being implemented, the more likely they would be to resist the change, and the greater the barriers there would be to unlearning old and established ways of working. Secondly, in terms of the final individual factor, it was found that the more people perceived the change to be positive and beneficial, the more likely they would be to unlearn and abandon old ways of working.

The two organizational-level factors that affected people's attitudes to unlearning were people's previous experiences of change in the same organization and the extent to which people were given formal support and training. In relation to previous experiences, it was found that the more people had negative previous experiences of change, the more likely they would be to resist any further change, and the less likely they would be to unlearn. Finally, unsurprisingly, the more formal support and training with which people were provided, the more positive their attitudes to unlearning were likely to be.

1. Based on this analysis, what recommendations and advice would you give to a company that was wanting to create a positive attitude to unlearning in respect to a forthcoming change initiative?

In terms of the relationship between change and unlearning, the vast majority of the unlearning literature suggests that unlearning is a precursor for or facilitator of change (see e.g. the example above from Becker 2010). However, only a few papers consider the relationship between unlearning and change in any depth. One such paper is Akgün *et al.*'s (2007*a*) conceptual paper. Akgün *et al.* (2007*b*) explicitly link to Lewin's (much criticized) three-stage model of change. This relatively simplistic model of change suggests that change happens via the sequential processes of unfreezing, change, and refreezing (Akgün *et al.* 2007*b*; Hayes 2002: 52). Akgün *et al.* assume that unlearning and learning together constitute the second stage in Lewin's model. Tsang and Zahra (2008) also examine the relationship

Table 8.1 Types of Unlearning

Type of Unlearning	Wiping	Deep Unlearning
Catalyst	Change programme	Unexpected individual experience
Level/type of impact	Typically focused on behaviours	Unlearning of behaviours and knowledge/values/beliefs
Speed of unlearning	Variable	Typically sudden
Emotional impact	Variable	Typically significant

Source: Rushmer and Davies 2004.

between learning, unlearning, and organizational change. They distinguish between two distinct types of change (continuous and episodic) and suggest that each type of change will involve a different form of unlearning. They define continuous change as change that is incremental, and gradual in character. By contrast, episodic change is typically discontinuous, infrequent, is greater in scope than continuous change.

Tsang and Zahra (2008) thus raise the idea that there may be different types of unlearning, which is an idea also examined by some other writers on the topic (see e.g. Akgün *et al.* 2007*a*). One of the most useful unlearning typologies, which is focused on individual rather than organizational unlearning, is developed by Rushmer and Davies (2004). While they distinguish three types of unlearning, which they label fading, wiping, and deep unlearning, fading, which involves the accidental and gradual loss of knowledge over time, is more akin to what is here defined as forgetting. Rushmer and Davies argue that each type of unlearning differs significantly (see Table 8.1).

For Rushmer and Davies, the typical catalyst for the type of unlearning they define as wiping is a change initiative external to the person (see e.g. Becker 2010). Wiping is thus a process of unlearning that results from a deliberate process of change that has been externally imposed on people. Wiping is deliberate and conscious and is typically focused on a relatively narrow practice or activity, where a person consciously gives up a particular way of behaving. The other type of unlearning referred to by Rushmer and Davies is deep unlearning. This radical form of unlearning is argued to occur rapidly as a result of an external event whose characteristics and/or outcomes are unexpected, and which suddenly bring into question some basic assumptions that people have. It is argued to have a significant impact on the individuals who experience it, leading them to question their values and beliefs. Deep unlearning may result in people experiencing strong emotions such as anxiety, fear, and confusion. However, the vast majority of the unlearning literature talks about unlearning in generic terms, and does not distinguish between different types of unlearning. Thus in the rest of the chapter no further reference will be made to different types of unlearning.

Antecedents of Unlearning

As has been outlined previously, research into unlearning suggests that there are many factors that influence the willingness of people and organizations to unlearn. The focus of this section is on examining these factors, the antecedents of unlearning, where it will be shown that a heterogeneous range of factors have been found to inhibit and facilitate people's willingness to unlearn. This section separates these factors into two distinct types. First to be examined are individual-level factors, those related to the character, personality, and attitude of people. The second type of factor to be considered is more related to the organizational context.

Individual-level antecedents of unlearning

The first potential individual-level barrier to unlearning is the negative emotion that unlearning and giving up knowledge can generate. As was highlighted in Chapter 6, learning of any type, while being potentially positive and enjoyable, can also stir up negative emotions in people. The feelings of fear and anxiety that unlearning can generate relate to admitting the limitations to, and giving up, knowledge and practices which may have provided a person with a sense of competence, self-identity, and self-esteem. For example, the studies of Lee and Sukoco (2011) and Becker (2010) both found that people's emotional state, and the extent to which people experience negative feelings of anxiety, was negatively related to their willingness to unlearn.

Research also suggests that unlearning which is related to admitting to and learning from failure can be an even more difficult process for people to undertake (Baumard and Starbuck 2005; Shepherd *et al.* 2011; Zhao 2011). One of the general conclusions of research in this area was that people do not like admitting to failure. This was partly due to the stigma that can be attached to being involved in or responsible for failure. Thus, Wilkinson and Mellahi (2005) suggest this typically means that failure is a brush to be tarred with rather than something to be admitted and learnt from. Cannon and Edmondson's (2005) research suggests that deep psychological factors related to the importance people attach to both sustaining feelings of self-competence and to how their esteem and competence is judged by others help explain why people are unwilling to admit to and learn from failure. Thus they suggest that 'being held in high regard by other people, especially those with whom one interacts in an ongoing manner, is a strong fundamental human desire, and most people tacitly believe that revealing failure will jeopardize this esteem', and that as a consequence, 'most people have a natural aversion to disclosing or even publicly acknowledging failure' (Cannon and Edmondson 2005: 302).

 Time to reflect   Admitting to and learning from failure

In your own experience, is admitting to failure and using it as a positive learning experience uncommon? Can you think of examples of where failure has been regarded in this way and where people have been willing to admit responsibility for failure?

Another general factor which can act as an individual-level barrier to unlearning relates to how people may perceive undertaking a process of unlearning as threatening and undermining their self-interest through the way it may impact not only their status and esteem, but also the power they possess, and the interests they are trying to pursue. Fundamentally, if people perceive that unlearning threatens to reduce the power they possess, this may inhibit them from doing this. This links to a point made in Chapter 11 by Carlile (2002, 2004), in relation to cross-community knowledge processes. Carlile, adopting a practice-based perspective on knowledge, suggested that the way in which people's knowledge is 'invested in practice' means that they may be reluctant to participate in processes they perceive will threaten their interests through requiring them to adapt and change their knowledge and practices.

In such situations, people may actively try and resist unlearning through carrying out what have been called defensive routines. Tranfield *et al.* (2000), based on an empirical study whose analysis built on Argyris's (1990) work on defensive routines, found that different groups of workers utilized particular defensive routines which acted as barriers to unlearning. Tranfield *et al.* (2000) define routines as 'habits', repetitive patterns of behaviour, which are often unconscious and which have cognitive, behavioural, and structural elements to them. Argyris (1990) defined a defensive routine as 'any policies or actions that prevent organizational players from experiencing embarrassment or threat while preventing the organization from uncovering the causes of the embarrassment or threat in order to reduce or get rid of them'. Defensive routines are thus repeated behaviours that allow people to avoid admitting to and dealing with any limitations that exist in their thinking and/or actions. Thus, if people are unwilling to unlearn, they might do more than passively resist engaging in such processes. They may proactively behave in ways that undermine attempts to unlearn, through reinforcing existing knowledge, behaviours, and practices.

Cognitive-level factors can also act as a potential barrier to unlearning, through blinkering people's thinking and creating a sense of cognitive myopia and inertia. Nystrom and Starbuck (2003) suggest that unlearning can be conceptualized as a process of cognitive reorientation, in which people need to give up traditional and accepted ways of understanding and embrace the need to develop and utilize new ones. However, people's cognitive structures shape how they see, interpret, and understand events. If particular views, values, ideas, and practices have been successful in the past, people can become (unconsciously) quite attached to them and be unwilling to give them up, and may become unaware how they blinker and constrain how they understand and interpret events. In the vocabulary of the learning literature, this can result in what may have previously been core competencies evolving into 'competency traps' (Shipton 2006), which trap people in past-focused ways of understanding the world.

Finally, when unlearning is linked to a change initiative, the attitude of people to the change process has been found to affect the extent to which people are prepared to engage in unlearning. For example Becker's (2010) study of unlearning during a process of change in an Australian organization (see illustration above) found that people's attitude to unlearning was affected both by the extent to which people felt change was necessary, and the extent to which they felt that the changes being implemented were a positive improvement. Thus, if people do not believe that change is necessary, or if they believe that the type of changes being implemented are not beneficial, this is likely to negatively affect their willingness to unlearn.

Organizational-level antecedents of unlearning

Research on unlearning also suggests that a number of factors related to the organizational context can also play a significant role in influencing whether people are willing to unlearn (Cegarra-Navarro *et al.*, 2011, 2012), and it is such organizational-level factors that are considered here.

Nystrom and Starbuck (2003) suggest that the embedding and institutionalization of knowledge, values, and practices in standard operating procedures and specific work practices can create an inertia that makes them difficult to change. Typically, the longer that work practices have been institutionalized, the more they become taken for granted and unquestioned, and the more difficult they are to change as people become unused to questioning the assumptions on which they work, and new staff members become socialized into particular ways of working. This links to the findings of Tsang's (2008) study (see illustration above), where the extent to which routines were socially embedded in an organization affected the extent to which people were prepared to unlearn existing ways of working and embrace new ones.

One of the findings from Baumard and Starbuck's (2005) study of fourteen failures in a single European telecommunications company was that the strong unwillingness among people to admit to involvement in or responsibility for failure produced a number of distortions in the organizational communication system which acted as a barrier to unlearning. Cegarra-Navarro *et al.* (2011) reinforce this and found that the nature of communication processes was an important element of the organizational context which affected people's attitude to unlearning. Some specific examples of the distorted forms of communication that Baumard and Starbuck (2005) found included:

- A failure to report any failures (often done in the hope/expectation that any problems would disappear over time).
- Findings/events which contradicted institutionalized beliefs/norms were often dismissed and ignored.
- The nature of any failures that were admitted were explained as having limited significance through being regarded as transitory 'blips' that would not be repeated.
- The exaggeration of small-scale successes.
- The general tendency to challenge/resist/subvert/hide analyses which implicated people as being in some way responsible for failure.

Another organizational-level factor which has been found to affect people's attitude to unlearning is the nature of their jobs. Lee (2011) examined the role that challenge and hindrance stressors had on people's attitude to unlearning. Both these factors relate to the nature of people's jobs. Challenge stressors include the complexity of people's jobs and the opportunities that jobs provide for people to be creative, and solve problems. Lee found that such stressors were positively linked to people's attitudes to unlearning. Hindrance stressors are more negative factors related to people's jobs, such as the extent to which administrative factors inhibit the completion of work tasks, or the degree of ambiguity that exists in people's roles. Lee (2011) found that such stressors were negatively related to people's attitude to unlearning. Thus, from a managerial point of view, the implications of Lee's (2011) study are that to facilitate unlearning, people should have clear unambiguous jobs, and should also have jobs that require people to routinely be creative and solve problems.

One means to actively facilitate unlearning involves deliberately introducing new, external ideas, knowledge, practices, and values into an organization with the objective of encouraging or forcing people to reflect on and question their existing values and assumptions. A number of specific ways that this can be done have been suggested. One of Nystrom and Starbuck's (2003) suggestions, which fits with their argument that senior management have a major responsibility for discouraging unlearning, is to sack senior management and replace them with a new senior management team. This radical way of facilitating unlearning is argued to work through bringing new, enthusiastic people into the organization, allowing senior management to carry the major responsibility for any problems and failures, and through encouraging existing staff to engage in a process of cognitive reorientation by engaging with the ideas brought into the organization by the new senior management team.

Two other less radical ways of introducing new ideas into an organization were identified by Tranfield *et al.* (2000), who found two specific enabling routines that facilitated unlearning by this means. First, the enabling routine titled 'envisioning what we might become' involved bringing external consultants into an organization who, through how they organized meetings and discussions, forced people to justify and reflect on their taken for granted assumptions and values. This is comparable with Akgün *et al.'s* (2006*b*) suggestion to challenge and undermine existing ideas through forcing work teams to deal with outsiders who played the role of a 'devil's advocate', deliberately questioning people's beliefs. Secondly, the enabling routine titled 'benchmark others achievements' by Tranfield *et al.* (2000) introduced new ideas to staff by organizing exchange visits with comparable firms who carry out their work differently, and organizing secondments that allow people to move between business units within the same organization to learn different business practices.

A number of suggestions have also been made regarding the way in which management can facilitate a process of unlearning and learning from failure. For example, Cannon and Edmondson (2005) and Provera *et al.* (2010) suggest that middle managers can do this via carrying out blameless discussions, and generally creating 'a safe environment where errors can be openly discussed' (Zhao 2011: 458).

Another general means of enhancing an organization's capacity to unlearn is through the retraining of existing staff. First, Akgün *et al.* (2006*b*) suggest that training staff in lateral thinking has the potential to endow workers with the capability to contemplate ideas that challenge their existing norms and values. Secondly, Becker (2010) found that providing access to training represented a way to facilitate attitudes to unlearning during change initiatives.

A couple of team-level factors have also been found to affect people's attitude to unlearning. Thus, one of the seven factors identified by Becker (2010) that positively affected the attitude of people to unlearning was the amount of informal support from peers that they received. Secondly, Lee and Sukoco (2011—see end of chapter case study) found that levels of reflexivity in teams, the ability of a team to question and reflect on the ongoing utility of existing knowledge and practices, were also positively related to team members' attitudes to unlearning.

 ## Conclusion

One of the key conclusions of the chapter is that, despite forgetting and unlearning being neglected topics in the knowledge management literature, they are crucially important to an organization's ability to adapt, change, and survive, as well as to its ability to access, develop, and utilize new knowledge. This is particularly the case with unlearning, the deliberate abandonment of existing knowledge and/or practices. Without being able to acknowledge the limitations of existing knowledge, values, norms, and practices, and without being prepared and able to give up established knowledge which may have become outdated, organizations are unlikely to be able to change and acquire or develop new knowledge. Thus, arguably, unlearning is as important an element of knowledge management as knowledge creation, codification, or knowledge-sharing processes.

While the ability to unlearn is a capability that is extremely useful for organizations to possess, there are a number of reasons which can make people unwilling to unlearn. These range from the threat to a person's self-esteem that can be associated with having to give up established forms of knowledge, the amount of stress and anxiety people experience, to the nature of people's job roles. Despite these challenges, the final section also highlighting the range of methods that organizations can utilize to improve their ability to unlearn.

 Case study   The impact of team reflexivity and stress on unlearning and innovation in new product development teams

Lee and Sokoco (2011) examined the impact of team reflexivity and perceptions of stress on both levels of unlearning and product innovation within new product development teams in Taiwan. In their paper they define unlearning as 'actively reviewing and breaking down the organization's long-held routines, assumptions and beliefs' (p. 412). The fundamental assumption they start with is that, due to the rapidly changing technological environment that high-technology companies have to deal with, the ability of new product development teams to reflect on and give up existing knowledge and beliefs (unlearning) is important to their innovativeness. Thus, one of the hypotheses that they test is that team unlearning is positively related to team innovation.

They also examine the impact of two other variables on both unlearning and innovation. The first of these factors is team reflexivity. Team reflexivity, the ability to critically reflect on taken for granted ideas and knowledge, is defined as 'a team's collective efforts to review and raise awareness toward task-related issues during the development of new products' (p. 411). They argue that the more teams are able to be reflexive, the more they are likely to be willing to unlearn and abandon existing knowledge or behaviours, thus they hypothesize that team-level reflexivity will be positively related to both unlearning and product innovation. The second factor they examined was team stress, which is defined as the extent to which teams have a sense of crisis or anxiety. They argue that teams which experience high levels of stress are likely to fear receiving negative feedback, selectively focus on what is regarded as threatening information, and tend to interpret unclear information in a negative way. They hypothesize that team stress will be positively linked to unlearning, but negatively linked to product innovation.

To test their hypotheses they conducted a survey-based study of new product development teams located in three science parks in Taiwan. Survey responses were received from 298 people, who were members of 77 different new product development teams, with the majority of these teams working in high-technology industries. All but one of their hypotheses were supported. As hypothesized, they found that unlearning was positively related to levels of product innovation. The ability to unlearn was found to be positively related to the performance of new product development teams. Further, as hypothesized, they found that team reflexivity was positively related to both unlearning and product innovation. In terms of the stress hypotheses, they found that stress levels were negatively related to levels of product innovation, but that, in contrast to what they hypothesized, team stress was also found to be negatively related to levels of unlearning. It appears that feelings of stress result in teams acting defensively, so they tend to rely upon what they perceive to have been traditionally successful beliefs and behaviours, which make them less willing to embrace change. Thus, they found that unlearning was facilitated by the team's ability to be reflexive, but inhibited by the extent to which teams experienced feelings of stress.

1. From an organizational point of view, can you think of ways that the levels of stress experienced by people in new product development teams can be reduced, and levels of reflexivity be developed and enhanced?

Source: Lee, L., and Sukoco, B. (2011). 'Reflexivity, Stress, and Unlearning in the New Product Development Team: The Moderating Effect of Procedural Justice', *R&D Management*, 41/4: 410–23.

 ## Review and Discussion Questions

1. If the distortion of communication is a barrier to unlearning what, if anything, can organizations do to address this issue? Is this an inevitable and unavoidable feature in business organizations?

2. One of the organizational-level barriers to learning from failure is that being involved in or responsible for failure is often punished, for example, via career opportunities being inhibited. Are you aware of or can you find any examples of where the opposite occurred, for example, where failure was not punished, or where active experimentation and learning from failure is encouraged?

3. The consequences of accidentally forgetting knowledge, such as through the loss of certain staff members, are usually regarded as negative. Can you think of any potentially positive consequences that might result from an organizational accidentally forgetting or losing some knowledge?

4. While opportunities to be creative and solve problems in people's jobs have been found to facilitate unlearning, feelings of stress and anxiety were found to inhibit unlearning. Is it possible that these factors could become interrelated if a person's work requires such high levels of creativity that this could be a source of stress?

 ## Suggestions for Further Reading

1. **E. Tsang and Zahra, S. (2008) 'Organizational Unlearning', *Human Relations*, 61/10: 1435–62.**
Conceptual paper which provides a comprehensive review of the literature on organizational unlearning, and which links unlearning explicitly to the topic of change.

2. **K. Becker (2010) 'Facilitating Unlearning during Implementation of New Technology', *Journal of Organizational Change Management*, 23/3: 251–68.**
Empirical case study of a single Australian company which examines the factors which facilitate and inhibit unlearning of individuals during a change process.

3. **L. Lee and Sukoco, B. (2011) 'Reflexivity, Stress, and Unlearning in the New Product Development Team: The Moderating Effect of Procedural Justice', *R&D Management*, 41/4: 410–23.**
An empirical study of the factors influencing unlearning and product innovation in Taiwanese new product development teams.

4. **E. Tsang (2008) 'Transferring Knowledge to Acquisition Joint Ventures: An Organizational Unlearning Perspective', *Management Learning*, 39/1: 5–20.**
Examines the role of unlearning and knowledge transfer in joint ventures using empirical data on joint ventures involving Chinese companies.

Take your learning further: Online Resource Centre

Visit the Online Resource Centre for resources which will extend your understanding of knowledge management in organizations. As well as web links to sites of interest, the author has provided case studies looking at knowledge management in virtual and knowledge-intensive firms, and in global multinationals. These will help you with your research, essays, and assignments; or you may find these additional resources helpful when revising for exams.

 www.oxfordtextbooks.co.uk/orc/hislop3e/

Part 4

Socio-Cultural Issues Related to Managing and Sharing Knowledge

While enormous numbers of companies have implemented knowledge management projects, many of them have been either partial successes or outright failures. Research consistently reveals that some of the main obstacles to success in such initiatives are social and cultural. Thus, for those concerned with achieving an intellectual understanding of the dynamics of knowledge management initiatives, as well as those concerned with making specific knowledge management projects successful, appreciating the significance of social and cultural factors is vital. The seven chapters in this section of the book all deal with this topic and thus arguably represent the core of the book.

While the early knowledge management literature arguably neglected socio-cultural aspects of knowledge management initiatives (Scarbrough and Swan 2001), this is less true of contemporary knowledge management literature. As the literature on knowledge management has evolved, greater recognition has been given to such issues. Thus, there now exists a significant body of writing which highlights the crucial role that socio-cultural factors play in shaping the character and dynamics of knowledge management initiatives. The chapters in this section of the book make use of this work.

Chapter 9 provides an overview of the important influence that a range of social and cultural factors have on the character and dynamics of organizational knowledge management processes and why it cannot be taken for granted that people will be willing to actively participate in such processes. One of the functions of Chapter 9 is to act as a springboard into the remaining chapters in this section, which each build from this overview, looking in depth at a range of social and cultural topics.

Chapter 10 examines the dynamics of knowledge-related processes within a homogeneous group context, in communities of practice, a form of organizing and interaction that is argued to facilitate knowledge sharing. Chapter 11 builds on this by examining the dynamics of knowledge sharing in a totally different context where, unlike in communities of practice, people have limited common knowledge and only a weak sense of shared identity. This can include knowledge processes within multidisciplinary teams, or knowledge processes which span functional, or organizational boundaries. Chapter 12 focuses on the topics of power, politics, and conflict, which, as will be seen, are under-researched areas in the knowledge management literature. Chapter 13 examines the impact and role of technology in knowledge management initiatives. Chapter 14 considers the role that a range of human resource management practices such as reward systems, or training and development systems, can have in shaping the dynamics of knowledge management processes. Part 4 of the book then concludes in Chapter 15 which considers the impact that organizational culture and leadership can have on knowledge management processes.

The Influence of Socio-Cultural Factors in Motivating Workers to Participate in Knowledge Management Initiatives

Introduction

As the topic of knowledge management has matured and evolved, so has interest in the human, cultural, and social dimensions of the topic. There is now a substantial body of writing and research on how these factors influence the character and dynamics of knowledge management processes, and workers' willingness to become involved in them. The aim of this chapter is to provide an overview and introduction to this literature, and the issues it addresses.

The importance of human, social, and cultural factors in shaping knowledge management processes is visible in a significant amount of case study evidence on knowledge management initiatives (see various examples presented throughout the chapter). This work shows that human, social, and cultural factors are often key in shaping the success or failure of knowledge management initiatives, and that a reluctance by workers to participate in knowledge management activities is not uncommon. For example, Lam's (2005) analysis of an Indian software development company's intranet-based knowledge management initiative found that the primary cause of its failure was the nature of the organizational culture, which was highly individualistic and which acted to inhibit workers from sharing knowledge with each other.

What is suggested here is that, whatever approach to knowledge management an organization adopts, the motivation of workers to participate in such processes is key to their success. The importance of human agency to the success of knowledge management initiatives flows largely from the character of organizational knowledge. Primarily, much organizational knowledge, rather than being explicit in a disembodied form is personal, tacit, and embodied in people. Thus, Kim and Mauborgne suggest, 'knowledge is a resource locked in the human mind' (1998: 323). The sharing and communication of knowledge therefore requires a willingness on the part of those who have it to participate in such processes. Or, as Flood *et al.* (2001: 1153) suggest, 'the tacit knowledge . . . employees possess may be exploited only if these workers decide to part with this knowledge on a voluntary basis'.

In exploring this topic the chapter begins by conceptualizing the decision workers face about whether to participate in knowledge management initiatives as being comparable to a 'public good dilemma'. After this, the next two sections examine how the context in which most knowledge management initiatives occur shapes workers' attitudes to knowledge management processes by influencing the nature of the relationship between employers/managers and workers, and also interpersonal relations between workers. The fourth and fifth sections look at the role of interpersonal trust and how a worker's sense of belonging to and identity with work groups shapes their willingness to codify and share knowledge with colleagues. The chapter closes by examining the literature which considers the influence that national culture and individual personality can have in shaping people's attitudes to participating in knowledge activities.

The Share/Hoard Dilemma

The decision workers face about whether to participate in knowledge-related activities has been compared to a classical public good dilemma, with the knowledge workers have access to in their organizations being considered a public good (Cabrera and Cabrera 2002; Fahey *et al*. 2007; Renzl 2008). A public good is a shared resource which members of a community or network can benefit from, regardless of whether they contributed to it or not, and whose value does not diminish through such usage. Collective organizational knowledge resources are thus a public good as anyone can utilize them, whether they have contributed to their development or not. In such situations there is thus the potential for people to 'free-ride', by utilizing such resources but never contributing to their development. The dilemma for the worker is that there are potentially positive and negative consequences to both sharing knowledge and contributing to the public good, and hoarding knowledge and acting as a free-rider. Thus in deciding how to act in such situations workers are likely to attempt to evaluate the potential positive and negative individual consequences of sharing or hoarding knowledge.

 Time to reflect   Knowledge as a public good?

If a public good is a shared resource whose value does not diminish through use, to what extent can knowledge be considered a public good? Does the use of shared knowledge diminish or affect its value? Is there a risk that sharing it with large numbers of people may reduce its value?

Some of the main potential benefits to workers of knowledge sharing are that doing so may be intrinsically rewarding, that there may be benefits at the group level (such as enhanced team or organizational performance), that there is some material reward (such as a pay bonus or a promotion), or that a person's status as an expert becomes enhanced (see Table 9.1). However, the negative consequences of contributing knowledge are that, first, doing so may be time-consuming. Secondly, there is the risk that workers are 'giving away' a source of individual power and status. Finally, there are also the rewards/benefits of hoarding to be accounted for. While the benefit of hoarding knowledge (free-riding) is that

Table 9.1 The Potential Advantages and Disadvantages to Workers of Sharing their Knowledge

Knowledge Sharing	Advantages	Intrinsic reward of process of sharing
		Group/organizational level benefits (such as improved group performance)
		Material reward (financial or non-financial)
		Enhanced individual status
	Disadvantages	Can be time consuming
		Potentially giving away a source of power and expertise to others
Knowledge Hoarding (Free-Riding)	Advantages	Avoids risk of giving away and losing a source of power/status
	Disadvantages	Extent of knowledge may not be understood or recognized

the worker avoids the risk of giving away knowledge, and the power and status that may accompany it, a potential negative consequence is that by doing so they never receive full recognition for what they do know.

There is some evidence in the knowledge management literature that people consider such issues and that their participation in knowledge management activities is shaped by such factors, with a number of studies finding that people's concerns about negative consequences from knowledge sharing actively inhibited them from participating in knowledge management initiatives (Lam 2005; Ardichvili *et al.* 2003; Martin 2006; Mooradian *et al.* 2006; Renzl 2008).

A potential limitation of this way of conceptualizing worker's knowledge-sharing/hoarding decisions is that it presents an over-rational view of how people think and act. Fundamentally, workers' behaviour and decisions are not only shaped by rational calculation. Spender (2003) develops an analysis which suggests that issues of emotion also shape people's decision-making processes. For Spender, emotions affect how people think and act when they have to deal with situations beyond their control and when uncertainty exists. The importance of the linkage between emotion and uncertainty is that uncertainty is argued to be a fundamental feature of organizational life. Spender suggests that the idea of emotion, uncertainty, and the limits to a person's knowledge are less compatible with the objectivist epistemology, which emphasizes objective knowledge, and is more compatible with the practice-based epistemology, which acknowledges and emphasizes the tacit, personal, and subjective nature of knowledge (see Chapters 2 and 3). From this perspective, there is always a subjective and personal element to a worker's knowledge, with it being impossible for workers to possess purely objective knowledge isolated from personal opinion.

In studies of knowledge management initiatives, the emotion of fear has been highlighted by a number of writers as inhibiting people from participating in knowledge management initiatives, with the workers studied fearing a number of things, including a loss of status and power, the loss of their jobs, and a fear of ridicule related to concerns that sharing knowledge may reveal its limitations to others (Ardichvili *et al.* 2003; Newell *et al.* 2007; Renzl 2008).

> ### ⬤ Illustration   The influence of emotion on people's attitude to knowledge sharing
>
> Van den Hooff *et al.* (2012) report the findings of a survey-based study into the impact emotion had on people's willingness to share knowledge. More specifically they examined the extent to which the emotions of pride and empathy affected people's eagerness and willingness to share knowledge. Empathy is defined as a person's ability to sympathetically react to the experiences of others, and is linked to the sense of shared identity with others. Pride is defined as a positive self-evaluation of one's own capabilities and skills. They hypothesized that both emotions would be positively linked to people's willingness and eagerness to share knowledge. In the case of empathy it was assumed that the stronger a person's group identity and level of empathy, the more likely they would be to share knowledge. In relation to pride on the other hand they argued that the greater the pride someone had in their knowledge, the happier they would be to share it with others.
>
> To evaluate this they analysed the results of a survey given to staff within a Dutch global IT company. Of the 450 employees approached, 252 completed it. The survey provided respondents with a number of hypothetical scenarios and asked people to indicate how they would respond to them. As hypothesized, they found that both levels of pride and levels of empathy were positively related to people's willingness and eagerness to share knowledge. Thus, in general terms, they concluded that people's emotional state could have a significant impact on their attitude to knowledge sharing.
>
> 1. Draw up a list of other emotions (such as fear, happiness, etc.) and think about whether they are likely to have a positive or negative impact on people's attitude to sharing knowledge with others.

In understanding the socio-cultural factors which shape workers' willingness to participate in organizational knowledge management initiatives it is also important to take account of the context in which such action takes place, as this shapes workers' relations with colleagues and their managers/employers, and as a consequence influences workers' knowledge sharing/hoarding decisions. The next section looks at the worker–manager relationship in the context of the employment relationship.

The Context of the Employment Relationship: Employer–Employee Relations in Business Organizations

The focus in this section is narrowly on one specific type of organization: private business organizations operating in capitalist markets. While the analysis here is of limited use in understanding the manager/employee relationship in other types of organization, such as public sector or voluntary organizations, it is arguable that the vast majority of knowledge management initiatives occur within private business organizations.

Much analysis in the knowledge management literature portrays the knowledge possessed by an organization's workforce as an economic asset which is owned by the employing organization, and which they have the power to manage. However, the knowledge that workers have can also be conceptualized as belonging to them rather than their employer. From this perspective, while workers may apply, develop, and use their knowledge towards the achievement of organizationally directed goals and objectives, the knowledge is fundamentally the workers', to use as, when, where, how, and if they want. This highlights the potential tension between workers and the organizations they work for over who owns and controls their knowledge, and points towards an important factor which may inhibit the willingness of workers to share their knowledge.

Arguably, the origin of this tension is the intrinsic character of the employment relationship in private business organizations. First, the employment relationship involves organizational management acting as the mediating agents of shareholders and typically places workers in a subordinate position, with no ability to shape corporate objectives and with one of management's key roles being to achieve their shareholder's objectives (for profit, market share, etc.) through controlling and directing workers' efforts (Contu and Willmott 2003; Tsoukas 2000). The issue of power in the employment relationship is returned to and examined in more detail in Chapter 12. Secondly, embedded in the employment relationship is the potential for conflict between the interests of managers/shareholders and workers.

In the context of workers' knowledge this tension relates not only to who 'owns' an employee's knowledge, but how and for what purposes such knowledge is used. For example, while management may perceive that it is the interests of the organization to encourage workers to codify their knowledge, workers may be reluctant to do so if they feel that such efforts will negatively affect them through diminishing their power and/or status. Such concerns explain the reluctance of some experienced middle and senior managers in the UK-based pharmaceutical company studied by Currie and Kerrin (2004) to participate in their organization's knowledge management efforts (which took place in the context of a downsizing initiative), as they were concerned that doing so would make it easier for their employer to get rid of them and replace them with younger, less experienced staff. These feelings were expressed by one manager as follows:

> The experience I have built up over the years is knowledge the organization needs. They have to keep me if they want to benefit from my years of experience. They can't replace me with a young kid and I'm certainly not going to help them do so by giving away to a young kid what I've learned through my years of experience. (p. 21)

Such concerns by workers mean that they may not participate in organizational knowledge management processes if they perceive there to be negative personal consequences from doing so.

One further indication that worker can perceive there to be differences between their interests and opinions and those of their managers relates to occasions/situations where they have been reluctant to express particular views. Both Hayes and Walsham (2000) and Ciborra and Patriotta (1998) found that concerns held by a number of workers about the visibility of their opinions to senior management actively inhibited them from participating in electronic knowledge exchange forums. These concerns were related to how this information/knowledge might be used or interpreted by senior managers. For example, Ciborra and Patriotta (1998: 50) showed that, in one of the groupware systems they studied, contribution levels changed dramatically following comments put on the system by a 'very senior manager'. Their research showed that '[t]his "intrusion" . . . provoked a panic reaction amongst employees and contributed to a freeze in the use of the system for some months'. Primarily, in both studies, workers were loath to express opinions which might be seen as not complying with managerial perspectives in forums which were transparent and widely used.

 Time to reflect   'Visibility' and behaviour

How typical are the findings of Hayes and Walsham and Ciborra and Patriotta? If workers are aware that their knowledge and values will be visible to senior management are they likely to censor or modify how they act and what they say?

It is also useful to acknowledge that factors other than the employment relationship affect a worker's relationship with their employer and can shape their knowledge-sharing attitudes. Kim and Mauborgne (1998) suggest that 'procedural justice' is one such factor. Procedural justice represents the extent to which organizational decision-making processes are fair, with fairness being related to how much people are involved in decision-making, the clarity of communication regarding why decisions are made, and clarity of expectations. Kim and Mauborgne (1998) suggest that, when all these factors are in place, workers will feel valued for their intellectual capabilities and skills and that experiencing such feelings can impact on workers' attitudes towards knowledge sharing, 'when they felt that their ideas and person were recognized through fair process, they were willing to share their knowledge and give their all' (1998: 332). Empirical support for these ideas are provided by Han *et al.* (2010), who present the findings of a study involving 260 knowledge-intensive Taiwanese companies. A key finding from this study was that employee participation in decision-making processes provided them with a sense of psychological ownership over the decisions. Further, this sense of psychological ownership was positively linked to employee levels of organizational commitment, which was in turn positively related to levels of knowledge sharing.

 Time to reflect   Expectations of equity?

What level of equity do workers expect from the organizations they work in? For example, with regards to involvement in decision-making, what type of decisions, and what levels of involvement, do workers regard as fair?

The Ubiquity of Conflict in Business Organizations and its Impact on Knowledge Processes

A general weakness of the mainstream knowledge management literature is that issues of conflict, power, and politics are generally neglected (see Chapters 1 and 12). However, such factors arguably can have a significant influence on the character and dynamics of knowledge processes in organizations. The purpose of this section is to highlight the important role that interpersonal and inter-group conflict can have on knowledge processes in organizations. Primarily, the actual or perceived differences of interest between individuals or groups in knowledge management projects may affect attitudes to participating in such activities. The analysis of how such factors influence organizational knowledge processes is returned to and developed in Chapter 12 by adding the issue of power into the analysis.

The contemporary knowledge literature is full of examples of where such conflicts have affected attitudes to knowledge sharing (Currie and Kerrin 2004; Hislop 2003; Newell *et al.* 2000). Hislop (2003) examined a number of case studies where organizational change was inhibited by a lack of willingness among staff to share knowledge across functional boundaries. This unwillingness to participate in cross-functional knowledge sharing was suggested to be partly due to a history of inter-functional conflict and rivalry (a similar situation is examined in the end of chapter case study). Other studies illustrate how issues of power and politics are intimately linked with processes of knowledge sharing. For example, Willem and Scarbrough (2006), in looking at the relationship between social capital and knowledge sharing, found that what they referred to as 'instrumental social capital' was often used politically through a very selective form of knowledge sharing.

 Illustration   The impact of task and relationship conflict on knowledge sharing

Chen *et al.* (2011*b*) conducted research with staff in two Chinese software companies to examine how conflict was related to knowledge sharing. In looking at this topic they examined both task and relationship conflict. Task conflict is defined as conflict in relation to work activities and tasks, for example, relating to work procedures, resource allocation, etc. Personality conflict relates conflict caused by significant differences in personality relating to issues such as interpersonal style or beliefs. In the paper, Chen *et al.* examine how both types of conflict impact on three psychological states (perceived meaningfulness of work, perception of safety to express dissenting views, perception of availability of resources to complete tasks), and how these psychological states impacted on people's level of work engagement, and knowledge sharing. Crucially, they hypothesized that task conflict would have a positive impact on the three psychological states, as this type of conflict facilitates positive dialogue and information sharing related to the completion of work tasks. In contrast they hypothesized that personality conflict would be negatively related to each of the psychological states, as this type of conflict was likely to distract people from work and create negative situations which may be difficult to resolve.

Chen *et al.* found that all the hypothesized relationships in their model were supported. Thus task conflict had a positive impact on people's psychological stages, while personality conflict had a negative one, people's psychological state was positively related to levels of work engagement, and finally, levels of work engagement were positively linked to knowledge sharing. Thus, conflict does not necessarily have a negative impact on knowledge sharing.

 Time to reflect   Conflicts of interest in knowledge sharing

Can you think of an example from your own experience where there was interpersonal, or inter-group conflict with regards to the sharing and utilization of some knowledge? What was the basis of the conflict?

The typical neglect of conflict (and power and politics) in the mainstream knowledge management literature is largely due to the assumptions of consensus and goal congruence in business organizations that exist in the majority of the knowledge management literature. For example, as outlined in Chapter 1, Schultze and Stabell (2004) suggest that one dimension against which the knowledge management literature can be characterized is the extent to which consensus in society and organizations predominates, with their analysis suggesting that consensus represents the mainstream perspective in the knowledge management literature. This perspective has echoes of Fox's unitarist framework on organizations, where everyone in an organization is assumed to have common interests and shared values (Fox 1985).

However, such a perspective on organizations can be challenged by evidence and analysis which suggest the opposite, that conflict is an inherent and unavoidable feature of business organizations. A radical version of this argument, similar to that developed in the previous section, can be found in knowledge management literature adopting what Schultze and Stabell (2004) label a dissensus perspective (see Figure 1.3) and suggests that potential conflict between management and workers is an inevitable part of the employment relationship. A less radical version of this argument aligns with what Fox (1985) labelled the pluralist perspective on organizations, where organizations are regarded as a coalition of different interest groups acting in a coordinated way. Marshall and Brady (2001: 103), reflecting such a perspective, refer to the 'frequent organizational reality of divergent interests, political struggles and power relations'. Empirical support for this perspective can also be found in the work of Buchanan (2008), where political behaviour has been found to be a common feature of organizational life.

However, the importance of taking account of how conflict (and power and politics) shapes people's willingness to participate in knowledge management processes is not just due to the fact that conflict is an inherent/common feature of organizational life. As will be shown in Chapter 12, it is also because the close inter-relationship that exists between power and knowledge means that knowledge can be used in a highly political way and is a resource people commonly draw on in dealing with situations of conflict.

Interpersonal Trust

This section highlights the crucial role that interpersonal trust can have in shaping people's attitudes to participating in organizational knowledge processes. As will be seen, it has been generally found that the lower the level of trust a person has in someone else, the less willing they will be to share knowledge with them. However, this section also highlights the complexity of the concept of trust, and thus after providing a general definition of it and outlining how levels of trust affect attitudes to knowledge sharing, the concept will be unpacked through considering both the distinction between trust and a person's 'propensity to trust', as well as the typologies of distinctive types of trust that have been developed.

The crucial role of trust in shaping people's willingness to participate in knowledge-related processes has also been recognized by a growing number of writers (Abrams *et al.* 2003; Andrews and Delahaye 2000; Ardichvili *et al.* 2003; Holste and Fields 2010; Levin and Cross 2004; Mooradian *et al.* 2006; Newell *et al.* 2007; Seba *et al.* 2012; Zhou *et al.* 2010). Fundamentally, a lack of trust between individuals is likely to inhibit the extent to which they are willing to share knowledge with each other. To understand why this is the case it is useful to formally define what trust is and how it shapes the character of interpersonal relationships.

Trust can be defined as 'the willingness of a party to be vulnerable to the actions of another party based on the expectation that the other will perform a particular action important to the trustor' (Mooradian *et al.* 2006: 524). Therefore, if trust exists, a person is likely to act on faith by the unilateral provision of resources, information, etc. (in this context giving knowledge), with the expectation that this action will be reciprocated at some point in the future. Thus trust involves an element of risk, where a person makes themselves vulnerable to another by providing knowledge prior to receiving anything in return (with one risk being that the other acts opportunistically and doesn't provide anything in return). The existence of trust in a person helps mediate and reduce the perception of risk people experience, and provides a level of confidence that their action will be reciprocated.

DEFINITION Trust

The belief people have about the likely behaviour of others, and the assumption that they will honour their obligations (not acting opportunistically). A trusting relationship is based on an expectation of reciprocity, or mutual benefit.

However, sharing knowledge on the basis of trust arguably involves an unavoidable element of uncertainty, and can thus be a process which produces and is shaped by emotion (see earlier section in this chapter for a discussion on the relationship between uncertainty and emotion). Knowledge sharing can be a time-consuming and uncertain process. Not only is there uncertainty whether someone will reciprocate a trust-based action, but even when there is reciprocation there will be an element of uncertainty regarding the utility of

 Illustration   Trust and the sharing and use of tacit knowledge

Holste and Fields (2010) investigated whether trust affected both the extent to which people share tacit knowledge with others, and the extent to which they used the tacit knowledge that had been provided by others. They conceptualized trust as having two forms: affect-based trust and competence-based trust. Affect-based trust is trust in the person, which is developed through personal relationships and knowledge of the person and a sense of mutual care existing in the relationship. Competence-based trust by contrast is trust in a person's level of competence and reliability to carry out particular tasks or activities. Holste and Fields conducted a survey-based study of some managerial staff in the headquarters of an international non-profit organization that supports the work of missionaries. Surveys were completed by 202 of the 263 people who were invited to participate in the study. While both forms of trust were positively related to the sharing and use of knowledge, affect-based trust was more strongly linked to the sharing of tacit knowledge, while competence-based trust was more strongly linked to the use of tacit knowledge. Thus they concluded that trust in the relationship with others played a key role in the sharing of tacit knowledge, but that when it came to using tacit knowledge that had been provided by others, people's trust in the competence of others was more fundamentally important.

Table 9.2 Newell and Swan's Three Types of Trust

Type of Trust	Description of Trust
Companion	Trust based on judgements of goodwill or friendship, built up over time
Competence	Trust based on perception of others' competence to carry out relevant tasks
Commitment	Trust stemming from contractual obligations

Source: Newell and Swan 2000, see also Newell *et al.* 2007.

the knowledge received. Acting on the basis of trust, due to the uncertainty involved, can therefore generate and produce strong emotions, both positive and negative, with, for example, someone feeling anger when their trust has been betrayed, or where someone feels a sense of happiness and joy when a trust-based action is effectively reciprocated.

Research has found trust to be a complex concept. One aspect of this is the distinction that can be made between a person's general propensity to trust others and specific instances where trust exists in particular people (Mooradian *et al.* 2006). Mooradian *et al.* conceptualize a person's propensity to trust as being a relatively enduring predisposition they have which is a facet of the personality trait, 'agreeableness', one of the five dimensions in the five-factor personality model (see later section in this chapter on the five-factor model). Thus the propensity to trust is a 'general willingness to trust others' (Mooradian *et al.* 2006: 525) which can vary significantly between people. In contrast, the act of trusting is a specific instance in a particular context and at a particular time, where trust is extended to or developed in a particular entity (person, group, organization). Mooradian *et al.* argue that the greater a person's propensity to trust, the more likely they will be to extend trust to others in specific contexts. As will be discussed later, they examine how a person's propensity to trust is related to knowledge-sharing attitudes and conclude that this personality variable can influence people's general willingness to share knowledge with others.

A number of analyses introduce another layer of complexity by suggesting that trust has multiple dimensions and that there is more than one type of trust. For instance Wang *et al.* (2006) distinguish between calculus-, knowledge-, and identification-based trust, Zhou *et al.* (2010) and Holste and Fields (2010) differentiate between affect- and competition-based trust, while Lee *et al.* (2010) talk of reliance and disclosure-based trust (see Chapter 15). Further, this work suggests that each type of trust is developed in quite different ways, and that they have a complex, mutually interdependent relationship. However, there is inadequate space here to fully describe, compare, and contrast these different typologies. Instead, one typology is examined to highlight a particular way of conceptualizing trust into different types.

In Newell and Swan's (2000) three-dimensional typology (see Table 9.2), companion-based trust represents typically the strongest form of trust that can exist. This form of trust is developed over time and is built up gradually based on perception of acts of goodwill and generosity. Thus this form of trust cannot develop quickly, and requires extensive interaction to occur between people. Competence-based trust is the second of Newell and Swan's trust types and relates to trust in a person's ability to carry out work tasks. Finally, the third form of trust in Newell and Swan's typology is commitment-based trust, which relates to trust stemming from contractual obligations that a person has made. For example, if someone has made an explicit commitment to help someone, or has committed to a formal contract to provide some resources or services, this can result in a form of commitment-based trust developing (based on the expectation that, if an explicit promise has been made, this means there is a reasonable chance the person is likely to keep it).

Typically, interpersonal relations at work with colleagues will involve elements of all three forms of trust. Thus, if two colleagues who have known each other for a number of years have to collaborate in a particular project team there may be an element of companion- and competence-based trust due to the personal relationship that may exist between them and their confidence in each other's ability from knowing how they have performed on previous projects. Further, there may be an element of commitment-based trust due to promises that may have been made to do particular tasks within particular timescales. However, interpersonal trust may also be based on one element alone.

The final issue touched on here is the fact that trust can be developed not only in individual people, but also in groups, teams, or organizations, and that these types of trust can have an equally important influence on a person's willingness to share knowledge with others. For example, Renzl (2008) found evidence that the greater the extent to which workers trusted their managers the more likely they would be to have a positive attitude to sharing knowledge with colleagues. Ardichvili *et al.* (2003) reached similar conclusions based on their analysis of what factors shaped workers' willingness to contribute knowledge within a virtual community of practice. They talked about institution-based trust, which referred to the extent to which people trusted the organization to provide a working environment conducive to positive knowledge sharing and where people were unwilling to act opportunistically or excessively selfishly. They found that workers were likely to contribute knowledge to the virtual community of practice when this form of trust existed, as they were confident that others wouldn't use this knowledge opportunistically. Finally, Usoro *et al.* (2007)—see following section, and the communities of practice literature more generally (see Chapter 10)—suggest that the greater a person's level of trust in and identification with a particular work group or community, the more likely they will be to be willing to share knowledge with others in that community/group.

The issue of trust links to themes examined in a number of the remaining chapters in this section of the book. First, it is relevant in Chapter 10 on communities of practice where the nature of interpersonal relations in communities of practice, where groups of people have shared identity and values, facilitates the development of high levels of trust among community members, which has positive consequences for intra-community knowledge sharing. Trust is also examined in Chapter 11, on group-based working where people do not have shared values and identity, which makes the development of trust more difficult. Finally, issues of trust are also engaged with in Chapter 13 on the role of information technology in knowledge management processes, where it is suggested that in situations where people have to collaborate and communicate extensively via electronic means, and where opportunities for face-to-face interaction are limited, the development of high levels of interpersonal trust may be difficult.

Group Identity

This section examines how issues of personal identity can affect the extent to which and ways in which workers participate in organizational knowledge processes. As will be seen, research has shown that the extent to which people feel a part of and identify with their organization, a project team, a work group, or a community of practice can significantly shape their willingness to participate in knowledge processes. For example, Chapter 6 noted how knowledge-intensive workers can identify strongly with the clients they work for, with Ravishankar and Pan (2008) presenting an example from an Indian IT consultancy firm of where the sense of identity some staff had with the client firm made them unwilling to participate in their employer's knowledge management initiative due to concerns that they would give away valuable client knowledge to colleagues.

Further, the extensive literature on communities of practice (see Chapter 10) suggests that when people feel a sense of identity with a community this facilitates the development of trust with other community members and is likely to create a positive attitude towards sharing knowledge with other community members. For example, Usoro *et al.* (2007), who examined a virtual, IT-mediated community of practice in a Fortune 500 global IT company, found that people's level of community trust was positively related to knowledge sharing.

Finally, a number of studies have shown how worker's identity with the particular functional group or business unit that they work in can influence their knowledge-sharing patterns, with it being common for people who have a strong sense of identity with their function or business unit being relatively unwilling to share knowledge with people from outside of these areas (see e.g. Hislop 2003). For example, Rosendaal (2009) found that the more people identified with the teams they worked in, the more likely they were to share knowledge with other team members. Further, Currie and Kerrin's (2003) study of the sales and marketing business of a UK-based pharmaceutical company found that the existence of strong subcultures within the sales and marketing divisions created an unwillingness among staff to share knowledge across these functional boundaries.

All this research thus suggests that one of the key effects of a worker's sense of identity is to influence who they are and are not willing to share knowledge with. The issues touched on here will be examined more extensively in Chapter 10 which looks at the characteristics of knowledge processes within communities of practices, where people have a strong sense of shared identity, and in Chapter 11, which examines knowledge processes where people do not have such a strong sense of shared identity, such as in cross-functional, or multidisciplinary team working.

National Culture

The extent to which national cultural characteristics shape people's attitude to participation in knowledge management activities is a subject that only partial and limited knowledge exists on as it has not been extensively or systematically researched.

Much of the analysis which links issues of national culture to knowledge management has come from studies of cross-national collaborations, where cultural differences have been found to play a significant role. For example, this was the case with Inkpen and Pien's (2006) study of Chinese–Singaporean collaboration (see Chapter 11), Li's (2010) study of IT-based communication between workers from the USA and China, and Chen *et al.*'s (2010) study of knowledge transfer between workers from Canada, the USA, and China.

The assumption that a person's cultural background will shape their attitude to knowledge, and knowledge management activities is something that is explicitly acknowledged within practice-based epistemology (see Chapter 3). Thus, as was outlined, this epistemology suggests that people's knowledge and understanding, what counts as valid types of knowledge, etc., will be shaped by cultural factors, including national cultural characteristics. This idea has been reinforced by a number of published studies which have looked specifically at how the characteristics of particular cultural values impact on people's knowledge management activities (see e.g. Huang *et al.* 2008; McAdam *et al.* 2012; Tong and Mitra 2009—see illustration). Kanzler (2010) on German and Chinese scientists is a good example of such research, showing how the attitudes of the scientists from both countries to knowledge sharing appeared to be shaped by national cultural characteristics. For example, in the study it was found that concerns about a loss of power were negatively related to the intention to share knowledge of the German, but not the Chinese scientists. Kanzler argued that this was because German society is more individualistic than Chinese society and so concerns about a loss of power due to sharing and 'giving up' knowledge were greater for the German scientists.

 Illustration   The influence of Chinese culture on knowledge sharing

Tong and Mitra (2009) conducted a qualitative case study of a Chinese mobile phone manufacturer to investigate the effect national cultural characteristics had on people's knowledge management practices. Data were collected via the observation of people at work, and also through conducting qualitative, semi-structured interviews with a range of managers and research and development staff from the company. One way in which they found Chinese culture to influence knowledge sharing was in interactions between experienced and more junior members of staff. Due to the level of hierarchy consciousness that exists within Chinese culture, it was normal for junior staff to be expected to follow the guidance and instructions of experienced staff, but typically not to challenge or contradict them, even when they believed them to be wrong. Thus, one junior member of staff said, 'I think this traditional teaching method . . . can force me to learn knowledge from an experienced staff member fast. But because he is my teacher, and I am new staff, I do not really want to disagree with his out-of-date suggestions.' This reluctance of junior employees to express opinions that challenged experienced workers was also due to cultural concerns about losing face. Another interviewee said, 'I believe nobody likes to be embarrassed in public. But this is a little bigger matter for the old employees.'

How national cultural factors influence cross-national collaborations and processes of knowledge sharing will be considered in Chapter 11 on cross-community knowledge processes, as cross-national collaboration can be conceptualized as a cross-community form of

Table 9.3 Characteristics of the Traits in the Five-Factor Personality Model

Trait	Characteristics
Openness (or openness to change)	The extent to which someone is imaginative, creative, and curious
Extraversion	The extent to which someone is sociable, talkative, enthusiastic, and assertive
Neuroticism	The extent to which someone experiences negative emotions such as anxiety, anger, or guilt
Conscientiousness	The extent to which someone is careful, self-disciplined, hard-working, dependable, and reliable
Agreeableness	The extent to which someone is generous, trustful, cooperative, and forgiving

collaboration. These issues are also touched on in Chapter 13 which considers the role of ICTs in knowledge management activities, where the not insignificant challenges of ICT-mediated cross-national knowledge processes are examined.

Personality

The final factor considered which may shape workers' attitudes to participating in knowledge management processes is not related to the socio-cultural characteristics of the work environment, but is concerned with personality. Fundamentally, some research suggests that people with certain personality traits may have a more positive attitude to knowledge sharing than others. However, in general, this is a very under-explored topic in the knowledge management literature.

A number of studies in this area have concluded that certain personality traits did appear to be positively related to knowledge-sharing attitudes. All the studies in this area (Cabrera and Cabrera 2005; Mooradian *et al.* 2006) make use of the five-factor personality model (see Matzler *et al.* illustration). This personality model, which is becoming the dominant way of conceptualizing personality, suggests that human personality can be understood to be made up of five broad traits: openness, conscientiousness, extraversion, agreeableness, and neuroticism (see Table 9.3).

However, despite these studies using the same personality model, they come to different conclusions about which personality traits are related to positive knowledge-sharing attitudes. Thus, Cabrera and Cabrera's (2005) research found that the 'openness to change' personality variable was related to a positive knowledge-sharing attitude. By contrast, Mooradian *et al.*'s (2006) study found a link between 'agreeableness' and positive knowledge-sharing attitudes. Further, all these studies are based on surveys conducted in single organizations, so their findings cannot be regarded as generalizable. Therefore research in this area is in its infancy and is inconclusive regarding exactly how personality relates to a person's propensity to share knowledge or their willingness to participate in any organizational knowledge processes.

Illustration   Personality traits and attitude to knowledge sharing

Matzler *et al.* (2011) found that the personality variables of agreeableness and conscientiousness were positively linked to knowledge-sharing activities. Matzler et al.'s analysis is based on a study of 150 workers from within an Austrian utility company. The conceptual model they tested suggested that agreeableness would be positively linked to levels of affective commitment to the organization, while conscientiousness would be positively linked to the extent to which people document their knowledge. The model also suggested that levels of affective commitment and the extent to which people document their knowledge would be positively linked to the extent to which people share knowledge. The statistical analysis they undertook of the survey data collected supported all the hypotheses that were tested, and provided support for the conceptual model. Thus, this study supports the idea that the personality variables of agreeableness and conscientiousness are linked to knowledge sharing.

 ## Conclusion

Fundamentally this chapter has shown that human, social, and cultural factors are typically key to the success of knowledge management initiatives. This is because they have a significant influence on the extent to which workers are willing to participate in such initiatives, and that without such willingness the knowledge management initiatives are unlikely to succeed, as the resource they are focused on managing and sharing, workers' knowledge, will remain locked in the worker's head.

The chapter conceptualized the decision workers face about whether to participate in such initiatives as being comparable to a public good dilemma, where people's actions are shaped by how they evaluate the potential consequences of the various options they have. However, a caveat was added by suggesting that account needs to be taken of emotion in decision-making as it was problematic to conceptualize workers as purely rational decision-makers.

The chapter highlighted a number of key socio-cultural factors which can play a crucial role in shaping workers' motivation to participate in knowledge management initiatives. First, the nature of the employment relationship means that in relation to knowledge management initiatives the interests of workers and their employers may not always be compatible. Secondly, the typically conflictual nature of intra-organizational relations was also found to shape the character of organizational knowledge management initiatives. Thirdly, interpersonal trust was found to be important, with a lack of trust likely to inhibit the extent to which people are willing to share knowledge with each other. Fourthly, the role of personal identity was also found to be important, with a person's identity often shaping who they were and were not willing to share knowledge with. Fifthly, national cultural characteristics have been found to shape people's attitudes to knowledge processes. Finally the role of personality in shaping people's general proclivity to share knowledge was also highlighted.

This chapter to some extent has acted as a springboard to the remaining chapter in this part by giving an introduction to key socio-cultural issues. Many of the factors examined here can be influenced by how management in an organization act. These issues have been deliberately avoided here as they are examined in Chapters 14 and 15 which consider the role that human resource management culture management, and leadership practices can play in dealing with these issues and encouraging workers to participate fully in organizational knowledge management initiatives.

Case study Problems with the management of patient safety knowledge within the UK's National Health Service

Currie *et al.* (2008) report the findings of a study into the effectiveness of an IT-based knowledge management system that was implemented within the UK's National Health Service and was concerned with improving patient safety (the National Reporting and Learning System, NRLS). The logic underpinning the implementation of the system was that levels of patient safety could be improved if information on safety-related incidents was recorded and disseminated via the NRLS, as the system would allow knowledge and experience on patient-safety issues to be shared throughout the NHS. However, the system did not meet its objectives because many people were unwilling to codify their knowledge and experience on the system, there were problems with recording or understanding the information that was recorded on the system, and there were also disputes about the status and validity of what was recorded on the system. Currie *et al.* characterize the failure of the system as being due to issues of epistemology, culture, and politics.

Currie *et al.*'s paper is based on a detailed qualitative study of how the NRLS was used within one hospital. Research data were collected via both direct observation of people and interviews with key personnel. Observations were done at a range of locations, from corporate-level activities down to the level of hospital wards and operating theatres, with about 500 hours of observation in all. Forty-three interviews were conducted with a range of staff including nurses, doctors/consultants, administrators, and medical managers. The data collected gave detailed insights into how the NRLS was actually used in practice.

Before giving an overview of one part of Currie *et al.*'s findings, it is necessary to provide some background information on the specific characteristics of the professional, cultural, and structural context of the NHS. Overall, this was a context in which the type of knowledge sharing required to make the NRLS successful was unlikely to occur. First, a modernization agenda has seen the implementation of managerialist principles. This agenda was often challenged and resisted by medical practitioners. Thus there was a 'them and us' culture between managers and medical practitioners, with practitioners being concerned that the primary focus of managers was the management of budgets rather than the provision of high-quality care. Secondly, in relation to the type of patient-safety incidents that the NRLS was intended to record, there was a predominant 'culture of blame', which meant that people were typically reluctant to share knowledge on patient-safety issues due to fears of being blamed for any problems. Finally, the knowledge possessed by medical staff was highly tacit, and the status/legitimacy of people's knowledge was often open to dispute due to the different professions and related bodies of knowledge that people drew upon.

These issues had a significant impact on the way the NRLS was used, which can be illustrated by looking at a couple of issues that emerged. One of the most fundamental challenges to the identification of safety-related incidents, which was both cultural and epistemological, was that the large number of professional groups involved in the provision of patient care meant that issues of risk and safety were perceived very differently by different people. Thus one person said: 'the way people think about risk, error and clinical governance varies across specializations'. One specific example of this was a dispute regarding sterilization procedures that existed between a surgeon and a nurse, with the surgeon choosing not to follow a sterilization procedure that the nurse regarded as vitally important. The nurse's attempts to have this incident recorded as an incident on the NRLS was prevented when the relevant clinical director supported the actions of the surgeon. Another example of the cultural, epistemological, and political issues affecting the use of the NRLS related to how information was captured. First, clinical staff did not like the closed-style questions on the system, which they felt prevented them from accurately recording incidents. As one interviewee said, 'you can't get all the relevant information on the forms'. Secondly, non-clinical staff were suspicious that clinical staff weren't providing accurate details of incidents, with one manager saying: 'people are biased in their presentation of events. They can present a select view of things, probably through a concern they might look like idiots'. Overall this meant that the accuracy and authenticity of the incidents that were recorded were disputed, with there often being conflicting perspectives developed by clinical and managerial staff regarding the same incidents.

1. Given the character of the cultural context within which the NRLS was implemented was its success always likely to be limited?

Source: Currie, G., Waring, J., and Finn, R. (2008) 'The Limits of Knowledge Management for UK Public Services Modernization: The Case of Patient Safety and Service Quality', *Public Administration*, 86/2: 363–85.

 ## Review and Discussion Questions

1. Based on your own experience, what has been the attitude of work colleagues to sharing their knowledge? Have you found them to be willing to share, or has hoarding been more typical? What are the most important factors which explain this behaviour?

2. How compatible have your and your employing organization's interests been with regard to how you have used your knowledge? Have the organization's goals and your own always been harmonious, or has there been any conflict and tension over how you use your knowledge?

3. Have you found trust to be an important factor underpinning attitudes to knowledge sharing? Have you had any experiences where a lack of trust has inhibited knowledge sharing, or where the existence of trust has facilitated it?

4. To what extent is people's behaviour at work (whether concerned with knowledge sharing or not) shaped by rationality and decision-making, and to what extent is it shaped by emotion and subjective feelings?

 ## Suggestions for Further Reading

1. B. Van den Hooff, A. Schouten, and S. Simonovski (2012). 'What one Feels and What one Knows: The Influence of Emotions on Attitudes and Intentions towards Knowledge Sharing', *Journal of Knowledge Management*, 16/1: 148–58.

2. K. Matzler, B. Renzl, T. Mooradian, G. von Krogh, and J. Mueller (2011) 'Personality Traits, Affective Commitment, Documentation of Knowledge and Knowledge Sharing', *International Journal of Human Resource Management*, 22/2: 296–310.

A study which highlights the role that personality plays in shaping people's general attitudes to knowledge sharing.

3. R. McAdam, S. Moffett, and J. Peng (2012) 'Knowledge Sharing in Chinese Service Organizations: A Multi Case Cultural Perspective', *Journal of Knowledge Management*, 16/1: 129–47.

A study of Chinese workers which highlights how national cultural characteristics shape the way they share and manage their personal knowledge.

4. S. Newell, G. David, and D. Chand (2007) 'An Analysis of Trust among Globally Distributed Work Teams in an Organizational Setting', *Knowledge and Process Management*, 14/3: 158–68.

Highlights the crucial role of interpersonal trust (of different types) in shaping attitudes to knowledge sharing within geographically dispersed and culturally diverse work teams.

Take your learning further: Online Resource Centre

Visit the Online Resource Centre for resources which will extend your understanding of knowledge management in organizations. As well as web links to sites of interest, the author has provided case studies looking at knowledge management in virtual and knowledge-intensive firms, and in global multinationals. These will help you with your research, essays, and assignments; or you may find these additional resources helpful when revising for exams.

 www.oxfordtextbooks.co.uk/orc/hislop3e/

Communities of Practice

Introduction

In the vast literature on knowledge management that has been produced, the concept of 'communities of practice' has been one of the most popular. This is evident in the large quantity of academic articles and books that have been published on the topic (see e.g. Amin and Roberts 2008, Hughes *et al.* 2008). The popularity of the term is largely because communities of practice are argued to facilitate interpersonal knowledge sharing (e.g. allowing IT professionals who work in different companies to share knowledge and ideas—see Moran 2010), can support and underpin innovation processes in organizations (Bertels *et al.* 2011), and have the potential to help improve organizational performance (Bradley *et al.* 2011). Thus, a growing number of writers suggest that developing communities of practice can provide an effective means for people and organizations to manage and share knowledge.

Communities of practice are informal groups of people who have some work-related activity in common. As will be seen, the communities of practice literature is most closely associated with the practice-based perspective on knowledge, as it assumes that the knowledge people have is embedded in and inseparable from the (collectively based) activities that people carry out. The informality of these communities stems from the fact that they emerge from the social interactions that are a necessary part of the work activities that people undertake. Further, while most of the literature on communities of practice focuses on organizationally specific communities, communities can span organizational boundaries (see the Bettiol and Sedita 2011 illustration). For example, Gittelman and Kogut (2003) conceptualize the researchers involved in the biotechnology industry in the USA as constituting a community of practice.

This chapter has a very specific focus, discussing and analysing the *internal dynamics* of communities of practice. The character and dynamics of inter-community knowledge processes are explored in Chapter 11. Chapters 10 and 11 can therefore be read together, as they both examine the dynamics of group-based knowledge processes. The reason for doing this in two chapters rather than one is that, as will be discussed more fully in Chapter 11, the character and dynamics of intra- and inter-community knowledge processes are qualitatively different. Further, the dynamics of knowledge processes within 'virtual' communities, where personal interactions are typically via electronic means rather than via face-to-face meetings, are discussed in Chapter 13.

Communities of Practice: Basic Characteristics

Communities of practice are groups of individuals who have some form of practice or activity in common, for example, an informal group of IT staff within an organization which has responsibility for designing and maintaining similar IT systems. These groups are typically informal, and *ad hoc* in nature, developing out of the communication and interaction which is a necessary part of most work activities. Unlike formalized work groups, and teams, they do not represent a part of the formal organizational structure and therefore typically do not appear on organization charts (see Table 10.1).

Historically, such groups have been treated with hostility by senior management, who may be concerned about how these groups may undermine formal structures and systems (Brown and Duguid 1991). However, due to the increasing acknowledgement of the role they can play in facilitating knowledge sharing, organizations have been attempting more and more often to deliberately support and develop communities of practice (see examples later, such as Borzillo *et al.* 2011). By their very nature, however, communities of practice are not easily amenable to deliberate management and control. The contradictions of attempting to formalize such inherently informal interactions are not insignificant, and will be discussed later.

Table 10.1 Difference between a CoP and Formal Work Groups

	Community of Practice	Organizational Work Group/Team
Objective	Evolving Shaped by common values Internally negotiated	Clear, formally defined Externally determined
Focus of Efforts	Collective practice/knowledge	Provide specific service and/or product
Membership	Voluntary	Typically formalized and delegated (though occasionally voluntary)
Government of Internal Structure	Consensually negotiated Non-hierarchical	Formalized division of labour Hierarchical structure Individualized roles and responsibilities
External System of Management and Control	Self-managing Informal, interpersonal relations	Formalized relations defined by organizational hierarchy Performance monitoring against specific targets, goals
Timeframe	Indefinite, internally negotiated	Permanent, or with finite timeframe/objective

Illustration A community of practice among designers in Turin

Bettiol and Sedita (2011) describe the characteristics of a community of practice that developed in Turin among graphic/industrial designers and architects in the city. The community started in the mid-2000s in the immediate aftermath of the Winter Olympics, and after Turin was nominated to be the first World Design Capital. Some designers in Turin decided to try and build/sustain the city's reputation for design that these events stimulated. A number of people were key in developing the community, which by 2009 involved 53 design studios and 119 designers. The aims of the community were to both help sustain Turin's reputation for design, and to also allow individual designers and studios to share knowledge and ideas with each other. One potential benefit to individual designers of participation in the community was that they could find out about job opportunities in different studios. Knowledge was shared among community members via formal events organized by community members and also informally, when community members met up individually or in groups at non-community events. The community also helped forge a sense of identity among the designers, with Bettiol and Sedita (p. 476) concluding that the community became a 'hotbed for sensemaking and building of meaningful relationships among people who share a common identity'.

DEFINITION Community of practice

A group of people who have a particular activity in common, and as a consequence have some common knowledge, a sense of community identity, and some element of overlapping values.

Communities of Practice: Origins, Features, and Dynamics

The community of practice concept is based on two central premises: the practice-based perspective on knowledge, and the group-based character of organizational activity. The primary relevance of the practice-based perspective on knowledge stems from the assumption in the communities of practice literature that knowing and doing are inseparable, as undertaking specific tasks requires the use and development of embodied knowledge. The second major premise is that organizational activities are typically collective, involving the coordinated interaction of groups of workers. Thus, one common feature of virtually every type of work imaginable, from office cleaning to management consulting, is that they involve an element of coordination and interaction with co-workers, subordinates, and/or supervisors.

Therefore, while the knowledge that members of a community of practice have and develop is highly personal, there is an extent to which much of this knowledge is simultaneously shared within a community. From an objectivist perspective on knowledge, the common knowledge shared by the workers in a community of practice is collective/group knowledge (with both tacit and explicit elements: see Table 2.3).

Lave and Wenger (1991), who are typically acknowledged as being instrumental in the development and elaboration of the community of practice concept, define them as a community of practitioners within which situational learning develops, which results in the community developing, 'a set of relations among persons, activity and the world' (p. 98).

Table 10.2 Generic Characteristics of Communities of Practice

Characteristics of a Community of Practice
Body of common knowledge/practice
Sense of shared identity
Some common, or overlapping values

Extrapolating from this definition, communities of practice can be seen to have three defining characteristics, all of which flow from the community members' involvement in some shared activities (Table 10.2). First, participants in a community possess and develop a stock of common, shared knowledge. Secondly, communities typically also develop shared values and attitudes, a common 'world-view'. Finally, and equally importantly, members of communities also possess a sense of communal identity (Brown and Duguid 2001; Bettiol and Sedita 2011). These elements of a community develop not only through the physical activities involved in collectively carrying out the communities' tasks, but also through language and communication. Thus, for example, stories, or specialist jargon can be regarded as a part of the collective knowledge of the group, whose use by group members contributes to their sense of collective identity and shared values.

A useful way to illustrate these characteristics is through an example. Trowler and Turner (2002) illustrate how the Deaf Studies group of an English university constitutes a community of practice. This group consisted of three hearing academics (who are fluent in sign language) and three deaf academics. The shared practice of this community constituted both the teaching of the Deaf Studies curriculum, as well as research conducted by the group on a range of issues affecting deaf people. This group had a strong sense of collective identity, as well as a belief in a common goal (contributing to the education of deaf people and their integration in society, raising awareness of the social issues affecting deaf people, and furthering knowledge on the issues which affect deaf people through carrying out research).

 Time to reflect   Language and communities of practice?

Are you or have you ever been a member of a community of practice? What role, if any did language, in the form of specialist jargon and shared stories, play in the development and reinforcement of the community?

Communities of practice are highly dynamic, evolving as new members become absorbed into a community, as existing members leave, and as the knowledge and practices of the community adapt with changing circumstances (e.g. Mørk et al. 2012). Learning and knowledge evolution are therefore inherent and fundamental aspects of the dynamics of communities of practice, which helps explain why one of the main contexts in which the community of practice concept originated and developed was in the organizational learning literature.

Lave and Wenger (1991) used the term 'legitimate peripheral participation' to characterize the process by which people learn and become socialized into being a member of a community. This process is based on 'triadic' group relations involving masters (or 'old timers'), young masters (or 'journeymen'), and apprentices (or 'newcomers'). Apprentices learn from watching and communicating with the master and other members of the community, and start as peripheral members, participating initially in relatively straightforward tasks. However, over time, as the apprentices become competent in these basic skills, they gradually become introduced to more complex tasks. Legitimate peripheral participation is thus the process by which newcomers to a community acquire the knowledge required to be a community member, through gradually increasing levels of *participation* in community activities, during which time they simultaneously move from being *peripheral* members of the community to become more central and *legitimate* members of it. Informal learning from other group members is a key element of this process, or as Trowler and Turner (2002: 242) suggest, 'learning to become an organizational member is far more a question of socialization than of formal learning'.

Communities of Practice and Intra-Community Knowledge Processes

Almost universally, the communities of practice literature considers communities of practice to be advantageous for both individuals and organizations. Thus they provide workers with a sense of collective identity, and a social context in which they are argued to have the potential to effectively develop and utilize their knowledge. For organizations, they can provide a vital source of innovation. The knowledge management literature, which has utilized the communities of practice concept, argues that they can facilitate organizational knowledge processes. The rest of this section considers the potential benefits in terms of knowledge processes that communities of practice can provide.

Communities of practice have the potential to provide benefits in two broad areas. First, communities of practice can underpin levels of organizational innovativeness through supporting and encouraging the creation, development, and use of knowledge. Thus, Orr (1990) showed how the community of practice that existed amongst Xerox's photocopy repair engineers allowed these workers to develop their knowledge and understanding through solving problems that could not be corrected by simply following the knowledge encoded in instruction manuals. Secondly, the common knowledge possessed by members of a community of practice, combined with their sense of collective identity, and system of shared values, means they have the potential to facilitate individual and group learning, and the sharing of knowledge within the community.

The advantages of communities of practice in enabling such knowledge processes are closely related to the elements that members of a community share (see Figure 10.1). As outlined earlier, members of a community of practice not only have a stock of common knowledge, but also have a shared sense of identity, and some overlapping, common values. The simultaneous existence of these elements enables knowledge processes, as they simplify the communication of knowledge that is inherently sticky: tacit knowledge.

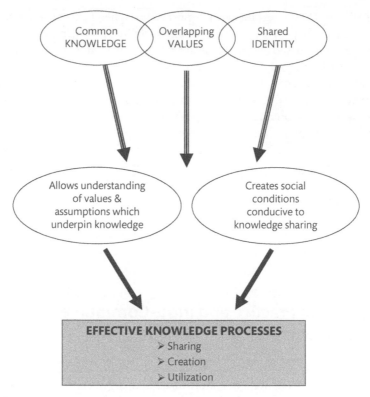

Figure 10.1 How Communities of Practice Underpin Knowledge Processes

First, the existence of these three elements make appreciating the taken for granted assumptions and values which underpin tacit knowledge easier to understand. Secondly, the existence of these elements is likely to produce and sustain trust-based relations, creating social conditions that are conducive to knowledge sharing (see Chapter 9 for a discussion of how identity and group-based identities can affect people's knowledge-sharing behaviours).

Managing Communities of Practice

In discussing how to explicitly manage communities of practice, the difficulties, contradictions, and risks of doing (or attempting to do) this need to be highlighted. The contradictions and difficulties related to managing communities of practice stem from their fundamentally informal, emergent, and somewhat *ad hoc* nature (see Table 10.1). These characteristics mean that communities of practice are not easily amenable to top-down control. Communities of practice are autonomous, self-managing systems, which can exist and flourish without the need for any senior management support (Baumard 1999). Managerial attempts to control and influence communities of practice may therefore conflict with a community's system of self-management. The risk in attempting to explicitly manage communities of practice is that such attempts may in fact have adverse effects on the community, and the very knowledge processes that such efforts are intended to support and develop become undermined (see e.g. Anand *et al.* 2007; Thompson 2005). For example, attempts to formalize a community may introduce rigidities which inhibit its innovativeness or adaptability.

However, despite these difficulties and potential problems, more and more organizations are attempting to develop and support communities of practice as part of their knowledge management initiatives. This section considers the ways in which this can be done. Due to the narrow focus of this chapter, only issues related to managing and supporting individual communities and intra-community knowledge processes are examined. The managerial implications of coordinating inter-community relations and knowledge processes are discussed separately, in Chapter 11.

The literature typically suggests that management should not play a role in initiating communities of practice, as this is contradictory to their fundamental character, but that there is scope to facilitate and manage communities that exist. In general terms, the knowledge management literature advocates two main ways in which communities of practice, once formed, can be managed and supported. First, it is argued that their management should be done with a 'light touch'. Secondly, all management interventions should reinforce the essential attributes of communities that make them so effective at facilitating knowledge processes.

Advocates of the 'light touch' approach to managing communities of practice include Anand *et al.* (2007), McDermott (1999), and Ward (2000). Thus, McDermott suggests that organizations should 'develop natural knowledge communities without formalizing them' (p. 110). Ward, utilizing a garden metaphor, argues that communities of practice require to be, 'tended and nurtured rather than commanded and controlled' (p. 4). The gardening metaphor, suggesting the communities of practice have organic qualities and are continually adapting and evolving, usefully captures the informal and emergent aspect of communities of practice. For example, Thompson (2005) suggests that managerial initiatives that are too directive or controlling of workers may inhibit communities. The limitation of this managerial advice is that it is often somewhat vague, and lacking in detail. Thus, the analyses that advocate such an approach typically fail to provide specific details on what the 'light touch' management approach looks like, or consists of.

More concrete is the second type of advice, to reinforce the best attributes of communities of practice. This advice covers a range of issues including:

- Emphasize practice-based, peer-supported learning methods rather than formalized, classroom-based methods as this reinforces the existing ways that communities learn and share knowledge (Brown and Duguid 1991; Stamps 2000).

- Have specific people within a community undertaking organizing roles which have the objective of sustaining and developing the community (see Borzillo *et al.* 2011 illustration).

- Due to the significant length of time required for communities of practice to develop (to allow the creation of a common perspective, and a stock of common knowledge, as well as a sense of collective identity) continuity is important (Baumard 1999). Overly discontinuous social relations are thus likely to hamper their development.

Illustration   Managing and supporting communities of practice

Borzillo *et al.* (2011) examined nine communities of practice within seven multinational corporations. While they varied in terms of the degree of management support provided, and also in terms of their size and characteristics (the smallest had 40 members and the largest 400) Borzillo *et al.* develop a general model of how people's relationships to and involvement with communities evolved over time. However, the focus here is on the various ways in which these communities were managed. Arguably, the main way that these communities were managed was via key community members (defined as 'core members') taking on organizing roles within the communities. These roles were community leaders, facilitators, content coordinators, and community supporters.

Specific roles played by facilitators include the advertising of community events to community members and non-members, as well as mentoring new members, and helping to network and link together community members who may have some specific shared interests. Content coordinators played the role of subject-matter experts, and provided knowledge and information in response to questions and queries. Finally, the community support role involved organizing or providing resources that facilitated community activities, such as IT resources. The most demanding and time-intensive role was that of community leader, with a community leader taking a lead in any activity deemed useful for sustaining or developing the community.

Borzillo *et al.* also found that communities that were supported by organizational management tended to integrate and involve new members more quickly than voluntary communities. This was for a number of reasons, including that management more actively marketed and advertised sponsored communities, that the financial resources provided to sponsored communities facilitated their development, and that with sponsored communities there were greater expectations placed on people to participate in them. However, Borzillo *et al.* conclude by suggesting that, for management, getting the balance right between providing autonomy to communities and managing/controlling is not straightforward.

● Find, nurture, and support existing communities (Borzillo *et al.* 2011). McDermott (1999) suggests that the best way to do this is reinforce each community's systems of self-management, for example strengthening their existing mechanisms for social interaction, and providing them with adequate autonomy to allow them to decide and control both what knowledge is important, as well as how it should be organized and shared.

Therefore, a significant amount of advice exists on how communities of practice can best be supported. Ironically, much of this advice suggests that the best way to manage communities is to provide them the autonomy to manage themselves.

 Time to reflect   Managing communities

In your work experience, what have management attitudes to communities of practice been? Were they aware of them? Were they hostile to them? Were they given autonomy to be self-managing? Or were attempts made to facilitate and manage them? Further, did these attitudes and behaviours facilitate or inhibit the operation of these communities?

Finally, it is worth concluding this section by highlighting how some of the features in many contemporary organizations create conditions which make developing and sustaining communities of practice difficult (Roberts 2006). First, Roberts, drawing on Bauman (2007), suggests that the contemporary trend in society towards an increasing sense of individualism, and away from collective and community forms of identity and action, may make people unlikely to develop community-based forms of identity at work. Roberts further suggests that the high level of dynamism and turbulence in many contemporary business and market sectors means the organizations which have to compete in them have to constantly change and adapt, which again may make it difficult to generate and sustain the type of long-term interpersonal relations and sense of community identity necessary for communities of practice to develop.

Critical Perspectives on Communities of Practice

As outlined earlier, much of the communities of practice literature presents communities in a very positive light, suggesting that in relation to knowledge processes they are largely or exclusively beneficial for organizations. The limitation of this idealistic characterization of communities is that it creates a blindness to their potential negative features and the range of ways in which they may inhibit organizational knowledge processes. Arguably much of the communities literature has thus provided a somewhat one-sided, and unbalanced analysis of communities of practice. However, increasingly, a number of writers are examining the ambiguities, problems, and difficulties with both the way communities of practice are conceptualized and their role in organizational knowledge processes.

Four specific issues are examined here. First, how issues of power and conflict can shape the internal dynamics of communities are considered. Secondly, how the diversity in types of community of practice mean that it is increasingly problematic to talk about communities of practice in general terms, and how it is thus important to differentiate between different types of community. Thirdly, there is brief consideration of the way that the popularity of the term means that it is sometimes misused in the literature. Finally, this section closes by considering the way that communities may develop 'blinkers' which can inhibit innovations and inter-community interaction.

Power, conflict, and the internal dynamics of communities

As will be seen in Chapter 12, one of the major criticisms of the majority of the mainstream knowledge management literature is the neglect of issues of power and conflict. The communities of practice literature is no exception to this, and thus, generally, issues of power and conflict within communities are either typically downplayed, or ignored. In *Situated Learning* (1991) Lave and Wenger do discuss these issues, but their appeal for future analyses to take greater account of 'unequal relations of power' (p. 42) within communities has typically been neglected by subsequent writers (the most notable exception being Contu and Willmott 2003; Fox 2000; and Mørk *et al*. 2010). Further, these issues have also been downplayed in some of their own later work, such as Wenger (1998), where, as Fox makes clear, issues of power and conflict are largely relegated to footnotes. While

Wenger *et al.* (2002) devote a whole chapter to the 'downside of communities', issues of power are ignored. One manifestation of this neglect of power and politics in the communities of practice literature is that it typically portrays them as idealistic communities of equals where conflict is rare and where homogeneity exists and consensus is the norm.

However, such perspectives arguably downplay the extent to which communities of practice have inherent tensions built into them which unavoidably result in them possessing an 'unequal distribution of power' (Lave and Wenger 1991: 42), and where what Fox (2000) described as 'power conflicts' are likely. The uneven distribution of power results from the, by definition, greater amount of community knowledge masters have compared to newcomers (Contu and Willmott 2003). While communities of practice do not have a formal hierarchical structure, this does not mean that all members of the community are equal. This uneven distribution of knowledge creates potential conflicts in processes of legitimate peripheral participation. For example, Lave and Wenger (1991: 57) argue that 'There is a fundamental contradiction in the meaning to newcomers and old-timers of increasing participation by the former; for the centripetal development of full participants . . . implies the replacement of old timers'.

Legitimate peripheral participation thus requires the 'old timers' to help develop the knowledge of the 'newcomers' who will, over time, take their place. The contradictions inherent in such a process are fundamental, and unavoidable (see Lave and Wenger 1991: 113–17). Another source of conflict within communities of practice relates to the 'contradictory nature of collective social practice' (Lave and Wenger 1991: 58). Although the members of a community work together collectively and cooperate, they are also simultaneously, to some extent, competing with each other inside their organizations, for example, for promotion opportunities (see the illustration).

◉ Illustration   Innovation, change, and power dynamics within a community of practice

Mørk *et al.* (2010) examined two cases where innovation in medical practices in Norway challenged some existing communities of practice, which resulted in conflict and power dynamics developing. The innovation examined was laparoscopic (keyhole) surgery, where surgical procedures are carried out via inserting a laparoscope and other surgical instruments into patients via small incisions. The advantage of laparoscopic surgery is that it is significantly less invasive than conventional open surgery. However, laparoscopic surgery requires the learning of special surgical techniques, and may thus be seen as threatening the established authority and knowledge of existing surgeons.

One of the cases examined was the use of laparoscopic surgery for treating prostate cancer. The treatment of prostate cancer had traditionally been the responsibility of urologists. However, the development of laparoscopic surgical techniques in this domain was initially done by a non-urological medical team based at the University Hospital in Oslo. To develop their knowledge and expertise in this surgical procedure, the plan was to collaborate with urologists from a range of hospitals. However, the urologists at one of the hospitals involved in initial collaborations with the laparoscopic team suddenly withdrew from the collaborative project, primarily because they wanted their hospital to become a national centre of excellence in this new procedure. This effectively ended the collaboration with the non-urological team from the University Hospital in Oslo. Mørk *et al.* argue that the urologists did this as they regarded the non-urological laparoscopic team from Oslo to be challenging their authority, knowledge, and expertise within the established urological community of practice, which they decided to resist, in order to retain a degree of control over knowledge and practice in this area.

The power conflicts that are an inherent aspect of communities take on greater importance when communities are faced with change, which over time they inevitably are. Change
that requires a community's practices/knowledge to adapt, threatens the status quo (the
reproduction of existing knowledge/practices), and can have contradictory implications for
different members of a community of practice (Fox 2000). Thus old-timers may see such
change as a threat to their status (see the illustration), power, and knowledge, whereas other
members of a community may see it as an opportunity to develop and increase their own
power, knowledge, and status (Handley *et al.* 2006). These insights have two implications
with regard to how communities of practice respond to change, which are both neglected
by the mainstream literature. First, communities of practice are as likely to resist as support
change, and secondly, it cannot be assumed that all the members of a community will
respond in the same way to change.

The heterogeneity of communities of practice

The generic nature of the way the concept of communities of practice is defined means
that it can be applied to an enormous range of different contexts. The growing popularity
and use of the term suggests that communities of practice exist almost everywhere.
However, a number of writers (Amin and Roberts 2008; Handley *et al.* 2006; Roberts
2006) suggest that it is becoming increasingly important to differentiate between types of
community as they may have different characteristics and dynamics. For example,
communities can vary in size from involving small numbers of people to involving
hundreds and even thousands of people (see e.g. Borzillo *et al.* 2011; Fahey *et al.* 2007).
Further, communities can also differ in terms of their geographic spread and means of
interaction, from communities where everyone is collocated on the same site and
communicate extensively via face-to-face interaction, to globally dispersed communities
where people interact largely via information technology (in virtual communities of
practice—see Ardichvili *et al.* 2003; Usoro *et al.* 2007). Finally, communities can vary from
being based within a single organization to spanning a whole industrial/business sector
(such as the biotechnology community in the USA examined by Gittelman and Kogut
2003).

The social and cultural characteristics of these communities and their knowledge-
sharing dynamics are likely to vary. However, the community of practice literature has only
just started to examine and acknowledge this diversity, and thus far, there have been
few attempts to systematically compare and contrast the characteristics of different types
of community.

The misuse of the community of practice concept

The third issue examined is the potential misuse or misapplication of the community of
practice concept. As it has grown in popularity and importance, the concept has been
applied and used in a diverse range of contexts. However, in some cases the work groups
examined do not appear to possess the attributes of a community of practice. Arguably,
fundamental characteristics of communities of practice are their self-initiating, *ad hoc*,

organic, and non-hierarchical features, but not all the work groups examined that have been described as communities of practice possess them.

For example, Chua (2006) charts the 'rise and fall' of a 'community of practice'. However, the details of the article reveal that the work group which is characterized as a community of practice wasn't self-initiating (it was set up by as part of a top–down management initiative); its membership didn't develop and evolve organically, as it was set up by a senior manager who approached various people to join it; and finally, it wasn't a non-hierarchical community of equals as there was a senior manager who managed and controlled it. Cross *et al.* (2006) present an analysis designed to help management improve the performance of the communities of practice in their organizations. However the advice given, which involves moving communities away from being informal and *ad hoc*, arguably eliminates the features of the work groups which make them a community of practice. Increasingly, caution is needed in reading analyses of what are articulated as communities of practice, as whether some of the work group examined constitute communities is open to dispute.

Blinkered and inward-looking communities

While the collective sense of identity and values that exist between members of a community can create a bond that may facilitate the development of trust and knowledge sharing, there are potential negative consequences if such bonds are too strong. For example, where too strong a sense of community identity exists this may provide a basis for exclusion, where those not part of the 'community' are ignored, and their knowledge not considered to be relevant or important to the community (Alvesson 2000; Baumard 1999). This can cause communities to become inward-looking, and unreceptive to ideas generated outside the community (Brown and Duguid 1998). In such circumstances a community's search processes may be limited rather than extensive, with consequent negative implications for the community's innovativeness (Leonard and Sensiper 1998). In such circumstances, the type of competency traps outlined in the unlearning and forgetting chapter (Chapter 8) can develop, where a community can fail to innovate, change, and adapt, with the risk that its ideas and practices eventually become outdated.

Such communities may not only neglect external ideas, but also people. Communities with a strong sense of identity may become exclusive clubs or 'cliques' (Wenger *et al.* 2002), where membership is tightly controlled, and the factors that define a community's identity are used to exclude entry to others. Just as with the neglect of external ideas, such practices can result in communities becoming poor at absorbing new, external knowledge and ideas.

 Time to reflect   'Not invented here' syndrome

Have you worked as part of a team, or community where there has been a hostility or blindness to ideas generated outside of it? If so, did this have any effect on group or organizational performance?

Conclusion

Communities of practice have been defined as informal groups that have some work activities in common. As a consequence, these communities develop:

1. a shared body of common knowledge
2. a shared sense of collective identity
3. some overlapping values.

The mainstream knowledge management literature portrays communities of practice as being effective vehicles for knowledge sharing and knowledge creation. Consequently, the existence of effectively operating communities of practice is typically argued to underpin individual- and organizational-level learning processes, as well as supporting high levels of organizational innovativeness. The effectiveness of communities of practice in this respect is because:

- the existence of common knowledge and a shared system of values makes sharing tacit knowledge easier, as group members have insights into the implicit assumptions and values embedded in each other's knowledge;
- the shared knowledge, values, and identity which exist also facilitate the development and maintenance of trust-based relations, which, as outlined in Chapter 9, create social conditions conducive to knowledge sharing.

However, the chapter also concluded that the mainstream literature on communities of practice portrays an overly optimistic image of them. To understand why communities of practice have the potential to inhibit as much as facilitate knowledge processes, account needs to be taken of issues of power and conflict within communities, as well as the way that too strong a sense of community identity may inhibit inter-community processes of knowledge sharing. This final conclusion points towards the dynamics of inter-community interaction, which is the topic dealt with in Chapter 11.

Case study   Communities of practice and career trajectories in the British advertising industry

McLeod *et al.* (2011) use the concept of communities of practice to understand how creative workers in the UK advertising industry use formal and informal collaboration, networking, and mentoring to develop and sustain their careers. The need for individuals to engage in this type of community practice is particularly important in this industry as opportunities for permanent employment are limited, and personal reputation and networks are crucially important in gaining work. McLeod *et al.* collected data by conducting life-history interviews with forty-eight people working in the industry, who talked about how they had developed their careers to date.

McLeod *et al.* identified five possible stages that advertising creative workers could progress through which could take them from unpaid, unqualified trainees to becoming creative directors within advertising agencies. While formal college education could play an important role in developing people's skills and networks, particularly at the early stages of a creative's career, most learning typically occurred on the job, via carrying out tasks, dialogue with experienced staff, and having their work critiqued by clients or more experienced advertising staff.

The first stage of career development, labelled the 'pre-peripheral' stage, involved developing a portfolio of work, which was achieved through both doing unpaid work placements in agencies (typically for between two and twelve weeks) or completing college-based assignments. Both types of activity could bring early career advertising staff into contact with experienced advertising staff who

(*continued*)

were able to offer advice and criticism to allow them to develop and refine their portfolios. At this stage such advice was typically given by junior rather than senior staff in agencies, who were able to draw on their own recent experience in mentoring those early-career people they saw as having potential.

The second career stage, labelled 'moving towards the periphery', involved the further development and refinement of portfolios through getting involved in paid work with agencies. Typically this was small-scale, low-prestige work that established agency staff were reluctant to undertake (such as small radio adverts). Learning at this stage involved working intensively on such projects and liaising with more established agency staff to get guidance and feedback on their work. People who were successful at this stage were able to develop a reputation for doing creative work, and build a personal network of contacts that could be useful for finding work in the future.

The third career stage, labelled 'on the periphery', was where people had achieved junior, paid roles within agencies. Learning and career development at this stage centred on developing 'craft skills', such as in photography, illustration, etc. These skills were important in allowing people to fully bring to life the creative ideas that had won pitches to clients. As careers were driven more by reputation and skills rather than formal qualifications, at this stage it was important to receive support and guidance from more senior advertising staff, and to be involved in award-winning campaigns.

The fourth career stage, labelled 'progressing from the periphery', involved junior advertising staff progressing towards middle-level and senior positions within agencies. This was achieved fundamentally through developing a reputation for doing creative work, and also through networking and the development of interpersonal skills. This often involved intense networking, through participating in work events, social activities, attending award ceremonies, etc., and could demand significant amounts of time.

The fifth and final career stage, labelled 'reaching the centre', is when advertising staff became senior staff, taking on creative director roles. This stage also involved learning by doing and learning via trial and error as people were changing to do less creative work and more managerial work, and their sense of identity was altering (from designer to manager).

1   Is this model of career development through networking and participating in occupational communities only relevant in industries where opportunities for the development of stable, organization-based careers are limited? To what extent is this type of insecure employment and individualized career development becoming common?

Source: McLeod, C., O'Donohue, S., and Townley, B. (2011) 'Pot Noodles, Placements and Peer Regard: Creative Career Trajectories and Communities of Practice in the British Advertising Industry', *British Journal of Management*, 22: 114–31.

 ## Review and Discussion Questions

1. If you are or have been a member of a community of practice, how were you socialized? How did you develop the knowledge, values, and identity that characterize membership? Did your socialization closely resemble the process of legitimate peripheral participation described by Lave and Wenger?

2. What if anything can be done to prevent communities developing a sense of identity that is so strong that it inhibits community members from accepting ideas generated outside of it?

3. To what extent is it possible to formalize legitimate peripheral participation and the socialization of new community members? Are there any potential risks for a community of formalizing such processes?

4. Based on any organizational experience you have had, what effect have communities of practice had on organizational knowledge processes? Have they been largely or purely positive and beneficial? Have there been any negative aspects to them (such as knowledge hoarding)?

Suggestions for Further Reading

1. E. Wenger, R. McDermott, and W. Snyder (2002) *Cultivating Communities of Practice* (Boston: Harvard Business School Press).

Presents a positive view of communities of practice and highlights a diversity of ways in which they can be managed.

2. B. Mørk, T. Hoholm, G. Ellingsen, B. Edwin, and M. Aanestad (2010) 'Challenging Expertise: On Power Relations within and across Communities of Practice in Medical Innovation', *Management Learning*, 41/5: 575–92.

An interesting case which highlights the power dynamics that can develop as communities evolve over time.

3. J. Roberts (2006) 'Limits to Communities of Practice', *Journal of Management Studies*, 43/3: 623–39.

Provides a comprehensive analysis of the limitations and criticisms of the community of practice concept.

4. S. Borzillo, S. Azner, and A. Schmitt (2011) 'A Journey through Communities of Practice: How and Why Members Move from the Periphery to the Core', *European Management Journal*, 29: 25–42.

Compares and contrasts the characteristics of managed and autonomous communities as well as highlighting some of the ways in which communities of practice can be managed.

Take your learning further: Online Resource Centre

Visit the Online Resource Centre for resources which will extend your understanding of knowledge management in organizations. As well as web links to sites of interest, the author has provided case studies looking at knowledge management in virtual and knowledge-intensive firms, and in global multinationals. These will help you with your research, essays, and assignments; or you may find these additional resources helpful when revising for exams.

 www.oxfordtextbooks.co.uk/orc/hislop3e/

Cross-Community, Boundary-Spanning Knowledge Processes

Introduction

The focus of this chapter is on knowledge processes in group contexts that are distinct from those examined in Chapter 10, communities of practice. Within communities of practice, as has been outlined, people have a shared sense of identity, common values, and some shared practice/knowledge. What is distinctive about the group contexts examined here is that they involve collaboration between people who, while having to collaborate, may have only a limited sense of shared identity and common knowledge. These contexts are referred to as cross-community, boundary-spanning group situations as they involve collaboration between people who have divergent identities, and whose collaboration thus involves the spanning of the boundaries between these groups or communities. As will be seen, cross-community, boundary-spanning knowledge processes encapsulate an enormous variety of contexts and can involve the spanning of community, occupational, organizational, functional, national, or project boundaries. While, as outlined in Chapter 10, there has been much interest within the knowledge management literature on communities of practice, what are here referred to as cross-community collaborations represent a more common form of group working in contemporary organizations.

The reason why these group contexts are examined separately from the intra-community knowledge processes examined in Chapter 10 is that the lack of much common knowledge and limited shared identity that exists in cross-community contexts makes them distinctive from the group dynamics and knowledge processes that are typical within communities of practice. For example, in terms of the knowledge dimension, Carlile (2002: 442), in the context of cross-functional working, argued that 'the characteristics of knowledge that drive innovative problem solving within a function actually hinder problem solving and knowledge creation across [functional] boundaries'. In relation to the identity dimension, the different identities that people have in cross-community contexts, as was highlighted in Chapter 9, can have a significant impact on the character and dynamics of interpersonal relations (such as the extent to which trust exists or can be developed), which influences the dynamics of interpersonal knowledge processes. Ultimately, due to such factors,

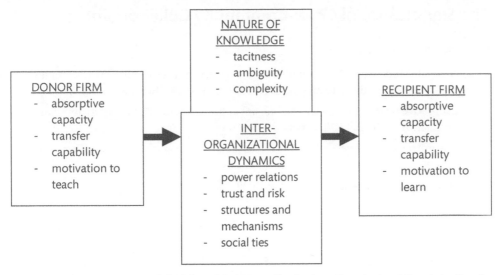

Figure 11.1 Easterby-Smith *et al.*'s (2008) Model of Factors Shaping Inter-Organizational Knowledge Transfer
Source: Adapted from Easterby-Smith *et al.* 2008: figure 1, p. 679.

cross-community knowledge processes are typically more complex and difficult to manage than those that occur within communities of practice.

This topic has been addressed by people adopting both objectivist and practice-based epistemologies. For example, Easterby-Smith *et al.* (2008), and all the contributors to the special issue of the *Journal of Management Studies* on knowledge sharing in intra- and inter-firm knowledge transfer processes, broadly adopt an objectivist perspective. This is visible in the way Easterby-Smith *et al.* model the character of inter-firm knowledge processes (see Figure 11.1), which utilizes the transmitter–receiver model of knowledge sharing outlined in Chapter 2. By contrast, other writers, such as Carlile (2002, 2004) and Oborn and Dawson (2010), examine this topic utilizing a practice-based epistemology.

In looking at this topic, the chapter has a relatively narrow focus, being concerned with how the nature of knowledge and the character of interpersonal dynamics shape the character of micro-level knowledge processes in cross-community contexts. Thus, the chapter has some, but only limited, engagement with the vast literature that exists on joint ventures and inter-firm alliances. Much of the writing in this area has adopted an organization-level analysis, looking at how firm performance is affected by participation in such alliances, and how the structuring of these alliances at the firm level shapes their likelihood of success. Such issues are not considered here.

In the following section we consider why cross-community collaboration is so important and widely used. After this, the chapter examines the character of cross-community knowledge processes, outlining how the lack of common knowledge and shared identity shape their dynamics. Next, Carlile's (2002, 2004) work is used to distinguish between the types of boundaries that can be involved in cross-community working, before considering the way that cross-community knowledge processes can be facilitated and managed, such as through the use of boundary objects and the management of cross-boundary social relations.

The Significance of Cross-Community Collaboration

Consider the following situations:

- Inter-organizational collaboration on the development and/or production of complex and high-technology products (Harryson *et al.* 2008; Lam 1997; Tallman and Phene 2007).

- Collaborative working that spans significant cultural boundaries (Inkpen and Pien 2006; Chen *et al.* 2010; Li 2010; Peltokorpi 2006).

- Cross-project knowledge-sharing processes (Scarbrough *et al.* 2004b; Cacciatori *et al.* 2012).

- Multidisciplinary working (Currie *et al.* 2008; McGivern and Dawson 2010; Oborn and Dawson 2010).

- Cross-occupational/functional collaboration (Bechky 2003; Carlile 2002, 2004; Majchrzak *et al.* 2012).

- Inter-organizational supply chain based collaboration (Dyer and Nobeoka 2000; Mason and Leek 2008).

- Cross-business collaboration *within* multinational corporations (Jonsson and Kalling 2007; Massingham 2010).

- The outsources of business services to third-party, external providers (Newell et al. 2007—see later illustration; Williams 2011, Zimmermann and Mayasandra 2011).

All these situations, while being diverse in character, have one thing in common: they all represent cross-community, boundary-spanning situations as they involve the sharing or joint utilization and development of knowledge among people who do not typically work together, and who have substantially different knowledge bases. One of the reasons why examining the dynamics of cross-community knowledge processes is so important is that the type of working practices outlined in these examples are becoming more and more common. For example, evidence suggests that the use of network-based forms of organizing, involving inter-organizational collaboration, has become widespread.

Another factor that signals the importance of cross-community knowledge processes is the growing acknowledgement that the knowledge bases of all organizations are to some extent fragmented into separate, specialized knowledge domains. This led Brown and Duguid (1991: 53) to refer to organizations as being comparable to a 'community-of-communities'. Carlile (2002, 2004), utilizing a practice-based epistemology, makes a similar argument in talking about the localized nature of knowledge that develops within particular functions of organizations (due to their focus on specific, distinctive problems, and the use of particular, localized practices), and argues that cross-functional collaboration constitutes a boundary-spanning process. Further, various writers have highlighted how the provision of healthcare services, or the development of medical innovations, even when occurring within single organizations, involves multidisciplinary, cross-professional collaboration (Currie et al. 2008; McGivern and Dawson 2010). Thus, the knowledge base of all organizations can be considered as being made up of a diversity of localized communities which have some over-lapping knowledge in common, but which also possess much specialized and specific knowledge.

From this perspective one of the general tasks of management is to coordinate these diverse internal communities, integrating, diffusing, and combining fragmented internal knowledge as necessary (Blacker *et al.* 2000; Brown and Duguid 2001; Tsoukas 1996). Thus, if the knowledge base of all organizations is constituted by a diverse collection of specialized knowledge domains, intra-organizational processes which require collaboration between across these domains can be conceptualized as cross-community, boundary-spanning situations as much as inter-organizational collaborations (Easterby-Smith *et al.* 2008; van Wijk *et al.* 2008).

 Time to reflect   Fragmented organizational knowledge bases

Is the level of fragmentation in an organization's knowledge base likely to be proportional to organizational size? Further, if so, are the difficulties of managing such a fragmented knowledge base likely to be greatest for large, global multinationals?

The importance of cross-community, boundary-spanning knowledge processes stems from the fact that the contemporary (re)structuring of organizations is placing a greater emphasis on such forms of working than has been traditional, and because many forms of intra-organizational collaboration can be conceptualized as involving cross-community interaction.

Characterizing Cross-Community Knowledge Processes

As illustrated by Figure 10.1, knowledge processes within communities of practice are facilitated by the high degree of common knowledge, overlapping values, and shared sense of identity that community members typically possess. This is because in such circumstances it is likely that the tacit assumptions underpinning people's knowledge, which are key to effective knowledge sharing, are likely to be well understood or commonly shared. Also, the level of trust and mutual understanding between people in this context is likely to be conducive to effective knowledge sharing. However, in cross-community collaborations, as has been outlined, the situation is somewhat different (see Table 11.1). In these circumstances people will have much less shared, common knowledge, they may only have a weak sense of shared identity, or may even have distinctive and separate identities, and finally, may have fundamentally different value systems. Thus, the social relations between people who are not members of the same group/community are much less conducive to effective knowledge sharing.

Table 11.1 Factors Making Cross-Community Knowledge Processes Difficult

Weak shared identity or different sense of identity
Knowledge-related differences:
1. lack of common knowledge
2. tacitness and context specificity make transferability difficult
3. epistemic differences: based on different assumptions, values, and world-view

The following two subsections consider in detail how the lack of a shared identity, and/or differences in knowledge can inhibit knowledge processes in cross-community contexts.

Identity

People from different teams, departments, organizations, sites, or functions who work together may have either a weak sense of common identity, or may have distinctive and separate identities. For example, Massingham (2010) found that collaboration across business units within one Australian multinational was influenced by the differences in identity that existed between host country nationals and parent country nationals.

This potentially weak sense of common identity arguably complicates knowledge processes through the potential for conflict this creates, as people with differing senses of identity may perceive differences of interest to exist between themselves and others. As was made apparent in Chapter 9 via a number of different examples, conflict or perceptions that differences of interest exist between people/groups have been found to play a crucial role in shaping whether, with whom, and how people are prepared to share knowledge. Further, people's identity can be aligned to different types of group, including particular business units, organizations, professions, or functions. Another type of identity that has to be considered is more culturally based—national forms of identity—as such forms of identity can affect the character and dynamics of cross-community knowledge processes. For example, van Wijk et al.'s (2008) meta-analysis of research on the antecedents of knowledge sharing in cross-organizational alliances found that the degree of culture distance that existed typically inhibited the level of knowledge sharing that occurred.

Most fundamentally, as was outlined in Chapter 3, those adopting a practice-based epistemology build on the assumption that all knowledge is culturally embedded, and that everyone's knowledge thus to some extent reflects the values, assumptions, and worldviews which predominate in the cultures they were socialized into (Jonsson and Kalling 2007; Chen et al. 2010). For example, Inkpen and Pien's (2006) analysis of the collaboration between Chinese and Singaporean organizations in the development of the Suzhou Industrial Park (SIP) found that cultural differences significantly inhibited knowledge sharing. Specifically, Chinese workers found it difficult to understand the intent and rationale underpinning the actions of the Singaporean workers, because the Singaporean workers couldn't articulate them as they were so deeply embedded in their cultural values.

At a more basic level, cross-cultural communication and knowledge sharing can also be inhibited by a lack of a shared language, misinterpretations due to variable language skills, or concerns about limitations in people's language competencies (see e.g. Li 2010). For example, Peltokorpi (2006) found that knowledge sharing between some Nordic managers working in Japan and the Japanese people they worked with were inhibited by the lack of a shared language with which to communicate. Peltokorpi further found that the knowledge-sharing behaviours of the Japanese workers were heavily influenced by their cultural values, so the strong respect they had for status hierarchies inhibited lower level workers from interacting with the Nordic managers.

> ### ⊙ Illustration   Comparing the transfer of knowledge between different cultures
>
> Chen *et al.* (2010) examined how issues of national culture affected the transfer of knowledge during some formal training activities. The training considered involved workers in the China-based IT technical service/support centre of a US corporation. The staff in the centre had the task of providing IT technical support by telephone to customers in the USA. The focus of the paper was on the training provided to the service centre staff. Research data were collected from company documentation, interviews, and the observation of some of the training activities.
>
> During the initial period, face-to-face classroom-based training was provided by staff from the USA to eighteen Chinese trainees and two Canadian trainees. (At a later stage, more experienced Chinese staff provided further training to more Chinese and Canadian workers, but this stage is not considered here.) According to Hofstede's conceptualization of national cultures, culture in the USA is similar to that in Canada, but there are significant culture differences between China and both the USA and Canada. For example, while culture in the USA and Canada is highly individualistic, in China there is a more collectivist or group orientation to culture. Thus, it was possible to consider how culture differences affected the transfer of knowledge to the support centre staff during the initial training period by looking for similarities and differences in the effectiveness of the training provided by the US trainers to the Chinese and Canadian trainees.
>
> In terms of the Canadian trainees it was found that the similarity in culture between the trainers from the USA and the Canadian trainees meant that issues of culture did not negatively impact on the training at all. The situation was different for the Chinese trainees. For example, culture differences were found to be responsible for difference in the teaching/learning styles of the US trainers and the Chinese trainees. The US trainers preferred to facilitate two-way training and communication where trainees were active in the learning process through asking questions and taking the initiative. This contrasted with the preferred learning style of the Chinese trainees which was more passive and one-way: it was assumed that trainers provided all relevant knowledge and trainees passively accepted/learnt it without challenging, probing, or questioning the knowledge. Ultimately, these culture differences in teaching/learning styles negatively impacted on the training of the Chinese workers.

A further way in which national culture has been found to shape knowledge sharing in cross-community contexts is that the strong collectivist nature of culture in many Asian countries, while facilitating in-group knowledge sharing, can act as a significant brake on cross-community knowledge sharing (Michailova and Hutchins 2006; Peltokorpi 2006; Weir and Hutchings 2005).

Knowledge

The difficulties of cross-community knowledge sharing, as outlined, are related to more than just the sense of identities that individuals possess. An equally important factor complicating such processes is the nature of the knowledge possessed by people in these situations. These difficulties stem from three interrelated factors (see Table 11.1).

First, as in any context, the sharing of knowledge may be inhibited by its tacitness. However, the sharing of tacit knowledge in cross-community contexts is made more difficult and complex by two other knowledge-related factors: the limited amount of common knowledge that can exist; and the significant epistemological differences that can exist in the knowledge people possess (i.e. their knowledge is based on different underpinning assumptions and values). Thus, for example, Currie *et al.* (2008) found that the differences in perceptions of risk and safety within UK hospitals was shaped by professional backgrounds, which often led to disagreements or misunderstandings over what constituted risky behaviour (see the case study at the end of Chapter 9).

The issue of epistemological differences is worth elaborating on, as such differences can have a profound effect on attempts to share or collectively utilize knowledge. Brown and Duguid (2001: 207) argue that, while the advantage of communities of practice is that 'common . . . practice . . . creates social-epistemic bonds', conversely, '[p]eople with different practices have different assumptions, different outlooks, different interpretations of the world around them, and different ways of making sense of their encounters'. Thus, in cross-community, boundary-spanning contexts people may not only have limited amounts of common, shared knowledge, but the knowledge they possess may be based on a fundamentally different system of values and assumptions (Majchrzak *et al.* 2012). Carlile (2002), in a similar vein, and adopting a practice-based epistemology, argued that such epistemic differences will always exist in cross-community contexts because people's knowledge is localized, being developed around and focused on the particular problems and issues in their day-to-day work. Carlile's analysis also suggests that the scope for conflict in such situations can be related to such knowledge-based differences. This is because he suggests that people's knowledge becomes 'invested in practice'. People's sense of competence relates to the knowledge they possess and the way it allows them to do their work. Thus, people can become committed and attached to particular types of knowledge and ways of doing things, and may be reluctant to adapt and change them due to the negative impact such change may have on their sense of individual competence.

The complexity of knowledge sharing in such circumstances stems from the fact that epistemological differences between people or groups can inhibit the development of even a fundamental understanding of the basic premises and values on which the knowledge of others is based. Newell and Swan (2000) suggest that the greater the epistemological difference between collaborating parties, the less chance there is that such collaborations will be successful, and the more likely that they will not be able to effectively integrate their different perspectives and knowledge bases. Further, in the example of cross-functional collaboration examined by Majchrzak *et al.* (2012), the knowledge differences that existed between people meant that effective collaboration took a significant amount of time and resources, and required extensive dialogue between people to 'transcend' the differences in knowledge that existed.

The embeddedness of knowledge in language means that epistemological differences in cross-community contexts can stem from national cultural and linguistic differences as much as from differences in people's work practices. For example, Peltokorpi's (2006) research suggested such differences had a significant negative impact on the ability of Norwegian managers to communicate and share knowledge with the Japanese people they worked with. First, Japanese is argued to be a 'high context' language (where non-verbal, tacit, and shared meanings are important) and meaning is determined as much by how things are said as by the words, while Western languages are 'low context' and meaning is determined more by what is said than how it is said. One illustration of how such factors inhibited communication and knowledge sharing was that the Nordic managers said they were often unclear what their Japanese subordinates meant when they said 'yes'.

Illustration The impact of 'knowledge gaps' on the transfer of knowledge within a multinational between 'parent' and 'host' country staff

For all multinationals, the transfer of knowledge across and between divisions, and between the corporate centre and different divisions, is important to their ongoing competitiveness and success. Massingham (2010) examined problems with the transfer of knowledge between parent and host country staff within a single Australian multinational company within the building materials sector, which had divisions in six Asian countries.

Massingham found that gaps between the knowledge of parent and host country staff inhibited the sharing of knowledge in four distinctive ways. One of these situations was where host country staff lacked sufficient knowledge to learn how to do a particular task that was being taught to them by parent country staff. One example of this was the inability of host country staff to make large-scale investment decisions. The knowledge on how to do this was transferred from parent country staff in the form of codified market research reports. However, host country staff lacked the tacit knowledge to utilize the knowledge in these reports to make effective investment decisions. Parent country staff interpreted this inability as incompetence on the part of host country staff—such tasks were routine to them due to the implicit and intuitive nature of the tacit knowledge they drew on in carrying out this work.

Massingham argued that the tacit knowledge required to make these investment decisions involved combining external market knowledge with internal knowledge of the company, which was knowledge that parent country staff had built up over time, through experience. The tacit nature of the knowledge used by parent country staff in making these decisions, combined with the lack of confidence they had in the ability of host country staff to learn how to carry out these tasks, meant that parent country staff were either unable or unwilling to share the necessary tacit knowledge with host country staff.

In conclusion, cross-community knowledge processes are inhibited by the differences in the knowledge possessed by the people involved in such processes. In general terms, the greater the degree of common knowledge that exists, the more straightforward knowledge processes are likely to be. Further, the character of knowledge processes in such circumstances are also affected by the degree of epistemological difference in the assumptions and values underpinning the knowledge bases involved, with a high level of epistemological difference likely to significantly increase the difficulty and complexity of such knowledge processes.

Identity, Knowledge, Trust, and Social Relations

One of the major conclusions to emerge from the previous section was that, where the common knowledge base is limited, or where people have a limited sense of shared identity, this means that the social relationship between parties is unlikely to be strong, and that the foundations for the existence of trust are relatively weak. Thus in such circumstances not only is the existence of strong trust unlikely, but the development of trust will typically be complicated and difficult (Janowicz-Panjaitan and Noorderhaven 2009). This section thus examines the topic of trust in cross-community, boundary-spanning contexts, which links back to Chapter 9, where the topic of trust was introduced and conceptualized.

At the most general level, and somewhat unsurprisingly, trust in these contexts has been found to significantly affect knowledge sharing, with levels of knowledge sharing typically being found to be directly related to levels of trust (Jonsson and Kalling 2007; van Wijk *et al.* 2008). More specifically, Becerra *et al.* (2008) found that trust was more closely related to the sharing of tacit, rather than explicit knowledge. Becerra *et al.*, whose analysis is based on surveys of Norwegian firms involved in inter-firm alliances, argue that, as was suggested in Chapter 9, trust is closely and inversely related to perceptions of risk. In inter-firm contexts, collaborators in one context or situation may be competitors in another. Thus, the risk with inappropriate knowledge sharing is that, once knowledge has been shared, control over it is lost and it may be used for purposes other than intended. One of Becerra *et al.'s* main findings was that trust was related to the extent to which a partner was prepared to take a risk, as perceptions of trust reduce the risk that people perceive they are taking.

 Illustration   Trust and knowledge sharing in a globally distributed work team

Newell *et al.* (2007) utilize Newell and Swan's (2000) typology of trust (see Chapter 9 and Table 9.2) to analyse how the evolution of trust affected work relations and knowledge sharing in globally dispersed software development teams in a company called GLOBALIS. The company examined had offices in a number of cities in the USA, but also in Ireland and India. Project management and strategic elements of the work were typically done in the USA, with more routine work being done in the 'offshore' offices in India and Ireland. In the context studied, the development of trust-based working relations was inhibited not just by the cross-cultural nature of the project teams, but also because most communication was electronic, with opportunities for face-to-face interaction being limited.

Working relations in the teams were also negatively affected by the perception among many of the American workers that their jobs were threatened by the use of offshore sites, due to the rapid rise in the use of 'offshoring' that had been undertaken. There was therefore a strong sense of 'us' versus 'them' in the project teams, rather than people identifying strongly with the project they worked on. This sense of 'them' and 'us' was reinforced by the strategy of knowledge hoarding adopted by many American workers, who believed this provided a way of protecting their position and knowledge, with the perception being that sharing knowledge would make it easier for the company to get rid of them. Because of these factors, levels of commitment trust, the extent to which people feel committed to the goals of their joint endeavour, were limited. For example, levels of commitment-based trust among the Irish and Indian workers was low as they felt excluded from the more interesting work, and did not like the lack of knowledge sharing by American workers. Further, the extent of the knowledge hoarding that was undertaken by the American workers meant that the Irish and Indian workers often found it difficult to do their jobs effectively, which inhibited the extent to which the American workers developed a sense of competence-based trust in them. Finally, the professional rather than collegial way in which work-related interactions were carried out, and the lack of opportunities for face-to-face interaction between Irish, Indian, and American workers, made the development of companion-based trust difficult as well.

1. Given the cost and difficulty of organizing face-to-face meetings among these workers, what, if anything, could management in GLOBALIS have done to address the lack of trust that existed in their software development teams?

What is of particular interest here is how strong trust based relations develop in cross-community contexts. Inkpen and Pien's (2006) study of the long-term collaboration between Singaporean and Chinese workers in the development of the Suzhou Industrial Park found that knowledge sharing in the early stages of the collaboration was inhibited to some extent due to low levels of trust. Despite the formalization of the collaboration in a number of written contracts, even levels of commitment-based trust (see Table 9.2) were initially low, as Singaporean staff were unhappy with the level of ambiguity that existed in the written contracts, which was greater than they were typically used to. However, over time, through face-to-face interaction, and close collaboration between Chinese and Singaporean workers, levels of companion- and competence-based trust developed significantly as these workers developed not only personal relationships (companion-based trust) with each other, but also a confidence in each other's abilities (competence-based trust).

Harryson *et al.*'s (2008) study of the development of new Volvo C70, which involved intensive collaboration between Swedish and Italian engineers, found that informal socialization provided another means via which trust-based working relations could be developed. The types of events that project team members participated in included attending football matches together, having wine-tasting events, regularly going out to dinner together, and weekend snowboarding trips. Thus trust-based working relations can be developed via collaboration on work-related activities and through interacting and socializing at non-work events. However, as the illustration in this section shows, the development of trust-based working relations is by no means easy or straightforward, especially when the groups collaborating perceive that their interests may be conflicting.

A Classification of Boundary Types

Thus far, while cross-community boundary-spanning contexts have been acknowledged as being highly diverse, no effort has been made to systematically differentiate between the different types of boundary that exist, and how the character of these boundaries influences the nature and dynamics of cross-community knowledge processes. This topic is addressed here, through using Carlile's (2002, 2004) framework of boundary types. The empirical focus of Carlile's work is predominantly on cross-functional working within single organizations. Adopting a practice-based perspective Carlile characterized such situations as involving boundary spanning as the knowledge possessed by staff working in different functional areas, even within the same organization, is understood to be quite different. For Carlile this is because the knowledge of staff in these functional areas is localized, being concerned with addressing the particular problems, and being embedded, in the particular work practices that each function is involved in and responsible for.

Carlile developed a typology distinguishing between three distinctive types of boundary: syntactic, semantic, and pragmatic (see Table 11.2) with the degree of novelty of the collective tasks being undertaken varying from low (syntactic boundaries) to high (pragmatic boundaries). Syntactic boundaries are assumed to be the easiest to work across as people share a common logic, set of values, and worldview. Thus, working across a syntactic boundary involves the relatively straightforward process of transferring knowledge and information from one community to the other. Semantic boundaries are more difficult to

Table 11.2 Carlile's (2002, 2004) Boundary Types and their Characteristics

	Syntactic	Semantic	Pragmatic
Degree of Novelty in Collaborative Activity	Low	Medium	High
Type of Activity Involved in Facilitating Boundary Activity	Common syntax/language/understanding exists. Focus on sharing and transferral of knowledge/information across boundary.	Existence of differing interpretations across boundary requires development of mutual understanding.	Dealing with conflicting interests which requires one party to adapt/change their knowledge.
Dominant Knowledge Process Involved	Transfer	Translation	Transformation

work across, as with them people do not have a shared logic or set of values. Instead, in such contexts people will have different understandings and interpretations of the same knowledge. In such contexts, successfully working across a semantic boundary involves people developing an understanding of and sensitivity to other people's understandings and interpretations.

Finally, pragmatic boundaries are the most complex and difficult type of boundary to work successfully across. In such contexts not only do people have different interpretations and understandings of issues/events, they also have different interests, and working successfully across a pragmatic boundary thus involves both developing some common, shared interests and (at least) one group/community being prepared to change and transform their knowledge. Due to the extent to which people and groups develop a sense of investment in and commitment to their knowledge/practices (see earlier), doing so is typically never straightforward.

A fundamental element in Carlile's typology is the role of boundary objects in facilitating cross-boundary working. Carlile suggests that to successfully work and share knowledge across each boundary type requires the use of appropriate boundary objects. This element in his analysis is examined and illustrated in the following section.

Facilitating/Managing Knowledge between Communities

Up to this point the chapter has emphasized the not insignificant difficulties in sharing knowledge in cross-community, boundary-spanning contexts. However, these difficulties are to some extent manageable. There is much that can be done to address them and facilitate cross-community knowledge processes. In general terms, this involves improving the level of mutual understanding and developing the social relationship between relevant people.

From a practice-based perspective, developing such an understanding involves the sort of perspective making and taking processes outlined in Chapter 3. While the practice-based perspective on knowledge assumes that processes of perspective making and taking are necessary for the sharing and communication of knowledge in *all* circumstances, the lack of common knowledge in cross-community contexts raises the importance of such proc-esses. These perspective making and taking processes do not result in the integration of the different knowledge bases into a coherent whole, but should instead involve a process of dialogue, where 'each community maintains its own voice while listening to the voice of the other' (Gherardi and Nicolini 2002: 421). Thus, perspective making and taking occurs through a process of talking, listening, acknowledging, and being tolerant to any differences identified.

Current writing suggests two broad ways in which this can be achieved. First, work can be invested in managing the social relationship between people, and secondly, the existing areas of overlap between people can be developed by means of boundary objects.

Relationship management

Relationship management actively involves key, strategic individuals in developing the social relationship between the people involved in a cross-community, boundary-spanning work situation. Brown and Duguid (1998) identified two roles that key individuals could take in the development of cross-community social relations: brokers and translators. The brokering role is relevant where there is some pre-existing overlap in the knowledge of the communities/people involved. A broker is someone who inhabits both communities, and uses their knowledge and understanding of both to facilitate the development of mutual understanding between other members of the communities. Gherardi and Nicolini (2002) argue that a broker is someone who has the ability to 'transfer and translate certain elements of one practice to another'. The role of translator is relevant where there is no overlapping common knowledge between communities/people. This requires the translator to have a detailed knowledge of both communities, and further, the translator has to be trusted by members of both communities as they play such a key role in interacting between them. Such roles are acknowledged to be extremely complex and difficult to manage successfully.

Finally, collaboration and knowledge sharing can be facilitated by efforts to develop the social relationship that exists between those involved in cross-community collaboration (see previous section on trust in this context). For example, Williams (2011) found that, with the offshoring of IS development work to India, collaboration was facilitated by the codifi-cation of explicit knowledge and the sharing of more tacit knowledge through what was referred to as 'client embedment' (developing an understanding of the client through either social interaction with client staff or spending time working at client sites).

Boundary objects

The third and final method discussed by Brown and Duguid (1998) to facilitate cross-community knowledge sharing involves the development and utilization of boundary objects, a concept initially developed by Star (1989). Boundary objects are entities that are common to a number of communities and can be either physical or linguistic/symbolic in character. An example of a physical boundary object is the new air traffic management system examined by Landry et al. (2010) which through providing a common interface to all those who used it, improved collaboration and communication among the diverse range of sites and organizations involved in the management of air traffic in the USA. An example of linguistic/epistemic boundary objects is provided by McGivern and Dawson (2010). In their study of attempts to translate genetics knowledge and science into medical practices that could be used to treat patients, the projects concerned were conceptualized as epistemic/knowledge objects, with control over them being a significant source of dispute among the various epistemic communities involved in the projects.

Boundary objects provide a focus for negotiation, discussion, or even shared activity between people from different communities, and thus can be utilized to help develop and improve the working relationship between people, and the mutual understanding they have of each other. The boundary object concept has proved popular and has been used by an increasing number of analysts to understand change processes (Fenton 2007), biomedical innovation (McGivern and Dawson 2010; Swan *et al.* 2007), and the sharing of project-specific knowledge (Sapsted and Salter 2004; Swan *et al.* 2007).

 Time to reflect   Face-to-face communication and trust

How important is face-to-face interaction for the development of trust and an effective working relationship between people from significantly different cultures? Can cross-cultural working relations be developed without any face-to-face interaction?

A more systematic analysis of the concept of boundary objects is developed by Carlile, as alluded to earlier. Carlile (2002) outlined a typology of distinctive types of boundary objects that was adapted from Star's (1989) work (see Table 11.3), and links this to his typology of boundary types (see Table 11.2) to suggest that successfully working across boundaries requires the use of boundary objects appropriate to the type of boundary being crossed (see Table 11.4). In the space available here it is only possible to sketch out the complex model developed over two detailed academic papers (Carlile 2002, 2004).

To successfully span syntactic boundaries, the fact that people have a shared syntax and language means repository type boundary objects, in the form of common data and information, can facilitate cross-boundary working. Thus, the primary knowledge process involved

Table 11.3 Carlile's Boundary Object Types

Boundary Object Type	Boundary Object Characteristics
Repository	Common data or information that provide shared reference point for groups involved in cross-boundary work.
Standardized forms/methods	Shared forms and methods of working allow differences of opinion across a boundary to be acknowledged, accounted for, and understood.
Objects/models	Complex representations (such as drawings, computer simulations) which can be observed, shared by groups involved in cross-boundary situations.
Maps	Representation of dependencies between groups involved in cross-boundary working.

Source: Carlile 2002, 2004.

Table 11.4 Carlile's Boundary Types and Appropriate Boundary Objects

Type of Boundary	Characteristics Required for Cross-Boundary Collaboration	Boundaries Objects that Allow Successful Cross-Boundary Working
Syntactic	Shared system and common set of data/information.	Repository
Semantic	Provide a means for people to specify and learn about cross-boundary differences and dependencies.	Standardized form and methods Objects/models Maps
Pragmatic	Provide a means whereby people develop a common sense of shared interests and a willingness to transform their knowledge to achieve them.	Objects/models Maps

Source: Carlile 2002, 2004.

in spanning syntactic boundaries is knowledge sharing, where repository type boundary objects are developed via the transferral and sharing of knowledge to allow the development of a common knowledge base, agreed upon and understood by all communities.

Successfully spanning semantic boundaries, where people do not have a shared syntax and language, and where people may have divergent interpretations and understandings, is more complex. To do this involves the development and use of boundary objects which facilitate a process of perspective making and taking, where people develop an increased understanding of the perspective of others. Carlile suggests that this can be achieved via the use of three types of boundary object. First, standardized forms and models can be used, where people gain insights into the perspective of others via understanding the different ways that common forms are used. Secondly, objects/models can be used, as the use of shared drawings etc. provides a way in which people's differences in perspective can be communicated and discussed. Finally, maps, which outline the interdependencies between communities can also be used, as they allow groups to understand how people's perspectives are shaped by their community interests and co-dependencies. Thus, with the spanning of semantic boundaries, the primary knowledge process is one of translation.

Finally, pragmatic boundaries are the most difficult and complex to span, due to the differences of interest that exist between communities, with Carlile arguing that both object/models and maps are appropriate boundary objects for this context. This is because the development and use of maps allow people to better understand and appreciate the differences of interest that exist, while the use of objects/models can provide a resource which not only allows people to develop a sense of shared interests and common endeavour, but also to transform their knowledge to achieve a collective goal. Thus, with the spanning of pragmatic boundaries, the primary knowledge process is one of transformation.

Carlile (2002) illustrated the role of boundary objects in facilitating boundary spanning via the analysis of a specific issue that developed and was eventually resolved in his ethnographic study of the development of a new car valve. While the development process involved collaboration among staff from four functions/communities (sales, manufacturing engineering, production, and design engineering), the focal issue involved the manufacturing and design engineering functions. A manufacturing engineer, who was responsible for transforming the design engineers' work into a manufacturable product, had a concern about the design that would potentially require a significant redesign to be undertaken. Thus, the boundary being spanned was a pragmatic one, requiring the transformation of knowledge. The manufacturing engineer's initial efforts at communicating his concerns to the design engineers failed, largely because, Carlile argued, the boundary object used, some out-of-date design drawings, represented an inappropriate boundary object that the design engineers couldn't effectively relate to—the drawings didn't reflect the latest version of the design they were familiar with. However, when the same manufacturing engineer later expressed the same concerns to the designers with up-to-date drawings, his efforts were successful, and the design engineers agreed to change the design. Carlile argued that the up-to-date drawings were a suitable boundary object as they allowed effective cross-community dialogue and communication. The outcome of these efforts was an effective boundary-spanning collaboration, as all concerned took account of the manufacturing engineer's concerns and undertook to change the design, even though this involved utilizing some new design principles and ideas that were novel to the company.

 ## Conclusion

This chapter has narrowly focused on cross-community, boundary-spanning knowledge processes. Arguably, the relevance and importance of cross-community knowledge processes has increased due to the changes in working practices that have emerged from the contemporary restructuring of work organizations. The difference between the social dynamics and knowledge processes that occur within cross-community knowledge processes and those that occur within communities of practice relate to the sense of shared identity and typically high level of common knowledge which exists within communities, but which tends to be absent from cross-community contexts (see Chapter 10). It may also be the case that not only are there limited amounts of common, shared knowledge between parties, but that there may be epistemic differences in the knowledge of the people and communities involved, where their knowledge is based on fundamentally different assumptions and values.

Typically, as illustrated by a number of examples, cross-community knowledge processes are likely to be more complex and difficult to make successful than intra-community processes. This is due to both the differences in identity, which may induce cross-community conflict, and the lack of common knowledge. Somewhat simplistically, the less common knowledge that exists, and the greater the level of epistemic difference, the more complicated and difficult the knowledge-sharing process will be.

Knowledge sharing across communities was shown to require two primary and closely interrelated elements, both of which are developed through a process of social interaction and communication. First, an adequate level of trust needs to be developed between the individuals from both communities. Secondly, people from both communities have to develop a basic understanding of the values, assumptions, and viewpoints which underpin each other's knowledge base. This process of perspective making and taking, which was also examined in Chapter 3, requires not a merging of these different knowledge bases, but an appreciation of, sensitivity to, and tolerance of the differences in perspective which emerge. Finally, cross-community knowledge processes can be facilitated through the use of boundary objects. However, Carlile's analysis suggests, for boundary objects to be effective, the type of boundary object has to be appropriate to the type of boundary being worked across.

Case study   The negotiation of meaning within multidisciplinary medical teams

Oborn and Dawson (2011) examine the power dynamics that shaped how meaning was negotiated in what can be conceptualized as a cross-community collaborative context: multidisciplinary medical teams. More specifically, the context they examined was a multidisciplinary urology cancer team that was based in a large UK hospital. While the team was under the leadership of a surgeon in the hospital's urology department, the team studied also included medical staff from a number of disciplines including surgery, radiotherapy, oncology, pathology, nursing, and radiology.

The researchers undertook a longitudinal qualitative study of this medical team, studying it over the course of seventeen months. The main source of data were observational data from a number of weekly multidisciplinary meetings. This was a weekly face-to-face meeting that involved the whole team, and which had the aim of agreeing diagnoses and treatment plans for the patients under the team's care.

The team studied represents a cross-community collaboration, as the different people involved in the team had their own distinctive knowledge bases and values, which were linked to their different professions and different work practices. In studying these teams, Oborn and Dawson adopt what is here labelled the practice-based epistemology, assuming that people's knowledge is closely linked to and inseparable from the work practices they carry out. Further, in acknowledging that knowledge is linked to power, and that the knowledge claims people made in negotiating meaning within the teams were closely linked to the 'discursive resources' that people drew up—how they justified and attempted to validate their 'knowledge claims'—they can also be aligned with the Foucaludian dialogic-discourse on power (see Chapter 12). To illustrate these issues, it is useful to present and examine some of the observational data from the team meetings that Oborn and Dawson collected and analysed.

The knowledge bases and practices of the different team members meant that they typically utilized different discursive resources in support of their knowledge claims. For example, due to the nature of the work of surgeons, which requires carrying out operations on patients and making quick 'real-time' decisions in theatre, they are able to utilize dramatic and vivid stories and language and can talk in terms of their 'life-saving' heroic actions. For example, in discussing the treatment of a patient one surgeon said, 'I saw multiple tumours on the bladder when I was putting the stent in . . . dark in colour . . . like polyps . . . I was sure it was [cancer]' (p. 1846). The power of this type of discursive resource/knowledge claim is that it is difficult for others to challenge due to their lack of involvement with the surgical procedures being described.

Other medical staff were able to draw on different resources in making knowledge claims. For example, in discussing a different patient, one radiologist was able to influence opinion within the team towards a particular treatment plan by making reference to research published in a reputable journal. Thus, the radiologist said, 'the chances of not being able to successfully complete the nephrostomy are very low. It is about 1–2% failure . . . I hate to put a number on it, because this patient may be that 1–2% . . . but there is a study on it that I read in [journal] which reported . . . it is a lot lower than you think' (p. 1842). The prestige of the journal that the radiologist referred to meant that the others in the meeting regarded his suggestion as valid, and as a result he was able to influence the diagnosis of the patient under discussion. Thus, in the multidisciplinary team that was studied, not only did people utilize different, professionally based knowledge bases, they also utilized distinctive knowledge resources in support of the knowledge claims they made that were linked to the nature of the work they did.

1. In the case of knowledge claims like the one made by the surgeon, which relate directly to personal experiences, what if anything can be done by other people who did not share the same experience to challenge or question such knowledge claims?

Source: Oborn, E., and Dawson, S. (2010) 'Knowledge and Practice in Multidisciplinary Teams: Struggle, Accommodation and Privilege', *Human Relations*, 63/12: 1835–57.

Review and Discussion Questions

1. The prevalence of inter-organizational networking can be gauged by a simple piece of research. Examine the business section from any serious daily newspaper and you are likely to find relevant examples. However, is this type of working practice likely to be more common in some business sectors more than others? What factors affect the extent to which inter-organizational networks are developed and utilized?

2. Reflect on any work experience that you have had. What, if anything, did you and your work colleagues most strongly feel a sense of identity with: your immediate work group, the function you worked in, the division you worked for, or the overall corporate group? Are these senses of identity likely to inhibit the development of an effective working relationship and the sharing of knowledge with people from different parts of the organization?

 ## Suggestions for Further Reading

1. P. Carlile (2004) 'Transferring, Translating and Transforming: An Integrative Framework for Managing Knowledge across Boundaries', *Organization Science*, 15/5: 555–68.
Develops a framework which differentiates between the distinctive ways that knowledge is managed across three different boundary types.

2. J. Chen, P. Sun, and R. McQueen (2010) 'The Impact of National Culture on Structured Knowledge Transfer', *Journal of Knowledge Management*, 14/2: 228–42.
A case which highlights how knowledge transfer processes can be influenced by differences in national cultures.

3. G. McGivern and S. Dawson (2010) 'Inter-Epistemic Power and Transforming Knowledge Objects in a Biomedical Network', *Organization Studies*, 31/12: 1667–686.
A study of how conflict and power dynamics emerged and were dealt with in a cross-community context concerned with biomedical innovation that involved a range of academics, medical practitioners, and government policy-makers.

4. M. Easterby-Smith, A. Lyles, and E. Tsang (2008) 'Inter-Organizational Knowledge Transfer: Current Themes and Future Prospects', *Journal of Management Studies*, 45/4: 677–90.
Introduction to a special issue of *JMS* on inter-organizational knowledge sharing which adopts an objectivist perspective on knowledge.

Take your learning further: Online Resource Centre

Visit the Online Resource Centre for resources which will extend your understanding of knowledge management in organizations. As well as web links to sites of interest, the author has provided case studies looking at knowledge management in virtual and knowledge-intensive firms, and in global multinationals. These will help you with your research, essays, and assignments; or you may find these additional resources helpful when revising for exams.

    www.oxfordtextbooks.co.uk/orc/hislop3e/

12 Power, Politics, Conflict, and Knowledge Processes

Introduction

One of the defining characteristics of the vast majority of the writing on knowledge management is that discussions of power are typically marginalized, if not completely absent (Kärreman 2010). Such an omission is puzzling, as a cursory glance outside the narrow confines of the knowledge management literature reveals both the need to understand issues of power in explaining organizational dynamics, as well as the close relationship between knowledge and power. However, the neglect of this topic is not total, because, as has already been shown in Chapters 10 and 11, a number of writers do take such issues seriously. This chapter argues that understanding the relationship between power and organizational knowledge processes is of fundamental importance.

While power has not been adequately dealt with in the knowledge management literature there has been a growing acknowledgement, as was outlined in Chapter 9, that conflict in relation to knowledge processes is not uncommon, and that such conflict can play an important role in shaping such processes, for example influencing who a person is willing and unwilling to share knowledge with. These issues are raised again here, but are explicitly linked to the topics of power and politics. Arguably, a missing link in the knowledge management literature is that it does not address the fundamental causes of such conflicts. To do so requires power to be accounted for, which reveals not only the inherent potential for conflict that exists in organizations but how power is structurally embedded in the employment relationship.

In the analysis presented, power and knowledge will be seen to be extremely closely interrelated, which is another reason why issues of power have to be accounted for in attempting to understand the dynamics of organizational knowledge processes. However, there is no consensus either how power should be defined or how its relationship to knowledge should be conceptualized. Here two different perspectives on power are examined, and linked to the two dissensus-based perspectives on knowledge management research identified by Schultze and Stabell (2004).

The chapter is structured into three major sections. The first section provides an overview of the two perspectives on power, and outlines how they link with Schultze and Stabell's framework. The following two sections then examine the two perspectives on power. First is the 'power as a resource' perspective, which links back to the topics of the employment relationship and intra-organizational conflict discussed in Chapter 9. The second perspective is Michel Foucault's distinctive perspective on power/knowledge.

Two Perspectives on Power and the Power/Knowledge Relationship

That two contrasting perspectives on power have been articulated in the knowledge management literature should not really be a surprise, as power is one of the most contested concepts in social theory. This section provides an overview of these two perspectives on power and power/knowledge relations, and links them with the two 'dissensus' perspectives in Schultze and Stabell's (2004) framework on knowledge management research articulated in Chapter 1 (see Figure 1.3).

In Schultze and Stabell's (2004) framework there were two dimensions: epistemology and social order. In terms of the social order dimension they differentiated between the consensus- and dissensus-based views. In Chapters 2 and 3, where the characteristics of the two epistemological perspectives that dominate in the knowledge management literature were presented, the focus was deliberately confined to epistemologies linked to the consensus-based perspective on social order (what Schultze and Stabell labelled the constructivist and neo-functional discourses). Part of the rationale for doing so was that the two consensus-based perspectives have been more extensively utilized, and interest in and use of either of the dissensus-based perspectives has been comparatively marginal and limited. However, in considering how power and politics link to knowledge processes in organizations it is necessary to make use of the two epistemologies/discourses on knowledge management that link to the dissensus-based perspective on social order (in Schultze and Stabell's terms, the dialogic and critical discourses). Thus the neglect of them is addressed here.

Before outlining the two perspectives on power, what differentiates them, and how they map onto the two dissensus-based perspectives on social order in Schultze and Stabell's framework, it is worth, briefly, (re)articulating what the two dissensus-based epistemologies/discourses have in common. Their primary common feature is that, in contrast to the consensus-based perspective, which assumes harmonious social relations typically predominate, the two epistemologies linked to the dissensus-based perspective on social order assume that antagonistic relations are an inherent feature of social dynamics both in business organizations, and society more widely. From this perspective societies are made up of groups whose interests are often oppositional and conflicting, where political behaviour motivated by the pursuit of such interests is common. One of the features common to both of the epistemologies/discourses linked to the dissensus-based perspective, and the reason they are both examined here, is that power and knowledge are conceptualized as being closely interrelated. Thus, from these perspectives, in examining the character and dynamics of organizational knowledge processes, it is fundamentally important and necessary to take account of power.

The primary reason why the two perspectives on power examined here map neatly on to the two dissensus perspectives in Schultze and Stabell's framework (the critical and dialogic

Table 12.1 Mapping of Two Perspectives on Power onto Critical and Dialogic Perspectives on Knowledge Management Research

	Critical Discourse	Dialogic Discourse
Character of Knowledge	A stable entity/resource that can exist independently of people	Knowledge largely tacit and provisional, being embodied by people and embedded in the activities they undertake
	Power as Resource	**Foucault's Power/Knowledge**
Character of Power	A stable resource (that has diverse forms) which exists independently of people, and which can be utilized by actors to influence people and/or events with the aim of achieving particular goals	A phenomenon which is embedded within and inseparable from social relationships and the discourses people articulate which people can utilize, but not possess, and which shapes (and legitimates) particular ways of acting and thinking
Relationship between Power and Knowledge	Knowledge is an important type of power resource that people can utilize in pursuit of particular interests	Power and knowledge are inseparable and mutually constituted

discourses) is that they conceptualize power in almost identical ways to how knowledge is conceptualized in these discourses (see Table 12.1). The 'power as resource' perspective (which maps onto the critical discourse perspective in Schultze and Stabell's framework) links to the influential resource-based tradition in the analysis of power (Bacharach and Baratz 1963; Dahl 1957; French and Raven 1959), as well as the more radical perspective on power developed by Lukes (1974). The alternative power/knowledge perspective (which maps onto the dialogic discourse) is embedded in the work of Foucault, whose distinctive understanding of power has grown in influence, and has been utilized and adopted by a number of writers to understand organizational knowledge processes.

As seen in Table 12.1, and as will be outlined more fully in subsequent sections, what differentiates these perspectives on power is not only how they define power, but how they conceptualize the relationship between power and knowledge. Thus the 'power as resource' perspective regards knowledge as a power resource that people can utilize politically, where conflict exists, in the pursuit of particular self-interested goals. By contrast the Foucauldian perspective on power, and the reason why the term power/knowledge is used, is that power and knowledge are regarded as being completely inseparable, with all acts of power being embedded in and to some extent perpetuating particular ways of understanding (knowledge), while all statements of knowledge involve the exercise of power (by implicitly and unavoidably privileging a particular perspective and simultaneously questioning the legitimacy of other claims to knowledge).

An important topic from both perspectives which links power and politics to knowledge is the process via which certain forms and types of knowledge come to be regarded as legitimate, while other knowledge claims become marginalized and regarded as having less legitimacy. Thus each of the following sections outlines how this process occurs from the viewpoint of the perspectives on power examined.

Power as a Resource and the Critical Discourse on Knowledge Management

As already highlighted, the perspective on power associated with the critical discourse on knowledge management aligns with the resource-based view on power (see Table 12.1). This perspective on power was first articulated over fifty years ago, in the late 1950s, and has been highly influential since then.

Theorizing power and power/knowledge relations

From this perspective, power is a resource that individuals can develop and utilize to influence the attitudes, values, and behaviour of others in the pursuit of particular objectives. Thus, Hales (1993: 20) defines power resources as 'those things which bestow the means whereby the behaviour of others may be influenced', while Liao (2008: 1882) similarly defines power as 'the ability of an agent to change or control the behaviours, attitudes, opinions, objectives, needs, and values of another agent'. The key feature of these definitions is that power is conceptualized as a discrete resource/entity that people can possess, or have access to. Hales argues that power resources have this ability through three specific properties they possess (see Table 12.2). First, they are relatively scarce and only available to some. Secondly, they are desired because they can satisfy certain wants. Finally, there are no alternatives available, in that the only way to satisfy these wants is via the use of particular power resources. Thus knowledge has the potential to be a power resource if it has these characteristics. For example, the specialist technical knowledge built up over time that an experienced engineer possesses will be a power resource available to the engineer who possesses it if it is scarce and only possessed by a small number of people, if it is important and useful to their employer, and if there are no alternative sources of similar expertise.

Table 12.2 Properties of Power Resources which Make them Influential

Property	Expert power-based example
Scarcity	Specialist knowledge/expertise which only a limited number of people possess. Knowledge which may be highly tacit, and which requires to be developed through experience.
Satisfy Wants	Knowledge which may satisfy individual wants through its possession or use (such as status, or rewards), or knowledge which satisfies organizational goals and objectives through its possession or use (such as providing organizations with status, profits, market share, or product/market innovations).
No Alternatives	Where there are no alternative sources of knowledge which can satisfy important wants (see above).

DEFINITION Power (resource-based perspective)

Power is a (scarce) resource whose use allows people to shape the behaviour of others.

This perspective assumes that there are five distinct types of power resource that people can utilize (see Table 12.3). The first two types of power represent contrasting ways of attempting to influence others. First, reward power utilizes a person's ability to offer rewards as a way of influencing behaviour. Rewards can take a variety of forms, from monetary to non-monetary (such as an award, praise, recognition). This power resource is thus available to anyone who has access to such rewards. However, the ability to shape someone's behaviour in this way depends on the extent to which they desire the reward that is offered. Fundamentally, the more desirable the reward is to a person, the more likely their behaviour is to be influenced by being offered it. In contrast, coercive power utilizes a person's ability to punish non-compliance as a way of influencing behaviour. As with rewards, such punishments can take a variety of forms including witholding a reward, providing a negative report on a person, or even the extreme of using physical threats. However, the ability to influence someone in this way is affected by the extent to which they regard the potential punishment as serious and important. Legitimate power refers to the ability to influence someone through being regarded as someone who has a legitimate right to give commands and control behaviour. The most obvious example of this is the authority possessed by a manager, due to their formal position, roles, and responsibilities in the organizational hierarchy. However, simply possessing managerial authority does not guarantee someone that they will have legitimate power. For example, if someone is deemed to have achieved their position by unfair means (such as favouritism), or if they abuse their authority (via bullying and threatening people), they may not be deemed as having legitimate power and may not be able to use their position to effectively influence others. The fourth type of power is reference power.

Table 12.3 Types of Power

Power Resource	Nature/Source of Influence
Reward power	Influencing others via the ability to administer rewards for particular behaviours.
Coercive power	Influencing others via the ability to administer a punishment for non-compliance with requests.
Legitimate power	Influencing others via persuading them of the legitimacy of someone's right to define and control behaviour.
Reference power	Influencing others via possessing and developing their admiration and desire to gain approval.
Expert power	Influencing others via the possession or use of particular knowledge, expertise or skill.

This source of power is based not on hierarchical position in an organization, but is instead on the extent to which people admire and respect someone and wish to gain their approval.

Of most relevance to the topic of knowledge management is the fifth and final type of power, expert power. A person has access to this type of power if they possess or utilize what are regarded as important and legitimate knowledge and skills. However, simply possessing knowledge and skills is not necessarily a source of expert power as the legitimacy of someone's knowledge may be open to dispute, or someone's competence in utilizing knowledge and skills may be questioned or compromised.

 Illustration   Resource-based power and knowledge sharing

Liao (2008) uses the resource-based model of power to examine the extent and ways in which managers are able to influence their subordinates' knowledge-sharing behaviours. Empirical data were collected from a survey of Research and Development staff in three Taiwanese computer companies. The theoretical model they tested considered both the direct effect that the five types of power available to managers had on employees' knowledge sharing, and also the indirect effect, when the relationship between the types of power and employee knowledge sharing was mediated by trust.

In terms of the direct effect, it was found that only reward and expert power had a direct influence on employees' knowledge sharing. In terms of the indirect relationship it was found that only reference and expert power had a positive relationship with employees' trust in their managers. Perhaps unsurprisingly, coercive power had neither a direct or indirect relationship with employees' knowledge sharing.

These findings have significant organizational implications. First, in terms of the direct relationship between power and knowledge sharing, the importance of reward power suggests that rewarding employees may be a useful way to motivate them to share knowledge. Secondly, in terms of the indirect relationship between power and knowledge sharing, the importance of reference and expert power in the development of trust suggests that manager should develop both types of power, through managing employees so that they respect both the expert knowledge of managers and them as individuals.

1. To what extent does this reinforce the idea that the use of coercive power is unlikely to be a successful way to influence people as its use is never likely to be regarded as legitimate?

2. Can you think of situations where the use of coercive power may be considered legitimate?

Linking power and knowledge to conflict and politics

To fully understand the role that power resources can play in organizational knowledge processes, it is necessary to consider the complex relationship that exists between power, knowledge, politics, and conflict in organizations. Figure 12.1 sums this relationship up diagrammatically. However, before explaining it more fully, it is necessary to define what is meant by politics. Political acts are those actions whereby people deliberately attempt to influence others through the use of power resources, with the aim of achieving particular goals (which may be in conflict with the goals of others).

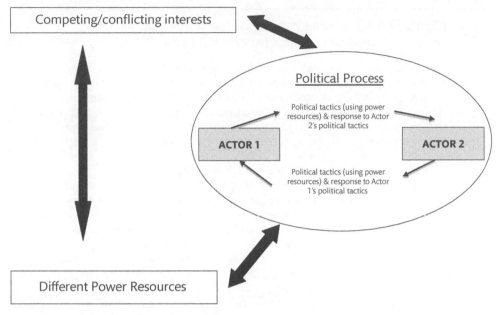

Figure 12.1 Linking Power, Politics, and Conflict

The political process in Figure 12.1 is a dynamic social situation where different actors (individuals or groups) who have competing or conflicting interests draw upon particular power resources, which are used as political tools aimed at achieving each group's objectives. The political process is a dynamic situation as it can evolve over time, with actors having scope to change what interests they purse, what power resources they draw upon in pursuit of their aims, and the particular political tactics they utilize. For example, in relation to expert power, there is a diverse range of political tactics by means of which this source of power can be utilized in attempting to influence others. For example, some could choose to share or hoard their expert knowledge, or may choose to selectively share it with only certain people. Thus, with every source of power, a diverse range of political tactics can be utilized.

A key part of the model outlined in Figure 12.1 is how the dynamics of political processes are shaped by the way actors respond to the political tactics and power resources of others. As outlined above in describing the character of power resources, the ability of people to use power resources to influence others depends on the extent to which they are regarded as important and legitimate by people. Such judgements have important implications for how actors behave, because if someone's power is deemed legitimate then people are more likely to comply than if it is regarded as being of dubious legitimacy. Thus while managerial power is, to some extent, a function of organizational position, it is one of the problematic aspects of management that such power cannot be assumed to be *automatically* deemed as legitimate by workers (Hislop *et al.* 2000). For example, behaviour such as verbally abusing workers, or not adequately consulting them, may undermine the extent to which power related to managerial position is deemed legitimate by workers.

Illustration   Disputed knowledge: 'pit sense' and the bureaucratization of risk assessment in coal mines

Kamoche and Maguire (2011) examined a political dispute within the UK coal industry regarding how risk assessment should be carried out, which centred on the legitimacy of 'pit sense', a form of sense-based, tacit knowledge developed by miners which they had traditionally used to evaluate risk. This tacit knowledge was developed over time, through working in mines, was never codified in any way, was regarded by miners as being fundamentally important to safe working, and was knowledge that management had little understanding of, or control over. Thus, in terms of the resource-based view of power, this was a dispute regarding the 'expert power' possessed by the miners in the form of specialized knowledge on risk assessment that was not possessed by management.

'Pit sense' involved being aware of unusual and suspicious noises or smells that may suggest a problem in a mine. This knowledge was defined as being concerned with 'how to look after yourself in a mine, knowing what to do and what not to do' (p. 732). However, over time, with the development of new, mechanized work practices, and more rule-based, bureaucratic working practices, management increasingly came to question the validity and legitimacy of 'pit sense'. Fundamentally, management wanted risk assessment to be more focused on using standardized health and safety procedures, and to be less driven by 'pit sense'. To help do this they implemented new health and safety procedures and simultaneously attempted to undermine the legitimacy of 'pit sense'. For example, it began to be referred to by some managers as 'old wives tales' (p. 736). However, due both to the miners' reluctance to give up 'pit sense' and to the lack of control that management had over the miners' working practices, they were not able to eliminate the use of 'pit sense'.

Instead, an uneasy compromise was reached by the miners and management, whereby the miners used the new rules, but had discretion to ignore them when they chose. An illustration of this was provided by one miner who said, 'you're supposed to wear ear muffs while you're bolting. Now if something is going to come over, usually it gives you a warning, you can hear something. When you've got ear muffs on you can't hear it coming. So more often than not we don't wear our ear muffs' (p. 736). The compromise made by management was to accept that this was done, but ignore it, as long as productivity levels were maintained at an acceptable level.

1. Analyse this case using the political model outlined earlier in the chapter and summarized in Figure 12.1. How would you characterize the political tactics utilized by both management and the miners?

2. Could the dispute have been resolved differently if either management or miners had utilized different sources of power, or used different political tactics?

Yanow (2004), in examining the nature of the knowledge possessed by bakery workers found that formal codified knowledge ('expert' knowledge) was typically privileged over the tacit knowledge possessed by bakery drivers ('local' knowledge). This privileging of codified knowledge (and simultaneous marginalization of tacit, 'local' knowledge) was a consequence of the greater legitimacy accorded formal, codified knowledge and the reduced legitimacy that was typically accorded more tacit, contextual, and local knowledge. Analysed in the context of the issues examined here, this process of privileging codified expert knowledge and marginalizing local, tacit knowledge is the outcome of a political process whereby the legitimacy of these different forms of knowledge has been disputed and resolved in a particular way. Overall, from a resource-based perspective on power, an actor's knowledge-based power resources are never automatically regarded as legitimate by others, and the extent to which they are will influence how others respond to them.

The critical discourse on knowledge management and the inevitability of power and conflict in business organizations

In examining the importance of power to knowledge processes from the perspective of a critical discourse on knowledge management and from a resource-based perspective on power it is necessary to return to two issues discussed in Chapter 9: the employment relationship, and the potential for conflict that exists between workers in organizations. It is due to both of these factors that those adopting a critical discourse on knowledge management believe knowledge processes in organizations typically produce conflict both between workers and management and between different workers (and groups of workers). As suggested previously and in Figure 12.1, issues of conflict, power, and politics are intimately interrelated. Thus, acknowledging that organizational knowledge processes often create conflict suggests that power and politics are an unavoidable element of such processes.

In terms of the employment relationship, while Chapter 9 highlighted the potential conflict between workers and organizational management that knowledge management processes can induce, what was only touched on was the extent to which the employment relationship is also a relationship of power. This section highlights issues of power embedded in the employment relationship.

As outlined in Chapter 9 there are tensions between workers and their employing organization over the ownership and control of workers' knowledge (Contu and Willmott 2003). On the one hand, their interests may be compatible, through the potential mutual benefits that workers and their employers may derive from the employer supporting and facilitating the workers' knowledge activities. On the other hand, simultaneously, the requirement of organizations to extract economic value from their workers' knowledge may conflict with their workers' individual objectives in this respect. Such tensions are amplified by the (potential) fragility of the employment relationship resulting from the ability of both parties to easily terminate the relationship, the worker through leaving or the employer through making workers redundant.

However, only when the employment relationship is located within the socio-economic context of capitalist relations of production does a structurally embedded power relationship become visible. For example, Tsoukas (2000), developing a realist conception of the employment relationship referred to the 'structural basis of managers' power' (p. 34), which places workers in a typically subordinate relationship to managers/superiors. From this perspective, management are the mediating agents of capital owners and shareholders, where organizations are shaped by demands to make profit and accumulate capital, which requires managers/superiors to control and simultaneously achieve the cooperation of workers in order to turn their labour power into actual, productive work effort. Such a perspective on the employment relationship is developed by Contu and Willmott (2003), who talk of the hierarchical organization of the employment relationship and how this places workers in a typically subordinate position to management.

At this point, a significant caveat is required when considering the situation of knowledge workers. The power of management over workers is contingent upon the specific character-istics of the organizational context, and the power of management can be diminished or enhanced by shifts in societal power relations (Tsoukas 2000). For knowledge workers two factors imbuing them with power are, first, the typical importance of their knowledge to the organizations they work for and, secondly, the general scarcity of their skills in labour mar-kets, which makes many knowledge workers highly sought after (Beaumont and Hunter 2002; Flood *et al.* 2001). These factors are thus likely to provide knowledge workers with significant amounts of power and may mean they are likely to be in a less subordinate posi-tion to management than other types of workers.

 Time to reflect   The power of knowledge workers

How unique is the situation of knowledge workers? Are they the only type of workers whose knowledge is important and valued? Can you think of other types of workers who have important knowledge that provides them with a source of power?

As also outlined in Chapter 9, for those adopting a dissensus-based perspective on social order the potential for conflict in organizations emanates from more than just the nature of the employment relationship. This potential flows from the different interests that exist within organizations between both individuals and groups. From this perspec-tive the social dissensus, conflict, and antagonism that is assumed to exist within socie-ties also exists within organizations. Thus, both the dissensus-based perspectives on knowledge management adopt, as outlined in Chapter 9, what Fox (1985) labelled a plu-ralist perspective, which assumes organizations can be conceptualized as being made up of a coalition of different interest groups acting in a coordinated way. This divergence of interests may come from individuals/groups competing over scarce organizational resources, or through clashes between the personal objectives and strategies that indi-vidual employees may pursue in order to sustain and develop their careers, such as receiving recognition for particular efforts/knowledge, receiving financial rewards, or gaining promotions.

 Time to reflect   The nature of organizations

What does your own experience say about the nature of organizations? Is conflict inevitable? Are power imbalances inherent?

As outlined in Chapter 9, despite the general neglect of issues of power, politics, and conflict in much knowledge management literature, there is a significant and growing body of empirical evidence which reinforces this perspective, as conflict, or perceived conflict, between individuals and groups has been found to play an important role in shaping the character and dynamics of organizational attempts to manage knowledge.

Power/Knowledge and the Dialogical Discourse on Knowledge Management

It is impossible to examine the relationship between power and knowledge without taking account of the work of the French philosopher Michel Foucault, as arguably he is the single most influential author in both the general business and management literature and in the area of human resource management (Barratt 2002; Introna *et al.* 2009; McKinlay and Starkey 1998; McKinlay *et al.* 2010; Motion and Leitch 2009; Townley 1994). As will be seen, Foucault's (1980) conceptualization of power, and characterization of the relationship between power and knowledge, is quite different from the resource-based perspective on power just elaborated. This section begins by giving a brief overview on the way Foucault theorizes power and its relationship with knowledge before subsequent subsections elaborate some of the key ways in which his work is relevant to the topic of knowledge management. As has been noted, only a small amount of writing on the topic of knowledge management draws on Foucault's work. Examples of studies on knowledge processes which explicitly utilize Foucauldian concepts are Hayes and Walsham (2000), Heizmann (2011), Marshall and Rollinson (2004), McKinlay (2000, 2002), and Sewell (2005).

Conceptualizing power/knowledge

To understand Foucault's particular way of conceptualizing power it is worth quoting him at length:

> the power exercised on the body is conceived not as a property, but as a strategy. . . . this power is exercised rather than possessed; it is not the 'privilege', acquired or preserved, of the dominant class, but the overall effect of its strategic positions—an effect that is manifested and sometimes extended by the position of those who are dominated.
>
> (Rabinow 1991: 174, quoting from Foucault's *Discipline and Punishment*)

Thus Foucault suggests that power, rather than being a discrete resource that social actors can utilize, is something which is produced and reproduced within and through the dynamics of evolving social relationships. This resonates with the practice-based episte-mology's conceptualization of knowledge as being embedded in particular contexts and work practices. Thus, power is not a resource that can be utilized at will by an actor, but is instead something that is embedded in the way people act, talk, and interact with others. In more simple terms, power is not a resource that actor 'a' can use autonomously to influence actor 'b' (as with the resource-based view of power), but is instead something that is constituted by actors 'a' and 'b' through how they interact with each other. Both actors play an equally fundamental role in the constitution of power.

Further, Foucault suggests that power and knowledge are so inextricably interrelated that they are fundamentally inseparable, and he coined the phrase power/knowledge to symbolize this (Foucault 1980). Further, the term power/knowledge symbolizes that not only are power and knowledge mutually constituted, but also that neither element should be privileged over the other. To properly appreciate Foucault in this respect, it is again worth quoting him at length:

> Power produces knowledge . . . power and knowledge directly imply one another; that there is no power relation without the correlative constitution of a field of knowledge, nor any knowledge that does not presuppose and constitute at the same time power relations.
>
> (Rabinow 1991: 17, quoting from Foucault's *Discipline and Punishment*)

The implication of this insight for understanding the dynamics of knowledge processes is therefore profound, as all uses of knowledge, or attempts to shape and manage knowledge within organizations, inevitably involve the use of power.

DEFINITION   Power (power/knowledge perspective)

Power is produced and reproduced through the evolution of social relations. Power is embedded in language and is implicated in struggles over truth claims whereby the veracity of certain knowledge or truth claims are negotiated.

Discourse, power/knowledge, and the legitimation of truth claims

A further consequence of the way power/knowledge is conceptualized is the importance of language and discourse. Fundamentally, power/knowledge claims are embedded in and expressed through language, as truth claims. Styhre (2003: 88) thus argues that 'discourses are always based on power, and are manifestations of power'. For Foucault, this is the case with all truth claims, and is evidence of a Nietzschean inspired scepticism with the apparent absolute truth claims that are based in taken for granted belief systems such as religion. For Foucault, as with Nietzsche, there is a rejection of all essentialisms as there is argued to be no basis on which absolute truth can be established.

The process via which certain claims to knowledge become established as legitimate, and others become marginalized and regarded as having limited legitimacy, is a collaborative social process of negotiation and struggle over meaning between actors articulating different truth claims. However, while with the resource-based perspective power resources are seen as relatively fixed and stable entities that actors utilize and draw upon in attempting to resolve political dynamics in a way favourable to them, from a Foucauldian perspective, power/knowledge claims have no such stable status, with the extent to which they are regarded as legitimate being an outcome of the process of negotiation over meaning that actors engage in. Such a process of negotiation is examined by both Marshall and Rollinson (2004), who examine the dynamics of conflict during a problem solving situation, and Heizmann (2011), who analysed power/knowledge disputes between HR practitioners within a single multinational corporation (this is utilized as the extended end of chapter example).

Sewell (2005) reinforces these ideas in his conceptual paper which outlines the character of a Foucauldian perspective on knowledge management. For Sewell such an approach would involve the three equally important processes of elicitation (identifying useful knowledge), representation (the codification of useful knowledge), and finally, legitimation (the process via which some knowledge claims come to be regarded as legitimate—and simultaneously the legitimacy of other knowledge claims becomes reduced). Sewell makes transparent his commitment to a dissensus-based perspective on organizations by placing at the centre of his analysis the idea that workers and managers are likely to have competing interests, and that a key part of the struggle produced by this conflict is the process via which management attempt to control how workers think and act through discursive strategies aimed at establishing the legitimacy of managerial truth claims.

 ## Conclusion

While two contrasting perspectives on power have been examined, they both point to the conclusion that to analyse and effectively understand the full dynamics of organizational knowledge processes power must be accounted for. The chapter has identified two key reasons why this is the case. From a resource-based perspective the importance of taking account of power is due to the extent to which conflict shapes organizational knowledge processes, and the role that power and politics play in shaping them. From a Foucauldian perspective, power has to be accounted for in knowledge management processes, as power and knowledge are inseparable and mutually constituted.

As a consequence, one of the most general conclusions of this chapter is that the centrality of power to knowledge processes means that any analyses of such processes that neglects to account for power are relatively impoverished. For example, taking account of power helps to explain and understand the human/social dimension of knowledge processes, such as whether people are willing or reluctant to participate in organizational knowledge processes. Thus, Walsham suggests (2001: 603): 'what we know affects how influential we are [thus] . . . there may be good reasons why individuals may not wish to participate in, or may modify some aspect of their sense-giving activities, for reasons related to organizational politics'.

Knowledge management was also shown to be concerned with more than simply managing all the knowledge that exists in organizations. Taking account of power helps reveal and make visible how knowledge management processes involve certain claims to knowledge becoming legitimated (and others marginalized), which often involves disputes and negotiations over competing knowledge claims. Thus, taking account of power helps address the typically neglected topic of why certain types and forms of knowledge become the focus of knowledge management initiatives.

 ### Case study   Power/knowledge struggles between HR practitioners

Heizmann (2011) utilizes Foucault's power/knowledge concept to analyse the dynamics of a conflict that developed between regional and corporate HR practitioners within a single multinational corporation. The central focus of the analysis is on the contradictory truth claims made by corporate and regional HR staff about each other that involved questioning and challenging each others' legitimacy. The organization that Heizmann studied was a large Australian insurance company, which had offices throughout Australia and employed about 8,000 workers in total. In terms of the HR function, it had sixty to seventy people based at the corporate headquarters, and a small number of staff at a few regional offices. The main source of data for Heizmann was semi-structured interviews, with twenty staff being interviewed in total, sixteen of them located at the corporate headquarters, and four at two separate regional offices.

Heizmann adopted a practice-based epistemology and assumed that the knowledge of HR staff was embedded in their (local) work practices and activities. In analysing interviewees' perspectives on the dispute between corporate and regional HR staff, Heizmann started from the assumption that what they said in the interviews, their 'discursive truth claims' (p. 382), were considered as 'power/knowledge claims' (p. 382). Further, it was assumed that in making these power/knowledge claims people were attempting to establish the legitimacy of their claims, while simultaneously questioning the legitimacy of conflicting power/knowledge claims. Presented below are some selective examples of the power/knowledge claims made by both corporate and regional HR staff.

(continued)

The power/knowledge claims made by corporate HR staff took the perspective that the HR function had a key role to play as change agents and strategic business partners. Further, due to the geographic proximity of corporate HR staff to senior corporate managers, they argued that corporate HR staff were successful in playing these roles, whereas regional staff were out of touch with these roles for the HR function. Thus, one corporate HR employee said: 'I guess the regional HR managers have been there a very long time and are old school as far as their HR approach . . . we're there to advise and support, but we're not there to manage people. We're there to support the leaders in managing people' (p. 385). Corporate HR staff claimed that part of the reason regional HR staff were disconnected from the corporate agenda was that they were too focused on meeting the needs of local clients. Thus, one interviewee from the corporate centre said: 'you can't always just pander to what the local clients want because what the business wants, what they think they want, might not be the right thing for the business' (p. 385).

In contrast, regional HR staff took a conflicting position, arguing that due to corporate HR's focus on strategic alignment with the business, the work of corporate HR staff was political and strategic, rather than being orientated towards the management of people. Thus one regional interviewee said: 'It's a much more political world in Big City A [corporate HQ], because you've got the major players, the executive managers, those sorts' (p. 385). Related to this a key element of the power/knowledge claims of regional HR staff was that corporate HR staff didn't understand the importance of addressing the needs of local clients, through customizing and adapting the corporate agenda to their specific needs. Implicit in the power/knowledge claims of regional staff was that they were more knowledgeable than corporate HR staff with respect to understanding client needs. Thus, one regional HR staff member said, 'whatever I get from Head office, I usually cut out half the slides. It's just too much detail and not client-focused. And I also change the language. Words like "capability identification" . . . my clients would simply leave the room' (p. 387).

As the article presented a 'static' viewpoint, outlining people's perspectives at one particular point in time only, it was not clear how this conflict evolved over time, and how, if at all, it was resolved. This dispute was found to have had a significant impact on knowledge-sharing practices between HR staff. The sharing of knowledge between regional and corporate staff was adversely affected, due largely to each group disputing and questioning the legitimacy of each other's knowledge.

1. What, if anything could be done to resolve these disputed claims (and who would be best placed to evaluate the claims and negotiate a resolution)?
2. To what extent are the types of regional versus head office disputes found in the case study relatively unavoidable in geographically dispersed organizations and common to all multinational corporations?

Source: Heizmann, H. (2011) 'Knowledge Sharing in a Dispersed Network of HR Practice: Zooming in on Power/ Knowledge Struggles', *Management Learning,* 42/4: 379–93.

 ## Review and Discussion Questions

1. In general, how compatible are the interests of workers and their employers over how workers' knowledge is used? Does the requirement by organizations to derive economic value from it mean conflict is likely or inevitable?

2. The chapter assumed that power and knowledge are closely related, if not inseparable. Can you think of any ways in which knowledge can be used in organizations which do not involve the use of power?

3. Foucault's perspective on power/knowledge suggests that all power/knowledge claims are open to dispute, and that it is never possible to establish any form of ultimate, objective 'true' knowledge. What implications does such an assumption have for the possibility of resolving disputes which occur within organizations?

Suggestions for Further Reading

1. **L.-F. Liao (2008) 'Knowledge Sharing in R&D Departments: A Social Power and Social Exchange Theory Perspective',** *International Journal of Human Resource Management*, 19/10: 1881–95.
Explicitly utilizes the resource-based perspective on power to consider the way in which managers can influence the knowledge-sharing behaviours of subordinates.

2. **H. Heizmann (2011) 'Knowledge Sharing in a Dispersed Network of HR Practice: Zooming in on Power/Knowledge Struggles',** *Management Learning*, 42/4: 379–93.
Utilizes a Foucauldian perspective on power to examine the dynamics of a conflict among the HR staff within one company which concerned disputes regarding the legitimacy of two different perspectives on the role of the HR function.

3. **A. Willem and H. Scarbrough (2006) 'Social Capital and Political Bias in Knowledge Sharing: An Exploratory Study',** *Human Relations*, 59/10: 1343–70.
Case study analysis of two Belgian companies which examined how politics moderates the relationship between social capital and knowledge sharing and can produce a very selective form of self-interested knowledge sharing.

4. **B. Mørk, T. Hoholm, G. Ellingsen, E. Maaninen-Olsson, and M. Aanestad (2012) 'Changing Practices through Boundary Organizing: A Case from Medical R&D',** *Human Relations*, 65/2: 263–88.
An interesting empirical case which examines the politics involved in 'boundary organizing' activities related to the implementation of changes in knowledge and practice.

Take your learning further: Online Resource Centre

Visit the Online Resource Centre for resources which will extend your understanding of knowledge management in organizations. As well as web links to sites of interest, the author has provided case studies looking at knowledge management in virtual and knowledge-intensive firms, and in global multinationals. These will help you with your research, essays, and assignments; or you may find these additional resources helpful when revising for exams.

 www.oxfordtextbooks.co.uk/orc/hislop3e/

Information and Communication Technologies and Knowledge Management

Introduction

Information and communication technologies (ICTs) have always played a prominent role in knowledge management processes and research. However, the reason for this interest has evolved over time. When interest in knowledge management began to develop in the late 1990s ICTs played a significant role in the vast majority of knowledge management initiatives. Thus, Ruggles (1998), reporting on a 1997 survey, found that the four most popular types of knowledge management projects involved the implementation of intranets, data warehouses, decision support tools, and groupware (i.e. technologies that support collaboration and communication). Scarbrough and Swan (2001) found that this emphasis was also reflected in academic research on knowledge management, with the vast majority of published research focusing on information technology-related issues. The reason for the significant role accorded to ICTs at this time was that there was a general optimism that much organizational knowledge could be codified, stored in, and distributed via ICTs. There was also a general optimism amongst many organizations that simply implementing a relevant ICT system would lead to the successful management of knowledge. Over time, both these assumptions have been questioned and challenged.

However, ICTs have still retained a high-profile role in knowledge management activities and research. This continued interest is arguably due to two, related factors. First, developments in ICTs have facilitated collaboration between people and teams which are geographically dispersed, with a variety of labels being used for this type of working, including virtual working and (globally) dispersed working. One significant strand of research into this type of collaboration has been concerned with understanding the character and dynamics of knowledge processes in such contexts. Since the mid-2000s there has been a significant amount of research on this broad topic (Chiravuri *et al.* 2011; Ho *et al.* 2011; Faraj *et al.* 2011; Kotlarsky *et al.* 2007; Mueller *et al.* 2011; Oshri *et al.* 2008; Robert *et al.* 2009; Wang and Haggerty 2009). Secondly, and relatedly, it has increasingly been acknowledged that ICTs can facilitate knowledge management activities, not just via the codification of knowledge, but through facilitating rich and interactive forms of communication. This is most visible in research into the role that Web 2.0 technologies can play in facilitating knowledge management activities, which is a topic examined more fully later in the chapter.

DEFINITION Information and communication technologies (ICTs)

ICTs are technologies which allow/facilitate the management and/or sharing of knowledge and information. Thus the term covers an enormous diversity of heterogeneous technologies including computers, telephones, e-mail, databases, data-mining systems, search engines, the internet, and video-conferencing equipment.

The chapter begins by providing an overview of the diversity of ways that ICTs can be used to facilitate knowledge management initiatives, which is done via linking back to the typologies of knowledge management examined in Chapter 4. One of the key conclusions of this section is that the role assigned to ICTs in knowledge management initiatives is significantly shaped by the assumptions about knowledge that are made. Before examining in detail the different ways in which ICTs can be used to facilitate the management of knowledge, the chapter briefly links back to issues raised in Chapter 9, to consider the importance of taking account of socio-cultural factors in all types of ICT-enabled knowledge management. Following this, two separate sections consider the role ascribed to ICTs in knowledge management initiatives when objectivist and practice-based perspectives on knowledge are adopted. The chapter concludes by considering two (related) debates regarding the character of ICT-mediated social processes that have implications for the role that ICTs can play in knowledge management. These debates centre on the extent to which ICTs can facilitate rich interaction and communication, and the extent to which trust can be developed and sustained in social relations mediated by ICTs.

Linking Knowledge Management and ICTs

As was discussed explicitly in Chapter 4, and what should be apparent implicitly throughout this book is that there are a vast range of ways in which organizations can attempt to manage their knowledge. A specific issue that was touched on in Chapter 4, and that is examined more fully here, is how the role that ICTs can play in such activities will vary significantly depending upon the particular approach to knowledge management an organization adopts. The objective of this section is to return to the knowledge management typologies outlined in Chapter 4 to consider the particular roles that ICTs play in them.

Hendriks (2001) described the bringing together of ICTs and knowledge management as involving the clash of two titans, as such an enormous amount of analysis has been devoted to both topics and the inter-relationship between them. Attempting to do justice to the scale and scope of the debate on these linkages in the space of one chapter is therefore a difficult task. Fundamentally, Hendriks challenges the assumption that knowledge management can simply be equated with the implementation and use of certain types of technology. Instead Hendriks suggests that there are five dimensions which affect the way ICTs are used to help manage knowledge in organizations, including the extent to which knowledge is important to organizational performance and the nature of organizational knowledge (whether it is largely tacit or explicit, etc.). Rather than attempt to articulate the full complexity of Hendriks's model of the ICT–KM relationship, the divergent roles that ICTs can play in organizational knowledge management initiatives are here considered by combining the epistemological distinctions between the objectivist and practice-based epistemologies with the knowledge management typologies outlined in Chapter 4 (see Table 13.1).

Table 13.1 Divergent Approaches to ICT-Enabled Knowledge Management

ICT-Enabled KM from Objectivist Perspective

Purpose	KM Strategies Linked with	Empirical Examples
Libraries of Codified Knowledge	Alvesson and Kärreman's extended library Earl's systems-based school Hansen et al.'s codification-based approach	Dixon et al. (2009): the use of knowledge codification to capture and store knowledge within a US public healthcare organization Lam (2005): a repository base knowledge management application within an Indian software company Gray and Durcikova (2005–6): knowledge repository used by technical support staff in a call centre environment
Task-Related Codified Knowledge Embedded in Documentation and Standard Operating Procedures	Alvesson and Kärreman's enacted blueprints Earl's engineering school	King and Marks (2008): an IT-based system for the sharing of 'best practices' between staff in a globally dispersed US military procurement company Hsaio et al. (2006): system to support work of engineers in a semiconductor fabrication equipment company

ICT-Enabled KM from Practice-Based Perspective

Purpose	KM Strategies Linked with	Empirical Examples
Mapping of Expertise	Earl's cartographic approach	Choi et al. (2010): The role of IT systems to create transactive memory and facilitate the sharing of knowledge within two South Korean companies Oshri et al. (2008): the importance of transactive memory to facilitate the sharing of knowledge within globally dispersed software development teams
Collaboration Tools to Facilitate ICT-Based Communication and Knowledge Sharing	Earl's organizational school Earl's spatial school	Teo et al. (2011): see end of chapter case study Li and Poon (2011): the use of Web 2.0 technologies for the sharing of knowledge on construction safety Kauppila et al. (2011): the sharing of knowledge between globally dispersed virtual teams in one Finnish company

Table 13.1 illustrates the extent of the role that ICTs can play in knowledge management processes, as articulated in the three different knowledge management typologies examined in Chapter 4. Specifically, one of Hansen *et al*.'s (1999) two knowledge management strategies, two of Alvesson and Kärreman's (2001) four approaches to knowledge management, and five of the seven schools of knowledge management developed by Earl (2001) all give a significant role to ICTs. It is suggested here that the roles allocated to ICTs by these different styles of knowledge management can be classified into four generic types, two of which relate to each epistemological perspective. Subsequent sections examine in more detail the different ways that ICTs can be used in organizational knowledge management processes through outlining how the epistemological assumptions of the objectivist and practice-based perspectives shape the way ICTs are used, examining the four generic roles that ICTs typically have in knowledge management processes, and illustrating the issues raised with examples.

The Importance of Accounting for Socio-Cultural Factors in ICT-Enabled Knowledge Management

Research suggests that many ICT-enabled knowledge management initiatives have been unsuccessful, arguably because they focused almost exclusively on technological issues and typically played down, if not completely ignored, social, cultural, and political factors which have since been shown to be key in influencing the willingness of people to participate in knowledge management initiatives (see Chapter 9). Examples of such situations include a number of cases including the failed virtual community of practice examined by Chua (2006), and the failed knowledge management initiative studied by Lam (2005). Other research has shown that while socio-cultural factors have not led to the failure of knowledge management initiatives, they have shaped their characteristics and dynamics. For example, Kauppila *et al*. (2011) and Li (2010) highlight how different cultural backgrounds and a weak sense of shared identity can influence the character of virtual knowledge sharing among teams with members from different countries and/or functional groups; Robert *et al*. (2009) consider issues of trust in virtual teams; King and Marks (2008) highlight how workers' relations with supervisors and managers impacted on workers' IT-based codification behaviours; Kotlarsky and Oshri (2005) highlighted the importance of issues such as rapport to knowledge sharing in globally distributed teams, and Paroutis and Al Saleh (2009), see illustration, found that various socio-cultural factors helped explain why some workers didn't participate in Web 2.0-based knowledge-sharing activities.

Fundamentally, there are two key conclusions to be drawn from these studies on ICT-enabled knowledge management initiatives. First, simply putting an ICT-based knowledge management system in place is not in and of itself going to make people utilize it. Secondly, as was highlighted in Chapter 9, the success of all knowledge management initiatives, whether they utilize ICTs or not, involves effectively taking account of the socio-cultural factors which influence people's willingness to share knowledge, such as conflict, trust, time, or concerns about loss of status.

Illustration   Factors influencing knowledge sharing via Web 2.0 technologies

Paroutis and Al Saleh (2009) examined the factors that influenced people's decisions regarding whether to codify and share knowledge via Web 2.0 technologies within a single technology and service-based multinational corporation. They interviewed both users and non-users to understand their different rationales. Among both groups they found that a number of socio-cultural factors inhibited their willingness to use the Web 2.0 system.

   One of the main barriers to some people using the Web 2.0 platform for knowledge sharing was a lack of time: it was perceived that using the Web 2.0 system to both search for and find relevant knowledge, or to codify and share knowledge, could be time-consuming. For example, one interviewee said, 'the risk is that you spend time contributing to them and that people do not use the information you publish' (p. 56). Secondly, they also had concerns about the quality and quantity of the knowledge that was posted on the Web 2.0 system, with one interviewee saying: 'I think there is information overload and much of it is useless' (p. 56). Finally, people's unfamiliarity with the relatively new Web 2.0 technology meant that they felt more comfortable sharing knowledge via methods that they had always used. Thus, one interviewee said, 'it is easier and more comfortable to do it [share knowledge] the old way. You've got a traditional way of accessing and gaining information and you know how to do it quickly. Its almost second nature . . . you automatically default into what you're used to'.

Objectivist Perspectives on ICT-Enabled Knowledge Management

The popularity of the objectivist perspective on knowledge management, and the idea that through codification ICTs can play a crucial role in knowledge management processes, is visible in the number of ICT-enabled knowledge management initiatives in which codification activities are central. Examples include Siemens' ShareNet initiative (Voelpel *et al.* 2005), the US public health organization examined by Dixon *et al.* (2009), the globally dispersed military procurement organization examined by King and Marks (2008), the semiconductor equipment company examined by Hsiao *et al.* (2006), and the World Bank, where the objective of its knowledge management strategy in the late 1990s was to make itself a 'technology broker, transferring knowledge from one place where it is available to the place where it is needed' (van der Velden 2002: 30).

Epistemological assumptions and ICTs

Chapter 2 outlined in detail both how the objectivist perspective on knowledge conceptualizes knowledge and how it characterizes knowledge-sharing processes. However, it is worth briefly restating some of the key assumptions of this perspective, as they help explain the roles that this perspective assumes ICTs can play in knowledge management processes. First, this perspective conceptualizes knowledge in entitative terms, with knowledge being regarded as a discrete object that can exist separately from the people who possess and use it. Secondly, there is an optimism embedded in this perspective that much knowledge either exists in an explicit form, or that it can be made explicit through a process of codification (Steinmueller 2000). Thirdly, this perspective conceptualizes knowledge sharing as being based on a transmitter–receiver or conduit model (see Figure 2.1), and assumes that it is relatively straightforward to share codified knowledge. Building from these assumptions those utilizing an objectivist perspective believe that ICTs can play a direct role in knowledge management processes, with ICTs simply representing one key channel/medium through which explicit knowledge can be shared.

Objectivist perspectives on knowledge and the two roles for ICTs in knowledge management

The meta-analysis of the role of ICT systems in the three knowledge management typologies examined in Chapter 4 is articulated in Table 13.1 above. This suggests that despite the diversity of approaches to knowledge management embedded in these typologies, when objectivist assumptions about the nature of knowledge (outlined above) are utilized, there are two specific ways in which ICTs can facilitate knowledge management processes. Both of these roles for ICT-enabled knowledge management build on the twin assumptions outlined above: that knowledge can be codified and that once codified it can be transferred and shared between people via ICTs.

The first role for ICTs is in creating searchable repositories or libraries of knowledge. As outlined in Table 13.1 this relates to three specific knowledge management strategies, including Hansen *et al.*'s codification approach, Earl's systems approach, and Alvesson and Kärreman's extended library approach. The rationale of such systems is that if people are looking for knowledge on a particular topic or issue then they can search the repository for it, rather than having to develop their own solutions. For such systems to be successful a number of factors are necessary. First, people must be willing to codify their knowledge. Secondly, a system of categorizing and structuring knowledge must be found which allows people looking for knowledge to find it. Finally, people must be willing to search such systems for knowledge when they require assistance (Bock *et al.* 2006; Gray and Durcikova 2005–6; Paroutis and Al Saleh 2009).

The second role for ICTs is in codified and documented knowledge which is task-specific. As outlined in Table 13.1 this relates to both the enacted blueprint approach of Alvesson and Kärreman and Earl's engineering school of knowledge management. With this approach task-related knowledge is codified into documents like standard operating procedures, troubleshooting checklists, protocols for decision-making, etc. The assumption is that once what is regarded as the 'best practice' way of completing a task has been identified, this knowledge can be codified and disseminated to all relevant staff who may need to use it. The case of the knowledge management initiative implemented in 'Chipfab', the Taiwanese division of a semiconductor equipment company in Hsiao *et al.* (2006), represents one example of such a system. With this case, the knowledge management initiative was a 'knowledge repository' (Hsaio *et al.* 2006: 1295) concerned with updating and sharing 'best practice' procedures for the installation and maintenance of equipment. Key objectives of the system were thus to allow engineers to codify and share their knowledge of how to improve work practices, and that provided engineers with up-to-date knowledge on the best working practices they should utilize. Another example is the system examined by King and Marks (2008) which was utilized by a globally dispersed military procurement company, whose aim was to create a '"best practices, lessons learned" Repository' (p. 136).

Illustration The codification of knowledge in a geographically dispersed, cross-functional virtual team

Kauppila *et al.* (2011) examined the creation of some relatively successful virtual teams within one Finnish company, VI, which designed, manufactured, and sold industrial measuring equipment. While VI was a Finnish-based company, with all manufacturing, development, and marketing work being done in Finland, its customer base was globally dispersed, which consequently meant that is sales force was spread across twenty-four offices in twelve different countries. Virtual teams were set up to enable communication and knowledge sharing between the Finnish-based R&D and marketing staff and the globally dispersed sales force. Kauppila *et al.* summarized the aim of the teams as providing a way to 'bridge the different knowledge contexts . . . to ensure everyone's access to all relevant knowledge, to encourage a culture that was conducive to the joint creation of new knowledge'. Kauppila *et al.* examined a wide range of factors affecting the implementation and use of the virtual team system. However, the focus here is on factors influencing the sharing of codified, explicit knowledge. In general terms, the virtual team initiative was successful, and did facilitate the sharing of knowledge.

  However, they found an interesting contradiction. While the sales staff found the virtual team system to be a useful source of codified knowledge, they did not themselves codify their own knowledge on the system. Equally, while marketing staff codified knowledge on the virtual team portal, they did not regard it as their main method of communication and knowledge sharing. One of the main explanations for this was differences in the nature of the knowledge held by the marketing and sales staff. While much of the knowledge of marketing staff was 'product-related knowledge [which] dealt with technological specifications' (p. 413) and was relatively straightforward to codify, the knowledge of sales people on customers and markets was 'highly heterogeneous, context specific, and nuanced' (p. 413), and was difficult to codify.

Practice-Based Perspectives on ICT-Enabled Knowledge Management

Even over the short space of time that knowledge management has been regarded as an important topic there has been a significant evolution in the role that ICTs are conceptualized as being able to play in such processes. Broadly speaking, this has seen practice-based perspectives on knowledge become more fully embraced. As will be seen, the practice-based perspective regards ICTs as having a less direct, but equally important role in supporting and facilitating the social interactions that underpin interpersonal knowledge processes. As will be seen, this involves dealing with the concept of 'transactive memory systems' and the use of Web 2.0 technologies.

Epistemological assumptions and ICTs

Most fundamentally, due to the way those writing from a practice-based perspective conceptualize knowledge, they believe that the codification and storage of knowledge in ICT-based repositories is unlikely to result in useful knowledge. This is because these processes of codification typically produce a denuded form of knowledge, as the tacit assumptions and values which underpin it are lost (Hislop 2002*b*; Walsham 2001). Thus, effectively, what is codified is only part of the knowledge people possess and its utility, on its own, is limited.

Further, as outlined in Chapter 3, those adopting a practice-based epistemology assume that the transmitter–receiver metaphor of knowledge sharing is inappropriate, as the sharing of knowledge does not involve the simple transferral of a fixed entity (explicit knowledge) between two people. Instead, the sharing of knowledge involves two people actively inferring and constructing meaning from a process of interaction (Hislop 2002*b*). This relates to the processes of perspective making and taking which were described in Chapter 3, where those interacting develop an understanding of the values, assumptions, and tacit knowledge which underpin each other's knowledge base (Walsham 2001). Communication processes in such interactions, to be successful, require to be relatively rich, open, and based on a certain level of trust.

The role which those writing from a practice-based perspective believe that ICTs can play in knowledge processes is thus somewhat indirect, being related to facilitating and supporting the social relationships and communication processes which underpin knowledge processes. Walsham (2001: 599) usefully summarized this by arguing that 'computer based systems can be of benefit in knowledge based activities . . . to support the development and communication of human meaning'.

Practice-based perspectives on knowledge and the two roles for ICTs in knowledge management

As outlined in Table 13.1, despite the diversity of approaches to knowledge embedded in the three typologies of knowledge examined in Chapter 4, there are two ways that those utilizing a practice-based perspective on knowledge consider ICTs can be used to facilitate organizational knowledge management activities. First, they can be used to produce 'expertise maps', allowing people looking for help to identify others with relevant knowledge and expertise, which is where the concept of transactive memory systems is relevant. Secondly, they can be used as tools to facilitate rich forms of communication and collaboration between people who are physically dispersed, which is where the use of Web 2.0 technologies is examined.

The use of ICTs for mapping expertise fits closely with Earl's cartographic school of knowledge management. From this perspective, ICTs can be used to support knowledge management activities by allowing people to search for and identify other people with expertise that they are looking for. This can be done through producing databases of expertise, searchable web portals, or electronic yellow pages. Where this approach to ICT-enabled knowledge management differs from the library/repository approach is that no attempt is made to codify knowledge and expertise. Instead, knowledge is shared via interpersonal communication and interaction, which can occur once someone looking for a particular type of expertise has found someone who possesses it. The benefit of this approach to knowledge management is that it allows people to establish and develop contacts with strangers who have relevant knowledge which would have been difficult to achieve by other means. Such a facility has the potential to be of much use in geographically dispersed teams or multinational organizations.

DEFINITION Transactive memory system

Knowledge relating to the distribution of expertise within teams whereby team members have an understanding of who possesses what specialist knowledge.

The importance of knowing where expertise is located within the context of geographically dispersed teams helps to explain why the concept of 'transactive memory systems' has largely been developed and researched in this context, with research interest in the topic developing in the late 2000s (Choi *et al.* 2010; Jarvenpaa and Majchrzak 2008; Kanawattan-achai and Yoo 2007; Oshri *et al.* 2008). Choi *et al.* (2010) formally define transactive memory systems (TMSs) as 'a specialized division of cognitive labour that develops within a team with respect to the encoding, storage and retrieval of knowledge from different domains' (p. 856). More informally, they say that in TMSs, 'team members know who knows what and who knows who knows what' (p. 856). Thus, it is a concept that it closely linked to the idea of expertise mapping. Research on transactive memory systems suggests that their existence is linked to and can facilitate the sharing and joint creation/application of knowledge within teams.

 Illustration   The relationship between IT support, transactive memory systems, and the sharing and application of knowledge within teams

Choi *et al.* (2010) examined the impact of IT support and transactive memory systems on knowledge processes and team performance in the context of two large South Korean firms, one an oil company and one a steel company, both of which had well-developed knowledge management systems. Research data were collected via surveys, with over 740 useable surveys involving people from 139 teams being analysed. The focus here is narrowly on the relationship between IT support, transactive memory systems, and the sharing and application of knowledge. In terms of the relationship between IT support and transactive memory systems, a positive relationship was found, which suggests that one effective way of developing transactive memory within teams is through investing effectively in IT systems. Secondly a positive relationship was found to exist between both IT support and the sharing and application of knowledge, and between transactive memory systems and the sharing and application of knowledge. This therefore suggests that if investments in IT support lead to the development of transactive memory, this can be an effective way to facilitate the sharing and application of knowledge.

The second practice-based use for ICTs in knowledge management activities is to facilitate interpersonal communication and collaboration. This type of usage fits with both Earl's organizational and spatial schools of knowledge management. Here ICTs, via a wide range of virtual/web-based platforms, forums, and conduits, such as e-mail, instant messaging, discussion boards, intranets, chatrooms, blogs, etc., create conditions where rich interpersonal interactions can take place between people who are geographically dispersed and who have limited opportunities for face-to-face interaction. One example of how this can be done is through the creation of virtual spaces or 'cafes' whose primary purpose is to stimulate and facilitate informal interactions and processes of knowledge sharing between people. The knowledge management initiatives studied by McKinlay (2002) and Alavi *et al.* (2005–6) both had such features to them. Secondly, the creation of virtual communities of practice, which research evidence suggests has been widespread, also represents a means of developing and encouraging rich forms of communication and knowledge sharing that are ICT-mediated (Ardichvili *et al.* 2003; Chua 2006; Fahey *et al.* 2007; McClure Wasko and Faraj 2000; Usoro *et al.* 2007). However, by the late 2000s one of the most common ways that ICTs were being argued as facilitating knowledge management initiatives was via the use of Web 2.0 technologies (Levy 2009; Li and Poon 2011; Matschke *et al.* 2012). Thus, in considering ICTs as a tool to facilitate communication and collaboration, the focus here is on Web 2.0 technologies.

Before considering the role that Web 2.0 technologies can play in knowledge management processes it is necessary to define what Web 2.0 is. Web 2.0 technology refers to web-based platforms and applications that are collectively created via ongoing user contributions. Two more formal definitions of Web 2.0 are those of Paroutis and Al Saleh (2009: 53), 'community-driven web services such as social networking sites, blogs, wikis, etc. which facilitate a more socially connected web where everyone is able to communicate, participate, collaborate', and Steininger *et al.* (2010: 511), 'a more mature internet, in which users collaborate, share information and create networks and scale effects in large communities'. Compared to first-generation websites and platforms, where interaction between the user and the site was largely one way, with users taking content from sites, with Web 2.0 platforms, users have a greater to degree of interactivity and play a more active role in contributing knowledge and the creation of the Web 2.0 platform (Allen 2010). Examples of Web 2.0 technologies include wikis (most famously Wikipedia), blogs, discussion forums, and social networking sites.

DEFINITION Web 2.0

Internet-based technologies and systems which facilitate interaction between people and whose content is created via ongoing user interactions and contributions.

In relation to knowledge management, Web 2.0 technologies are argued to have positive benefits for the workers who utilize them, and for the organizations that employ them. In terms of worker benefits, the interactivity of Web 2.0 technologies are argued to help empower workers through creating opportunities for them to participate in dialogue and discussion and contribute their knowledge to interpersonal and community discussions (Levy 2009; Li and Poon 2011). Through the type of user interactions that Web 2.0 technologies facilitate, they also provide opportunities for workers to share knowledge with relevant others. Organizationally, the knowledge-related benefits of using Web 2.0 technologies are that, through the extensive interpersonal communication and interaction that they produce, they facilitate the sharing and co-creation of knowledge among those who actively participate in Web 2.0 platforms. Further, the internet-based nature of these technologies means that people can participate in them irrespective of their geographic location. Overall therefore, Web 2.0 technologies are argued by many to facilitate rich communication and interaction which allow people to develop a sense of community and shared identity, and which may also even facilitate the sharing of tacit knowledge (Steininger *et al.* 2010). Examples of academic studies into knowledge sharing and creation via Web 2.0 technologies include the division of HP Analytics examined by Teo *et al.* (2011) which is the end of chapter case study, a study into the sharing of knowledge on construction safety (Li and Poon 2011), and Paroutis and Al Saleh's (2009) study on the use of Web 2.0 technologies within one multinational corporation.

Debates Regarding the Role of ICTs in Knowledge Management Processes

Despite the increasing rhetoric, relating particularly to the use of Web 2.0 technologies, that interactive forms of ICT-based communication can facilitate the sharing of knowledge, there are still a number of questions regarding the extent to which people can develop strong social relationships and effectively share knowledge via ICTs. Suggested limitations to ICT-based knowledge sharing are the challenges of developing trust when much interpersonal communication is ICT-mediated and the richness of ICT-based communication compared to face-to-face interactions. Both these issues are considered here.

ICTs and communication/media richness

The first area of debate relates to the question of whether ICTs can facilitate the rich interaction and processes of perspective making and taking that those adopting a practice-based perspective suggest is necessary for interpersonal knowledge sharing to be successful. Walsham (2001) answers this question in the positive, and believes that ICT-mediated communication does have the potential to facilitate such processes of perspective making and taking. Boland *et al.* (1994) also believe that it could be possible to design IT systems to do this, suggesting: 'information technology can support distributed cognition by enabling individuals to make rich representations of their understanding, reflect upon those representations, engage in dialogue with others about them, and use them to inform action' (p. 457). DeSanctis and Monge (1999: 696) also take a positive view regarding the ability of ICTs to allow a rich form of interaction, by arguing that, rather than the loss of social cues which occurs when communicating via most ICTs being negative, such a loss may in fact facilitate understanding 'by removing the distraction of irrelevant stimuli'.

 Time to reflect   The communication benefits of having limited social cues

Is a potential advantage of ICT-mediated communication that people are less likely to judge others on potentially superficial factors such as looks? How does the process of making initial judgements of strangers vary between face-to-face situations and ICT-mediated situations?

However, other writers are more critical, fundamentally arguing that the difficulties of facilitating rich interactions via ICTs should not be underestimated (Hislop 2002*b*). This is primarily because many of the social cues which facilitate face-to-face communication (tone and pace of voice, gesture, facial expression) are lost or become degraded when people communicate via ICTs. For example e-mail communication is text only, which means that factors such as voice tone or facial expression cannot be utilized to support communication. As a consequence of the limited richness of ICT-based communication a number of people suggest this can negatively impact on the effectiveness and extent to which knowledge can be shared via ICT-based communication (Goodall and Roberts 2003; Roberts 2000; Symon 2000).

Looking in more detail, it can also be seen that different ICTs have different communication characteristics and have varying degrees of richness dependent upon the type and number of social cues which can be shared between those who are communicating. Information richness theory (IRT) suggests that different media have fixed and static levels of information richness, where 'communication richness (or leanness) is an invariant, objective property of communication media' (Ngwenyama and Lee 1997: 147). From this perspective, it is possible to rank different communication media in terms of their levels of information richness, with face-to-face interaction being the richest, and e-mail being one of the leanest (see Table 13.2).

Table 13.2 Characteristics of Various Communication Media

	Medium	Communication Characteristics
↑	*Face-to-Face Interaction*	Information rich (social cues such as facial expression, voice, gestures visible; plus, synchronous communication, potential for rapid high-quality feedback/interaction) Most relevant for sharing of tacit knowledge Spontaneous/informal interactions possible when people geographically proximate Conditions amenable to development of trust (other factors excluded) Expensive when people geographically dispersed
	Video Conferencing	Information rich (social cues, and virtually real time, synchronous medium) Expensive to set up Set-up time inhibits spontaneity
	Telephone	Intermediate information richness (tone of voice conveys some social cues, but gestures, expression invisible; also synchronous, facilitating detailed, immediate feedback) Cost variable Spontaneous/informal interactions possible irrespective of geographic proximity Can facilitate development of trust where face-to-face interaction difficult
	E-mail	Suitable for sharing of highly codified knowledge Relatively low information richness (all social cues lost) Inexpensive (cost unrelated to geographic proximity) Asynchronous, with variable feedback speed Spontaneous/informal interactions possible irrespective of geographic proximity Permanent record of interaction exists Development of trust based on e-mail alone difficult

Increasing information richness (vertical label on left)

Time to reflect

To what extent does any type of communication medium have a fixed and static level of richness? Is the richness of ICT-mediated communication (such as e-mail) also affected by both a person's competence at using it and their willingness to invest time and effort in communicating their views?

Finally, some acknowledge that when people collaborate and communicate over extended periods of time they rarely use only one type of communication medium. Even when people are geographically dispersed, and when opportunities for meetings are limited (such as with the virtual teams examined by Kauppila *et al.* (2011), over time they are likely to communicate with remote colleagues via multiple methods including e-mail, telephone calls, and face-to-face meetings. Thus, to understand the richness of any interaction that occurs between people it is necessary to take account of all the various types of communication that people have previously utilized to interact. Further, the richness of an ICT-based interaction between people will be affected by whether they have met face-to-face and have some knowledge of each other. Maznevski and Chudoba (1999) reach such a conclusion in their study of global virtual teams, suggesting that 'effective global virtual teams . . . generate a deep rhythm of regular face-to-face incidents interspersed with less intensive, shorter incidents using various media' (p. 473). The positive impact of occasional face-to-face meetings on knowledge sharing and communication within virtual teams is something that has also been found in a number of more recent studies (Jarvenpaa and Majchrzak 2008; Kauppila *et al.* 2011; Oshri *et al.* 2008).

ICTs and developing/sustaining trust

The second area of debate examined is the extent to which trust can be developed and sustained in social relations where people communicate either solely or predominantly via ICTs. Much of the research on this topic has been on virtual or dispersed teams, where opportunities for face-to-face interaction between team members may be limited. The importance of trust to the performance of virtual/dispersed teams, and the challenges involved in developing it, is illustrated by the significant number of studies on the topic (Chang *et al.* 2011; Kimble 2011; Malhotra *et al.* 2007; Muethel *et al.* 2012; Sarker *et al.* 2011).

The literature on this topic shows that the extent of face-to-face interaction that occurs between people affects more than just their ability to develop an understanding of each other. It also affects the basic nature of the social relationship, and the extent to which trust can be developed and sustained. However, there are divergent perspectives on the extent to which trust can be developed and sustained by electronically mediated communication alone (for a review of the literature on trust in online transactions see Li *et al.* 2012).

One school of thought suggests that it is not possible to develop and maintain trust in social relations mediated purely by ICTs. Roberts (2000) thus argues that face-to-face contact is a vital element in the establishment of a relationship of trust. This research generally suggests that the development and maintenance of trust in ICT-mediated communication is facilitated by occasional face-to-face meetings between people (Kauppila *et al.* 2011; Malhotra *et al.* 2007). For example, research conducted by Maznevski and Chudoba (1999)

Illustration   Trust, computer-mediated communication, and the performance of globally dispersed teams

Muethel *et al.* (2012) conducted a survey of some globally dispersed new product development teams in the software development industry to examine the extent to which a number of variables (including national diversity, geographic dispersal, and computer-mediation of communication) moderated the relationship between trust and team performance. The focus here is narrowly on the moderating role of computer-mediated communication. Muethel's hypothesis was that the computer mediation of team communication would increase the importance of the relationship between trust and team performance. They tested this hypothesis (among others) on the results of a survey completed by almost 400 members of software development teams who worked in five different software development companies. Muethel found that this hypothesis was supported and that the computer mediation of communication significantly increased the importance of the relationship between trust and team performance.

reinforces this perspective, as their study found that successful virtual teams were the ones which had occasional face-to-face meetings as these meetings helped to improve the social relationship and the level of trust that existed amongst project team members.

Some writers are more positive, and argue that it is possible to build and sustain trust in interpersonal relations that are totally mediated by ICTs. Pauleen and Yoong (2001), in a study on the role of ICTs for relationship building in virtual teams, argue that social relations can be developed and built amongst strangers by the strategic use of a range of electronic communication media such as telephone, e-mail, and video conferencing. They also suggest that the specific balance of the most appropriate communication media is likely to vary between contexts, and will be shaped by factors such as national and organizational cultural norms, individual personality, and the range of media available.

 Time to reflect   The relationship between ICT-mediated and face-to-face knowledge processes

Do you agree with Pauleen and Yoong's conclusion that through the judicious use of a range of ICT-based communication mechanisms it is possible to develop effective working relations with strangers who have different cultural values without any face-to-face interaction?

Jarvenpaa and Leidner (1999) are also positive that trust can be developed in totally virtual social relations, though they found that the type of trust developed in temporary virtual teams was extremely fragile. The virtual teams examined by Jarvenpaa and Leidner were 'separated by time and culture', as they involved remote interaction between people of different nationalities who not only had no previous knowledge of each other, but who had no opportunities to meet face to face. In the teams examined, time was not available for the development of personal-based trust, but with some groups what has been labelled as swift trust developed, which allowed them to work together effectively. Swift trust is utilized in situations where there isn't the luxury of time to develop social relations, and is typically, inferred presumptively, based on the limited information that team members

Table 13.3 Trust Facilitating Behaviours and Actions

Communication Behaviours and Actions that Facilitated Trust in Early Group Life	Communication Behaviours and Actions which Helped Maintain Trust Over Time
Social communication	Predictable communication
Demonstrate enthusiasm	Substantial and timely responses
Cope with technical uncertainty	Successful transition from social to procedural to task focus
Show individual initiative	Positive leadership
	Phlegmatic response to crises

Source: Adapted from Leidner 1999: 807, table 4.

have of each other. For example, Robert *et al.* (2009) found that, in contexts where people had limited knowledge of each other, swift trust was developed based on the perception of other people having similar general characteristics (such as age, gender, nationality, occupation), but that over time, as people developed more understanding of each other, trust became more based on people's knowledge of the actual behaviours and competencies of others. The topic of swift trust, and its role in facilitating interpersonal relations and the sharing of knowledge, has also been examined by a number of others (Gammelgaard 2009; Xu *et al.* 2007).

Jarvenpaa and Leidner (1999: 807) found that certain actions and behaviours facilitated the development of this type of trust (see Table 13.3). For example, in the early stage of a group's life, trust is more likely to be developed if group members communicate an enthusiasm for the task to be undertaken, and show a willingness to engage in social communication to establish a more personal basis to social relations. Further, they found that at more mature stages of a group's working life, trust was sustained if group members provided timely responses to queries, and if groups were able to manage the transition from social-based interactions to task-based interactions. Thus, Jarvenpaa and Leidner conclude that (a weak form of) trust can be developed in ICT-mediated social relations if people behave and act in certain ways.

Conclusion

One of the key objectives of the chapter has been to highlight and explain why there is such a diversity of perspectives regarding the role that ICTs can play in organizational knowledge management activities. Thus, rather than attempt to present a unitary perspective, this chapter has attempted to do justice to the debate by presenting a range of perspectives.

One contrast in the literature can be made between analyses utilizing objectivist and practice-based perspectives. Writing which utilizes an objectivist conceptualization of knowledge typically argues that ICTs can have an important and direct role in knowledge processes, for example in the structuring, storage, and dissemination of codified knowledge. This perspective on ICT-enabled knowledge management was quite dominant within the early knowledge management literature (up until the early 2000s). Over time, a growing number of people challenged the assumptions and utility of this way of using ICTs to facilitate knowledge management activities, emphasizing the difficulty of both codifying knowledge, and sharing codified knowledge electronically. Analyses which built on this critique utilized concepts such as transactive memory systems, and often advocated the use of collaborate Web 2.0 technologies and platforms for the management and sharing of knowledge. Thus this perspective tended to suggest that ICTs can have a more indirect role in knowledge processes, facilitating interpersonal interaction and processes of perspective making/taking, which is more aligned with the practice-based epistemology.

However, one general conclusion that can be made on this topic is that, whatever the role that ICTs have in knowledge processes, for such systems to be effective, their development and use requires sensitivity to the socio-cultural context in which they are being implemented. The danger of not doing this, as was well demonstrated by the high failure rate of the earliest technology-led knowledge management projects, is that the chances of such projects succeeding are relatively low.

 Case study   Using Web 2.0 technology to help build a knowledge-sharing culture

Teo *et al.* (2011) report on a study into the successful use of a range of Web 2.0 technologies to facilitate the development of a knowledge-sharing culture within HP Analytics, a business unit in Hewlett Packard's global business services division that is responsible for providing shared services and other business process expertise to different HP divisions. HP Analytics is based in offices in the Indian cities of Bangalore and Chennai, and by 2010 had about 900 employees. The company decided to invest in IT to facilitate knowledge sharing between employees, but the aim was not to create a 'static', centralized knowledge repository or library, but instead to utilize IT to facilitate a process of ongoing interaction and knowledge sharing. Further, it was recognized that this would require a change in culture, with it being hoped that the use of Web 2.0 technologies would facilitate this culture change. Thus, Teo *et al.* (2011: 11) said that the key aim of the Web 2.0 initiative was to 'promote knowledge sharing behaviours that over time would become part of the organizational culture'.

The web-based knowledge-sharing platform that was developed had a number of components to it, but it was accessed through a single portal. There were four main components within the platform which were a website with links, an online document repository, a blog, and online discussion forums. The main focus of Teo *et al.*'s case study is on the blogging and discussion forum elements of the initiative. With both these elements, there were opportunities for people to discuss both work and non-work issues.

The blog was intended to be a central focus for discussion where people could post comments and contribute to discussions on any topic that they wanted. While the discussion forums had the same broad objective, they were more decentralized and focused, with discussion forums being set up on specific topics and themes. The idea with the forums was to create small, more specialized interest groups to share knowledge on specific topics. These interest groups could be formed around work-related issues (such as cloud computing), or non-work-related, with forums being set up on topic related to personal interests and hobbies, such as sport and cricket. There were two reasons for allowing people to discuss non-work issues on the blogs and forums. It was felt this would help motivate people to participate in the Web 2.0 collaborative platform and allowing people to discuss non-work issues was also seen as helping the development of a sense of community identity and good interpersonal relations.

User participation and involvement with the collaborative platform was developed via a number of means. First, knowledge management ambassadors were recruited to the project from a wide range of different parts of the business. The people selected were those who were passionate about the initiative. The aim of having ambassadors was to help 'sell' the benefits to employees of the initiative, and to also provide a decentralized source of technical support that people could utilize. Secondly, particularly in relation to the blogging component, various things were done to encourage participation. For example, some fun competitions were set up to encourage people to both post and read blogs. One such competition took the form of the TV shows *Pop Idol/X-Factor*, where awards were given to the best blogs, with the decision on which blogs were best being made by employees reading the blogs who then voted for them. Winners were announced at a special ceremony where they were given rewards and recognition for the popularity of their blogs. Finally, the topics for forums were decided via a process of discussion—the aim was only to set up forums on topics that people were interested in and likely to contribute to.

Overall, the initiative succeeded in facilitating knowledge sharing, with one interviewee saying, 'collaborative technologies help information flow freely so that people can get their information from various sources, all across the world, at the touch of a button'.

1. While the use of 'fun' competitions may provide a way of generating interest in the platform, is there a risk that using fun and humour to do this may undermine the seriousness and importance of the initiative's objectives?

2. How important is it to allow the discussion of non-work-related topics/themes on this type of platform? Is this likely to encourage people to participate in this type of initiative, or is it likely to distract people from the work-related elements of the initiative? Finally, should there be limits and/ or controls on the type of non-work topics that can be included?

Source: Teo, T., Nishant, R., Goh, M., and Agarwal, S. (2011) 'Leveraging Collaborative Technologies to Build a Knowledge Sharing Culture at HP Analytics', *MIS Quarterly Executive*, 10/1: 1–18.

 ## Review and Discussion Questions

1. Is it impossible to share tacit knowledge via ICTs irrespective of how much trust exists between people or how rich the communication process is?

2. To what extent is the time it takes to codify knowledge likely be a significant factor influencing people's willingness to codify their knowledge? Further, is the codification of knowledge likely to be a time-consuming process? Finally, what factors are likely to influence the time it takes to codify knowledge? (Its complexity? Its inter-relatedness to other knowledge?)

3. How rich a form of communication can Web 2.0 technologies facilitate, and where on Table 12.2 would you locate them?

4. Is an important factor influencing the richness of any ICT-mediated interaction the extent to which people know each other, with richer forms of ICT-mediated communication being possible between people who are very familiar with each other compared to people who have limited knowledge of each other?

5. To what extent is swift trust important in the development of social relations between people who are relatively unfamiliar? Are people more likely to assume a relatively unknown stranger is trust-worthy if they have some characteristics which are similar to each other?

 ## Suggestions for Further Reading

1. T. Teo, R. Nishant, M. Goh, and S. Agarwal (2011) 'Leveraging Collaborative Technologies to build a Knowledge Sharing Culture at HP Analytics', *MIS Quarterly Executive*, 10/1: 1–18.
Interesting case study of the successful use of Web 2.0 technologies to facilitate the development of a knowledge-sharing culture.

2. O.-P. Kauppila, R. Rajala, and A. Jyrämä (2011) 'Knowledge Sharing through Virtual Teams across Borders and Boundaries', *Management Learning*, 42/4: 395–418.

Interesting case study of a cross-community virtual knowledge-sharing initiative that highlights the importance of socio-cultural factors.

3. I. Oshri, P. Fenema, and J. Kotlarsky (2008) 'Knowledge Transfer in Globally Distributed Teams: The Role of Transactive Memory', *Information Systems Journal*, 18/6: 596–616.

Case study of how the existence of transactive memory within global virtual teams facilitated the sharing of knowledge.

4. M. Muethel, F. Siebdrat, and M. Hoegle (2012) 'When do we Really Need Trust in Globally Dispersed New Product Development Teams', *R&D Management* 42/1: 31–46.

Examines how factors such as the computer mediation of communication and team diversity affects the role of trust in the performance of dispersed teams.

5. S. Newell, M. Bresnen, L. Edelman, H. Scarbrough, and J. Swan (2006) 'Sharing Knowledge across Projects: Limits to ICT-Led Project Review Practices', *Management Learning*, 37/2: 167–85.

Presents case study evidence suggesting there are limits to the role that ICTs can play in the sharing of project-specific knowledge.

Take your learning further: Online Resource Centre

Visit the Online Resource Centre for resources which will extend your understanding of knowledge management in organizations. As well as web links to sites of interest, the author has provided case studies looking at knowledge management in virtual and knowledge-intensive firms, and in global multinationals. These will help you with your research, essays, and assignments; or you may find these additional resources helpful when revising for exams.

 www.oxfordtextbooks.co.uk/orc/hislop3e/

Facilitating Knowledge Management via the Use of Human Resource Management Practices

Introduction

As the introduction to Part 4 and Chapter 9 detail, social and cultural issues have been found to play a key role in affecting the dynamics and likely success of knowledge management initiatives. This is primarily because such factors have increasingly been recognized as playing a fundamental role in determining whether workers will be willing to actively participate in knowledge management initiatives. Inevitably, this has led to organizations deliberately attempting to use different types of managerial practices to encourage workers to participate in knowledge management activities and initiatives. The focus of this chapter is on how different human resource management (HRM) practices can impact on workers' attitudes towards and participation in knowledge management activities.

In broad terms the attitudes and behaviours that are relevant to knowledge management initiatives are outlined in Table 14.1. Thus, the use of HRM practices can be seen to be concerned not only with attempting to create a positive attitude towards, and a willingness to participate in, organizational knowledge management activities, but also with making workers committed and loyal to their employer. This is fundamentally because, if workers are not committed and loyal to their organizations, there is a risk that organizations will lose any tacit knowledge these workers possess through staff turnover. As was touched on in Chapter 5, knowledge loss through staff turnover is often a problem experienced by knowledge-intensive firms. Thus HRM practices concerned with supporting organizational knowledge management efforts should be concerned as much with developing the commitment and loyalty of workers as they are with persuading workers to share, codify, or create knowledge.

The chapter begins by outlining three possible reasons why HRM practices can be used to support organizational knowledge management activities that link back to the concept of the share/hoard dilemma outlined in Chapter 9, as well as how HRM practices are linked to organizational commitment, and finally, through the way that HRM practices can influence the 'social architecture' within organizations (the character of interpersonal relations between staff). The next major section examines how a range of specific HRM practices such as job design, recruitment and selection, and training can all be used to reinforce and support organizational knowledge management efforts. The third and final major section

Table 14.1 Attitudes and Behaviours Relevant to Knowledge Management Initiatives

Attitudes	Behaviours
Positive attitude towards knowledge management initiatives	Active participation in knowledge management initiatives
Level of loyalty and commitment to the organization, and the goals it is pursuing	Having continuous employment for significant periods

considers the importance of staff loyalty and retention to organizational knowledge management activities and considers a range of ways that organizations can attempt to develop the loyalty of their staff and thus help to prevent the loss of potentially vital sources of knowledge through the loss of staff.

Why HRM Practices are Important to Knowledge Management

This section considers three separate reasons why HRM practices can help produce the type of behaviours and attitudes that are necessary to make knowledge management initiatives successful. First, making links between the share/hoard dilemma outlined in Chapter 9, and the concept of motivation, HRM practices can be used to positively motivate workers to participate in knowledge management activities. The second potential way in which HRM practices can be utilized to support and facilitate organizational knowledge management activities is through developing employees' organizational commitment, with it being suggested that commitment may be an important variable which mediates the relationship between HRM practices and knowledge management activities. Third and finally, it is suggested that HRM practices can facilitate knowledge management activities through positively influencing the type of socio-cultural factors which have been shown to be crucial to employee participation in knowledge management activities.

In considering the motivational role of HRM practices it is useful to link back to the hoard/share dilemma which was outlined in Chapter 9 (see Table 9.1). This dilemma suggested that the willingness of workers to participate in organizational knowledge management activities depends on what they perceive as the likely positive and negative consequences of doing so. If the positive benefits are likely to outweigh the negative ones, then they are likely to participate in knowledge management activities. Whereas if they feel the opposite, they are more likely to 'hoard' their knowledge and not participate in knowledge management activities. Chapter 9 highlighted some of the most important factors that the knowledge management literature has found can influence workers' share/hoard decisions, which include the extent to which they perceive their interest to be in conflict with that of their employers, the extent of group and community identity they feel, and how much they trust colleagues. HRM policies have the potential to play a crucial role influencing how workers resolve such share/hoard decisions through providing positive motivation for participating in knowledge management activities.

In talking about motivation, it is necessary to distinguish between intrinsic and extrinsic motivation. Intrinsic motivation refers to the pleasures and positive feelings people can derive from simply carrying out a task or activity, rather than for any reward derived from doing so. Thus if a software engineer derives pleasure from the process of writing computer code which is efficient and effective, they are intrinsically motivated to carry out this activity. In contrast, extrinsic motivation refers to the external rewards people derive from carrying out a task, such as money. Thus, a software engineer is extrinsically motivated to write computer code if the main reason they do it is for the salary they are paid. In terms of linking HRM practices, motivation, and knowledge management, HRM practices can be utilized to provide both intrinsic and extrinsic motivations for undertaking knowledge management activities. For example, as will be shown later, in terms of intrinsic motivation, HRM practices can be used to design jobs that are intrinsically interesting and challenging, and which thus encourage and motivate workers to utilize and share their knowledge. In contrast, HRM practice such as reward systems can be used to extrinsically motivate workers to participate in knowledge management activities through offering financial incentives.

The second way to understand why HRM practices can positively influence workers' knowledge-related attitudes and behaviours is via linking to the concept of organizational commitment. As highlighted in Chapters 9, 10, and 11, people's sense of identity as being part of group, team, or organization can significantly influence their willingness to participate in knowledge management activities. In broad terms, the greater the strength of a person's identity with a team or group, the more likely they are to participate in knowledge management activities which involve other group/team members, or which are perceived to benefit the group. Thus, the more a worker identifies with and it committed to the organization they work for, the more likely they will be to participate in organizational knowledge management activities. In this context, the role of HRM practices is therefore to help develop employees' levels of organizational commitment.

DEFINITION Organizational commitment

The sense of emotional attachment that people feel to the organizations they work for, which may be reflected in the alignment of individual and organizational values and objectives.

A number of writers suggest that the level of commitment workers feel for the organizations they work in may affect their knowledge-sharing attitudes and behaviours as well as their level of loyalty (Byrne 2001; Hislop 2002a; O'Neill and Adya 2007; Storey and Quintas 2001; Scarbrough and Carter 2000). Several empirical studies have provided evidence in support of these arguments. Thus, Robertson and O'Malley Hammersley (2000) found that levels of organizational commitment affected employee retention levels and attitudes to knowledge processes. Secondly, Han *et al.* (2010), in a study involving staff working in eight high-technology Taiwanese companies, found this to be the case with employees' participation in organizational decision-making processes. Thus, they found that levels of participation in decision-making processes were positively related to the sense of psychological ownership workers felt over such decisions, with levels of psychological ownership being positively linked to employees' levels of organizational commitment and knowledge sharing. Finally, Camelo-Ordaz *et al.* (2011) found that certain types of HRM practice influenced employees' levels of knowledge sharing indirectly, affecting their levels of organizational commitment (see the illustration). An alternative way of developing workers' organizational commitment is via managing an organization's culture, which is a topic examined in the following chapter.

 Illustration High-involvement HRM, organizational commitment, and knowledge sharing

Camelo-Ordaz *et al.* (2011) looked at the relationship between HRM practices, organizational commitment, and knowledge sharing in a study of innovative, research-intensive manufacturing companies in Spain. This involved surveying companies in the five most innovative industries (including chemical, motorized vehicle, and electronic equipment industries) that had more than fifty employees and an R&D department. Eighty-seven completed surveys were analysed. In terms of the HRM practices they examined, their focus was on what was defined as high-involvement HRM, which is HRM practice focused on employee development and growth. More specifically, this included recruitment and selection practices intended to select people on the basis of their fit with the organization, the use of team-based reward and appraisal systems, reward systems which encourage knowledge sharing, and the provision of extensive training and development opportunities. They hypothesized that utilizing these types of HRM practices was likely to be positively linked to organizational commitment, with organizational commitment being positively linked to levels of knowledge sharing. In the analysis of the completed surveys they found that all hypotheses were supported, and that high-involvement HRM practices were positively linked to organizational commitment and levels of knowledge sharing.

Finally, the third way in which HRM practices may facilitate worker's participation in knowledge management activities is via influencing the socio-cultural environment within a firm. As was shown in Chapter 9, factors such as the existence of interpersonal trust were found to play a crucial role in shaping people's willingness to share knowledge with others. If HRM practices can affect such socio-cultural factors they may affect people's willingness to participate in knowledge management activities. An example of how HRM practices can impact interpersonal relations is through providing training which brings employees together to learn collectively, or designing jobs so that interpersonal collaboration is encouraged. The best illustration of this perspective on the relationship between HRM and knowledge management is the end of chapter case study.

HRM Practices and Knowledge Management

This section examines how some specific HRM practices can be used to shape attitudes and behaviours towards organizational knowledge management activities, with a number of relevant examples being used to illustrate and support the points being made.

Recruitment and selection

The knowledge management literature suggests that there are two ways in which recruitment and selection processes can be utilized to support knowledge management activities. They can be used to recruit people whose values are compatible with the existing organizational culture, and they can be used to select people with personalities that are conducive to knowledge sharing.

In relation to the first topic both Swart and Kinnie (2003) and Robertson and Swan (2003) suggest that recruiting people whose values are aligned with those of the company was an important factor in the success of the companies they examined. Both papers presented an analyses of a single successful knowledge-intensive firm, which were successful not only in narrow economic and business terms, but also in terms of having happy and committed workers, which meant neither organization had significant turnover problems. The way such forms of recruitment reinforce and sustain organizational knowledge activities is that by recruiting people whose values and norms are compatible with those that exist in an organization new recruits are likely to be able to develop a strong sense of identity with their employer and work colleagues and that a good foundation for the development of strong trust-based relations between new recruits and their colleagues should exist. The only empirical study which has examined this topic, and which did find a positive link between 'fit' based recruitment and attitudes to knowledge sharing, was conducted by Chen *et al.* (2011a—see the example).

As outlined in Chapter 9, the way in which personality relates to knowledge-sharing attitudes is a topic that is significantly under-researched, with very few empirical studies being done into this topic. Further, while all the studies in this area (Cabrera and Cabrera 2005; Matzler *et al.* 2011; Mooradian *et al.* 2006) use the five-factor personality model, they reach different conclusions about which personality traits are related to positive knowledge-sharing attitudes. Thus, Cabrera and Cabrera's (2005) research, which is based on a survey of a single Spanish organization, found that the 'openness to change' personality variable was related to a positive knowledge-sharing attitude. By contrast, Mooradian *et al.*'s (2006) study, which was also based on a survey of a single organization, found a link between 'agreeableness' and positive knowledge-sharing attitudes. Finally, Matzler *et al.*'s (2011) study, which is based on a survey conducted within a single Austrian company, found that both agreeableness and conscientiousness were positively related to knowledge-sharing attitudes. Another limitation of these studies, which affects their generalizability, is the fact that they are all based on single-organization studies. To more effectively test the generalizability of the findings of these studies, the same research questions would need to be tested on a wider population.

If the premise of these studies is accepted (that personality traits can influence people's general attitudes to knowledge sharing, making certain types of people generally more open to doing so than others) then attempting to recruit people with appropriate personality traits may represent another way in which recruitment and selection processes can be used to support organizational knowledge activities. However, the scarcity of research on this topic, and the contradictory findings of the studies that have been done, means that, at the moment, using personality tests to identify positive knowledge-sharing attitudes needs to be done with caution.

Job design

In the area of job design, there is a strong consensus about the best way to structure jobs to facilitate appropriate knowledge-sharing attitudes. In general terms, work should have three key features: it should be interesting and challenging, secondly, workers should have high levels of autonomy with regard to decision-making and problem-solving, and finally it should encourage and require interpersonal collaboration. For example, Chen *et al.*'s (2011*b*) study into the link between conflict and knowledge sharing conducted in some Chinese software companies, recommended that interpersonal knowledge sharing would be encouraged if workers had both challenging and meaningful work tasks, and had high levels of autonomy. In terms of the first feature, not only should work be challenging and fulfilling, providing opportunities for workers to effectively utilize their existing skills and knowledge, but it should also provide opportunities for workers to continuously develop their knowledge and skills (Robertson and O'Malley Hammersley 2000; Swart and Kinnie 2003). The importance to knowledge workers of having interesting and challenging work is supported by the findings of Horowitz *et al.*'s (2003) study of Singaporean knowledge workers, which found that providing challenging work was ranked as the most important factor by managers for helping to retain their knowledge workers. Relatedly, Han *et al.* (2010), as outlined above, found that involvement in decision-making was positively linked to levels of organizational commitment and knowledge sharing.

In terms of autonomy, available evidence also suggests that knowledge workers also place a lot of importance on having high levels of autonomy at work (Khatri *et al.* 2010). Thus, in the scientific consultancy examined by Robertson and Swan (2003), autonomy was found to be important to the consultants, and extended to the projects they worked on (the consultants had the autonomy to freely choose which project they worked on so long as they reached their annual revenue targets), the selection of the training and development activities they undertook (consultants identified their own development needs, with funding being available for virtually all training requests), work clothing, and work patterns. Finally, Kuo and Lee's (2011) study into empowering leadership concluded that providing workers with high levels of autonomy was likely to help with the development of a knowledge-sharing culture.

The third feature of work tasks argued to encourage workers' participation in knowledge management activities is that they should require and/or encourage collaboration amongst people. This is because collaborative working makes knowledge sharing a central feature of work activities and it is likely to facilitate the development of the type of strong interpersonal relations which are conducive to interpersonal knowledge sharing (Holste and Fields 2010; Kase *et al.* 2009—see end of chapter case study for more details).

Training

While, as outlined, providing opportunities for self-development can be integrated into the way people's work activities are organized, it can also be achieved through providing appropriate opportunities to undertake formal training. Thus, research suggests that knowledge workers regard the provision of such opportunities by their employers as crucially important (Hunter et al. 2002; Robertson and O'Malley Hammersley 2000). While the provision of such opportunities is a potentially double-edged sword for employers (as such activities make it easier for staff to leave), without supporting continuous development staff may be likely to leave anyway. Garvey and Williamson (2002) suggest that the most useful sort of training to support a culture of learning and knowledge development is not investing in 'narrow' skills-based training, but training with a broader purpose to encourage reflexivity, learning through experimentation, and how to conduct critical dialogues with others. Hansen *et al.* (1999) suggest that the type of training provided should reflect the particular approach to knowledge management an organization adopts (see Chapter 4). For example, in relation to their distinction between codification- and personalization-based approaches to knowledge management, they argue that the provision of IT-based training is relevant for organizations pursuing a codification-based strategy, whereas training to develop interpersonal skills and team working is most appropriate for organizations pursuing a personalization-based knowledge management strategy.

Reinforcing this point about linking the type of training provided to the approach to knowledge management, a number of the studies into the role of Web 2.0 technologies to facilitate knowledge management (see Chapter 13) suggest that the provision of training on the use of these technologies is likely to encourage workers to utilize them for knowledge sharing (Paroutis and Al Saleh 2009; Teo *et al.* 2011). Finally, as outlined in more detail in the end of chapter case study, Kase *et al.* (2009) suggest that one of the knowledge-related benefits of training is that it facilitates the development of good interpersonal relations between those undertaking it, which may encourage such people to share knowledge with each other in the future.

Coaching and mentoring

A growing body of literature also suggests that the use of coaching and mentoring in organizations can facilitate the informal sharing of knowledge (Garvey and Williamson 2002; Harrison and Kessels 2004; Karkoulian *et al.* 2008; Kets de Vries 1991; Orlikowski 2002). What coaching and mentoring have in common is that they are both concerned with the sharing of knowledge between a relatively experienced person, the mentor or coach, and someone less experienced, the mentee (Wilson and Elman 1990). However, they can be distinguished from each other on a number of dimensions. First, while mentoring typically has an indefinite timescale, coaching is usually undertaken for a set duration. Secondly, coaching is typically more structured in the way it is organized, for example, occurring at set regular times, for specific time periods. Finally, while coaching is typically concerned with the development of relatively narrow and specific skills and knowledge, mentoring is less focused in this way.

However, both coaching and mentoring can take many forms. For example, mentoring can be done in highly formalized ways, or relatively informally, and coaching can be done on a one-to-one basis or in groups. The knowledge-sharing benefits of mentoring and coaching can be provided by a number of brief examples. First, in the software company examined by Swart and Kinnie (2003), mentoring was used to facilitate cross-project knowledge sharing. Secondly, Kets de Vries (1991) in evaluating a single, intensive group coaching activity found that the development of trust among participants in this activity facilitated interpersonal knowledge sharing. Thirdly, Karkoulian *et al.* (2008), in a study of mentoring in Lebanese banks, found that informal mentoring had a positive impact on knowledge-sharing behaviours. Finally, in the study of leadership undertaken by Lee *et al.* (2011), which is examined in the following chapter, one of the ways team leaders developed intra-team trust and knowledge sharing was via a process of mentoring that involved linking experienced team members with less experienced ones. Thus, setting up and facilitating both coaching and mentoring activities represents another way for organizational management to facilitate interpersonal knowledge sharing.

Reward and performance appraisal

In the area of reward, there is no consensus regarding how reward systems can best be used to support knowledge management activities. Some suggest that rewarding people for appropriate knowledge-related behaviours and embedding knowledge-related attitudes and behaviours in performance appraisal processes represent a potentially important way to use HRM practices to underpin organizational knowledge management efforts (Cabrera and Cabrera 2005; Oltra 2005). It is also agreed that such reward systems should reflect the particular knowledge management strategy adopted by an organization and the type of knowledge processes associated with it. For example, Hansen et al. (1999) argue that, if a codification strategy is pursued, the pay and reward systems should acknowledge employee efforts to codify their knowledge, and search for the knowledge of others, while with a personalization strategy, pay and reward systems should recognize the efforts of workers to share their tacit knowledge with each other.

However, this perspective is challenged by a number of writers who suggest that there may be negative consequences to directly linking individual, financial rewards to knowledge behaviours. For example, Osterloh and Frey (2000), in distinguishing between extrinsic forms of motivation (largely financial), and intrinsic forms of motivation (motivation related to the benefits derived from carrying out an activity itself), conclude that financial rewards may inhibit the sharing of tacit knowledge. Fahey et al. (2007) and Milne (2007) both reach a similar conclusion and argue that directly linking individual rewards to knowledge sharing may mean people develop instrumental attitudes to such processes whereby they only participate in knowledge processes when they derive some form of financial reward from doing so, which may inhibit knowledge sharing when such rewards are not available.

Another area of debate concerns whether individual or group-based rewards provide the best way to facilitate positive knowledge-related attitudes and behaviours. Thus, some research suggests that individually focused financial rewards can play a positive role. For example, Horowitz et al.'s survey of Singaporean knowledge workers found that providing a 'highly competitive pay package' (2003: 32) was ranked as the second most effective way to help retain knowledge workers. Further, Kankanhalli et al. (2005) and Huang et al. (2008) also found that individually focused reward systems support participation in knowledge management activities.

Others suggest that such individually focused rewards can inhibit knowledge sharing through not only creating an instrumental attitude to knowledge sharing but also through the way such reward mechanisms may undermine people's sense of team or community spirit (Nayir and Uzunçarsili 2008). For example, in the organization studied by Lam (see the earlier illustration) the use of individually focused rewards contributed importantly to the individualistic culture which existed, which meant that people were unwilling to codify and share knowledge with colleagues. Thus some suggest that the best way to develop group focused knowledge sharing is through making knowledge related rewards group, rather than individually, focused (Cabrera and Cabrera 2005). The research of Chen et al. (2011a—see the example) also reinforces these conclusions.

Finally a growing number of writers suggest that non-financial rewards such as recognition can play an important role in facilitating and encouraging appropriate knowledge behaviours in people (Nayir and Uzunçarsili 2008; O'Dell and Hubert 2011; Teo et al. 2011).

> ⊙ **Illustration**   HRM practices to facilitate intra-team knowledge sharing
>
> Chen *et al.* (2011*a*) investigated how a range of different HRM practices affected the willingness of people within R&D teams in Taiwan to share knowledge. All the R&D teams surveyed were in high-technology industries (electronics, communications, precision machinery, semiconductors, and optoelectronics). They analysed the surveys of over 200 employees from over fifty separate R&D teams. Overall they found that most of the HRM practices examined did affect people's knowledge-sharing behaviours.
>
> First, they found that recruiting people who fitted with the existing culture and values of the teams promoted knowledge sharing. Secondly, people's willingness to share knowledge was positively related to the extent to which they perceived that their employer paid attention to their long-term career development. Finally, they found performance appraisals which were focused on the individual inhibited people's willingness to share knowledge within teams. Thus, in the type of team-based contexts that they examined, team-focused, rather than individually focused performance appraisals are likely to facilitate knowledge sharing. Finally, one hypothesis they tested that was not supported by the study was that the use of reward systems would increase people's willingness to share knowledge. Thus this study undermines the argument that financial rewards can be used to motivate people to share knowledge.

While Huang *et al.* (2008) found that financial rewards did encourage knowledge sharing among the Chinese workers they studied, they found that people's attitudes to knowledge sharing were more strongly influenced by non-financial rewards. Paroutis and Al Saleh's (2009) study of what motivates people to share knowledge using Web 2.0 technology concluded that 'companies involved in implementing Web 2.0 should consider introducing soft rewards like praise and recognition to encourage employee participation. For instance having a recognition programme where "the most active blog", "top-rated blog post" or "best wiki contribution" is publicized on the company's intranet or newsletter is one effective way to recognize employees' contributions.'

HRM, Staff Retention, and Knowledge Management

Retaining workers who possess valuable knowledge should arguably be as important an element in an organization's knowledge management strategy as motivating workers to participate in knowledge activities. This is because the tacit and embodied nature of much organizational knowledge means that when employees leave an organization, they take their knowledge with them. Staff turnover means an inevitable leakage and loss of knowledge (Schmitt *et al.* 2012). As Byrne (2001: 325) succinctly put it, 'without loyalty knowledge is lost'. However, paradoxically, while many writers comment on the importance of retention, very few knowledge management studies examine the topic of retention in any detail (Martins and Meyer 2012).

This raises the question of what organizational management can do to induce high levels of commitment and loyalty among their workers. Developing high levels of commitment is not a simple matter. However, empirical evidence suggests that a number of factors within managerial control can affect commitment levels including: employee voice and employee trust in management (Farndale *et al.* 2011); the provision of training (Bulut and Culha 2010); and levels of organizational support (He *et al.* 2011).

In general, the literature on knowledge workers and knowledge-intensive firms (see Chapter 5) suggests that developing the loyalty of knowledge workers is particularly problematic. This is to a large extent because labour market conditions, where the skills and knowledge of knowledge workers are typically relatively scarce, create conditions for knowledge workers which are favourable to mobility. In relation to knowledge workers, Joo (2010) found in a study based on a survey administered to a diverse range of South Korean companies that organizational commitment was facilitated by workers having strong and supportive supervision from managers, and by the organization having a learning culture. The most comprehensive study of factors influencing employee commitment levels was undertaken by Giauque *et al.* (2010), and it is described as an illustrated example.

 Illustration   Factors influencing the organizational commitment of Swiss knowledge workers

Giauque *et al.* (2010) report the findings of their study into factors influencing levels of organizational commitment among knowledge workers in some Swiss companies. They surveyed small and medium companies in the French-speaking parts of Switzerland and analysed 200 completed surveys from staff in thirty different companies. They investigated the impact that six separate factors had on employees' commitment levels. These included levels of organizational support (perception that organization is interested in and supports employee well-being, for example, via providing some flexible working), procedural justice (perceived fairness of organizational decision-making processes), participation in organizational decision-making, organizational reputation, satisfaction with pay, and skills development.

Of these six factors the only ones that were found to be positively linked to levels of organizational commitment were organizational reputation, procedural justice, and organizational support. They found, somewhat surprisingly and in contradiction to what they expected, that organizational commitment levels among staff surveyed were not influenced by satisfaction with pay, skill development levels, or participation in organizational decision-making. This study suggests that the best way to develop commitment levels among knowledge workers is to develop organizational reputation, ensure a sense of fairness in organizational decision-making (procedural justice), and provide good levels of support to employees.

Having a high turnover rate is a potentially significant problem for knowledge-intensive firms (Alvesson 2000; Beaumont and Hunter 2002; Flood *et al.* 2001). First, this is a potential problem because the knowledge possessed by knowledge workers is typically highly tacit. Therefore, when they leave an organization, they take their knowledge with them. For example, one key source of knowledge possessed by knowledge workers is social capital— their knowledge of key individuals (see the illustration on client organizations in Chapter 5). The need for knowledge workers to work closely with client organizations means that they often develop close relations with important client staff. When such workers leave, there is a risk for their employer that they will lose their clients as well. The second main reason why poor retention rates may be a problem for knowledge-intensive firms is that the knowledge, skills, and experience possessed by knowledge workers are often a crucial element in organizational performance.

 Time to reflect   The weakness of instrumental loyalty?

Instrumental based loyalty, derived through pay and financial rewards is argued to be a weak form of loyalty. Do you agree? How significant is pay, and related financial reward, in the development of organizational loyalty and commitment?

Alvesson (2000) argues that one of the best ways to deal with the turnover problem is to create a sense of organizational loyalty in staff, particularly through developing their sense of organizational identity. Alvesson identifies two broad types of loyalty, and four strategies for developing them (see Table 14.2). The weakest form of loyalty is argued by Alvesson to be instrumental-based loyalty, which is when a worker remains loyal to their employer for as long as they receive specific personal benefits, with one of the most effective ways of developing such loyalty being through pay and working conditions. The second, and what Alvesson argues is a stronger form of loyalty, is identification-based loyalty, which is loyalty based on the worker having a strong sense of identity as being a member of the organization, and where the worker identifies with the goals and objectives of their organization. The three strategies for developing identification-based loyalty are illustrated in Table 14.2. This type of loyalty is typically not developed through financial rewards, and is instead built through developing a culture that workers can buy into, creating a sense of community amongst staff, or both.

Table 14.2 Type of Loyalty and Strategies for Developing Them

Type of Loyalty	Strategy for Development	Means of Development
Instrumental-Based Loyalty	Financial strategy	Providing employees with good pay and fringe benefits.
Identification-Based Loyalty	Institutional-based strategy	Developing a vision and set of values and encouraging employees to identify with them. Achieved through culture management, vision building, use of stories.
	Communitarian-based strategy	Developing a sense of community and social bonding amongst workers. Achieved through use of social events and meetings which bring people together and allow them to develop strong relations with, and knowledge of each other.
	Socially integrative strategy	A combination of the institutional- and communitarian-based strategies.

Source: Alvesson 2000.

⊕ Conclusion

The central focus of this chapter has been on how HRM practices have the potential to facilitate and support organizational knowledge management activities. The chapter began by presenting various explanations for why they have this potential which relate to their role in motivating workers to behave in certain ways, in developing interpersonal relations between workers, or developing people's level of organizational commitment. Broadly however, organizational management can use HRM practices to facilitate knowledge management initiatives by dealing with the problems and challenges that can often make workers unwilling to participate in knowledge management activities (see Chapter 9). The chapter also illustrated roles that specific HRM practices such as reward systems, job design, or training can having in shaping the attitudes and behaviours of workers to knowledge initiatives. In general terms, with the exception of reward systems, where evidence is contradictory and opinion is divided, there is a broad consensus regarding specifically how HRM practices should be utilized to support knowledge management initiatives.

Finally, the chapter also showed how attempting to develop the commitment and loyalty of workers can be a key part of an organization's knowledge management strategy. Not only does the typically tacit and embodied nature of knowledge mean that when workers leave an organization they take much of their knowledge with them, but that the level of commitment a worker feels towards their employer is also likely to affect their willingness to participate in knowledge management initiatives. However, developing such commitment and attitudes is by no means straightforward.

 Case study   The impact of HR practices on interpersonal relations and knowledge processes

Kase *et al.* (2009) examined the impact that a range of HR practices had on both interpersonal relations between workers and the extent to which workers were willing to share or source knowledge from each other. In doing this they developed a conceptual model that explained how HRM practices could be positively linked to knowledge processes. In terms of knowledge processes they were specifically interested in knowledge sharing (the extent to which people are prepared to share their own knowledge with colleagues) and knowledge sourcing (the extent to which people are prepared to look for and use the knowledge of colleagues). One of their most fundamental premises was that people's willingness to share knowledge with or source knowledge from colleagues was shaped by the quality of interpersonal relations that existed between people. The conceptual model they developed hypothesized that, if HR practices positively influenced the nature of interpersonal relations between colleagues, then they may indirectly be linked to knowledge processes.

In terms of the HR practices they examined, their focus was on HR practices which had 'relational implications' (p. 619), that is, HR practices which positively impacted on the nature of interpersonal relations between colleagues. In particular they focused on three types of HR practice: the design of work processes which encourage and facilitate collaboration (such as team working, job rotation), team/group-based pay which encourages/rewards people on the basis of group performance, and collaborative training and development activities which bring together groups of workers in a collective learning environment. To examine interpersonal relations they utilized the concept of social capital which, as outlined in Chapter 5, has three dimensions. Social capital refers to the network of social relations that people possess as well as the resources that they can gain access to through such networks. The three dimensions of social capital are structural (the number/quantity of people involved in a network), affective (the quality or character of the interpersonal relations between people—such as the level of trust), and the cognitive (the degree of common knowledge that people share with others in their network).

The conceptual model that Kase *et al.* (2009) developed, which linked together three types of HR practice (job design, incentives/pay, training), the three dimensions of social capital (structural, affective, cognitive), and the two types of knowledge process (sharing, sourcing) was very complex, and constraints of space mean that it isn't possible to outline the model and all its hypotheses in detail, or examine the results of all the hypotheses that were tested. Thus what are presented here are some selected highlights of their empirical findings. The conceptual model was empirically tested within some Slovenian knowledge-intensive firms. Empirical data, in the form of web-based surveys, were collected from employees in four organizations which operated in the IT, web-services, communication, and professional services sectors. Participating firms employed between 50 and 200 employees and very high response rates were achieved in all four organizations.

The key results worth highlighting here are as follows. Of the three types of HR practice examined, work design and training, but not incentives, were found to have a significant impact on either people's levels of social capital or their willingness to share/source knowledge with each other. In terms of the impact of HR practices on social capital, it was found that both collaborative work design and training were positively related to the structural dimension of social capital. Thus, collaborative work design and training helps people to develop their social networks through involving them in interpersonal collaboration with colleagues. In contrast, the hypothesis that collective incentives would facilitate the development of the affective dimension of social capital was not supported.

Further, with respect to the mediating impact of social capital on the relationship between HR practices and levels of knowledge sharing/sourcing, again the hypotheses relating to work design and training were supported, while those related to collective incentives were not. Thus, social capital was found to mediate the relationship between work design and both the sourcing and sharing of knowledge, and was also found to mediate the relationship between training and knowledge sourcing. Overall therefore, the general conclusion of Kase *et al.*'s (2009) study was that the most effective HR practices for supporting the development of social capital within firms, and for facilitating interpersonal knowledge sharing and sourcing, were collaborative work design and training processes.

1. These findings suggest that one of the benefits of face-to-face training with groups is the social relations between people that occur. To what extent, if at all, is it possible to achieve similar benefits from online learning or distant learning, where opportunities for interpersonal interactions between students are more limited?

Source: Kase R., Paauwe, J., and Zupan, N. (2009) 'HR Practices, Interpersonal Relations and Intrafirm Knowledge Transfer in Knowledge Intensive Firms: A Social Network Perspective', *Human Resource Management*, 48/4: 615–39.

 ## Review and Discussion Questions

1. The research presented suggests that having interesting and challenging work is more likely than pay to motivate people to participate in organizational knowledge activities. To what extent do you agree with this?

2. The end of chapter case found that the provision of training and the use of collective work design practices facilitated the development of socio-cultural relations between employees, which had positive effects on their knowledge-sharing behaviours. Can you identify other HRM practices which could also be used to positively affect interpersonal relations between colleagues?

3. In Giauque *et al.*'s (2010) study organizational support was one of the factors linked to levels of commitment. What types of support for non-work commitments and responsibilities are likely to be most attractive to employees?

Suggestions for Further Reading

1. R. Kase, J. Paauwe and N. Zupan (2009) 'HR Practices, Interpersonal Relations, and Intrafirm Knowledge Transfer in Knowledge Intensive Firms: A Social Network Perspective', *Human Resource Management*, 48/4: 615–39.

An empirical study which examines the impact of work design, incentive, and training practices on interpersonal relations and knowledge processes within firms.

2. W.-Y, Chen, B.-F., Hs, M.-L., Wang, and Y.-Y. Lin (2011) 'Fostering Knowledge Sharing through Human Resource Management in R&D Teams', *International Journal of Technology Management*, 53/2–4: 309–30.

An empirical study which examines the impact of a range of diverse HR practices on knowledge sharing within R&D teams with Taiwanese companies.

3. D. Giauque, F. Resenterra, and M. Siggen (2010) 'The Relationship between HRM Practices and Organizational Commitment of Knowledge Workers: Facts Obtained from Swiss SMEs', *Human Resource Development International*, 13/3: 185–205.

An empirical study which presents some surprising findings from a study into the impact of a range of different HR practices on the level of organizational commitment of some knowledge workers.

4. E. Martins and H. Meyer (2012) 'Organizational and Behavioural Factors that Influence Knowledge Retention', *Journal of Knowledge Management*, 16/1: 77–96.

Highlights a range of factors which influence the extent to which organizations are able to retain important knowledge.

Take your learning further: Online Resource Centre

Visit the Online Resource Centre for resources which will extend your understanding of knowledge management in organizations. As well as web links to sites of interest, the author has provided case studies looking at knowledge management in virtual and knowledge-intensive firms, and in global multinationals. These will help you with your research, essays, and assignments; or you may find these additional resources helpful when revising for exams.

 www.oxfordtextbooks.co.uk/orc/hislop3e/

Leadership, Organization Culture Management, and Knowledge Management

Introduction

This chapter examines the closely interrelated topics of leadership and organizational culture and how they can impact on knowledge management initiatives. The vast majority of the literature on these topics argues that certain leadership styles or types of organizational culture can support and facilitate knowledge management activities. Thus, as with Chapter 14, which examined the use of human resource management practices, the primary focus here is relatively practical, considering the way that leadership and culture management activities can be utilized to persuade workers to take part in knowledge management activities.

There are two fundamental reasons why these topics are considered together in the same chapter. First, they are closely interrelated in that the attitudes, values, and behaviours of organizational leaders can have a significant impact on the type of culture that exists within an organization. This is particularly true within small companies where the leader and/or founder of the organization can have a profound impact in shaping the nature of organizational culture. For example, Pan and Scarbrough (1999) argue that Bob Buckman played an instrumental role in the development of the knowledge-sharing culture that developed within his company Buckman Laboratories (see illustration), and the end of chapter case study also highlights the relationship between leadership, culture, and knowledge management. The second reason why leadership and organizational culture are examined in the same chapter is that the adoption of certain leadership styles and attempts to manage organizational cultures have some characteristics in common. Thus, in contrast to the types of HRM processes examined in the previous chapter, which are broadly focused on short-term timescales and the management of workers' day-to-day (knowledge-related) behaviours, both leadership and culture management activities can be regarded as relatively strategic in nature and medium-term in their focus, being concerned with the development of visions and values that will inspire and motivate workers to behave in certain ways.

Both topics have been the focus of a significant amount of research and debate, with a vast academic literature existing on both. While the development of interest in the topic of

> **Illustration**   Leadership and knowledge-based culture at Buckman Laboratories
>
> Pan and Scarbrough (1999) argue that appropriate knowledge cultures can be developed, but admit that doing so is a complex, daunting, and time-consuming process. Their argument is based on a detailed examination of one organization—Buckman Laboratories. Buckman Laboratories has, in the words of one top manager interviewed by Pan and Scarbrough (1999: 369), 'created a culture of trust encouraging active knowledge sharing across time and space among all of the company's employees across the world'. Central to the efforts of Buckman Laboratories to develop a knowledge-sharing culture was the development and implementation of a technological system for codifying and sharing knowledge (K'Netix). However, it was also recognized by senior management that, to create an effective knowledge-sharing culture, management had to be proactive in the transformation of the company's culture, and they developed a culture change programme to achieve this. Pan and Scarbrough argue that key to the success of this programme was the role played by the organization's leader, Bob Buckman. He is described as a 'pioneering figure' (p. 369), who initiated and strongly championed the idea of developing a knowledge-sharing culture. Bob Buckman was argued to understand the importance of considering long-term concerns such as developing a future vision of the company and creating conditions which would allow it to be achieved. This was acknowledged by one senior manager who was interviewed who said that the 'climate we create as leaders has a major impact on our ability to share knowledge across space and time' (p. 370).

culture management has been relatively recent, becoming of great interest in the early 1980s, the study of leadership by contrast has a much longer heritage, with academic interest in the topic beginning in the first decades of the twentieth century. While brief links are made to both of these literatures, the central focus here is on the contemporary knowledge management literature that examines the impact of leadership and organizational culture on knowledge management activities.

The chapter begins by examining the topic of organizational culture and its relationship to knowledge management, before then considering the impact the leadership can have on knowledge processes. There are two separate sections on the topic of organizational culture, with the first one focusing on the relationship between organizational culture and knowledge management processes, and the second examining the different perspectives on the debate regarding the extent to which knowledge-based cultures can be created within organizations. The topic of leadership is also divided into two sections, with the first giving a brief overview of the way in which the conceptualization of leadership has evolved over time, and the second section looking more narrowly at the relationship between leadership and knowledge management activities.

The Impact of Organizational Culture on Knowledge Management Activities

This section both defines organizational culture and gives insights into the impact that organizational culture can have on knowledge management activities. An enormous quantity of the knowledge management literature that examines the topic of organizational culture argues that it can significantly influence organizational knowledge management activities (Al-Alawi *et al.* 2007; Chang and Lee 2007; Donate and Guadamillas 2010; Lee and Chen 2005; Rai 2011; Stock *et al.* 2010). While in many papers such statements are made without the support of empirical evidence (Cabrera and Cabrera 2005; De Long and Fahey 2000; du Plessis 2008; Milne 2007), in an increasing number of papers detailed and strong empirical data are presented to illustrate how organizational culture can impact on people's willingness to participate in knowledge management and innovation activities (Alavi *et al.* 2005–6; Chang and Lee 2007; Lam 2005; Liao *et al.* 2012; Nayir and Uzunçarsili 2008; Sanz-Valle *et al.* 2011; Suppiah and Singh Sandhu 2011). Finally, while the vast majority of this literature suggests that organizational culture can positively influence knowledge management activities and initiatives, there have been a number of studies, as will be shown later, which have highlighted the negative impact that certain types of organizational culture can have on knowledge management activities (Lam 2005; Rai 2011; Sanz-Valle *et al.* 2011; Suppiah and Singh Sandhu 2011).

Before proceeding any further it is necessary to define what organizational culture is. While every piece of writing on culture typically gives its own specific definition, a useful one is that provided by Huczynski and Buchanan (2001: 624), who define organizational culture as 'the collection of relatively uniform and enduring values, beliefs, customs, traditions and practices that are shared by an organization's members'.

This definition is useful as it highlights two key features of organizational culture. First, it emphasizes the collective nature of organizational culture, as for culture to be organizational it needs to be shared by a significant proportion of organizational staff. Secondly, the definition makes explicit that culture exists both at the level of ideas and values (such as the importance of good customer service, being innovative and creative) and behaviours (such as the particular ways that work processes are carried out, how and when team meetings are organized, how people are rewarded and recognized, etc.).

> **DEFINITION   Organizational culture**
>
> The beliefs and behaviours shared by an organization's members regarding what constitutes an appropriate way to think and act at work.

While there are debates within the organizational culture literature regarding the nature of organizational culture, and the extent to which it can be managed (Harris and Ogbonna 2002; Mathew and Ogbonna 2011), there is a significant proportion of literature which argues both that organizational culture can be managed and that there are a number of benefits that can be derived from having a strong, clear organizational culture. At the level of values and ideas, having a strong, clear culture means that employees should clearly understand what the key organizational values are. Further, if employees accept the validity and importance of the values of the culture this may mean that employees will be loyal and committed to the company and this also has the potential to create amongst staff a strong sense of collective organizational or team/group identity. At the level of behaviour, if employees believe in and accept an organization's culture this is argued to help make them behave in ways which support and reinforce the culture. For example, if the culture of the organization emphasizes the importance of innovation and creativity, if employees believe in these values they are likely to behave in innovative and creative ways, such as collaborating with people to produce new products or services.

Two of the factors identified in Chapter 9 that influence the attitudes of workers regarding their participation in organizational knowledge management activities are the relationship between workers and management and the extent to which workers have a sense of group identity. Culture management activities are argued to support organizational knowledge management efforts by addressing both these issues, through developing workers' trust in and commitment to management in their organization, and the organization more generally, and through helping develop the workers' sense of team and/or group identity.

A general weakness of much of the literature which examines the link between culture and knowledge management is that it is often relatively vague regarding the characteristics of organizational culture which facilitate knowledge management activities. Thus, for example, O'Dell and Hubert (2011) simply talk about a 'knowledge sharing' culture, while Donate and Guadamillas (2010) talk about a 'knowledge-centred' culture'. Within this literature, however, there is a broad consensus on the general characteristics of an organizational culture likely to facilitate knowledge management activities. These characteristics are that, first, knowledge sharing is regarded as a norm, second, that organizational staff have a strong sense of collective identity, third, that colleagues have a high level of trust in and respect for each other, fourth, that organizational processes are regarded as fair, and finally that staff have high levels of trust in and commitment to management.

However, by around 2009 a number of writers on knowledge management had begun to be more specific regarding the characteristics of 'good' and 'bad' organizational cultures. This has typically been done through using academic typologies of organizational culture to identify which ones best support knowledge management activities. While various typologies of organizational culture exist, the one that has been used most frequently in the knowledge management literature is that developed by Cameron and Quinn (see e.g. Sanz-Valle *et al.* 2011; Stock *et al.* 2010; Suppiah and Sandhu 2011). Thus, before looking at the research into the impact of these culture types on knowledge management and learning, it is necessary to give a brief overview of Cameron and Quinn's organization culture typology.

Cameron and Quinn's typology (2006) uses two dimensions to develop a typology which distinguishes between four distinctive organizational culture types (see Figure 15.1). In this framework, one dimension is flexibility/adaptability versus stability/continuity, while the other dimension examines whether the culture is focused internally within the organization, or whether its primary focus is externally, on the market and general business environment. Using these dimensions Cameron and Quinn distinguish between what they refer to as a clan culture, a culture of adhocracy, a hierarchical culture, and a market-focused culture. The characteristics of a clan culture are that it is a culture which is flexible and adaptable and which is primarily internally focused, being concerned with facilitating collaboration amongst staff and the development of a strong sense of group and team identity among staff. A culture of adhocracy is also flexible and adaptable, but is more focused on the market and the external business environment. This type of culture is suited to companies that operate in dynamic markets, and emphasizes values of creativity and innovation. A hierarchical culture is one that is both internally focused and concerned with stability and continuity. The characteristics of this culture are a focus on adhering to

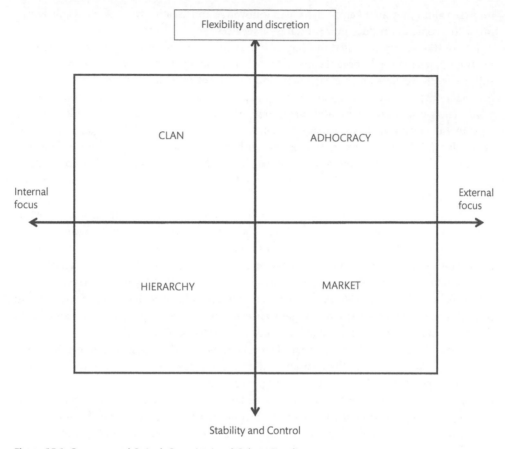

Figure 15.1 Cameron and Quinn's Organizational Culture Typology

organizationally defined rules and norms within organizations that have clearly defined authority structures. Finally, a market-based culture is one which is externally focused, but where the emphasis is on stability and continuity. This culture is appropriate to business environments which are not characterized by high levels of change, and where the focus of the culture is on factors such as consistency, incremental innovation or change, and maintaining or developing levels of competitiveness in business markets.

Recent writing on organizational culture types shows a remarkable degree of consensus regarding the types of organizational culture that facilitate and inhibit knowledge processes in organization. This research has been done on a heterogeneous range of different types of organization, including seven public and private sector Malaysian organizations (Suppiah and Sandhu 2011), hospitals in the USA (Stock *et al.* 2010), Taiwanese banks and insurance companies (Liao *et al.* 2012), and firms in south-east Spain (Sanze-Valle *et al.* 2011—see the example). The type of culture which most strongly facilitates knowledge management activities is a culture of adhocracy, with Sanz-Valle *et al.* (2011) finding this culture type to be positively related to levels of organizational learning, and Liao *et al.* (2012) finding a culture of adhocracy to be positively related to levels of organizational innovation. The type of organizational culture which inhibits knowledge management activities is generally found to be a hierarchical or bureaucratic culture, with Stock *et al.* (2010) finding this culture type to be negatively related to levels of knowledge dissemination within organizations, Sanz-Valle *et al.* (2011) finding it to be negatively related to levels of organizational learning, Liao *et al.* (2012) finding it to be negatively linked to levels of organizational innovation, and Sappiah and Sandhu (2011) finding it to be negatively related to the sharing of tacit knowledge among employees.

 Illustration   Organizational culture types and organizational learning

Sanz-Valle *et al.* (2011) use Cameron and Quinn's organizational culture typology to examine the impact that different types of culture have on levels of organizational learning and technical innovation within organizations. This topic was empirically investigated through carrying out a survey among a diverse population of companies from the south-east of Spain, with over 450 completed surveys being returned (out of 1,600 sent). While the hypotheses regarding the direct relationship between culture and technical innovation were not supported, the study did find that a culture of adhocracy was positively related to levels of organizational learning, while a hierarchical culture was negatively related to levels of organizational learning. Finally, no relationship was found to exist between clan or market-based cultures and organizational learning. Thus, on the basis of this study, organizational learning is best facilitated by a culture of adhocracy, where the culture is externally focused on the business environment, where the culture of flexible and adaptable is emphasized, and where values of creativity and innovation are encouraged and rewarded.

Creating and Managing an Organizational Culture to Support Knowledge Management Activities

A general limitation of much of the literature on this topic is that it provides little indication of either what organizations require to do to achieve such cultures, or what barriers may exist to their development. In the literature which does consider how appropriate cultures can be created, there is disagreement on whether organizational cultures should be changed to create appropriate knowledge behaviours and values, or whether knowledge management efforts should be designed to reflect an organization's existing cultural values.

The mainstream perspective in the knowledge management literature is that organizational cultures can be changed to produce appropriate knowledge related behaviours and values (see e.g. Teo *et al.* 2010, at the end of Chapter 13). Analysis based on this assumption therefore argues that one of the key tasks likely to underpin the success of knowledge management initiatives is the modification of an organization's culture in ways that encourage and support desired knowledge behaviours and attitudes (De Long and Fahey 2000; Ribiere and Sitar 2003). Pan and Scarbrough (1999) argue that appropriate knowledge cultures can be developed, but admit that doing so is a complex, daunting, and time-consuming process. Their argument is based on a detailed examination of one organization, Buckman Laboratories (see opening illustration in this chapter).

An alternative perspective is supported by McDermott and O'Dell, who suggest that organizations which are successful with their knowledge management initiatives, 'build their knowledge management approach to fit their culture' (2001: 77). This is because organizational cultures are much more resilient than any knowledge management initiative, thus organizations which attempt to shape the culture to fit with their knowledge management initiative, rather than vice versa, are likely to find that their knowledge management initiatives fail (see also O'Dell and Hubert 2011). The success of such initiatives is also predicated on organizations having suitable knowledge cultures already in place. Thus, embedded in McDermott and O'Dell's analysis is a pessimism about the achievement of large-scale culture change, and that if appropriate knowledge behaviours are not a part of the existing culture it is likely to be very difficult to change the culture to make them so.

 Time to reflect   How controllable is organizational culture?

Do management have the power to control and influence organizational culture, or is culture something beyond the control of management?

To align a knowledge management initiative with the organization's culture they argue that it is necessary to link it to both the visible and invisible elements of the culture (see Table 15.1). In terms of visible elements, the knowledge management initiative needs to be focused on addressing existing business problems, to match the existing 'style' of the organization (such as the degree of bureaucratic rigidity), and reward and appraisal systems need to make visible the importance of appropriate knowledge behaviours. In terms of the invisible aspects of an organization's culture, knowledge management initiatives should reflect existing core values, and should link into existing networks of social relations. In a similar vein Schulze and Boland (2000) argue that knowledge management initiatives are likely to fail if they involve the development and use of work practices which are incongruent with existing work practices.

These two perspectives on the manageability of knowledge-related cultures reflect similar debates in the wider culture literature (Harris and Ogbonna 2002; Mathew and Ogbonna 2011). Finally, again reflecting a theme in the wider culture management literature, some

Table 15.1 Linking Knowledge Management Initiatives to Organizational Culture

Visible Elements of Culture	Invisible Elements of Culture
KM initiative should link to existing business problems	KM initiatives should link to core organizational values
KM initiatives should reflect existing organizational style	KM initiatives should link into existing networks of social relations
HR practices should link to appropriate knowledge behaviours	

Source: McDermott and O'Dell 2001.

analysis acknowledges that organizations may not have coherent and unitary cultures, and that distinctive subcultures may exist which shape the characteristics and dynamics of organizational knowledge-sharing processes (Alavi *et al.* 2005–6; De Long and Fahey 2000). For example, Currie and Kerrin's (2003) case study of a pharmaceuticals company found that the existence of strong subcultures within the sales and marketing divisions inhibited the sharing of knowledge between staff in them, despite a number of management initiatives aimed at changing this knowledge sharing/hoarding pattern. Finally, the literature on cross-community knowledge processes (see Chapter 11) that considers intra-company situations, such as cross-functional collaboration, or collaboration between business units within the same company, also suggests that significant differences can exist in the culture of different parts of an organization. However, in the literature which examines the relationship between organizational culture and knowledge management, innovation, or learning, this does not represent the mainstream perspective, with this literature typically assuming, implicitly, that organizations have unitary and coherent cultures.

 Illustration   The impact of subcultures on organizational knowledge management activities

Alavi *et al.* (2005–6) examined how organizational culture shaped knowledge management practices in an American-based global IT company. The knowledge management initiative, which had a large technological emphasis, consisted of two main elements. First, there were centralized 'enterprise repositories' through which a range of knowledge was available to staff globally. Secondly, there was a technological infrastructure which consisted of both a content management tool (Lotus Notes) and a communication/collaboration tool (which included e-mail, calendaring, and online chat facilities where project teams could communicate and interact in private, virtual spaces).

In general terms they found that distinctive subcultures existed within the business and that they had a significant impact on how its KM tools were used. Primarily the existence of these subcultures meant that the standardized knowledge management tools were used quite differently by staff who were members of different subcultures. For example, use of the virtual collaborative spaces (online chatrooms for project teams) varied significantly between subcultures. They were typically used most extensively by subcultures that had strong collaborative values as they allowed them to connect and communicate with each other. In contrast the subcultures whose values were more focused around innovation made greater use of a different range of tools, such as portals, search engines, and expert locators, as they facilitated the development and accumulation of intellectual capital.

A consequence of this differentiated pattern of use was that different people and groups experienced different outcomes from their use of the knowledge management tools. Thus the staff in the subcultures which used the knowledge management tools to facilitate their interpersonal collaboration typically felt a greater sense of team identity as a result of using the knowledge management tools. In contrast, the people in the subcultures with innovation-related values perceived that their use of the knowledge management tools allowed them to work more effectively, and increased the likelihood that they would experience the benefits of serendipitous innovation.

1. Are all large organizations likely to have distinctive subcultures rather than a single, coherent corporate culture and does this mean that the way people share, manage, and create knowledge within such organizations is likely to vary?

The Conceptualization of Leadership in the Academic Business and Management Literature

Before examining the knowledge management literature that deals with the topic of leadership it is useful to begin by providing some context to this work through, briefly, engaging with the general academic literature on leadership. Given both the amount of writing that has been produced on the topic of leadership, as well as the diversity of perspectives and theories that have been developed, it is impossible in the space available here to provide a comprehensive overview. All that is provided is a schematic outline of how the theorization of leadership has historically evolved and some detail on what represents the mainstream contemporary perspective on leadership.

Serious interest in the topic of leadership in the academic business literature dates back to the early twentieth century. At this time, what was characterized as the 'trait' theory of leadership dominated (see Table 15.2). This perspective suggested that great and successful leaders possess particular personality traits and characteristics that distinguished them

Table 15.2 Historical Overview of Diverse Perspectives on Leadership

Leadership Theory	Assumptions about Leadership	Contemporary Status/Relevance
Trait Approach	Great leaders are born, not created, and possess particular inherent characteristics that distinguish them from other people—such as charisma, the ability to communicate effectively, emotional intelligence	Most popular in 1930s and 1940s but re-emerged in 1970s. Discredited as empirical studies found no agreed relationship between particular traits and successful leadership. Also criticized for neglecting context
Behaviour-Based Theories	Focus on what leaders do, attempt to identify behaviours of successful leadership	Developed in 1950s but still utilized by some researchers. Has been criticized for lacking adequate theorization and empirical methodologies used to measure and investigate behaviours
Contingency Approach (including Fiedler's contingency theory and path-goal theory)	What constitutes appropriate leadership is shaped by the nature of the organizational context	Developed in late 1960s with general growth in popularity of contingency theory. Has been criticized on a number of issues including lack of consistent empirical support
'New Leadership' Theories (including charismatic leadership theory, and transformational/transactional leadership theory)	Concerned with how leaders' action and talk motivates followers to act	Developed in late 1970s and have grown in popularity since. Have been criticized for universalistic assumptions which neglect importance of context

from others, such as high levels of charisma. From this perspective, great leaders are people born with particular traits that distinguish them from 'ordinary people'. However, over time, this perspective became subject to a number of criticisms, not least that empirical evidence has provided questionable support for it. Since then a number of different perspectives on leadership were developed (see Table 15.2), which themselves became subject to a number of criticisms. A useful starting point for those interested in gaining a more detailed understanding of how the theorization of leadership has evolved is to read relevant books or book chapters on the topic (see e.g. Densten 2008; Northouse 2007; Yukl 2008).

As suggested in Table 15.2, 'new leadership' theories represent the most popular contemporary perspective on leadership in the academic business literature. It is worth elaborating on this perspective in a little depth, not only because of its contemporary popularity, but also because, as will be seen later, it represents one of the perspectives on leadership most widely used by writers on knowledge management.

 Time to reflect   Applying leadership theories

Think of an example of a high-profile and successful leader (either from a business organization or from some other context, such as a sports team or a political party). Which leadership theory best explains their success?

Arguably Burns's (1978) development of the concept of transformational leadership represents the starting point of what has subsequently been labelled 'new leadership'. However, various terms such as strategic leadership, charismatic leadership, and visionary leadership have been utilized by others to refer to a very similar style of leadership. Typically, all these concepts are categorized as together representing 'new leadership' theory (Vera and Crossan 2004). Arguably, one of the key features of transformational leadership (and all 'new leadership' theories) is that it represents a form of leadership and people management that is distinctive from more traditional forms of management. Thus, transformational leadership is often defined in parallel with, and as the virtual opposite of, management (what might be referred to as micro-management, which is referred to by various writers as instrumental leadership, e.g. Nadler and Tushman (1990), and as transactional leadership, Burns (1978)). As outlined in Table 15.3 transformational leadership is fundamentally concerned with motivating and inspiring followers by developing long-term strategic visions and persuading people to buy into them and work towards their achievement. Transformational leaders thus motivate workers through providing them with intellectual stimulation and inspiring them to work towards these corporate visions and values.

While this literature places a central emphasis on the strategic importance of transformational leadership, there is also an acknowledgement that this form of leadership is not enough on its own to successfully motivate and manage workers. Thus, it is usually argued that transformational leadership has to be used in parallel with other forms of leadership and management that are more focused on the day-to-day management of workers and operational issues. Thus for example Burns talked of transformational and transactional leadership, and Nadler and Tushman (1990) refer to charismatic and instrumental leadership.

Table 15.3 Distinguishing Leadership from (Micro) Management

	Leadership	(Micro) Management
Timescale Focus	Long term	Short term
Primary Role	Strategic	Operational
Key Task	Development and communication of long-term vision	Day-to-day management of people towards work objectives
People Management Role	Motivate by providing inspiring vision and providing intellectual stimulation	Day-to-day management of people towards short- and medium-term work objectives through goal setting and reward management
Impact on Culture, Values, and Structure	Develop new values and vision with aim of sustaining long-term competitiveness	Reinforce existing culture, values, and structures through operating within them

---

DEFINITION Transformational leadership

A mode or style of leadership focused on the development of long-term visions, values, and goals which also involves persuading workers to become attached to them and to work towards achieving them.

However, while there is an enormous corpus of writing on the topic of leadership, and while it represents a relatively mature subject area, there is a lack of consensus on the questions of what leadership fundamentally consists in and whether and how links can be made between the leadership styles and behaviours of key individuals, and organizational performance (see e.g. Kelly 2008; Northouse 2007). Further, the mainstream literature on leadership has been criticized on such fundamental issues as making universalist assumptions about the relevance of certain leadership styles which neglect to adequately account for context, being weakly theorized, making use of questionable research methods, and of providing weak empirical support for the claims that are made (Barker 2001; Güldenberg and Konrath 2006; Yukl 2008). Despite this lack of consensus the vast majority of knowledge management literature, as will be seen in the following section, adopts a relatively uncritical stance on contemporary perspectives on transformational leadership.

Knowledge Management and Leadership

There now exists a reasonable body of writing on the relationship between leadership and knowledge management processes. Thus, for example, von Krogh *et al.* (2012) undertook a systematic literature review of the literature on leadership and knowledge management and identified forty-eight journal articles on the topic that were published between 1997 and 2009. Since then a number of other papers have also been published (see e.g. Kuo and Lee 2011; Lee *et al.* 2010; Nguyen and Mohamed 2011). The main perspective on leadership adopted by the knowledge literature is the strategic/transformational leadership perspective. For example, in von Krogh *et al.*'s (2012) analysis, the vast majority of the forty-eight articles they identified focused centrally on either transformational/transactional or strategic leadership styles.

This literature can be characterized by two features. First, the claims it makes with regard to the relationship between knowledge management or learning and leadership, and secondly, the claims made regarding the type of style of leadership necessary to facilitate knowledge management and learning. With regards to the link between leadership and knowledge management this literature typically makes a relatively strong claim that effective leadership can play an important role in facilitating learning and knowledge

 Illustration   Leadership, trust, knowledge sharing, and team performance

Lee *et al.* (2010) examined the relationship between a certain type/style of leadership, and the level of knowledge sharing within teams, as well as team performance. The empirical study they undertook was carried out within one Australian automotive company. The type of team leadership behaviour they examined was quite specific, being labelled as the 'knowledge builder role'. The behaviours associated with this leadership role include providing technical advice to team members, developing expertise within the team, searching beyond the team for new ideas, monitoring the quality of the team's work, and initiating the development and implementation of new working practices. The following interview quotation from a team leader also illustrates the nature of this role: 'I try to encourage them to challenge each team members' input into the design work and not just accept what they're told. I try and bring to the table different ways for them to look at things and to look outside their functions' (p. 483).

The conceptual model that they tested hypothesized that the team knowledge builder role was potentially directly related to levels of knowledge sharing within teams. The model also hypothesized that the relationship between knowledge builder behaviours and knowledge sharing in teams was mediated by trust in the team leader or trust in the team. Further, with both leadership and team-based trust, they suggested that two forms of knowledge-based trust existed. These were reliance trust, where people are willing to rely on the knowledge of others, and disclosure trust, where people are willing to share sensitive knowledge or information with other team members.

Lee *et al.*'s (2010) model was tested via a survey-based study of thirty-four project teams within the automotive company, with almost 200 team members and leaders completing the survey. In testing their theoretical model, Lee *et al.* found that knowledge builder behaviours were positively linked to knowledge sharing in teams, but that the relationship was mediated by team-based trust (but not leadership-based trust). Thus Lee *et al.* (2010) conclude that knowledge builder behaviours, by developing levels of reliance and disclosure-based trust in team members, are indirectly but positively related to levels of team-based knowledge sharing. Finally, the hypothesis that levels of knowledge sharing in teams were positively related to team performance was also supported.

1. The knowledge builder style of leadership seems particularly appropriate leadership style for relatively small teams/groups. To what extent is this style of leadership relevant to organizational-level leadership?

management activities in organizations. For example, both Huang *et al.* (2008) and Yang (2007) found that various leadership roles were positively related to knowledge sharing in organizations. Due to the assumptions made in this literature regarding the importance of knowledge processes to organizational performance, effective leadership is also assumed to help contribute to competitive advantage and organizational performance. Thus, Hinterhuber and Stadler (2006: 237), argue that 'leadership and strategy are the immaterial competencies which contribute most to a company's value'. Empirical studies which substantiate the relationship between leadership, knowledge management, and team performance are provided by Lee *et al.* (2010) and Srivastava *et al.* (2006), who focus on different styles of leadership (see illustrations).

The data presented by many of the studies on this topic that do empirically examine how leadership impacts on knowledge management processes can be questioned. For example, the generalizability of some of the empirical data that are presented can be questioned, as they are either anecdotal or case study evidence related to a single organization case study (such as Nonaka *et al.* 2006; Pan and Scarbrough 1999; Singh 2008). Further, studies that have collected and analysed quantitative, survey-based data in an attempt to statistically measure the relationship between leadership and knowledge management processes have largely failed to provide strong convincing evidence (Crawford 2005; Güldenberg and Konrath 2006; Politis 2002; Singh 2008). For example, Politis (2002) developed and tested (via a survey) seven hypotheses concerning the relationship between transformational and transactional leadership and both knowledge acquisition and team performance in an Australian manufacturing company. However, the results did not support the hypotheses developed, and with respect to the relationship between team performance and transformational leadership concluded that transformational leadership 'may not be the prime impetus for moving team performance forward' (p. 187).

On the style of leadership argued to be necessary to facilitate knowledge management activities, the strategic/transformational perspective on leadership is by far the dominant one. This literature talks about the importance of leaders who are concerned with developing long-term strategy and vision. Secondly, in relation to people management this literature emphasizes the ability of the leader to inspire and motivate rather than to micro-manage workers. For example, Nonaka *et al.* (2006: 1192) talk about leadership as being concerned with 'interpreting, nurturing and supporting the knowledge vision', and that in relation to their SECI model of knowledge creation (see Chapter 7) should be about 'enabling knowledge creation—not controlling and directing it'. However, despite the dominance of these perspectives on leadership, a number of papers have examined other styles/forms of leadership, and found them to facilitate knowledge management activities. Thus, for example, Lee *et al.* (2010) examine leadership concerned with 'knowledge building' in teams (see illustration immediately above). Others have also examined the impact of empowering leadership on knowledge management activities (see e.g. Kuo and Lee, 2011; Srivastava *et al.* 2006—see illustration). Empowering leadership is a form of leadership where power is shared with subordinates (such as via participative decision-making) which is argued to increase people's level of intrinsic motivation to work, and in relation to knowledge management, share knowledge and participate in the co-creation of knowledge with colleagues.

Illustration The relationship between empowering leadership, knowledge sharing, and the performance of management teams

Srivastava *et al.* (2006) examined the intervening role that knowledge sharing had on the relationship between empowering leadership and the performance of management teams. The study also examined the intervening role of team efficacy, but this aspect of the paper isn't examined here. Empowering leadership, through encouraging subordinates to express and share their opinions, was hypothesized as having the potential to play a crucial role in facilitating knowledge-sharing processes. With respect to the relationship between team knowledge sharing and team performance, it was hypothesized that team performance would be positively related to knowledge sharing. The hypotheses that were developed were tested via a survey of management teams from various regions in the USA. Of the 550 management teams that the survey was sent to, data from 102 teams were used. The statistical analysis of the survey data supported all the hypotheses examined, thus the empirical data did find that not only was empowering leadership positively related to intra-team knowledge sharing, but also that team performance was also positively related to intra-team knowledge sharing.

1. The empowering style of leadership examined by Srivastava *et al.* appears closer to what has been called (micro) management, rather than transformational leadership (see Table 15.3). Does this suggest that *both* effective (micro) management and transformational styles of leadership have a role to play in facilitating organizational knowledge management processes?

 ## Conclusion

This chapter has been concerned with providing an overview of how organizational culture and leadership in organizations can impact on organizational knowledge management activities. As outlined, the assumption that typically underpins much of the literature on this topic is that both can have a very positive role in facilitating and supporting knowledge management activities.

The culture of an organization was shown to be an important factor shaping the attitudes of workers to knowledge management initiatives, and the extent to which they are prepared to use and share their knowledge. In general terms, cultures of adhocracy are found to facilitate knowledge management, whereas bureaucratic or hierarchical cultures were generally found to inhibit knowledge management activities. However, it was also shown that there is an active debate on this topic, with some writers raising questions regarding the extent to which effective knowledge cultures can be achieved through culture management initiatives. While the majority of writers suggest that knowledge management activities can be facilitated by the development of appropriate cultures, McDermott and O'Dell (2001) suggest that attempting to modify an organization's culture to fit in with the objectives of a knowledge management initiative is likely to be a recipe for failure.

In terms of leadership, while transformational leadership is the dominant perspective in the knowledge management literature, there are also a number of papers that consider the relationship between other leadership styles and knowledge management. The transformational leadership perspective makes a relatively sharp distinction between leadership and management, arguing that while management is focused upon operational issues and is concerned with the day-to-day management of people and resources, transformational leadership by contrast is more focused on strategic issues and long-term matters such as developing and communicating a future vision that people can be inspired and motivated by. As has been shown here, a growing body of empirical evidence suggests that various leadership styles are positively related to level of knowledge sharing within organizations, which suggests that knowledge management initiatives can be facilitated by effective and appropriate leadership.

Case study   Leadership, culture, and knowledge management within Australian SMEs

Nguyen and Mohamed (2011) examined the extent to which leadership was positively related to knowledge management activities. They also investigated the extent to which organizational culture moderated this relationship. They suggest that the role and challenge for leaders was to encourage, demand, and motivate others to participate in knowledge management activities. They conceptualized leadership in terms of the transformational/transactional framework. They define transactional leadership as being concerned with managing others to perform desired behaviours via offering rewards, or threatening punishments. In contrast, transformational leaders are argued to influence the behaviour of others via creating knowledge-based vision and values and developing people's trust, loyalty, and admiration. They hypothesized that both forms of leadership would be positively related to knowledge management activities. Further, they argued due to the close inter-relationship that exists between leadership and organizational culture, with them being 'two sides of the same coin' (p. 209), that organizational culture will moderate the relationship between both leadership styles and knowledge management activities.

Nguyen and Mohamed tested these hypotheses in a survey-based study of some Australian SMEs involved in a wide range of industries. The survey produced a relatively low response rate, with 1,000 surveys being distributed, and 157 usable surveys being analysed. The size of the SMEs studied varied significantly, with 20 per cent having less than twenty-five employees and 33 per cent having between 200 and 500 employees. In terms of knowledge management activities, the survey had seventeen questions which examined a range of different knowledge management activities (such as knowledge exchange and knowledge internalization).

In terms of the hypotheses tested, they found that a positive relationship existed between both leadership styles and knowledge management activities. Thus both leadership styles were found to facilitate people's participation in knowledge management activities. These findings also suggest that organizational knowledge management activities are facilitated by more than one style of leadership, thus organizations should utilize both forms of leadership to facilitate knowledge management activities, rather than simply focusing on one style of leadership.

However, while organizational culture was found to moderate the relationship between transactional leadership and knowledge management activities, it was not found to moderate the relationship between transformational leadership and organizational culture. A potential explanation put forward for these findings was that organizational culture moderates the relationship between transactional leadership and knowledge management, as this style of leadership operates within, and is linked with, the existing organizational culture, and is not concerned with or focused on developing or changing organizational culture. The lack of a moderating relationship of culture in the relationship between transformational leadership and knowledge management was argued to be potentially due to the fact that this style of leadership is more concerned with shaping behaviour by developing an organization's culture, than with utilizing the existing culture.

1. Is the relationship between leadership, culture, and KM found by Nguyen and Mohamed likely to be particularly strong due to the fact that they conducted their research on SMEs? Is the moderating effect of culture on the relationship between leadership and knowledge management activities likely to be less in larger organizations?

Nguyen, H., and S. Mohamed, S. (2011) 'Leadership Behaviours, Organizational Culture and Knowledge Management Practices: An Empirical Investigation', *Journal of Management Development*, 30/2: 206–21.

Review and Discussion Questions

1. One critique of much of the leadership literature, including the concept of transformational leadership that is widely used in the knowledge management literature, is that it makes universalistic assumptions that such forms of leadership are appropriate in all contexts and situations. Thus, much of the knowledge management literature on leadership implies that transformational leadership is appropriate to all knowledge-intensive firms and the management of all knowledge workers. Do you agree with this argument, or do you think that context matters and that, while transformational leadership may be useful in some contexts, different types of situation require different styles of leadership?

2. If an organization does NOT have a culture of collaboration and knowledge sharing, how easy is it likely to be to develop such a culture?

3. Is the existence of distinctive subcultures within an organization likely to be related to organizational size, or the extent to which people in the organization are geographically dispersed?

 ## Suggestions for Further Reading

1. R. Sanz-Valle, J. Naranjo-Valencia, D. Jimenéz-Jimenéz, L. Perez-Caballero (2011) 'Linking Organizational Learning with Technical Innovation and Organizational Culture', *Journal of Knowledge Management*, 15/6: 997–1015.
A study which uses Cameron and Quinn's typology of organizational cultures to examine the relationship between different types of organizational culture and organizational learning among Spanish companies.

2. H. Nguyen and S. Mohamed (2011) 'Leadership Behaviours, Organizational Culture and Knowledge Management Practices: An Empirical Investigation', *Journal of Management Development*, 30/2: 206–21.
Examines how transformational and transactional styles of leadership affect knowledge management activities in Australian SMEs and also the extent to which organizational culture moderates these relationships.

3. P. Lee, N. Gillespie, L. Mann, and A. Wearing (2010) 'Leadership and Trust: Their Effect on Knowledge Sharing and Team Performance', *Management Learning*, 41/4: 473–91.
An empirical study which examines how knowledge-based team leadership affects levels of knowledge sharing within teams, and how this impacts on team performance.

4. G. Yukl (2008) *Leadership in Organizations* (London: Pearson Education).
A good introduction to and critical review of the diverse literature on leadership.

Take your learning further: Online Resource Centre

Visit the Online Resource Centre for resources which will extend your understanding of knowledge management in organizations. As well as web links to sites of interest, the author has provided case studies looking at knowledge management in virtual and knowledge-intensive firms, and in global multinationals. These will help you with your research, essays, and assignments; or you may find these additional resources helpful when revising for exams.

 www.oxfordtextbooks.co.uk/orc/hislop3e/

Reflections on the Topic of Knowledge Management

Introduction

The objective of this concluding chapter is to reflect on two general topics in the body of writing on knowledge management which both connect back to themes touched on in the first chapter of the book. First, the chapter links back to Schultze and Stabell's (2004) framework on knowledge management to draw some conclusions regarding the general character, and focus of the literature on knowledge management. Secondly, the chapter links to issues raised in Chapter 1 regarding the extent to which interest in the topic of knowledge management has been sustained since the initial explosive growth of interest in the mid-to-late 1990s. This is done by using Abrahamson's work on management fashions to consider the extent to which knowledge management constitutes a management fashion whose time has come (and possibly gone). This section is focused more on the production of knowledge on knowledge management than the extent to which it is consumed and used by business organizations. However, there is a brief discussion on the challenges of understanding the extent to which the business world is attempting to manage the knowledge of their workforces and an illustrative example that examines the extent to which academic knowledge on knowledge management is utilized by knowledge management practitioners in their work. Further, in looking at the production of knowledge on knowledge management, the chapter considers the roles of academics and of large global consultancy/professional service firms.

Reflection on the Character and Focus of the Academic Knowledge Management Literature

This section of the chapter links back to the framework on knowledge management research that was developed by Schultze and Stabell (2004) that was outlined in Chapter 1. The purpose of doing so is to expand on the comments made there to give a sense of how the general focus and character of academic literature on knowledge management has evolved over time. It is unnecessary to repeat the dimensions of Schultze and Stabell's framework as their four perspectives on knowledge management are outlined in Figure 1.3. Chapter 1 highlighted that, of the four perspectives on knowledge management that existed, the one which had been predominant was the neo-functionalist discourse, which was characterized by an objectivist perspective on knowledge, combined with a consensus-based perspective on social relations. This perspective typically assumes that knowledge can exist in the form of a codified object, and due to assumptions of consensus regarding social relations, typically ignores issues of conflict, politics, and power.

Reflecting on the character of the literature utilized in this current edition of the book, both some change and some continuity in this focus can be identified. First, in terms of change, as was highlighted in Chapter 3, and in various other chapters (such as Chapter 10 on communities of practice, Chapter 11 on cross-community knowledge processes, and Chapter 12 on power), a growing number of academic papers utilize a practice-based perspective on knowledge. This is reflective of the fact that over time this perspective on knowledge has grown in prominence and popularity (Corradi *et al.* 2010). Arguably, the neo-functionalist perspective may no longer be as dominant as it used to be, and both what are labelled the 'constructivist' and 'neo-functionalist' perspectives on knowledge management are both utilized by a significant proportion of academics.

The area of continuity that exists relates to the dominance of a consensus-based perspective on social relations and the continuing marginality of knowledge management literature that utilizes a dissensus-based perspective on social relations. Thus there is still a relatively limited amount of scholarship on knowledge management that adopts what Schultze and Stabell (2004) label a 'critical' or 'dialogical' perspective on knowledge management. The dialogical perspective is one that in particular is very rarely utilized, despite the relevance of Foucault's writing on power/knowledge.

An indication of this can be taken from an analysis of Easterby-Smith and Lyle's (2011*a*) *Handbook on Organizational Learning and Knowledge Management*. This book was deliberately designed to provide an overview of key debates, issues, and themes in the field of knowledge management. The analysis involved examining the book's index for the extent to which dissensus-based topics such as conflict, politics, or power were referred to, and revealed that in a book which includes twenty-nine chapters and extends to 680 pages, the topic of conflict was mentioned six times (within four separate chapters), the topic of politics was mentioned nine times (within five separate chapters), and that the topic of power was examined seven times (within five separate chapters). It should also be noted that there was no specific chapter devoted to these issues and that there was only one reference to Foucault (a key writer linked to the 'dialogic' perspective) in the whole book, with this reference being a one-sentence footnote. This vividly illustrates the relative marginality of dissensus-based perspectives in the knowledge management literature. Thus, the inclusion of a chapter on the topics of power, politics, and conflict here (Chapter 12), while drawing on important and useful studies, may give a false impression regarding the extent to which these issues are regarded as important within the knowledge management literature. The lead taken by those writers examined in Chapter 12 to account for such issues is a path that has not been followed by a significant number of writers.

The final issue touched on here, which does not link to Schultze and Stabell's framework, is the extent to which the literature on knowledge management focuses on issues of IT or human, social, and cultural factors. Scarborough and Swan's (2001) analysis of the early knowledge management literature found that while 70 per cent of the literature they examined focused on IT/IS-related issues, only 5 per cent focused on human resource and people-related issues.

Thus, their broad conclusion was that human/social issues were generally neglected and under-examined in this early literature. However, analysis of more contemporary literature suggests that this focus has substantially changed over time. Hislop's (2010) analysis of literature on knowledge management published in 2008 found that, while only 8 per cent focused on IS/IT-related issues, more than a quarter (27 per cent) focused on people-related issues. Thus, over time, there has been a significant growth of interest in people-related issues in academic writing on knowledge management. This is reinforced by the wide range of literature on this broad topic that is examined in Part 4 of the book (see Chapters 9–15).

Knowledge Management as a Fashion?

This section begins by considering another general critique of knowledge management: that it represents the latest in an apparently endless succession of management fads and fashions and that interest in the topic is likely to wane rapidly. As outlined in Chapter 1, this is a perspective adopted by a number of writers. In looking at this topic the main focus is on the production, rather than the consumption, of knowledge on knowledge management. This focus is partly pragmatic, as it is generally easier to quantify the extent to which knowledge on knowledge management is produced than it is to quantify the extent to which it is consumed and used within business organizations. However, there is a brief subsection on the consumption and use of knowledge on knowledge management by business organizations towards the end of the chapter. In examining the production of knowledge on knowledge management, the production of knowledge by both academics and global consulting and professional service firms is examined. This is because there has been an increasing tendency for global consulting and professional service firms to become involved in the production of management knowledge (Suddaby and Greenwood 2001).

Conceptualizing management fashions

Before examining how patterns on the production and consumption of knowledge on knowledge management have evolved, it is useful to elaborate a little on Abrahamson's (1996) perspective on management fashion, whose focus is on the uptake of fashions in the business world. Abrahamson starts from the assumption that management behaviour is shaped by norms of rationality and progress. The norm of rationality suggests that management will always use the techniques and ways of organizing which they regard as the most efficient. The norm of progress on the other hand suggests that, as knowledge improves and develops over time, managers will adopt new techniques and practices as they become available. Thus, the process of fashion setting involves fashion setters attempting to utilize the norms of progress and rationality to shape the 'collective beliefs' of managers in the business world that the particular technique they are currently advocating both represents an advance on existing knowledge and also the most effective current technique available.

Abrahamson defines a management fashion as, 'a relatively transitory collective belief, disseminated by fashion setters, that a management technique leads to rational management progress' (1996: 257). The transitoriness of fashions represents one of their defining characteristics, where interest in a particular topic grows quickly, but then wanes equally rapidly. Thus, for Abrahamson, management fashions are identifiable by 'rapid bells-shaped swings' and 'waves of interest in management techniques' (p. 256). Thus, if interest in a topic over time is plotted on a graph, a wave-shaped pattern will be produced which resembles a normal distribution curve. The question addressed here, now that it is almost twenty years since interest in the topic of knowledge management began to take off, is whether there has been the telltale rapid decline of interest in the topic which would allow knowledge management to be labelled a transitory management fashion.

The evolution of academic interest in knowledge management

As outlined in Chapter 1, Scarbrough and Swan (2001) undertook one of the most thorough analyses to determine whether the explosive growth of interest that has occurred in knowledge management could be understood as a fashion. They argued that the growth of interest in knowledge management that occurred in the late 1990s did resemble the start of a fashion, with there being a sudden ramping up of interest in the topic which resembled the first half of a normal distribution curve. While Scarbrough and Swan (2001) challenge and question various aspect of Abrahamson's (1996) fashion-setting model, they concluded that it was likely that interest in knowledge management would follow the bell-shaped curve that Abrahamson suggests is evidence of a fashion, predicting that levels of interest in knowledge management were likely to decline sharply and rapidly.

However, Scarbrough and Swan's analysis was speculating on how future interest in knowledge management would evolve. The data presented in Table 16.1, which extends Scarbrough and Swan's analysis by eight years to record the number of articles published on the topic of knowledge management per year up to 2008, makes it possible to more accurately judge whether interest in knowledge management has followed the normal distribution patterns symptomatic of a management fashion. This evidence is taken from Hislop's (2010) analysis of the academic database Proquest, which was searched for articles on knowledge management using a range of search terms (including 'knowledge management', 'knowledge sharing', 'knowledge transfer', and 'knowledge capture'). The evidence presented in Table 16.1 challenges the idea that knowledge management is a management fashion—rather than interest in the topic showing a rapid decline after 1998, the number of academic publications on the management of knowledge within organizations has steadily increased during the first eight years of the twenty-first century. According to this evidence, knowledge management does not represent a transitory management fashion, as since 1998 there has been a sustained level of academic interest in the topic.

Both Hislop (2010) and Serenko et al. (2010) go further than this and argue that there is evidence of knowledge management maturing into a recognized scholarly discipline (Serenko et al. 2010: 16–17), and becoming 'institutionalized' (Hislop 2010: 785). Evidence for

Table 16.1 Number of Peer-Reviewed Academic Articles on Knowledge Management 2000–8

	2000	2002	2004	2006	2008
Number of peer-reviewed academic articles published	207	281	361	415	440

Source: Hislop 2010.

this is the fact that, as outlined in Chapter 1, not only are there a number of regular, annual conferences on knowledge management, but there are at least twenty specific journals with an exclusive focus on knowledge management, learning, and intellectual capital. This therefore suggests that the level of academic interest in the topic is likely to be sustained, at least in the short and medium term.

One issue identified by Serenko *et al.*'s (2010) analysis of publications on knowledge management between 1994 and 2008 connects with the following two sections on the production and consumption of knowledge on knowledge management by the business community. Serenko *et al.*'s (2010) analysis found that between 1994 and 2008 there had been a significant decline in the number of practitioners involved in the publication of articles on knowledge management. Thus during the early phase of interest in knowledge management (1994–8), the percentage of practitioners who were authors was about 30 per cent, while by 2007 and 2008, this figure had declined to just over 10 per cent. Thus Serenko *et al.* warn that there is a risk of knowledge management becoming a purely academic discipline that is disconnected from the business world. This topic is returned to later in the chapter, when looking at the extent to which business people utilize academic literature on knowledge management in their work.

Finally, a quite distinctive approach on the question of whether knowledge management represents a fashion is adopted by Spender (2008), who not only rejects this idea, but turns it on its head. Spender argues that knowledge management represents a potentially very important subject area which not only opens up new ways of theorizing about the nature of organizations, but also has the potential to be highly relevant to the interests of the business world in improving business performance. To achieve this he suggests that more 'robust' models of knowledge than those that currently predominate need to be developed.

The evolving interest of global consultants and professional service firms in knowledge management

When considering the production of knowledge on knowledge management it is also necessary to consider the role of global consulting and professional service firms like McKinseys and KPMG, because, as outlined earlier, they have begun to play an increasingly significant role in the production of management knowledge. The evolution of their interest in the specific topic of knowledge management provides a sharp contrast with the case of academics examined in the previous section. In the late 1990s and early 2000s their interest in knowledge management was relatively high. At this time not only were they actively promoting IT-based knowledge management services (Scarbrough and Swan 2001), but they were also involved in publishing books (Kluge *et al.* 2001), and surveys on knowledge management (KPMG 2000, 2003). However, it appears that their interest in knowledge management has declined significantly since then. Analysis of the content of web-pages from six companies in 2009 (McKinsey, Boston Consulting Group, KPMG, Deloitte & Touche, Ernst & Young, and PricewaterhouseCoopers) found little evidence that knowledge management was a key topic on which any of them were providing consulting services (Hislop 2010). Thus, in contrast to the sustained interest of academics in knowledge management, levels of interest amongst global consulting and professional service firms have declined to an almost insignificant level.

The interest of business organizations in managing knowledge

The focus of previous sections has been on the production of knowledge on knowledge management, rather than its consumption. The focus of these sections has been to identify how the production of knowledge on knowledge management has evolved over time. This has shown that, while academic interest in the topic was sustained between the mid-1990s and 2010, this was not the case with global consulting and professional service firms. This final section attempts to consider how the consumption and use of knowledge on knowledge management by the business community has evolved over the same time period. However, finding accurate data on this topic is very difficult.

One potential source of information are large-scale surveys which record the experiences of firms in implementing knowledge management initiatives. In the late 1990s and early years of the twenty-first century a number of such surveys were conducted (such as KPMG 2000, 2003; Ruggles 1998). Since then a number of other 'overview' surveys have also been conducted (Coakes *et al.* 2010; Griffiths and Moon 2011; Rusanow 2006). Such surveys provide anecdotal evidence that many companies are making active efforts to manage knowledge. For example, the global online survey conducted by Coakes *et al.* (2010) was completed by over 700 participants. However, such surveys are more useful for providing insights into the issues experienced by companies that are actively trying to manage knowledge than they are at revealing the general level of interest in the topic of knowledge management within the business community.

Another complicating factor, which increases the difficulty of identifying the extent to which business interest in knowledge management has evolved, is that organizations may be actively managing the knowledge of their workers, but not labelling these activities explicitly as 'knowledge management'. This was a finding made by Nicolini *et al.*'s (2008) review of knowledge management in the healthcare sector which found that, despite the lack of initiatives which were explicitly labelled 'knowledge management', the 'healthcare sector reflects all the time on the nature and ways of managing what is known' (p. 258).

This fits with an argument developed by Schultze (2008), whose conclusions are based on limited anecdotal evidence: conversations with a number of friends in the business world. She argues that the apparent declining level of interest in knowledge management that she felt had occurred between 2000 and 2008 could be explained by a change in the way organizations managed their knowledge. Effectively her argument is that interest by business organizations in managing knowledge has not declined, but that these activities have just become less visible. Initial interest in knowledge management within the business world was visible as it often involved the implementation of high-profile, large-scale knowledge management initiatives, which often had a significant IT element to them. She argues that interest in this type of approach to knowledge management has declined significantly, but that it has been replaced by an approach to managing knowledge that is more focused on addressing the micro-level day-to-day knowledge-related challenges and problems experienced by workers as they carry out their work.

Finally, another method that can be utilized to give a partial insight into the extent to which business organizations are interested in knowledge management, which connects the production of knowledge examined in the previous section to its consumption, is to look at the extent to which knowledge management practitioners make use of academic knowledge on the topic. This is done by looking at the (somewhat pessimistic) results of a single study conducted by Booker *et al.* (2008) into the use of academic knowledge on knowledge management by knowledge management professionals (see illustrated example).

 Illustration   The limited relevance of knowledge management research to knowledge management professionals

Booker *et al.* (2008) report the findings of a study whose primary purpose was to identify the relevance of academic research on knowledge management to knowledge management professionals in the public and private sector. This was done through conducting semi-structured interviews with a sample of twelve people. The sample was generated through 'snowball sampling' whereby initial contacts were asked to provide names of other relevant people. Interviewees all worked in either the USA or Canada, with eight participants working in the public sector and four working in the private sector.

Overall the study found that, for various reasons that will be elaborated upon, the professionals interviewed made little use of academic publications on knowledge management. The first reason provided for their lack of use of academic research on knowledge management was a lack of time. All participants argued that their high workload precluded them from having the time to read what they regarded as lengthy academic studies. Further, a significant proportion of interviewees identified problems in the writing style of academic articles which they found to be difficult to understand, and which were not expressed in language that they were familiar with. One interviewee commented: 'I see that very often around me where people don't understand a lot of articles or the way that it is communicated' (p. 238). Interviewees felt that the reason for difficulties in understanding these articles was that, despite many of them including practitioner recommendations, the primary audience they are written for is the academic rather than the business community.

Finally, the professionals interviewed did not find the practitioner recommendations in these articles to be useful to them either. This was for two reasons. First, the applicability of recommendations to the particular work context of practitioners was often not seen as being relevant. Secondly, these recommendations were not seen as effectively reflecting the true complexities involved in dealing with such issues. Thus one interviewee said: 'I hate to use the word naïve—but they're more simplistic—the recommendations. They are a bit idealistic. The reality is far from that, I'm afraid' (p. 239).

1. Based on your understanding of the academic knowledge management literature, as well as of the challenges faced by organizations in managing knowledge, do you agree that academic studies are often limited in the relevance of their findings to the business world?

Overall therefore, while various methods can provide some insights into the level of interest in the business community in knowledge management, it is virtually impossible to accurately gauge the extent to which interest in the topic of knowledge management within the business community has evolved over time.

 ## Conclusion

The focus of this final chapter has been to reflect on two aspects of the topic of knowledge management in general. The first issue addressed, utilizing the framework on knowledge management by Schultze and Stabell (2004) that was introduced in Chapter 1, reflected on the changing character and focus of the academic literature on knowledge. This review highlighted three features of the academic literature on knowledge management. First, the growth of interest in the practice-based perspective on knowledge has meant that what Schultze and Stabell label the 'neo-functionalist' discourse has become less dominant. Secondly, the assumptions of consensus that typically predominate in the knowledge management mean that issues of power, politics, and conflict are still relatively neglected in the majority of studies. Finally, while the early knowledge management literature was dominated by a focus on IT-related issues and a neglect of human/social factors, this has changed, with the knowledge management literature evolving to place a greater emphasis on the key human/social factors which have been shown to be crucial in shaping whether and how people participate in knowledge management activities.

The second question examined was whether knowledge management is a contemporary example of a transient management fashion. The contradictory and partial nature of the evidence that exists on this topic means that it is impossible to give a simple unequivocal answer. On the one hand, in relation to academic interest in the topic, knowledge management was not found to be a transient management fashion. This is because, rather than interest in the topic rising and falling quickly, there was a relatively high level of sustained interest in the topic in the decade between 1998 and 2008. Further, the embryonic evidence of the institutionalization of knowledge management as a recognized academic discipline suggests that this interest is likely to be sustained, at least in the medium term. However, in relation to the interest of the business world in knowledge management, the evidence is more uncertain and equivocal. In general there is a lack of detailed evidence to determine with any degree of accuracy the extent to which the business world remains interested in the topic of knowledge management. What can be said with some degree of certainty is that global consulting and professional service firms do not regard knowledge management as a topic of significance in the way that they did in the late 1990s and early 2000s. However, evidence on the extent to which the business world is concerned with actively managing the knowledge of its workers is much more equivocal and uncertain.

Suggestions for Further Reading

1. J.-C. Spender (2008) 'Organizational Learning and Knowledge Management: Whence and Whither?', *Management Learning*, 39/2: 158–76.

A beautifully written and highly insightful analysis of the relationship between the literatures on knowledge and learning that makes suggestions for how the knowledge management literature should develop.

2. L. Booker, N. Bontis, and A. Serenko (2008) 'The Relevance of Knowledge Management and Intellectual Capital Research', *Knowledge and Process Management*, 15/4: 235–46.

Reports the findings of a small-scale study into the extent to which knowledge management professionals make use of academic knowledge on knowledge management in carrying out their work.

3. D. Hislop (2010) 'Knowledge Management as an Ephemeral Management Fashion?', *Journal of Knowledge Management*, 14/6: 779–90.

Uses the concept of management fashion to evaluate the extent to which the production of knowledge on knowledge management, by both academics and global consulting and professional service firms, has evolved over time.

Take your learning further: Online Resource Centre

Visit the Online Resource Centre for resources which will extend your understanding of knowledge management in organizations. As well as web links to sites of interest, the author has provided case studies looking at knowledge management in virtual and knowledge-intensive firms, and in global multinationals. These will help you with your research, essays, and assignments; or you may find these additional resources helpful when revising for exams.

 www.oxfordtextbooks.co.uk/orc/hislop3e/

References

Abrahamson, E. (1996) 'Management Fashion', *Academy of Management Review*, 21/1: 254–85.

Abrams, L., Cross, R., Lesser, E., and Levin, D. (2003) 'Nurturing Interpersonal Trust in Knowledge-Sharing Networks', *Academy of Management Executive*, 17/4: 64–77.

Akgün, A., Byrne, J., Keskin, H., and Lynn, G. (2006a) 'Transactive Memory System in New Product Development Teams', *IEEE Transactions on Engineering Management*, 53/1: 95–111.

—— Lynn, G., and Byrne, J. (2006b) 'Antecedents and Consequences of Unlearning in New Product Development Teams', *Journal of Product Innovation Management*, 23/1: 73–88.

—— Byrne, J., Lynn, G., and Keskin, H. (2007a) 'Organizational Unlearning as Changes in Beliefs and Routines in Organizations', *Journal of Organizational Change Management*, 20/6: 794–812.

—— Byrne, J., Lynn, G., and Keskin, H. (2007b) 'New Product Development in Turbulent Environments: Impact of Improvisation and Unlearning on New Product Development', *Journal of Engineering Technology Management*, 24: 203–30.

Al-Alawi, A., Al-Marzooqi, N., and Mohammed, Y. (2007) 'Organizational Culture and Knowledge Sharing: Critical Success Factors', *Journal of Knowledge Management*, 11/2: 22–42.

Alavi, M., Kayworth, T., and Leidner, D. (2005–6) 'An Empirical Examination of the Influence of Organizational Culture on Knowledge Management Practices', *Journal of Management Information Systems*, 22/3: 191–224.

Allen, J. (2010) 'Knowledge-Sharing Successes in Web 2.0 Communities', *IEEE Technology and Society Magazine* (Spring), 58–64.

Almeida, P., Hohberger, J., and Parada, P. (2011) 'Informal Knowledge and Innovation', in M. Easterby-Smith and M. Lyles (eds), *Handbook of Organizational Learning and Knowledge Management* (Chichester: John Wiley), 383–402.

Alvesson, M. (1995) *Management of Knowledge Intensive Firms* (London: de Gruyter).

—— (2000) 'Social Identity and the Problem of Loyalty in Knowledge-Intensive Companies', *Journal of Management Studies*, 37/8: 1101–23.

—— (2001) 'Knowledge Work: Ambiguity, Image and Identity', *Human Relations*, 54/7: 863–86.

—— (2011) 'De-Essentializing the Knowledge Intensive Firm: Reflections on Sceptical Research Going Against the Mainstream'. *Journal of Management Studies*, 48/7: 1640–61.

—— and Kärreman, D. (2001) 'Odd Couple: Making Sense of the Curious Concept of Knowledge Management', *Journal of Management Studies*, 38/7: 995–1018.

—— and Willmott, H. (2001) 'Identity Regulation as Organizational Control: Producing the Appropriate Individual', *Journal of Management Studies*, 39/5: 691–44.

Amara, N., Landry, R., and Doloreux, D. (2009) 'Patterns of Innovation in Knowledge-Intensive Business Services', *Service industries Journal*, 29/4: 407–30.

Amin, A., and Roberts, J. (2008) *Community, Economic Creativity, and Organization* (Oxford: Oxford University Press).

Anand, N., Gardner, H., and Morris, T. (2007) 'Knowledge-Based Innovation: Emergence and Embedding of New Practice Areas in Management Consulting Journals', *Academy of Management Journal*, 50/2: 406–28.

Andreeva, T., and Ikhilchik, I. (2011) 'Applicability of the SECI Model of Knowledge Creation in Russian Cultural Context: Theoretical Analysis', *Knowledge and Process Management*, 18/1: 56–66.

Andrews, K., and Delahaye, B. (2000) 'Influences on Knowledge Processes in Organizational Learning: The Psychosocial Filter', *Journal of Management Studies*, 37/6: 797–810.

Andrikopoulos, A. (2010) 'Accounting for Intellectual Capital', *Knowledge and Process Management*, 17/4: 180–7.

Antonacopoulou, E. (2006) 'The Relationship Between Individual and Organizational Learning: New Evidence from Managerial Learning Practices', *Management Learning*, 37/4: 455–73.

—— (2009) 'Impact and Scholarship: Unlearning and Practising to Co-Create Actionable Knowledge', *Management Learning*, 40/4: 421–30.

Ardichvili, A., Page, V., and Wentling, T. (2003) 'Motivation and Barriers to Participation in Virtual Knowledge-Sharing Communities of Practice', *Journal of Knowledge Management*, 7/1: 64–77.

Argyris, C. (1990) *Overcoming Organizational Defences* (Needham Heights, Mass.: Allyn and Bacon).

Argyris, C. and Schön, D. (1996) *Organizational Learning II: Theory, Method, and Practice* (Reading, Mass.: Addison-Wesley).

Bacharach, P., and Baratz, M. (1963) 'Decisions and Nondecisions: An Analytical Framework', *American Political Science Review*, 57: 632–42.

Barker, R. (2001) 'The Nature of Leadership', *Human Relations*, 54/4: 469–94.

Barratt, E. (2002) 'Foucault, Foucauldianism and Human Resource Manage-ment', *Personnel Review*, 31/2: 189–204.

Bauman, Z. (2007) *Liquid Modernity* (Cambridge: Polity Press).

Baumard, P. (1999) *Tacit Knowledge in Organizations* (London: Sage).

—— and Starbuck, W. (2005) 'Learning from Failures: Why it May Not Happen', *Long Range Planning*, 38/3: 281–98.

Beaumont, P., and Hunter, L. (2002) *Managing Knowledge Workers* (London: CIPD).

Becerra, M., Lunnan, R., and Huemer, L. (2008) 'Trustworthiness, Risk, and the Transfer of Tacit and Explicit Knowledge between Alliance Partners', *Journal of Management Studies*, 45/4: 691–713.

Bechky, B. (2003) 'Sharing Meaning across Occupational Communities: The Transfor-mation of Understanding on a Production Floor', *Organization Science*, 14/3: 312–30.

Becker, K. (2008) 'Unlearning as a Driver of Sustainable Change and Innovation: Three Australian Case Studies', *International Journal of Technology Management*, 42/1–2: 89–106.

—— (2010) 'Facilitating Unlearning during Implemen-tation of New Technology', *Journal of Organizational Change Management*, 23/3: 251–68.

—— Hyland, P., and Acutt, B. (2006) 'Considering Unlearning in HRD Practices: An Australian Study', *Journal of European Industrial Training*, 30/8: 608–21.

Bell, D. (1973) *The Coming of Post-Industrial Society* (Harmondsworth: Penguin).

Berends, H., and Lammers, I. (2011) 'Explaining Discontinuity in Organizational Learning: A Process Analysis', *Organization Studies*, 31/8: 1045–68.

Berman, S. L., Down, J., and Hill, C. W. L. (2002) 'Tacit Knowledge as a Source of Competitive Advantage in the National Basketball Association', *Academy of Management Journal*, 45/1: 13–31.

Bertels, H., Kleinschmidt, E., and Koen, P. (2011) 'Communities of Practice versus Organizational Climate: Which One Matters More to Dispersed Collaboration in the Front End of Innovation?', *Journal of Product Innovation Management*, 28/5: 757–72.

Bertoin Antal, A., Dierkes, M., Child, J., and Nonaka, I. (2001) 'Organizational Learning and Knowledge: Reflections on the Dynamics of the Field and Challenges for the Future', in M. Dierkes, A. Bertoin Antal, J. Child, and I. Nonaka (eds), *Handbook of Organizational Learning and Knowledge* (Oxford: Oxford University Press), 921–40.

Bettiol, M. and Sedita, S. (2011) 'The Role of Community of Practice in Developing Creative Industry Projects', *International Journal of Project Management*, 29: 468–79.

Bettis, R., and Prahalad, C. (1995) 'The Dominant Logic: Retrospective and Extension', *Strategic Management Journal*, 16/1: 5–14.

Blackler, F. (1995) 'Knowledge, Knowledge Work and Organizations: An Overview and Interpretation', *Organization Studies*, 16/6: 1021–46.

—— Crump, N., and McDonald, S. (2000) 'Organizing Processes in Complex Activity Systems', *Organization*, 7/2: 277–300.

Bock, G., Kankanhalli, G., and Sharma, S. (2006) 'Are Norms Enough? The Role of Collaborative Norms in Promoting Organizational Knowledge Seeking', *European Journal of Information Systems*, 15/4: 357–67.

Bogner, W., and Bansal, P. (2007) 'Knowledge Manage-ment as the Basis of Sustained High Performance', *Journal of Management Studies*, 44/1: 165–88.

Boland, R., and Tenkasi, R. (1995) 'Perspective Making and Perspective Taking in Communities of Knowing', *Organization Science*, 6/4: 350–72.

—— —— and Te'eni, D. (1994) 'Designing Information Technology to Support Distributed Cognition', *Organization Science*, 5/3: 456–75.

Bolisani, E., and Scarso, E. (2000) 'Electronic Communi-cation and Knowledge Transfer', *International Journal of Technology Management*, 20/1–2: 116–33.

Booker, L., Bontis, N., and Serenko, A. (2008) 'The Relevance of Knowledge Management and Intellectual Capital Research', *Knowledge and Process Management*, 15/4: 235–46.

Borzillo, S., Aznar, S., and Schmitt, A. (2011) 'A Journey through Communities of Practice: How and Why Members Move from the Periphery to the Core', *European Management Journal*, 29: 25–42.

Bosch-Sijtsema, P., Ruohomäki, V., and Vartiainen, M. (2010) 'Multi-Locational Knowledge Workers in the Office: Navigation, Disturbances and Effectiveness', *New Technology, Work and Employment*, 25/3: 183–95.

Bouty, I., and Gomez, M.-L. (2010) 'Dishing up Individual and Collective Dimensions of Organizational Knowing', *Management Learning*, 41/4: 545–59.

Bradley, K., Mathieu, J., Cordery, J., Rosen, B., and Kukenberger, M. (2011) 'Managing a New Collaborative

Entity in Business Organizations: Understanding Organizational Communities of Practice Effectiveness', *Journal of Applied Psychology*, 96/6: 1234–45.

Brown, J., and Duguid, P. (1991) 'Organization Learning and Communities of Practice: Towards a Unified View of Working, Learning and Innovation', *Organization Science*, 2/1: 40–57.

———and——— (1998) 'Organizing Knowledge', *California Management Review*, 40/3: 90–111.

———and——— (2001) 'Knowledge and Organization: A Social Practice Perspective', *Organization Science*, 12/2: 198–213.

Buchanan, D. (2008) 'You Stab My Back, I'll Stab Yours: Management Experience and Perceptions of Organization Political Behaviour', *British Journal of Management*, 19/1: 49–64.

Bui, H., and Baruch, Y. (2011) 'Learning Organizations in Higher Education: An Empirical Evaluation within an International Context', *Management Learning* (publ. via Onlinefirst, doi: 10.1177/1350507611431212).

Bulut, C., and Culha, O. (2010) 'The Effects of Training on Organizational Commitment', *International Journal of Training and Development*, 14/4: 309–22.

Bunderson, J., and Reagans, R. (2011) 'Power, Status and Learning in Organizations', *Organization Science*, 22/5: 1182–94.

Bunker Whitington, K., Owen-Smith, J., and Powell, W. (2009) 'Networks, Propinquity, and Innovation in Knowledge-Intensive Industries', *Administrative Science Quarterly*, 54: 90–122.

Burns, J. (1978) *Leadership* (New York: Harper & Row).

Burrell, G., and Morgan, G. (1979) *Sociological Paradigms and Organisational Analysis: Elements of the Sociology of Corporate Life* (London: Heinemann Educational).

Byrne, R. (2001) 'Employees: Capital or Commodity?', *Career Development International*, 6/6: 324–30.

Cabrera, A., and Cabrera, E. (2002) 'Knowledge Sharing Dilemmas', *Organization Studies*, 23/5: 687–710.

Cabrera, E., and Cabrera, A. (2005) 'Fostering Knowledge Sharing through People Management Practices', *International Journal of Human Resource Management*, 16/5: 720–35.

Cacciatori, E., Tamoschus, D., and Grahber, G. (2012) 'Knowledge Transfer across Projects: Codification in Creative, High-Tech and Engineering Industries', *Management Learning*, 43/3: 309–31.

Camelo-Ordaz, C., García-Cruz, J., Sousa-Ginel, E., and Valle-Cabrera, R. (2011) 'The Influence of Human Resource Management on Knowledge Sharing and Innovation in Spain: The Mediating Role of Affective Commitment', *International Journal of Human Resource Management*, 22/7: 1442–63.

Cameron, K., and Quinn, R. (2006) *Diagnosing and Changing Organizational Culture: Based on the Competing Values Framework* (Reading, Mass.: Addison-Wesley).

Cannon, M., and Edmondson, A. (2005) 'Failing to Learn and Learning to Fail (Intelligently): How Great Organizations Put Failure to Work to Innovate and Improve', *Long Range Planning*, 38/3: 299–319.

Carleton, K. (2011) 'How to Motivate and Retain Knowledge Workers in Organizations: A Review of the Literature', *International Journal of Management*, 28/2: 459–68.

Carlile, P. (2002) 'A Pragmatic View of Knowledge and Boundaries: Boundary Objects in New Product Development', *Organization Science*, 14/4: 442–55.

———(2004) 'Transferring, Translating and Transforming: An Integrative Framework for Managing Knowledge across Boundaries', *Organization Science*, 15/5: 555–68.

Carroll, J., Hatakenaka, S., and Rudolph, J. (2006) 'Naturalistic Decision Making and Organizational Learning in Nuclear Power Plants: Negotiating Meaning between Managers and Problem Investigation Teams', *Organization Studies*, 27/7: 1037–57.

Casillas, J., Acedo, F., and Barbero, J. (2010) 'Learning, Unlearning and Internationalisation: Evidence from the Pre-Export Phase', *International Journal of Information Management*, 30: 162–73.

Castells, M. (1998) *The Rise of Network Society* (Oxford: Basil Blackwell).

Cegarra-Navarro, J.-G., Wensley, A., and Sanchez-Polo, M.-T. (2010) 'An Application of the Hospital-in-the-Home Unlearning Context', *Social Work and Healthcare*, 49: 895–918.

———Sánchez-Vidal, M., and Cegarra-Leiva, D. (2011) 'Balancing Exploration and Exploitation of Knowledge through an Unlearning Context: An Empirical Investigation in SMEs', *Management Decision*, 49/7: 1099–1119.

———Eldridge, S., and Sanchez A. (2012) 'How an Unlearning Context Can Help Managers Overcome the Negative Effects of Counter-Knowledge', *Journal of Management and Organization*, 18/2: 981–1005.

Cha, H., Pingry, D., and Thatcher, M. (2008) 'Managing the Knowledge Supply Chain: An Orgaanizational Learning Model of Information Technology Offshore Outsourcing', *MIS Quarterly*, 32/2: 281–305.

Chang, H., Chuang, S.-S., and Chao, S. (2011) 'Determinants of Cultural Adaptation, Communication Quality, and Trust in Virtual Teams' Performance', *Total Quality Management and Business Excellence*, 22/3: 305–29.

Chang, S., and Lee, M. (2007) 'The Effects of Organizational Culture and Knowledge Management

Mechanisms on Organizational Innovation: An Empirical Study in Taiwan', *Business Review*, 7/1: 295–301.

Chaundy, C. (2005) 'Creating a Good Practice Centre at the BBC', *KM Review*, 8/2: 24–7.

Chen, J., Sun, P., and McQueen, R. (2010) 'The Impact of National Culture on Structured Knowledge Transfer', *Journal of Knowledge Management*, 14/2: 228–42.

Chen, W.-Y. Hsu, B.-F., and Lin, Y.-Y. (2011*a*) 'Fostering Knowledge Sharing through Human Resource Management in R&D Teams', *International Journal of Technology Management*, 53/2–4: 309–30.

Chen, Z., Zhang, X., and Vogel, D. (2011*b*) 'Exploring the Underlying Processes between Conflict and Knowledge Sharing: A Work-Engagement Perspective', *Journal of Applied Social Psychology*, 41/5: 1005–33.

Child, J. (2001) 'Learning through Strategic Alliances', in M. Dierkes, A. Bertoin Antal, J. Child, and I. Nonaka (eds), *Handbook of Organizational Learning and Knowledge* (Oxford: Oxford University Press), 657–80.

Chiravuri, A., Nazareth, D., and Ramamurthy, K. (2011) 'Cognitive Conflict and Consensus Generation in Virtual Teams during Knowledge Capture: Comparative Effectiveness of Techniques', *Journal of Management Information Systems*, 28/1: 311–50.

Chiva, R., and Allegre, J. (2005) 'Organizational Learning and Organizational Knowledge: Towards the Integration of Two Approaches', *Management Learning*, 36/1: 49–68.

Choi, S., Lee, H., and Yoo, Y. (2010) 'The Impact of Information Technology and Transactive Memory Systems on Knowledge Sharing, Application and Team Performance: A Field Study', *MIS Quarterly*, 34/4: 855–70.

Chua, A. (2006) 'The Rise and Fall of a Community of Practice: A Descriptive Case Study', *Knowledge and Process Management*, 13/2: 120–8.

Ciborra, C., and Patriotta, G. (1998) 'Groupware and Teamwork in R&D: Limits to Learning and Innovation', *R&D Management*, 28/1: 1–10.

Coakes, E., Amar, A., and Grandos, M. (2010) 'Knowledge Management, Strategy, and Technology: A Global Snapshot', *Journal of Enterprise Information Management*, 23/3: 282–304.

Collins, H. (2007) 'Bicycling on the Moon: Collective Tacit Knowledge nd Somatic-Limit Tacit Knowledge', *Organization Studies*, 28/2: 257–62.

Contu, A., and Willmott, H. (2003) 'Re-Embedding Situatedness: The Importance of Power Relations in Learning Theory', *Organization Science*, 14/3: 283–96.

—— Grey, C., and Örtenblad, A. (2003) 'Against Learning', *Human Relations*, 56/8: 931–52.

Cook, S., and Brown, J. (1999) 'Bridging Epistemologies: The Generative Dance between Organizational Knowledge and Organizational Knowing', *Organization Science*, 10/4: 381–400.

—— and Yanow, D. (1993) 'Culture and Organizational Learning', *Journal of Management Enquiry*, 2/4: 373–90.

Coopey, J. (1995) 'The Learning Organization, Power, Politics and Ideology', *Management Learning*, 26/2: 193–213.

—— (1998) 'Learning the Trust and Trusting to Learn: A Role for Radical Theatre', *Management Learning*, 29/3: 365–82.

—— and Burgoyne, J. (2000) 'Politics and Organizational Learning', *Journal of Management Studies*, 37/6: 869–85.

Corradi, G., Gherardi, S., and Verzelloni, L. (2010) 'Through the Practice Lens: Where is the Bandwagon of Practice-Based Studies Heading?', *Management Learning*, 41/3: 265–83.

Crawford, C. (2005) 'Effects of Transformational Leadership and Organizational Position on Knowledge Management', *Journal of Knowledge Management*, 9/6: 6–16.

Cross, R., Laseter, T., Parker, A., and Valasquez, G. (2006) 'Using Social Network Analysis to Improve Communities of Practice', *California Management Review*, 49/1: 32–60.

Crossan, M., Lane, H., and White, R. (1999) 'An Organizational Learning Framework: From Intuition to Institution', *Academy of Management Review*, 24/3: 522–37.

—— Maurer, C., and White, R. (2011) 'Reflections on the 2009 AMR Decade Award: Do we have a Theory of Organizational Learning?', *Academy of Management Review*, 36/3: 446–60.

Cruz, N., Pérez, V. and Cantero, C. (2009) 'The Influence of Employee Motivation on Knowledge Transfer', *Journal of Knowledge Management*, 13/6: 478–90.

Cuervo-Cazurra, A., and Un, A. (2010) 'Why Some Firms Never Invest in Formal R&D', *Strategic Management Journal*, 31: 759–79.

Currie, G., and Kerrin, M. (2003) 'Human Resource Management and Knowledge Management: Enhancing Knowledge Sharing in a Pharmaceutical Company', *International Journal of Human Resource Management*, 14/6: 1027–45.

—— and —— (2004) 'The Limits of a Technological Fix to Knowledge Management', *Management Learning*, 35/1; 9–29.

—— Waring, J., and Finn, R. (2008) 'The Limits of Knowledge Management for UK Public Services Modernization: The Case of Patient safety and Service Quality', *Public Administration*, 86/2: 363–85.

Cutcher-Gershenfeld, J., Nitta, M., and Barrett, B. (1998) *Knowledge-Driven Work* (Oxford: Oxford University Press).

Cyert, R., and March, J. (1963) *A Behavioural Theory of the Firm* (Englewood Cliffs, NJ: Prentice Hall).

Dahl, R. (1957) 'The Concept of Power', *Behavioural Scientist*, 2: 201–15.

Dawes, S., Cresswell, A., and Pardo, T. (2009) 'From "Need to Know" to "Need to Share": Tangled Problems, Information Boundaries, and the Building of Public Sector Knowledge Management Networks', *Public Administration Review*, 69/3: 392–402.

Deetz, S. (1998) 'Discursive Formations, Strategized Subordination and Self-Surveillance', in A. McKinlay and K. Starkey (eds), *Foucault, Management and Organization Theory* (London: Sage), 151–72.

DeFillippi, R., Arthur, M., and Lindsay, V. (2006) *Knowledge at Work: Creative Collaboration in the Global Economy* (London: Blackwell).

De Holan, P., and Phillips, N. (2004) 'Remembrance of Things Past? The Dynamics of Organizational Forgetting', *Management Science*, 50/11: 1603–13.

De Long, D., and Fahey, L. (2000) 'Diagnosing Cultural Barriers to Knowledge Management', *Academy of Management Executive*, 14/4: 113–27.

Densten, I. (2008) 'Leadership: Current Assessment and Future Needs', in S. Cartwright and C. Cooper (eds), *The Oxford Handbook of Personnel Psychology* (Oxford: Oxford University Press).

DeSanctis, G., and Monge, P. (1999) 'Introduction to the Special Issue: Communication Processes for Virtual Organizations', *Organization Science*, 10/6: 693–703.

Dixon, B., McGowan, J., and Cravens, G. (2009) 'Knowledge Sharing Using Codification and Collaboration Technologies to Improve Health Care: Lessons from the Public Sector', *Knowledge Management Research and Practice*, 7: 249–59.

Donate, M., and Guadamillas, F. (2010) 'The Effect of Organizational Culture on Knowledge Management Practices and Innovation', *Knowledge and Process Management*, 17/2: 82–94.

Dovey, K. (1997) 'The Learning Organization and the Organization of Learning: Learning, Power, Transformation and the Search for Form in Learning Organizations', *Management Learning*, 28/3: 331–49.

Driver, M. (2002) 'The Learning Organization: Foucauldian Gloom or Utopian Sunshine?', *Human Relations*, 55/1: 33–53.

Dul, J., Ceylan, C., and Jaspers, F. (2011) 'Knowledge Workers' Creativity and the Role of the Physical Work Environment', *Human Resource Management*, 50/6: 715–34.

du Plessis, M. (2008) 'What Bars Organisations from Managing Knowledge Successfully?', *International Journal of Information Management*, 28: 285–92.

Durcikova, A., and Gray, P. (2009) 'How Knowledge Validation Processes Affect Knowledge Contribution', *Journal of Management Information Systems*, 25/4: 81–107.

Dyer, J., and Nobeoka, K. (2000) 'Creating and Managing a High-Performance Knowledge-Sharing Network: The Toyota Case', *Strategic Management Journal*, 21/3: 345–67.

Earl, M. (2001) 'Knowledge Management Strategies: Towards a Taxonomy', *Journal of Management Information Systems*, 18/1: 215–33.

Easterby-Smith, M. (1997) 'Disciplines of Organizational Learning: Contributions and Critique', *Human Relations*, 50/9: 1085–1113.

—— and Lyles, M. (2011*a*) *Handbook of Organizational Learning and Knowledge Management* (London: John Wiley).

—— and —— (2011*b*) 'In Praise of Organizational Forgetting', *Journal of Management Inquiry*, 20/3: 311–16.

—— Crossan, M., and Nicolini, D. (2000) 'Organizational Learning: Debates Past, Present and Future', *Journal of Management Studies*, 37/6: 783–96.

—— Lyles, A., and Tsang, E. (2008) 'Inter-Organizational Knowledge Transfer: Current Themes and Future Prospects', *Journal of Management Studies*, 45/4: 677–90.

Ebbers, J., and Wijnberg, M. (2009) 'Organizational Memory: From Expectations Memory to Procedural Memory', *British Journal of Management*, 20: 478–90.

Elias, P., and Gregory, M. (1994) *The Changing Structure of Occupations and Earnings in Great Britain 1975–1990: An Analysis Based on the New Earnings* (Warwick: Institute for Employment Relations).

Elkin, G., Zhang, H., and Cone, M. (2011) 'The Acceptance of Senge's Learning Organization Model among Managers in China: An Interview Study', *International Journal of Management*, 28/4: 354–64.

Empson, L. (2001*a*) 'Introduction: Knowledge Management in Professional Service Firms', *Human Relations*, 54/7: 811–17.

Empson, L. (2001b) 'Fear of Exploitation and Fear of Contamination: Impediments to Knowledge Transfer in Mergers between Professional Service Firms', *Human Relations*, 54/7: 839–62.

Fahey, R., Vasconcelos, A., and Ellis, D. (2007) 'The Impact of Rewards within Communities of Practice: A Study of the SAP Online Global Community', *Knowledge Management Research and Practice*, 5/3: 186–98.

Faraj, S., Jarvenpaa, S., and Majchrzak, A. (2011) 'Knowledge Collaboration in Online Communities', *Organization Science*, 22/5: 1224–39.

Farndale, E., Van Ruiten, J., Kelliher, C., and Hope-Hailey, V. (2011) 'The Influence of Perceived Employee Voice on Organizational Commitment: An Exchange Perspective', *Human Resource Management*, 50/1: 113–29.

Felstead, A., Ashton, D., and Green, F. (2000) 'Are Britain's Workplace Skills Becoming More Unequal?', *Cambridge Journal of Economics*, 24/6: 709–27.

Fenton, E. (2007) 'Visualizing Strategic Change: The Role and Impact of Process Maps as Boundary Objects in Reorganization', *European Management Journal*, 25/2: 104–17.

Fleming, P., Harley, B., and Sewell, G. (2004) 'A Little Knowledge is a Dangerous Thing: Getting Below the Surface of the Growth of "Knowledge Work" in Australia', *Work Employment and Society*, 18/4: 725–47.

Flood, P., Turner, T., and Hannaway, C. (2000) *Attracting and Retaining Knowledge Employees: Irish Knowledge Employees and the Psychological Contract* (Dublin: Blackhall).

—— —— Ramamoorthy, N., and Pearson, J. (2001) 'Causes and Consequences of Psychological Contracts among Knowledge Workers in the High Technology and Financial Services Industry', *International Journal of Human Resource Management*, 12/7: 1152–65.

Foss, N., and Mahnke, V. (2011) 'Knowledge Creation in Firms: An Organizational Economics Perspective', in M. Easterby-Smith and M. Lyles (eds), *Handbook of Organizational Learning and Knowledge Management* (London: John Wiley), 125–51.

Fosstenløkken, S., Løwendahl, B., and Revang, O. (2003) 'Knowledge Development through Client Interaction: A Comparative Study', *Organization Studies*, 24/6: 859–80.

Foucault, M. (1979) *Discipline and Punishment* (Harmondsworth: Penguin).

—— (1980) *Power/Knowledge: Selected Interviews and Other Writings 1972–1977* (London: Harvester Wheatsheaf).

Fox, A. (1985) *Beyond Contract: Work, Power and Trust Relations* (London: Faber).

Fox, S. (2000) 'Practice, Foucault and Actor-Network Theory', *Journal of Management Studies*, 37/6: 853–68.

French, J., and Raven, B. (1959) 'The Bases of Social Power', in D. Cartwright (ed.), *Studies in Social Power* (Ann Arbor: University of Michigan Press), 150–67.

Frenkel, S., Korczynski, M., Donohue, L., and Shire, K. (1995) 'Re-constituting Work: Trends towards Knowledge Work and Info-normative Control', *Work, Employment and Society*, 9/4: 773–96.

Friedman, V., Lipshitz, R., and Overmeer, W. (2001) 'Creating Conditions for Organizational Learning', in M. Dierkes, A. Bertoin Antal, J. Child, and I. Nonaka (eds), *Handbook of Organizational Learning and Knowledge* (Oxford: Oxford University Press), 757–74.

Gallie, D., White, M., Cheng, Y., and Tomlinson, M. (1998) *Restructuring the Employment Relationship* (Oxford: Clarendon Press).

Gammelgaard, J. (2010) 'Knowledge Retrieval through Virtual Communities of Practice', *Behaviour and Information Technology*, 29/4: 349–62.

Garvey, B., and Williamson, B. (2002) *Beyond Knowledge Management: Dialogue, Creativity and the Corporate Curriculum* (Harlow: Financial Times/Prentice Hall).

Geertz, C. (1973) *The Interpretation of Cultures*. New York: Basic Books.

Gherardi, S. (2006) *Organizational Knowledge: The Texture of Workplace Learning* (Oxford: Blackwell).

—— and Nicolini, D. (2002) 'Learning in a Constellation of Interconnected Practices: Canon or Dissonance?', *Journal of Management Studies*, 39/4: 419–36.

Giauque, D., Resenterra, F., and Siggen, M. (2010) 'The Relationship between HRM Practices and Organizational Commitment of Knowledge Workers: Facts Obtained from Swiss SMEs', *Human Resource Development International*, 13/3: 185–205.

Gibson, C., and Birkinshaw, J. (2004) 'The Antecedents, Consequences, and Mediating Role of Organizational Ambidexterity', *Academy of Management Journal*, 47/2: 209–26.

Giddens, A. (1979) *Central Problems in Social Theory* (London: Macmillan).

—— (1991) *Modernity and Self Identity: Self and Society in the Late Modern Age* (Cambridge: Polity Press).

Gilbert, E., Morabito, J., and Stohr, E. (2010) 'Knowledge Sharing and Decision Making in the Peace Corps', *Knowledge and Process Management*, 17/3: 128–44.

Gittelman, M., and Kogut, B. (2003) 'Does Good Science Lead to Valuable Knowledge? Biotechnology Firms and the Evolutionary Logic of Citation Patterns', *Management Science*, 49/4: 366–82.

Glazer, R. (1998) 'Measuring the Knower: Towards a Theory of Knowledge Equity', *California Management Review*, 40/3: 175–94.

Glisby, M., and Holden, N. (2003) 'Contextual Constraints in Knowledge Management Theory: The Cultural Embeddedness of Nonaka's Knowledge Creating Company', *Knowledge and Process Management*, 10/1: 29–36.

Goles, T., and Hirschheim, R. (2000) 'The Paradigm is Dead, the Paradigm is Dead . . . Long Live the

Paradigm: The Legacy of Burrell and Morgan', *Omega*, 28/3: 249–68.

Goodall, K., and Roberts, J. (2003) 'Repairing Managerial Knowledgeability over Distance', *Organization Studies*, 24/7: 1153–76.

Gourlay, S. (2006) 'Conceptualizing Knowledge Creation: A Critique of Nonaka's Theory', *Journal of Management Studies*, 43/7: 1415–36.

Grant, R. (1996) 'Towards a Knowledge Based Theory of the Firm', *Strategic Management Journal*, 17 (Winter Special Issue), 109–22.

Grant, R. (2000) 'Shifts in the World Economy: The Drivers of Knowledge Management', in C. Despres and D. Chauvel (eds), *Knowledge Horizons: The Present and the Promise of Knowledge Management* (Oxford: Butterworth-Heinemann), 27–54.

Gray, P., and Durcikova, A. (2005–6) 'The Role of Knowledge Repositories in Technical Support Environments: Speed versus Learning in User Performance', *Journal of Management Information Systems*, 22/3: 159–90.

Griffiths, D., and Moon, B. (2011) 'The State of Knowledge Management: A Survey Suggests Ways to Attain More Satisfied Users', *KM World*, http://www.kmworld.com/Articles/PrintArticle.aspx?ArticleID=78481 (accessed Sept. 2012).

Grimshaw, D., and Miozzo, M. (2009) 'New Human Resource Management Practices in Knowledge-Intensive Business Service Firms: The Case of Outsourcing with Staff Transfer', *Human Relations*, 62/10: 1521–50.

Güldenberg, S., and Helting, H. (2007) 'Bridging "The Great Divide": Nonaka's Synthesis of "Western" and "Eastern" Knowledge Concepts Reassessed', *Organization*, 14/1: 101–22.

——— and Konrath, H. (2006) 'Bridging Leadership and Learning in Knowledge-Based Organizations', in B. Renzl, K. Matzler, and H. Hinterhuber (eds), *The Future of Knowledge Management* (Basingstoke: Palgrave Macmillan), 219–36.

Haas, M., and Hansen, M. (2007) 'Different Knowledge, Different Benefits: Towards a Productivity Perspective on Knowledge Sharing in Organizations', *Strategic Management Journal*, 28: 1133–53.

Hales, C. (1993) Managing *through Organization: The Management Process, Forms of Organisation and the Work of Managers* (London: Routledge).

Han, T.-S., Chiang, H.-H., and Chang, A. (2010) 'Employee Participation in Decision Making, Psychological Ownership and Knowledge Sharing: Mediating Role of Organizational Commitment in Taiwanese High-Tech Organizations', *International Journal of Human Resource Management*, 21/12: 2218–33.

Handley, K., Sturdy, A., Fincham, R., and Clark, T. (2006) 'Within and Beyond Communities of Practice: Making Sense of Learning through Participation, Identity and Practice', *Journal of Management Studies*, 43/3: 641–53.

Hansen, M., Nohria, N., and Tierney, T. (1999), 'What's Your Strategy for Managing Knowledge?', *Harvard Business Review*, 77/2: 106.

Harris and Ogbonna (2002) 'The Unintended Consequences of Culture Interventions: A Study of Unexpected Outcomes', *British Journal of Management*, 13(1): 31–49.

Harrison, R., and Kessels, J. (2004) *Human Resource Development in a Knowledge Economy* (Basingstoke: Palgrave Macmillan).

——— and Leitch, C. (2000) 'Learning and Organization in the Knowledge-Based Information Economy: Initial Findings from a Participatory Action Research Case Study', *British Journal of Management*, 11/2: 103–19.

Harryson, S., Dudkowski, R., and Stern, A. (2008) 'Transformation Networks in Innovation Alliances: The Development of Volvo C70', *Journal of Management Studies*, 45/4: 745–73.

Hayes, J. (2002) *The Theory and Practice of Change Management* (Basingstoke: Palgrave).

Hayes, N., and Walsham, G. (2000) 'Safe Enclaves, Political Enclaves and Knowledge Working', in C. Prichard, R. Hull, M. Chumer, and H. Willmott (eds), *Managing Knowledge: Critical Investigations of Work and Learning* (London: Macmillan).

He, Y., Lai, K., and Lu, Y. (2011) 'Linking Organizational Support to Employee Commitment: Evidence from Hotel Industry in China', *International Journal of Human Resource Management*, 22/1: 197–217.

He, Z.-L., and Wong, P.-K. (2004) 'Exploration vs. Exploitation: An Empirical Test of the Ambidexterity Hypothesis', *Organization Science*, 15/4: 481–94.

——— and ——— (2009) 'Knowledge Interaction with Manufacturing Clients and Innovation of Knowledge-Intensive Business Services Firms', *Innovation: Management, Policy and Practice*, 11/3: 264–78.

Hecker, A. (2012) 'Knowledge Beyond the Individual? Making Sense of a Notion of Collective Knowledge in Organization Theory', *Organization Studies*, 33/3: 423–45.

Heizmann, H. (2011) 'Knowledge Sharing in a Dispersed Network of HR Practice: Zooming in on Power/Knowledge Struggles', *Management Learning*, 42/4: 379–93.

Hemetsberger, A., and Reinhardt, C. (2006) 'Learning and Knowledge-Building in Open-Source Communities: A Social-Experiential Approach', *Management Learning*, 37/2: 187–214.

Hendriks, P. (2001) 'Many Rivers to Cross: From ICT to Knowledge Management Systems', *Journal of Information Technology*, 16/2: 57–72.

Hindmarsh, J., and Pilnick, A. (2007) 'Knowing Bodies at Work: Embodiment and Ephemeral Teamwork in Anaesthesia', *Organization Studies*, 28/9: 1395–1416.

Hinterhuber, H., and Stadler, C. (2006) 'Leadership and Strategy as Intangible Assets', in B. Renzl, K. Matzler, and H. Hinterhuber (eds), *The Future of Knowledge Management* (Basingstoke: Palgrave Macmillan), 237–53.

Hislop, D. (2002*a*) 'Linking Human Resource Management and Knowledge Management: A Review and Research Agenda', *Employee Relations*, 25/2: 182–202.

—— (2002*b*) 'Mission Impossible? Communicating and Sharing Knowledge via Information Technology', *Journal of Information Technology*, 17/3: 165–77.

—— (2003) 'The Complex Relationship between Communities of Practice and the Implementation of Technological Innovations', *International Journal of Innovation Management*, 7/2: 163–88.

—— (2008) 'Conceptualizing Knowledge Work Utilizing Skill and Knowledge-Based Concepts: The Case of Some Consultants and Service Engineers', *Management Learning*, 39/5: 579–97.

—— (2010) 'Knowledge Management as an Ephemeral Management Fashion?', *Journal of Knowledge Management*, 14/6: 779–90.

—— Newell, S., Scarbrough, H., and Swan, J. (2000) 'Networks, Knowledge and Power: Decision Making, Politics and the Process of Innovation', *Technology Analysis and Strategic Management*, 12/3: 399–411.

Ho, S.-C., Ting, P.-H., Bau, D.-Y., Wei, C.-C. (2011) 'Knowledge Sharing Intention in a Virtual Community: A Study of Participants in the Chinese Wikipedia', *CyberPsychology, Behaviour and Social Networking*, 14/9: 541–5.

Hoegl, M., and Schultze, A. (2005) 'How to Support Knowledge Creation in New Product Development: An Investigation of Knowledge Management Tools', *European Management Journal*, 23/3: 263–73.

Holste, J., and Fields, D. (2010) 'Trust and Tacit Knowledge Sharing and Use', *Journal of Knowledge Management*, 14/1: 128–40

Hong, F., and Snell, R. (2008) 'Power Inequality in Cross-Cultural Learning: The Case of Japanese Transplants in China', *Asia Pacific Business Review*, 14/2: 253–73.

Hong, J. (2012) 'Glocalizing Nonaka's Knowledge Creation Model: Issues and Challenges'. *Management Learning*, 43/2: 199–215.

—— Heikkinen, J., and Blomqvist, K. (2010) 'Culture and Knowledge Co-Creation in R&D Collaboration between MNCs and Chinese Universities', *Knowledge and Process Management*, 17/2: 62–73.

Horowitz, F., Heng, C., and Quazi, H. (2003) 'Finders, Keepers? Attracting, Motivating and Retaining Knowledge Workers', *Human Resource Management Journal*, 13/4: 23–44.

HR Magazine (2009) 'Leveraging HR and Knowledge Management in a Challenging Economy', *HR Magazine* (June).

Hsiao, R.-L., Tsai, S., and Lee, C.-F. (2006) 'The Problem of Embeddedness: Knowledge Transfer, Coordination and Reuse in Information Systems', *Organization Studies*, 27/9: 1289–1317.

Huang, Q., Davison, R., Liu, H., and Gu, J. (2008) 'The Impact of Leadership Style on Knowledge-Sharing Intentions in China', *Journal of Global Information Management*, 16: 67–91.

Huang, T.-P. (2011) 'Comparing Motivating Work Characteristics, Job Satisfaction, and Turnover Intention of Knowledge Workers and Blue-Collar Workers and Testing a Structural Model of the Variables' Relationships in China and Japan', *International Journal of Human Resource Management*, 22/4: 924–44.

Huczynski, A., and Buchanan, D. (2001) *Organizational Behaviour: An Introductory Text* (Harlow: Financial Times/Prentice Hall).

Hughes, J., Jewson, N., and Unwin, L. (2008) *Communities of Practice: Critical Perspectives* (London: Routledge).

Hume, C., and Hume, M. (2008) 'The Strategic Role of Knowledge Management in Nonprofit Organizations', *International Journal of Nonprofit and Voluntary Sector Marketing*, 13/2: 129–40.

Hunter, L., Beaumont, P., and Lee, M. (2002) 'Knowledge Management Practice in Scottish Law Firms', *Human Resource Management Journal*, 12/2: 4–21.

Hutchinson. V., and Quintas, P. (2008) 'Do SMEs do Knowledge Management? Or Simply Manage What they Know?', *International Small Business Journal*, 26/2: 131–54.

Huzzard, T., and Ostergren, K. (2002) 'When Norms Collide: Learning Under Organizational Hypocrisy', *British Journal of Management*, 13: S47–59.

Ichijo, K., and Nonaka, I (2006) *Knowledge Creation and Management: New Challenges for Managers* (New York: Oxford University Press).

Inkpen, A., and Pien, W. (2006) 'An Examination of Collaboration and Knowledge Transfer: Chinese-Singapore Suzhou Industrial Park', *Journal of Management Studies*, 43/4: 779–811.

Introna, L., Hayes, N., and Dimitra, P. (2009) 'The Working out of Modernization in the Public Sector: The Case of an E-Government Initiative in Greece', *International Journal of Public Administration*, 33/1: 11–25.

Iverson, R., and Buttigieg, D. (1999) 'Affective, Normative, and Continuance Commitment: Can the "Right Kind" of Commitment be Managed?', *Journal of Management Studies*, 36/3: 307–33.

Janowicz-Panjaitan, M., and Noorderhaven, N. (2009) 'Trust, Calculation, and Interorganizational Learning of Tacit Knowledge: An Organizational Roles Perspective', *Organization Studies*, 30/10: 1021–44.

Jarvenpaa, S., and Leidner, D. (1999) 'Communication and Trust in Global Virtual Teams', *Organization Science*, 10/6: 791–815.

—— and Majchrzak, A. (2008) 'Knowledge Collaboration among Professionals Protecting National Security: Role of Transactive Memories in Ego-Centred Knowledge Networks', *Organization Science*, 19/2: 260–76.

Jasimuddin, S., Connell, N., and Klein, J. (2012) 'Knowledge Transfer Frameworks: An Extension Incorporating Knowledge Repositories and Knowledge Administration', *Information Systems Journal*, 22: 195–209.

Jonsson, A., and Kalling, T. (2007) 'Challenges to Knowledge Sharing across National and Intra-Organizational Boundaries: Case Studies of IKEA and SCA Packaging', *Knowledge Management Research and Practice*, 5: 161–72.

Joo, B.-K. (2010) 'Organizational Commitment for Knowledge Workers: The Roles of Perceived Organizational Learning Culture, Leader-Member Exchange Quality, and Turnover Intention', *Human Resource Development Quarterly*, 21/1: 69–85.

Kamoche, K., and Maguire, K. (2011) 'Pit-Sense: Appropriation of Practice-Based Knowledge in a UK Coalmine', *Human Relations*, 64/5, 725–44.

Kanawattanachai, P., and Yoo, Y. (2007) 'The Impact of Knowledge Coordination in Virtual Team Performance over Time', *MIS Quarterly*, 31/4: 783–808.

Kang, S.-C., and Snell, S. (2008) 'Intellectual Capital Architectures and Ambidextrous Learning: A Framework for Human Resource Management', *Journal of Management Studies*, 46/1: 65–92.

Kankanhalli, A., Tan, B., and Wei, K. (2005) 'Contributing Knowledge to Electronic Knowledge Repositories: An Empirical Investigation', *MIS Quarterly*, 29: 113–43.

Kanzler, S. (2010) 'Knowledge Sharing in Heterogeneous Collaborations: A Longitudinal Investigation of a Cross-Cultural Research Collaboration in Nanoscience', *Journal of Business Chemistry*, 7/1: 31–45.

Karkoulian, S., Halawi, L., and McCarthy, R. (2008) 'Knowledge Management, Formal and Informal Mentoring: An Empirical Investigation of Lebanese Banks', *The Learning Organization*, 15/5: 409–20.

Kärreman, D. (2010) 'The Power of Knowledge: Learning from "Learning by Knowledge-Intensive Firm"', *Journal of Management Studies*, 47/7: 1405–16.

Kase, R., Paauwe J., and Zupan, N. (2009) 'HR Practices, Interpersonal Relations, and Intrafirm Knowledge Transfer in Knowledge Intensive Firms: A Social Network Perspective', *Human Resource Management*, 48/4: 615–39.

Kasper, H., Lehrer, M., Mühlbacher, J., and Müller, B. (2009) 'Integration-Responsiveness and Knowledge-Management Perspectives on the MNC: A Typology and Field Study of Cross-Site Knowledge-Sharing Practices', *Journal of Leadership and Organizational Studies*, 15/3: 283–303.

—— and —— (2010) 'Thinning Knowledge: An Interpretive Field Study of Knowledge Sharing Practices of Firms in Three Multinational Contexts'. *Journal of Management Inquiry*, 19/4: 367–81.

Kauppila, O.-P., Rajala, R., and Jyrämä, A. (2011) 'Knowledge Sharing through Virtual Teams across Borders and Boundaries', *Management Learning*, 42/4: 395–418.

Kazuo, I., Nonaka, I., and von Krogh, G. (1997) 'Develop Knowledge Activists!', *European Management Journal*, 15/5: 475–84.

Kelly, S. (2008) 'Leadership: A Categorical Mistake?', *Human Relations*, 61/6: 763–82.

Kets de Vries, M. (1991) 'Whatever Happened to the Philosopher King? The Leader's Addiction to Power', *Journal of Management Studies*, 28/4: 339–51.

Khatri, N., Baveja, A., Agarwal, N., and Brown, G. (2010) 'HR and IT Capabilities and Complementarities in Knowledge Intensive Services', *International Journal of Human Resource Management*, 21/15: 2889–2909.

Kim, W., and Mauborgne, R. (1998) 'Procedural Justice, Strategic Decision Making, and the Knowledge Economy', *Strategic Management Journal*, 19/4: 323–38.

Kimble, C. (2011) 'Building Effective Virtual Teams: How to Overcome Problems of Trust and Identity on Virtual Teams', *Global Business and Organizational Excellence*, 30/2: 6–15.

King, W., and Marks Jr., P. (2008) 'Motivating Knowledge Sharing through a Knowledge Management System', *Omega*, 36: 131–46.

Kluge, J., Stein, W., and Licht, T. (2001) *Knowledge Unplugged: The McKinsey Survey on Knowledge Management* (Basingstoke: Palgrave).

Knights, D., Murray, F., and Willmott, H. (1993) 'Networking as Knowledge Work: A Study of Strategic Interorganzational Development in the Financial Service Industry', *Journal of Management Studies*, 30/6: 975–95.

Kofman, F., and Senge, P. (1993) 'Communities of Commitment: The Heart of Learning Organizations', *Organizational Dynamics*, 22/2: 5–23.

Kogut, B., and Zander, U. (1996) 'What Do Firms Do? Coordination, Identity and Learning', *Organization Science*, 7/5: 502–18.

Kothari, A., Hovanec, N., Hastie, R., and Sibbald, S. (2011) 'Lessons from the Business Sector for Successful Knowledge Management in Healthcare: A Systemic Review', *Health Services Research*, 11: 173–84.

Kotlarsky, J., and Oshri, I. (2005) 'Social Ties, Knowledge Sharing and Successful Collaboration in Globally Distributed System Development Projects', *European Journal of Information Systems*, 14: 37–48.

—— —— Hillegsersberg, J., and Kumar, K. (2007) 'Globally Distributed Component-Based Software Development: An Exploratory Study of Knowledge Management and Work Division', *Journal of IT*, 22: 161–73.

KPMG (2000) *Knowledge Management Research Report* (London: KPMG Consulting).

KPMG (2003) *Insights from KPMG's European Knowledge Management Survey 2002/2003* (Amstelveen: KPMG Knowledge Advisory Services, The Netherlands).

Kumar, J., and Ganesh, L. (2011) 'Balancing Knowledge Strategy: Codification and Personalization during Product Development', *Journal of Knowledge Management*, 15/1: 118–35.

Kumar, K. (1995) *From Post-Industrial to Post-Modern Society: New Theories of the Contemporary World* (London: Blackwell).

Kunda, G. (1992) *Engineering Culture: Control and Commitment in a High-Tech Corporation* (Philadelphia: Temple University Press).

Kuo, R.-Z., and Lee, G.-G. (2011) 'Knowledge Management System Adoption: Exploring the Effects of Empowering Leadership, Task-Technology Fit and Compatibility', *Behaviour and Information Technology*, 30/1: 113–29.

Kusunoki, K. Nonaka, I., and Nagata, A. (1998) 'Organizational Development in Product Development of Japanese Firms: A Conceptual Framework and Empirical Findings', *Organization Science*, 9/6: 699–718.

Lam, A. (1997) 'Embedded Firms, Embedded Knowledge: Problems in Collaboration and Knowledge Transfer in Global Cooperative Ventures', *Organization Studies*, 18/6: 973–96.

Lam, W. (2005) 'Successful Knowledge Management Requires a Knowledge Culture: A Case Study', *Knowledge Management Research and Practice*, 3/4: 206–17.

Landry, S., Levin, K., Rowe, D., and Nickelson, M. (2010) 'Enabling Collaborative Work across Different Communities of Practice through Boundary Objects: Field Studies in Air Traffic Management', *International Journal of Human Computer Interaction*, 26/1: 75–93.

LaPolombara, J. (2001) 'Power and Politics in Organizations: Public and Private Sector Comparisons', in M. Dierkes, A. Bertoin Antal, J. Child, and I. Nonaka (eds), *Handbook of Organizational Learning and Knowledge* (Oxford: Oxford University Press), 557–81.

Lave, J., and Wenger, E. (1991) *Situated Learning: Legitimate Peripheral Participation* (Cambridge: Cambridge University Press).

Lee, C., and Chen, W.-J. (2005) 'The Effects of Internal Marketing and Organizational Culture on Knowledge Management in the Information Technology Industry', *International Journal of Management*, 22/4: 661–72.

Lee, L. (2011) 'The Effects of Challenge and Hindrance Stressors on Unlearning and NPD Success: The Moderating Role of Team Conflict', *African Journal of Business Management*, 5/5: 1843–56.

—— and Sukoco, B. (2011) 'Reflexivity, Stress, and Unlearning in the New Product Development Team: The Moderating Effect of Procedural Justice', *R&D Management* 41/4: 410–23.

Lee, P., Gillespie, N., Mann, L., and Wearing. A. (2010) 'Leadership and Trust: Their Effects on Knowledge Sharing and Team Performance', *Management Learning*, 41/4: 473–91.

Leonard, D., and Sensiper, S. (1998) 'The Role of Tacit Knowledge in Group Innovation', *California Management Review*, 40/3: 112–32.

Levin, D., and Cross, R. (2004) 'The Strength of Weak Ties You Can Trust: The Mediating Role of Trust in Effective Knowledge Transfer', *Management Science*, 50/11: 1477–90.

Levinthal, D., and March, J. (1993) 'The Myopia of Learning', *Strategic Management Journal*, 14 (Special Issue): 95–113.

Levitt, B., and March, J. (1988) 'Organizational Learning', *Annual Review of Sociology*, 14: 319–40.

Levy, M. (2009) 'Web 2.0 Implications on Knowledge Management', *Journal of Knowledge Management*, 13/1: 120–34.

Li, F., Pienkowski, D., van Moorsel, A., and Smith, C. (2012) 'A Holistic Framework for Trust in Online Transactions', *International Journal of Management Reviews*, 14/1: 85–103.

Li, R., and Poon, S. (2011) 'Using Web 2.0 to Share Knowledge of Construction Safety: The Fable of Economic Animals', *IEA Economic Affairs* (Mar.), 73–9.

Li, W. (2010) 'Virtual Knowledge Sharing in a Cross-Cultural Context', *Journal of Knowledge Management*, 14/1: 38–50.

Liao, L.-F. (2008) 'Knowledge Sharing in R&D Departments: A Social Power and Social Exchange Theory Perspective', *International Journal of Human Resource Management*, 19/10: 1881–95.

Liao, S.-H., Chang, W.-J., Hu, D.-C., and Yueh, Y-L. (2012) 'Relationships among Organizational Culture, Knowledge Acquisition, Organizational Learning, and Organizational Innovation in Taiwan's Banking and Insurance Industries', *International Journal of Human Resource Management*, 23/1: 52–70.

Lin, H.-F. (2011) 'The Effect of Employee Motivation, Social Interaction, and Knowledge Management Strategy on KM Implementation Level', *Knowledge Management Research and Practice*, 9: 263–75.

Lindblom, A., and Tikkanen, T. (2010) 'Knowledge Creation and Business Format Franchising', *Management Decision*, 48/2: 179–88.

Littler, C., and Innes, D. (2003) 'Downsizing and Deknowledging the Firm', *Work, Employment and Society*, 17: 73–100.

Lloria, M. (2008) 'A Review of the Main Approaches to Knowledge Management', *Knowledge Management Research and Practice*, 6: 77–89.

López, S. P., Peón, J. M. M., and Ordás C. J. V. (2004) 'Managing Knowledge: The Link between Culture and Organizational Learning', *Journal of Knowledge Management*, 8/6: 93–104.

Lukes, S. (1974) *Power: A Radical Perspective* (London: Macmillan).

Luo, X., and Deng, L. (2009) 'Do Birds of a Feather Flock Higher? The Effects of Partner Similarity on Innovation in Strategic Alliances in Knowledge-Intensive industries', *Journal of Management Studies*, 46/6: 1005–30.

McAdam, R., and McCreedy, S. (2000) 'A Critique of Knowledge Management: Using a Social Constructivist Model', *New Technology, Work and Employment*, 15/2: 155–68.

—— Moffett, S. and Peng, J. (2012) 'Knowledge Sharing in Chinese Service Organizations: A Multi Case Cultural Perspective', *Journal of Knowledge Management,* 16/1: 129–47.

McClure Wasko, M., and Faraj, S. (2000) '"It is What One Does": Why People Participate and Help Others in Electronic Communities of Practice', *Journal of Strategic Information Systems*, 9/1: 155–73.

McDermott, R. (1999) 'Why Information Technology Inspired But Cannot Deliver Knowledge Management', *California Management Review*, 41/1: 103–17.

—— and O'Dell, C. (2001) 'Overcoming Cultural Barriers to Knowledge Sharing', *Journal of Knowledge Management*, 5/1: 76–85.

McGivern, G., and Dawson, S. (2010) 'Inter-Epistemic Power and Transforming Knowledge Objects in a Biomedical Network', *Organization Studies*, 31/12: 1667–86.

Machlup, F. (1962) *The Production and Distribution of Knowledge in the US* (Princeton: Princeton University Press).

McKinlay, A. (2000) 'The Bearable Lightness of Control: Organisational Reflexivity and the Politics of Knowledge Management', in C. Prichard, R. Hull, M. Chumer, and H. Willmott (eds), *Managing Knowledge: Critical Investigations of Work and Learning* (London: Macmillan), 107–21.

—— (2002) 'The Limits of Knowledge Management', *New Technology, Work and Employment*, 17/2: 76–88.

—— (2005) 'Knowledge Management', in S. Ackroyd, R. Batt, and P. Thompson (eds), *The Oxford Handbook of Work and Organization* (Oxford: Oxford University Press), 242–62.

—— and Starkey, K. (1998) *Foucault, Management and Organization Theory* (London: Sage).

—— Carter, C., Pezet, E., and Clegg, S. (2010) 'Using Foucault to Make Strategy', *Accounting, Auditing and Accountability Journal*, 23/8: 1012–31.

McLeod, C., O'Donohue, S., and Townley, B. (2011) 'Pot Noodles, Placements and Peer Regard: Creative Career Trajectories and Communities of Practice in the British Advertising Industry', *British Journal of Management*, 22: 114–31.

Majchrzak, A., More, P., and Faraj, S. (2012) 'Transcending Knowledge Differences in Cross-Functional Teams', *Organization Science*, 23/4: 951–70.

Malhotra, A., Majchzek, A., and Rosen, B. (2007) 'Leading Virtual Teams', *Academy of Management Perspective*, 21/1: 60–70.

Malhotra, N., Mossis, T., and Smets, M. (2010) 'New Career Models in UK Professional Service Firms: From Up-or-Out to Up-and-Going-Nowhere?', *International Journal of Human Resource Management*, 21/9: 1396–413.

Mandelson, P. (2009) *The Future of Universities in a Knowledge Economy* (London: Department for Business Innovation and Skills).

Mansell, R., and SteinMueller, W. (2000) *Mobilizing the Information Society: Strategies for Growth and Opportunity* (Oxford: Oxford University Press).

March, J., and Simon, H. (1993) *Organizations*, 2nd edn. (Oxford: Blackwell).

Marcos, J., and Denyer, D. (2012) 'Crossing the Sea from They to We? The Unfolding of Knowing and Practicing in Collaborative Research', *Management Learning* (publ. via Onlinefirst doi: 10.1177/1350507612440232).

Marshall, N., and Brady, T. (2001) 'Knowledge Management and the Politics of Knowledge: Illustrations from Complex Product Systems', *European Journal of Information Systems*, 10/2: 99–112.

—— and Rollinson, J. (2004) 'Maybe Bacon had a Point: The Politics of Collective Sensemaking', *British Journal of Management*, 15 (Special Issue): S71–86.

Martin, J. (2006) 'Multiple Intelligence Theory, Knowledge Identification and Trust', *Knowledge Management Research and Practice*, 4/3: 207–15.

Martins, E. and Meyer, H. (2012) 'Organizational and Behavioural Factors that Influence Knowledge Retention', *Journal of Knowledge Management*, 16/1: 77–96.

Mason, K., and Leek, S. (2008) 'Learning to Build a Supply Network: An Exploration of Dynamic Business Models', *Journal of Management Studies*, 45/4: 774–99.

Massingham, P. (2004) 'Linking Business Level Strategy with Activities and Knowledge Resources', *Journal of Knowledge Management*, 8/6: 50–62.

—— (2008) 'Measuring the Impact of Knowledge Loss: More than Ripples on a Pond?', *Management Learning*, 39/5: 541–60.

—— (2010) 'Managing Knowledge Transfer between Parent Country Nationals (Australia) and Host Country Nationals (Asia)', *International Journal of Human Resource Management*, 21/9: 1414–35.

Mathew, J., and Ogbonna, E. (2011) 'Organisational Culture and Commitment: A study of an Indian Software Organisation', *International Journal of Human Resource Management*, 20/3: 654–75.

Matschke, C., Moskaliuk, J., and Cress, U. (2012) 'Knowledge Exchange Using Web 2.0 Technologies in NGOs', *Journal of Knowledge Management*, 16/1: 159–76.

Matson, E., and Prusak, L. (2010) 'Boosting the Productivity of Knowledge Workers', *McKinsey Quarterly*, 4: 93–6.

Matsudaira, Y. (2010) 'The Continued Practice of "Ethos": How Nissan Enables Organizational Knowledge Creation', *Information Systems Management*, 27: 226–37.

Matzkin, D. (2008) 'Knowledge Management in the Peruvian Non-Profit Sector', *Journal of Knowledge Management*, 12/4: 147–59.

Matzler, K., Renzl, B., Mooradian, T., von Krogh, G., and Mueller, J. (2011) 'Personality Traits, Affective Commitment, Documentation of Knowledge and Knowledge Sharing', *International Journal of Human Resource Management*, 22/2: 296–310.

Maznevski, M., and Chudoba, K. (1999) 'Bridging Space over Time: Global Virtual Team Dynamics and Effectiveness', *Organization Science*, 11/5: 473–92.

Mehrizi, M., and Bontis, N. (2009) 'A Cluster Analysis of the KM Field', *Management Decision*, 47/5: 792–805.

Meroño-Cerdan, A., Lopez-Nicolas, C., and Sabater-Sànchez, R. (2007) 'Knowledge Management Strategy Diagnosis from KM Instruments Use', *Journal of Knowledge Management*, 11/2: 60–72.

Michailova, S., and Hutchins, K. (2006) 'National Cultural Influences on Knowledge Sharing: A Comparison of China and Russia', *Journal of Management Studies*, 43/3: 383–405.

Milne, P. (2007) 'Motivation, Incentives and Organisational Culture', *Journal of Knowledge Management*, 11/6: 28–38.

Mintzberg, H., Ahlstrand, B., and Lampel, J. (1998) *Strategy Safari: The Complete Guide through the Wilds of Strategic Management* (Harlow: Financial Times/Prentice Hall).

Mooradian, T., Renzl, B., and Matzler, K. (2006) 'Who Trusts? Personality Trust and Knowledge Sharing', *Management Learning*, 37/4: 523–40.

Moran, J. (2010) 'Doing More with Less: How a Multicompany Community of Practice Shares Knowledge and Saves Money', *Global Business and Organizational Excellence* (Sept./Oct.), 50–6.

Mørk, B., Hoholm, T., Ellingsen, G., Edwin, B., and Aanestad, M. (2010) 'Challenging Expertise: On Power Relations within and across Communities of Practice in Medical Innovation', *Management Learning*, 41/5: 575–92.

—— —— —— Maaninen-Olsson, E., and Aanestad, M. (2012) 'Changing Practices through Boundary Organizing: A Case from Medical R&D', *Human Relations*, 65/2: 263–88.

Morris, T. (2001) 'Asserting Property Rights: Knowledge Codification in the Professional Service Firm', *Human Relations*, 54/7: 819–38.

—— and Empson, L. (1998) 'Organization and Expertise: An Exploration of Knowledge Bases and the Management of Accounting and Consulting Firms', *Accounting, Organizations and Society*, 23/5–6: 609–24.

Motion, J., and Leitch, S. (2009) 'The Transformation Potential of Public Policy Discourse', *Organization Studies*, 30/10: 1046–61.

Mueller, J., Hutter, K., Fueller, J., and Matzler, K. (2011) 'Virtual Worlds as Knowledge Management Platform: A Practice Perspective', *Information Systems Journal*, 21/6: 479–501.

Muethel, M., Siebdrat, F., and Hoegl, M. (2012) 'When do we Really Need Interpersonal Trust in Globally Dispersed New Product Development Teams', *R&D Management*, 42/1: 31–46.

Nadler, D., and Tushman, M. (1990) 'Beyond the Charismatic Leader: Leadership and Organizational Change', *California Management Review* (Winter), 77–97.

Nag, R., and Gioia, D. (2012) 'From Common to Uncommon Knowledge: Foundations of Firm-Specific Use of Knowledge as a Resource', *Academy of Management Journal*, 55/2: 421–57.

Nahapiet, J., and Ghoshal, S. (1998) 'Social Capital, Intellectual Capital and the Organizational Advantage', *Academy of Management Review*, 23/2: 242–66.

Nakamori, Y. (2006) 'Designing, Utilizing and Evaluating "Technology-Creating Ba" in a Japanese Scientific Research Institute', *Systems Research and Behaviour Science,* 23: 3–19.

National Skills Task Force (2000) *Skills for All: Research Report from the National Skills Task Force* (London: Department for Education and Employment).

Nayir, D., and Uzunçarsili, Ü. (2008) 'A Cultural Perspective on Knowledge Management: The Success Story of Sarkuysan Company', *Journal of Knowledge Management,* 12/2: 141–55.

Neef, D. (1999) 'Making the Case for Knowledge Management: The Bigger Picture', *Management Decision,* 37/1: 72–8.

Newell, S., and Swan, J. (2000) 'Trust and Inter-Organizational Networking', *Human Relations,* 53/10: 1287–1328.

—— Scarbrough, H., Swan, J., and Hislop, D. (2000) 'Intranets and Knowledge Management: De-centred Technologies and the Limits of Technological Discourse', in C. Prichard, R. Hull, M. Chumer, and H. Willmott (eds), *Managing Knowledge: Critical Investigations of Work and Learning* (London: Macmillan), 88–106.

—— David, G., and Chand, D. (2007) 'An Analysis of Trust among Globally Distributed Work Teams in an Organizational Setting', *Knowledge and Process Management,* 14/3: 158–68.

Nguyen, H., and Mohamed, S. (2011) 'Leadership Behaviours, Organizational Culture and Knowledge Management Practices: An Empirical Investigation', *Journal of Management Development,* 30/2: 206–21.

Ngwenyama, O., and Lee, A. (1997) 'Communication Richness in Electronic Mail: Critical Social Theory and the Contextuality of Meaning', *MIS Quarterly,* 21/2: 145–67.

Nicolini, D. (2007) 'Stretching Out and Expanding Medical Practices: The Case of Telemedicine', *Human Relations,* 60/6: 889–920.

—— (2011) 'Practice as the Site of Knowing: Insights from the Field of Telemedicine', *Organization Science,* 22/3: 602–20.

—— Powell, J., Conville, P., and Martinez-Solano, L. (2008) 'Managing Knowledge in the Healthcare Sector: A Review', *International Journal of Management Reviews,* 10/3: 245–63.

Nishikawa, M. (2011) '(Re)defining Care Workers as Knowledge Workers', *Gender, Work and Organization,* 18/1: 113–36.

Nonaka, I. (1991) 'The Knowledge-Creating Company', *Harvard Business Review* (Nov.–Dec.), 96–104.

—— (1994) 'A Dynamic Theory of Organizational Knowledge Creation', *Organization Science,* 5/1: 14–37.

—— Byosiere, P., Borucki, C., and Konno, N. (1994) 'Organizational Knowledge Creation Theory: A First Comprehensive Test', *International Business Review,* 3–4: 337–52.

—— and Konno, N. (1998) 'The Concept of "Ba": Building a Foundation for Knowledge Creation', *California Management Review,* 40/3: 40–55.

—— and Peltokorpi, V. (2006) 'Objectivity and Subjectivity in Knowledge Management: A Review of 20 Top Articles', *Knowledge and Process Management,* 13/2: 73–82.

—— —— and Hisao, T. (2005) 'Strategic Knowledge Creation: The Case of Hamamatsu Photonics', *International Journal of Technology Management,* 30/3–4: 248–64.

—— and Takeuchi, H. (1995) *The Knowledge Creating Company* (Oxford: Oxford University Press).

—— and —— (1998) 'A Theory of Organizational Knowledge Creation', *International Journal of Technology Management,* 11/7–8: 833–46.

—— and Toyama, R. (2002) 'A Firm as a Dialectical Being: Towards a Dynamics Theory of the Firm', *Industrial and Corporate Change,* 11/5: 995–1009.

—— and —— (2005) 'The Theory of the Knowledge-Creating Firm: Subjectivity, Objectivity and Synthesis', *Industrial and Corporate Change,* 14/3: 419–36.

—— and —— (2007) 'Strategic Management as Distributed Practical Wisdom (Phronesis)', *Industrial and Corporate Change,* 16/3: 371–94.

—— —— and Hirata, T. (2008) *Managing Flow: A Process Theory of the Knowledge-Based Firm* (Basingstoke: Palgrave Macmillan).

—— —— and Konno, N. (2000) 'SECI, "Ba" and Leadership: A Unified Model of Dynamic Knowledge Creation', *Long Range Planning,* 33/1: 5–34.

—— —— and Nagata, A. (2002) 'A Firm as a Knowledge-Creating Entity: A New Perspective on the Theory of the Firm', *Industrial and Corporate Change,* 9/1: 1–20.

—— and von Krogh, G. (2009) 'Tacit Knowledge and Knowledge Conversion: Controversy and Advancement in Organizational Knowledge Creation Theory', *Organization Science,* 20/3: 635–52.

—— —— and Voelpel, S. (2006) 'Organizational Knowledge Creation Theory: Evolutionary Paths and Future Advances', *Organization Studies,* 27/8: 1179–1208.

Northouse, P. (2007) *Leadership: Theory and Practice,* 4th edn. (London: Sage).

Nystrom, P., and Starbuck, W. (2003) 'To Avoid Organizational Crises, Unlearn', in K. Starkey, S. Tempest, and A. McKinlay (eds), *How Organizations Learn: Managing the Search for Knowledge* (London: Thomson), 100–11.

Oborn, E., and Dawson, S. (2010) 'Knowledge and Practice in Multidisciplinary Teams: Struggle, Accommodation and Privilege', *Human Relations*, 63/12: 1835–57.

O'Dell, C., and Hubert, C. (2011) 'Building a Knowledge-Sharing Culture', *Journal of Quality and Participation* (July), 22–6.

Ogbonna, E., and Harris, L. (2002) 'Managing Organisational Culture: Insights from the Hospitality Industry', *Human Resource Management Journal*, 12/1: 33–53.

Oltra, V. (2005) 'Knowledge Management Effectiveness Factors: The Role of HRM', *Journal of Knowledge Management*, 9/4: 70–86.

O'Neill, B., and Adya, M. (2007) 'Knowledge Sharing and the Psychological Contract: Managing Knowledge Workers across Different Stages of Employment', *Journal of Managerial Psychology*, 22/4: 411–36.

Orlikowski, W. (2002) 'Knowing in Practice: Enacting a Collective Capability in Distributed Organizing', *Organization Science*, 13/3: 249–73.

Orr, J. (1990) 'Sharing Knowledge, Celebrating Identity: War Stories and Community Memory in a Service Culture', in D. Middleton and D. Edwards (eds), *Collective Remembering: Memory in a Society* (London: Sage).

—— (1996) *Talking about Machines: An Ethnography of a Modern Job* (Ithaca, NY: ILR Press).

Oshri, I., Van Fenema, P., and Kotlarsky, J.(2008) 'Knowledge Transfer in Globally Distributed Teams: The Role of Transactive Memory', *Information Systems Journal*, 18/6: 593–616.

Osterloh, M., and Frey, B. (2000) 'Motivation, Knowledge Transfer, and Organizational Forms', *Organization Science*, 11/5: 538–50.

Pan, S., and Scarbrough, H. (1999) 'Knowledge Management in Practice: An Exploratory Case Study', *Technology Analysis and Strategic Management*, 11/3: 359–74.

Paroutis, S., and Al Saleh, A. (2009) 'Determinants of Knowledge Sharing Using Web 2.0 Technologies', *Journal of Knowledge Management*, 13/4: 52–63.

Pauleen, D., and Yoong, P. (2001) 'Relationship Building and the Use of ICT in Boundary-Crossing Virtual Teams: A Facilitators Perspective', *Journal of Information Technology*, 16/4: 205–20.

Pawlovsky, P. (2001) 'The Treatment of Organizational Learning in Management Science', in M. Dierkes, A. Bertoin Antal, J. Child, and I. Nonaka (eds), *Handbook of Organizational Learning and Knowledge* (Oxford: Oxford University Press), 61–88.

Pedler, M., Burgoyne, J., and Boydell, T. (1997) *The Learning Company: A Strategy for Sustainable Development*, 2nd edn. (London: McGraw-Hill).

Peltokorpi, V. (2006) 'Knowledge Sharing in a Cross Cultural Context: Nordic Expatriates in Japan', *Knowledge Management Research and Practice*, 4: 138–48.

Polanyi, M. (1958) *Personal Knowledge* (Chicago: University of Chicago Press).

—— (1969) *Knowing and Being* (London: Routledge and Kegan Paul).

—— (1983) *The Tacit Dimension* (Gloucester, Mass.: Peter Smith).

Politis, J. (2002) 'Transformational and Transactional Leadership Enabling (Disabling) Knowledge Acquisition of Self-Managed Teams: The Consequences for Performance', *Leadership and Organization Development Journal*, 23/4: 186–97.

Provera, B., Montefusco, A., and Canato, A. (2010) 'A "No Blame" Approach to Organizational Learning'. *British Journal of Management*, 21: 1057–74.

Rabinow, P. (1991) *The Foucault Reader* (London: Penguin Books).

Rai, K. (2011) 'Knowledge Management and Organizational Culture: A Theoretical Integrative Framework', *Journal of Knowledge Management*, 15/2: 779–801.

Raisch, S., Birkinshaw, J., Probst, G., and Tuckman, M. (2009) 'Organizational Ambidexterity: Balancing Exploitation and Exploration for Sustained Performance', *Organization Science*, 20/4: 685–95.

Ravishankar, M., and Pan, S. (2008) 'The Influence of Organizational Identification on Organizational Knowledge Management (KM)', *Omega*, 36: 221–34.

Raz, A., and Fadlon, J. (2006) 'Managerial Culture, Workplace Culture and Situated Curricula in Organizational Learning', *Organization Studies*, 27/2: 165–82.

Reich, R. (1991) *The Work of Nations: Preparing Ourselves for 21st-Century Capitalism* (London: Simon and Schuster).

Renzl, B. (2008) 'Trust in Management and Knowledge Sharing: The Mediating Effects of Fear and Knowledge Documentation', *Omega*, 36: 206–20.

Ribeiro, R., and Collins, H. (2007) 'The Bread-Making Machine: Tacit Knowledge and Two Types of Action', *Organization Studies*, 28/9: 1417–33.

Ribiere, V., and Sitar, A. (2003) 'Critical Role of Leadership in Nurturing a Knowledge-Supporting Culture', *Knowledge Management Research and Practice*, 1/1: 39–48.

Rifkin, J. (2000) *The End of Work: The Decline of the Global Workforce and the Dawn of the Post-Market Era* (London: Penguin).

Ripamonti, S., and Scaratti, G. (2011) 'Weak Knowledge for Strengthening Competencies: A Practice-Based

Approach in Assessment Management', *Management Learning*, 43/2: 183–97.

Robert, jun., L., Dennis, A., and Hung, Y.-T. (2009) 'Individual Swift Trust and Knowledge-Based Trust in Face-to-Face and Virtual Team Members', *Journal of Management Information Systems*, 26/2: 241–79.

Roberts, J. (2000) 'From Know-How to Show-How? Questioning the Role of Information and Communication Technologies in Knowledge Transfer', *Technology Analysis and Strategic Management*, 12/4: 429–43.

—— (2006) 'Limits to Communities of Practice', *Journal of Management Studies*, 43/3: 623–39.

Robertson, M., and O'Malley Hammersley, G (2000) 'Knowledge Management Practices within a Knowledge-Intensive Firm: The Significance of the People Management Dimension', *Journal of European Industrial Training*, 24/2–4: 241–53.

—— and Swan, J. (2003) '"Control—What Control?" Culture and Ambiguity within a Knowledge Intensive Firm', *Journal of Management Studies*, 40/4: 831–58.

Ron, N., Lipshitz, R., and Popper, M. (2006) 'How Organizations Learn: Post-Flight Reviews in an F-16 Fighter Squadron', *Organization Studies*, 27/8: 1069–89.

Rosendaal, B. (2009) 'Sharing Knowledge, Being Different and Working as a Team', *Knowledge Management Research and Practice*, 7: 4–14.

Ruggles, R. (1998) 'The State of the Notion: Knowledge Management in Practice', *California Management Review*, 40/3: 80–9.

Rusanow, G. (2006) 'Global Law Firms Knowledge Management Survey 2006', downloaded from: http://www.llrx.com/features/kmsurvey2006.htm (July 2012).

Rushmer, R., and Davies, H. (2004) 'Unlearning in Healthcare: Nature, Importance and Painful Lessons', *Quality and Safety in Healthcare*, 13: 10.–15.

Sadler, P. (2001) 'Leadership and Organizational Learning', in M. Dierkes, A. Bertoin Antal, J. Child, and I. Nonaka (eds), *Handbook of Organizational Learning and Knowledge* (Oxford: Oxford University Press), 415–27.

Salaman, G. (2001) 'A Response to Snell: The Learning Organization. Fact or Fiction?', *Human Relations*, 54/3: 343–60.

Sanz-Valle, R., Naranjo-Valencia, J., Jimenéz-Jimenéz, D., and Perez-Caballero, L. (2011) 'Linking Organizational Learning with Technical Innovation and Organizational Culture', *Journal of Knowledge Management*, 15/6: 887–1015.

Sapsted, J., and Salter, A. (2004) 'Postcards from the Edge: Local Communities, Global Programs and Boundary Objects', *Organization Studies*, 25/9: 1515–34.

Sarker, S., Ajuja, M., Sarker, S., and Kirkeby, S. (2011) 'The Role of Communication and Trust in Global Virtual Teams: A Social Network Perspective', *Journal of Management Information Systems*, 28/1: 273–309.

Scarbrough, H. (1998) 'Path(ological) Dependency? Core Competencies from an Organizational Perspective', *British Journal of Management*, 9/3: 219–32.

—— and Carter, C. (2000) *Investigating Knowledge Management* (London: CIPD).

—— and Swan, J. (2001) 'Explaining the Diffusion of Knowledge Management', *British Journal of Management*, 12/1: 3–12.

—— Bresnan, M., Edelman, L., Laurent, S., Newell, S., and Swan, J. (2004*a*) 'The Process of Project-Based Learning: An Exploratory Study', *Management Learning*, 35/4: 491–506.

—— Swan, J., Laurent, S., Bresnen, M., Edelman, L., and Newell, S. (2004*b*) 'Project-Based Learning and the Role of Learning Boundaries', *Organization Studies*, 25/9: 1579–1600.

Schmitt, A., Borzillo, S., and Probst, G. (2012) 'Don't Let Knowledge Walk Away: Knowledge Retention during Employee Downsizing', *Management Learning*, 43/1: 53–74.

Schultze, U. (2008) 'W(h)ither Knowledge Management?', in D. Barry and H. Hansen (eds), *The Sage Handbook of New Approaches in Management and Organization* (London: Sage), 526–7.

—— and Boland, R. (2000) 'Knowledge Technology and the Reproduction of Knowledge Work Practices', *Journal of Strategic Information Systems*, 9: 193–212.

—— and Stabell, C. (2004) 'Knowing What You Don't Know: Discourse and Contradictions in Knowledge Management Research', *Journal of Management Studies*, 41/4: 549–73.

Seba, I., Rowley, J., and Delbridge, R. (2012) 'Knowledge Sharing in the Dubai Police Force', *Journal of Knowledge Management*, 16/1: 114–28.

Seetharaman, A., Soori, H., and Saravanan, A. (2002) 'Intellectual Capital Accounting', *Journal of Intellectual Capital*, 3/2: 128–48.

Senge, P. (1990) *The Fifth Discipline* (New York: Doubleday).

Serenko, A., Bontis, N., Booker, L., Sadeddin, K., and Hardie, T. (2010) 'A Scientometric Analysis of Knowledge Management and Intellectual Capital Academic Literature (1994–2008)', *Journal of Knowledge Management*, 14/1: 3–23.

Sewell, G. (2005) 'Nice Work? Rethinking Managerial Control in an Era of Knowledge Work', *Organization*, 12/5: 685–704.

Shepherd, D., Patzelt, H., and Wolfe, M. (2011) 'Moving Forward from Project Failure: Negative Emotions, Affective Commitment, and Learning from the Experience', *Academy of Management Journal*, 54/6: 1229–59.

Shieh, C.-J. (2011) 'Study on the Relations among Customer Knowledge Management, Learning Organization, and Organizational Performance', *Service Industries Journal*, 31/5: 791–807.

Shipton, H. (2006) 'Confusion or Cohesion? Towards a Typology for Organizational Learning Research', *International Journal of Management Reviews*, 8/4: 233–52.

—— and Sillince, J. (2012) 'Organizational Learning and Emotion: Constructing Collective Meaning in Support of Strategic Themes', *Management Learning* (publ. onlinefirst, doi: 10.1177/135050761245057).

Singh, S. (2008) 'Role of Leadership in Knowledge Management: A Study', *Journal of Knowledge Management*, 12/4: 3–15.

Snell, R. (2001) 'Moral Foundations of the Learning Organization', *Human Relations*, 54/3: 319–42.

Song, J. (2008) 'The Effects of Learning Organization Culture on the Practices of Human Knowledge-Creation: An Empirical Research Study in Korea', *International Journal of Training and Development*, 12/4: 265–81.

Spender, J.-C. (1996) 'Organizational Knowledge, Learning and Memory: Three Concepts in Search of a Theory', *Journal of Organizational Change Management*, 9/1: 63–78.

—— (2003) 'Exploring Uncertainty and Emotion in the Knowledge-Based Firm', *Information Technology and People*, 16/3: 266–88.

—— (2008) 'Organizational Learning and Knowledge Management: Whence and Whither?', *Management Learning*, 39/2: 158–76.

—— and Scherer, A. (2007) 'The Philosophical Foundations of Knowledge Management: Editors' Introduction', *Organization*, 14/1: 5–28.

Srivastava, A., Bartol, K., and Locke, E. (2006) 'Empowering Leadership in Management Teams: Effects on Knowledge Sharing, Efficacy, and Performance', *Academy of Management Journal*, 49/6: 1239–51.

Stamps, D. (2000) 'Communities of Practice: Learning is Social, Training is Irrelevant?', in E. Lesser, M. Fontaine, and J. Slusher (eds), *Knowledge and Communities* (Oxford: Butterworth-Heinemann), 53–64.

Star, S. (1989) The Structure of Ill-Structured Solutions: Boundary Objects and Heterogeneous Distributed Problem Solving', in M. Huhns, and L. Gasser (eds), *Readings in Distributed Artificial Intelligence* (Menlo Park, Calif.: Morgan Kaufman).

Starbuck, W. (1993) 'Keeping a Butterfly and an Elephant in a House of Cards: The Elements of Exceptional Success', *Journal of Management Studies*, 30/6: 885–921.

Starkey, K., Tempest, S., and McKinlay, A. (2003) *How Organizations Learn: Managing the Search for Knowledge* (London: Thomson Learning).

Steininger, K., Rückel, D., Dannerer, E., and Roithmayr, F. (2010) 'Healthcare Knowledge Transfer through a Web 2.0 Portal: An Austrian Approach', *International Journal of Healthcare Technology and Management*, 11/1–2: 13–30.

Steinmueller, W. (2000) 'Will New Information and Communication Technologies Improve the Codification of Knowledge?', *Industrial and Corporate Change*, 9/2: 361–76.

Stock, G., McFadden, K., and Gowen III, C. (2010) 'Organizational Culture, Knowledge Management, and Patient Safety in U.S. Hospitals', *QMJ* 17/2: 7–26.

Storey, J., and Quintas, P. (2001), 'Knowledge Management and HRM', in J. Storey (ed.), *Human Resource Management: A Critical Text* (London: Thomson Learning), 339–63.

Strati, A. (2007) 'Sensible Knowledge and Practice-Based Learning', *Management Learning*, 38/1: 61–77.

Styhre, A. (2003) *Understanding Knowledge Management: Critical and Postmodern Perspectives* (Copenhagen: Liber, Copenhagen Business School).

—— Josephson, P.-E., and Knauseder, I. (2006) 'Organization Learning in Non-Writing Communities: The Case of Construction Workers', *Management Learning*, 37/1: 83–100.

Suchman, L. (2003) 'Organizing Alignment: The Case of Bridge-Building', in D. Nicolini, S. Gherardi, and D. Yanow (eds), *Knowing in Organizations: A Practice-Based Approach* (London: M. E. Sharpe).

Suddaby, R., and Greenwood, R. (2001) 'Colonizing Knowledge: Commodification as a Dynamic of Jurisdictional Expansion in Professional Service Firms', *Human Relations*, 54/7: 933–53.

Sullivan, D., and Marvel, M. (2011) 'Knowledge Acquisition, Network Reliance, and Early-Stage Technology Venture Outcomes', *Journal of Management Studies*, 48/6: 1169–93.

Suppiah, V., and Sandhu, M. (2011) 'Organizational Culture's Influence on Tacit Knowledge-Sharing Behaviour', *Journal of Knowledge Management*, 15/3: 462–77.

Swan, J., Bresnen, M., Newell, S., and Robertson, M. (2007) 'The Object of Knowledge: The Role of Objects in Biomedical Innovation', *Human Relations,* 60/12: 1809–1837.

Swart, J. (2011) 'That's Why it Matters: How Knowing Creates Value', *Management Learning,* 42/3: 319–32.

——— and Kinnie, N. (2003) 'Sharing Knowledge in Knowledge-Intensive Firms', *Human Resource Management Journal*, 13/2: 60–75.

——— and ——— (2010) 'Organisational Learning, Knowledge Assets and HR Practices in Professional Service Firms', *Human Resource Management Journal*, 20/1: 64–79.

——— ——— and Purcell, J. (2003) *People and Perform-ance in Knowledge-Intensive Firms: A Comparison of Six Research and Technology Organizations* (London: CIPD).

Symon, G. (2000) 'Information and Communication Technologies and the Network Organization: A Critical Analysis', *Journal of Occupational and Organizational Psychology*, 73/4: 389–414.

Szulanski, G. (1996) 'Exploring Internal Stickiness: Impediments to the Transfer of Best Practice within the Firm', *Strategic Management Journal*, 17 (Winter Special Issue): 27–43.

Tallman, S., and Phene, A. (2007) 'Leveraging Knowledge across Geographic Boundaries', *Organization Science*, 18/2: 252–60.

Teece, D. (2008) 'Foreward: From Management of R&D to Knowledge Management, Some Contributions of Ikujiro Nonaka to the Field of Strategic Management', in I. Nonaka, R. Toyama, and T. Hirata (eds), *Managing Flow: A Process Theory of the Knowledge-Based Firm* (Basingstoke: Palgrave Macmillan), pp. ix–xvii.

Teo, T., Nishant, R., Goh, M., and Agarwal, S. (2011) 'Leveraging Collaborative Technologies to Build a Knowledge Sharing Culture at HP Analytics', *MIS Quarterly Executive*, 10/1: 1–18.

Thomas, J., Sussman, S., and Henderson, J. (2003) 'Understanding "Strategic Learning": Linking Organizational Learning, Knowledge Management and Sensemaking', *Organization Science*, 1/3: 331–45.

Thompson, M. (2005) 'Structural and Epistemic Parameters in Communities of Practice', *Organization Science*, 16/2: 151–64.

Thompson, P., Warhurst, C., and Callaghan, G. (2001) 'Ignorant Theory and Knowledgeable Workers: Interrogating the Connections between Knowledge, Skills and Services', *Journal of Management Studies*, 38/7: 923–42.

Tong, J., and Mitra, A. (2009) 'Chinese Cultural Influences on Knowledge Management Practice', *Journal of Knowledge Management*, 13/3: 49–62.

Townley, B. (1994) *Reframing Human Resource Management: Power, Ethics and the Subject at Work* (London: Sage).

Tranfield, D., Duberley, J., Smith, S., Musson, G., and Stokes, P. (2000) 'Organisational Learning—It's Just Routine!', *Management Decision*, 38/4: 253–60.

Trowler, P., and Turner, G. (2002) 'Exploring the Hermeneutic Foundation of University Life: Deaf Academics in a Hybrid "Community of Practice"', *Higher Education*, 43: 227–56.

Tsang, E. (1997) 'Organizational Learning and the Learning Organization: A Dichotomy between Prescriptive and Descriptive Research', *Human Relations*, 50/1: 73–89.

——— (2008) 'Transferring Knowledge to Acquisition Joint Ventures: An Organizational Unlearning Perspective', *Management Learning*, 39/1: 5–20.

——— and Zahra, S. (2008) 'Organizational Unlearning', *Human Relations*, 61/10: 1435–62.

Tsoukas, H. (1996) 'The Firm as a Distributed Knowledge System: A Constructionist Approach', *Strategic Management Journal*, 17 (Winter Special Issue), 11–25.

——— (2000) 'What is Management? An Outline of a Metatheory', in S. Ackroyd and S. Fleetwood (eds), *Realist Perspectives on Management and Organisations* (London: Routledge), 26–44.

——— (2003) 'Do We Really Understand Tacit Knowl-edge?', in M. Easterby-Smith and M. Lyles (eds), *The Blackwell Handbook of Learning and Knowledge Management* (Malden, Mass.: Blackwell), 410–27.

Turner, N., and Lee-Kelley, L. (2012) 'Unpacking the Theory on Ambidexterity: An Illustrative Case on the Managerial Architectures, Mechanisms and Dynamics', *Management Learning*, doi: 1350507612444074.

Usoro, A., Sharratt, M., Tsui, E., and Shekar, S. (2007) 'Trust as an Antecedent to Knowledge Sharing in Virtual Communities of Practice', *Knowledge Management Research and Practice*, 5: 199–212.

Van den Hooff, B., Schouten, A., and Simonovski, S. (2012) 'What One Feels and What One Knows: The Influence of Emotions on Attitudes and Intentions towards Knowledge Sharing', *Journal of Knowledge Management*, 16/1: 148–58.

Van der Velden, M. (2002) 'Knowledge Facts, Knowledge Fiction: The Role of ICTs in Knowledge Management for Development', *Journal of International Development*, 14: 25–37.

van Wijk, R., Jansen, J., and Lyles, M. (2008) 'Inter and Intra-Organizational Knowledge Transfer: A Meta-Analytic Review and Assessment of its Antecedents and Consequences', *Journal of Management Studies*, 45/4: 830–53.

Vera, D., and Crossan, M. (2004) 'Strategic Leadership and Organizational Learning', *Academy of Management Review*, 29/2: 222–40.

Vince, R. (2001) 'Power and Emotion in Organizational Learning', *Human Relations*, 54/10: 1325–51.

——— Sutcliffe, K., and Olivera, F. (2002) 'Organizational Learning: New Direction', *British Journal of Management*, 13: S1–6.

Voelpel, S., Dous, M., and Davenport, T. (2005) 'Five Steps to Creating a Global Knowledge-Sharing System: Siemens' ShareNet', *Academy of Management Executive*, 19/2: 9–23.

Von Hayek, F. (1945) 'The Use of Knowledge in Society', *American Economic Review*, 25/4: 519–30.

Von Krogh, G., Nonaka, I., and Ichijo, K.(1997) 'Develop Knowledge Activists!', *European Management Journal*, 15/5: 475–84.

——Ichijo, K., and Nonaka, I. (2000) *Enabling Knowledge Creation: How to Unlock the Mystery of Tacit Knowledge and Release the Power of Innovation* (Oxford: Oxford University Press).

——Nonaka, I., and Aben, M. (2001) 'Making the Most of Your Company's Knowledge: A Strategic Framework', *Long Range Planning*, 34/4: 421–39.

—— —— and Rechsteiner, L. (2012) 'Leadership in Organizational Knowledge Creation', *Journal of Management Studies*, 49/1: 240–77.

Von Nordenflycht, A. (2010) 'What is a Professional Service Firm? Towards a Theory and a Taxonomy of Knowledge-Intensive Firms', *Academy of Management Review*, 35/1: 155–74.

Von Zedtwitz, M. (2002) 'Organizational Learning through Post-Project Reviews in R&D', *R&D Management*, 32/3: 255–68.

Walby, S. (2011) 'Is the Knowledge Society Gendered?', *Gender, Work and Organization*, 18/1: 1–29.

Walsham, G. (2001) 'Knowledge Management: The Benefits and Limitations of Computer Systems', *European Management Journal*, 19/6: 599–608.

Wang, H., He, J., and Mahoney, J. (2009) 'Firm-Specific Knowledge Resources and Competitive Advantage: The Role of Economic- and Relationship-based Employee Governance Mechanisms', *Strategic Management Journal*, 30: 1265–85.

Wang, J., K., Asleigh, M., and Meyer, E. (2006) 'Knowledge Sharing and Team Trustworthiness', *Knowledge Management Research and Practice*, 4: 75–186.

Wang, Y., and Haggerty, N. (2009) 'Knowledge Transfer in Virtual Settings: The Role of Individual Virtual Competency', *Information Systems Journal*, 19/6: 571–93.

Ward, A. (2000) 'Getting Strategic Value from Constellations of Communities', *Strategy and Leadership*, 28/2: 4–9.

Warhurst, C., and Thompson, P. (2006) 'Mapping Knowledge in Work: Proxies or Practices', *Work, Employment and Society*, 20/4: 787–800.

Waring, J., and Currie, G. (2009) 'Managing Expert Knowledge: Organizational Challenges and Managerial Futures for the UK Medical Profession', *Organization Studies*, 30/7: 755–78.

Watson, T. (1994) *In Search of Management: Culture, Chaos and Control in Managerial Work* (London: Routledge).

Webster, F. (1996) *Theories of the Information Society* (London: Routledge).

Weick, K., and Westley, F. (1996) 'Organizational Learning: Affirming an Oxymoron', in S. Clegg, C. Nord, and W. Nord (eds), *Handbook of Organization Studies* (London: Sage), 440–58.

Weir, D., and Hutchins, K. (2005) 'Cultural Embeddedness and Cultural Constraints: Knowledge Sharing in Chinese and Arab Cultures', *Knowledge and Process Management*, 12/2: 89–98.

Wenger, E. (1998) *Communities of Practice: Learning, Meaning and Identity* (Cambridge: Cambridge University Press).

——McDermott, R., and Snyder, W. (2002) *Cultivating Communities of Practice* (Boston: Harvard Business School Press).

Werr, A., and Stjernberg, T. (2003) 'Exploring Management Consulting Firms as Knowledge Systems', *Organization Studies*, 24/6: 881–908.

Wilkinson, A., and Mellahi, K. (2005) 'Organizational Failure: Introduction to Special Issue', *Long Range Planning*, 38/3: 233–8.

Willem, A., and Scarbrough, H. (2006) 'Social Capital and Political Bias in Knowledge Sharing: An Exploratory Study', *Human Relations*, 59/10: 1343–70.

Williams, C. (2011) 'Client–Vendor Knowledge Transfer in IS Offshore Outsourcing: Insights from a Survey of Indian Software Engineers', *Information Systems Journal*, 21: 335–56.

Wilson, J., and Ellman, N. (1990) 'Organizational Benefits of Mentoring', *Academy of Management Executive*, 4/4: 88–94.

Wilson, T. (2002) 'The Nonsense of "Knowledge Management"', *Information Research*, 8/1.

Wong, P., Cheung, S., Yiu, R., and Hardie, M. (2012) 'The Unlearning Dimension of Organizational Learning in Construction Projects', *International Journal of Project Management*, 30/1: 94–104.

Xu, G., Feng, Z., Wu, H., and Zhao, D. (2007) 'Swift Trust in a Virtual Temporary System: A Model Based on the Dempster-Shafer Theory of Belief Functions', *International Journal of Electronic Commerce*, 12/1: 93–126.

Yakhlef, A. (2010) 'The Corporeality of Practice-Based Learning', *Organization Studies*, 31/4: 409–30.

Yang, J.-T. (2007) 'Knowledge Sharing: Investigating Appropriate Leadership Roles and Collaborative Culture', *Tourism Management*, 28: 530–43.

Yanow, D. (2004) 'Translating Local Knowledge at Organizational Peripheries', *British Journal of Management*, 15 (Special Issue), S71–86.

Yildiz, H., and Fey, C. (2010) 'Compatibility and Unlearning in Knowledge Transfer in Mergers and Acquisitions', *Scandinavian Journal of Management* 26: 448–56.

Yli-Renko, H., Autio, E., and Sapienza, H. (2001) 'Social Capital, Knowledge Acquisition, and Knowledge Exploitation in Young Technology-Based Firms', *Strategic Management Journal*, 22: 587–613.

Yukl, G. (2008) *Leadership in Organizations*, 6th edn. (London: Pearson Education).

Zack, M. (1999) 'Developing a Knowledge Strategy', *California Management Review*, 41/3: 125–45.

Zahra, S., Abdelgawad, S., and Tsang, E. (2011) 'Emerging Multinationals Venturing into Developed Economies: Implications for Learning, Unlearning, and Entrepreneurial Capability', *Journal of Management Inquiry*, 20/3: 323–30.

Zhao, B. (2011) 'Learning from Errors: The Role of Context, Emotion, and Personality', *Journal of Organizational Behaviour*, 32: 435–63.

Zhou, S., Siu, F., and Wang, M. (2010) 'Effects of Social Tie Content on Knowledge Transfer', *Journal of Knowledge Management*, 14/3: 449–63.

Zietsma, C., Winn, M., Branzei, O., and Vertinsky, I. (2002) 'The War of the Woods: Facilitators and Impediments of Organizational Learning Processes', *British Journal of Management*, 13: S61–74.

Zimmermann, A., and Mayasandra, R. (2011) 'Collaborative IT Offshoring Relationships and Professional Role Identities: Reflections from a Field Study', *Journal of Vocational Behavior*, 78/3: 351–60.

Zuboff, S. (1998) *In the Age of the Smart Machine: The Future of Work and Power* (Oxford: Heinemann Professional).

Index

(Page numbers in **bold** type refer to tables and figures)